ARGONAUT LIBRARY OF ANTIQUITIES

ANCIENT SHIPS

ANCIENT SHIPS

by

Cecil Torr

Edited with an Introduction by

Anthony J. Podlecki, Ph.D.
Department of Classics, Northwestern University

**WITH AN APPENDIX CONTAINING A SERIES OF ARTICLES ON
THE GREEK WARSHIP AND THE GREEK TRIREME**

by

W. W. Tarn, A. B. Cook, Cecil Torr, Wigham Richardson,
and Philip H. Newman

ARGONAUT, INC., PUBLISHERS
CHICAGO   MCMLXIV

Library of Congress Catalog Card Number: *LC 64-23437*

INTRODUCTION

I must go down to the seas again, to the lonely sea and the sky,
And all I ask is a tall ship, and a star to steer her by . . .
John Masefield: "Sea-Fever"

Until comparatively recent times, the sea appeared to most men endlessly fascinating, and exercised upon them an attraction almost irresistible; the ancient Greeks were no exception. But they too, perhaps more than other men, knew the sea's loneliness. They knew, from that first day buried deep in pre-history, when one of their number hardier than his fellows set out from land on a willow-tied raft, that the allure of the sea, all silver ripples and beckoning glints one moment, might change to pounding swells and swallowing gray troughs the next. The expansiveness of the Greek genius can be explained in part as the result of their willingness to venture forth, to turn their backs on the familiar in search of the uncharted and unknown. But this in turn required the conquering, again and again before each new venture, of their fear of the sea's treachery and caprice; to say that they 'loved the sea' or were 'natural sailors' is simply untrue.

In part then, the growth of Greek genius, and especially that part of it which nourished itself by confronting and Hellenizing the new and exotic, is a history of the Greek coming to terms with the sea; a history, in short, of the Greek ship. The half-legendary figure of the Cretan Minos and his naval empire gave way to the supremacy of his Mycenean counterparts on the mainland, whose naval interests are tangibly attested by the elaborate cataloguing of rowers in the Pylos Linear B tablets. On the poetic side, we are told of the sea-borne adventures of Odysseus, returning from

Troy with his fleet of twelve ships. Even the raft, man-made but goddess-inspired, which he fashioned on Calypso's isle, deserves its place in the history of ships, for it shows us what the Greek sailor may have used in his pre-historic confrontations with the sea. The next man we hear of is thoroughly historical and has a name: Ameinocles, the Corinthian shipwright, who, Thucydides tells us, built ships for the Samians shortly before 700 B.C. He may have been the architect of the ships which carried Corinthian settlers to Sicily, to the hub of the western Corintho-Chalcidic mercantile empire which was later to become a name for Athens to contend with and to rue, Syracuse.

In the next century, ships carried the influence of the Ionian cities, and especially of Miletus, to the northeast, as far as the shores of the Black Sea. The might of sixth-century Samos must have been based in large part on the supremacy of her fleet, even if some of the exploits of Polycrates and his predecessors could hardly be distinguished from pirate raids. In the fifth century, the importance of the merchantman was surpassed by that of the warship. Themistocles made the Athenians a nation of sailors; the ships which he persuaded them to build were the 'wooden wall' which Delphi had said would withstand the Persians. And it was a combination of Themistocles' skill and the technical excellence of the ships which he inspired that brought about the destruction of the much larger fleet of Xerxes in the straits of Salamis on a clear September day in 480 B.C.

Athens' empire, which some (both ancient and modern) could chafe against, while others held it out as a blessing, was based on her superiority by sea. Pericles knew, and told the Athenians, that as long as they maintained this supremacy, they might lose all their land-holdings in Attica to Sparta, and still emerge victorious in the Peloponnesian War. Pericles' predictions were verified in a double victory by the Athenian Phormio against a numerically superior Peloponnesian fleet off Naupactus in the Corinthian Gulf at the beginning of the war (429 B.C.). But as the war dragged wearily on, and Athens had grown by turns over-confident, lazy and impatient, the tide began to turn. The great Athenian expedition to Sicily, some 350 ships including reinforcements, was destroyed in a series of naval defeats off Syracuse in the spring and summer of

413 B.C. Athens fought on, but her morale was broken. There remained only for the Spartan Lysander to issue the *coup de grace* to an Athenian fleet of over 170 ships near Aegospotami in the Hellespont (405 B.C.).

Greek naval history, of course, does not end there, and the development of Roman naval power presents a fascinating picture all its own, but enough has perhaps been said to show how important is a thorough knowledge of the ship to an understanding of ancient history. Cecil Torr's *Ancient Ships* is a monument of scholarship which presents, in a fashion which is both compact and yet complete, all the information on every aspect of the ancient ship. Because every original authority is cited in full, the work provides the indispensable tools for any serious student to make his own assessment of the evidence and reach his own conclusions.

A word must be said on the plan of the book. It is written as a continuous narrative; there are no chapter divisions. But at the top of each page there is a heading describing the contents of that page. Any reader who uses these headings, together with the numerous and very complete indices, will find that he can quickly locate any particular word, topic or author to which he might wish to refer.

Torr's overriding service was in collecting and discussing the ancient evidence. But some of his own theories on points of detail, particularly where the evidence is contradictory or inconclusive (as, for example, in the knotty question of the position of the oars in a trireme), have not gone unchallenged. For this reason, the present edition also contains a series of interrelated articles and letters which appeared after the publication of the first edition of *Ancient Ships*. The first is *"The Greek Warship"* by W. W. Tarn, one of the first scholars to attempt to refute Torr's theories[1] on this subject. It is followed by Torr's comments. The second article is *"Triremes"* by A. B. Cook, which attempts to present a new theory and partially opposes those of both Torr and Tarn. This is supported by Wigham Richardson's *"Sectional Half Model of a Trireme,"* a technical study on shipbuilding, which is again followed by Torr's commentary on these two studies. The fourth article

[1]After the first edition of Ancient Ships, 1894, revised in the article "Navis" in Daremberg-Saglio, *Dictionnaire d'Antiquites Grecques et Romaines.* IV. 1. Paris 1904, pp. 246-406.

is *"Thrănite, Zugite and Thalamite,"* also by W. W. Tarn who
defends his interpretations of the source evidence, followed by
Torr's remarks, a letter by Philip H. Newman and a letter con-
cluding the discussion signed by Torr. This material forms a lively
and brilliant discussion, in print, by the foremost scholars on the
subject of ancient ships and by studying these carefully, the reader
can, if he chooses, observe the techniques of theoretical reconstruction from evidence which is scanty and at times defective. In addition to Torr's original plates, this edition is supplied with a new
series of plates illustrating antiquities and research models of ancient
ships. The photographs for these plates were kindly supplied by the
Franklin Institute Museum of Philadelphia, the Board of Trade
and Conventions, Commercial Museum Division, also of Philadelphia, the British Museum, the Naval Museum of Greece and The
Mariners Museum of Newport News, Virginia.

Because so much of Torr's argumentation is based on the
fourth-century Athenian naval catalogues *(Tabulae Curatorum
Navalium),* it has been thought useful to provide at the end of
the present edition a table of parallel references to the *Corpus
Inscriptionum Atticarum* (CIA)[2], which Torr cites, and the
collection known as "editio minor" of *Inscriptiones Graecae*
(IG, II[2]), now the standard reference edition for the naval
catalogues. Mention has also been made of several inscriptions
supplementing the original Tabulae which have been published in
the *Supplementum Epigraphicum Graecum* (SEG)[3]. For those
who wish to follow the scholarly controversies on points of detail,
as well as theories on ancient ships based on more recent archaeolog-
ical studies and discoveries, a select bibliography (which, however,
makes no pretense to completeness) has been specially compiled for
this edition. In it there are also listed works of a more general
nature, some antedating Torr, as a help to reference for further
study by those interested in ancient naval theory and practice.

ANTHONY J. PODLECKI

NORTHWESTERN UNIVERSITY
JUNE, 1964

[2]Incorporated by decision of the Academy of Berlin (1903) in the general
series *Inscriptiones Graecae*. The three volumes of the CIA (I, II, III)
became thereafter, for reference purposes, IG, I; IG, II; IG, III. See the
table of concordance, pp. 222 of the present edition.
[3]Published by I. Hondius, Vol. I (1923) - XIa (1939) and by A. G. Wood-
head XIb (1954) ———.

PREFACE.

FOR some while I have been at work upon a history of
ancient shipping; and the following pages are meant
to form a portion of that history. Assuming that ancient
shipping means shipping in the Mediterranean between
1000 B.C. and 1000 A.D., and that a history of shipping should
deal with everything connected with ships, I find that I have
upon my hands a task of no small magnitude; and I do not
quite know when this task will be accomplished. That being
so, I am bringing out this portion of the work before the rest;
this portion being tolerably complete already, and dealing
with a question that may conveniently be discussed apart
from any other, namely, the character of the ships themselves.

Ancient ships have already formed the subject of dozens
of books and pamphlets; and I necessarily have made myself
acquainted with the bulk of this literature, from Dr Assmann's
latest article in the *Archäologisches Jahrbuch* back to the
treatise *De Re Navali* published by L. de Baif in 1536. I do
not wish to underrate my obligations to previous writers on
the subject, for they have informed me of many things that
I was not at all likely to discover for myself. But, taking
them altogether, I have found their works more voluminous
than valuable. As a rule, they have relied too much upon
their predecessors. A great many of their works are nothing
more than careless compilations from those of earlier date;
and hardly any of them fail to repeat a few exploded

blunders. And then a great deal of energy has been mis-directed. Author after author has written as though the question was simply how he would set to work, if he were called upon to build a trireme; and accordingly there has been a crop of so-called restorations, which are principally works of the imagination, and do not always agree with the evidence on the few points that happen to be known for certain. And while many of the writers on the subject have thus contented themselves with a very slender knowledge of the evidence available, nearly all of them have shewn more zeal in collecting evidence than in sifting it sufficiently to ascertain its value.

The best of the written evidence comes from inscriptions. In digging the foundations for a building at the Peiræus in 1834, the workmen came upon a Roman or Byzantine drain, and found that it was lined with slabs of marble covered with inscriptions. These were some of the inventories of the Athenian dockyards, and a few others have come to light since then, the earliest of them dating from 373 and the latest from 323 B.C. or thereabouts. Unhappily, these inscriptions are shattered and defaced in many places; but where the reading is clear, their testimony is conclusive[a].

Next in importance are the statements that occur in ancient literature: but, unfortunately, very few of these are more than passing allusions; and the only one that enters into details is open to suspicion. This is the account that Athenæos gives of some stupendous ships that were built about 400 years before his time. In my opinion, this account is not to be accepted as a description of those particular ships: but I imagine that its authors based their statements on what they knew of ships in general; so that, with due allowance for exaggerations and anachronisms, every detail is

---

[a] All these inscriptions are printed in the *Corpus Inscriptionum Atticarum*, vol. ii, nos. 789—812. The original set were edited by August Böckh in 1840 from copies by Ludwig Ross.

admissible as evidence in dealing with the ships of ancient times[b]. Of course, the literary evidence has all to be subjected to the ordinary tests, each statement being estimated by the value that we put upon its author and his means of information about the matter in hand. And peculiar difficulties arise when a thing is mentioned only once in literature, the question being whether this is due to chance, or must be taken to imply that the thing was not in vogue for any length of time. But that conclusion is not inevitable, even when a thing is mentioned several times by authors of one period and never once by those of earlier or later date; for those authors may only be repeating a simile or illustration that had struck the fancy of their generation. And, conversely, authors might go on repeating phrases that were no longer applicable; just as Plutarch and Lucian talk about akatian sails, although these sails had probably gone out of use some centuries before: the explanation being that the akatians were mentioned in a famous saying of Epicuros[c].

There are also the statements of the scholiasts and lexicographers: but their evidence may be rejected altogether. So far as their assertions relate to matters that admit of proof, they are oftener wrong than right; and there is no reason for supposing that they were any better informed on matters that do not admit of proof. Such people felt bound to find a meaning for every word or phrase that came within their range; and if they did not happen to know, they simply had to guess.

The evidence from written sources is supplemented by evidence from material sources. There are the ruins of the docks at Athens to give a notion of the dimensions and proportions of the war-ships: and there are some rams and

---

[b] Athenæos, v. 37—39, quoting Callixenos, and v. 40—44, quoting Moschion. See especially pp. 9, 10 and 27 to 29 as to the reasons for suspecting these descriptions; and also note 118 on p. 50 for an example of the mode of dealing with such evidence.   [c] See p. 86 as to this.

figure-heads and anchors, but practically no other remnants
of the ships themselves. A few models have been found:
but these are all too rough to be instructive; and the chances
are against our finding the splendid model that Lysander
placed at Delphi—a trireme, three feet long, and made of
ivory and gold[d]. There are plenty of pictures of the ships on
painted vases and in frescos and mosaics, and figures of them
on reliefs and coins and gems and works of art of every class;
for they were constantly in favour with the artists of antiquity.
But these works of art must all be taken at a discount. In
dealing with so large a subject as a ship, an ancient artist
would seize upon some characteristics, and give prominence
to these by suppressing other features; and then would
modify the whole design to suit the space at his disposal.
Moreover, the treatment would vary with the form of art,
painters and sculptors seeing things from different points of
view; and it would vary also with the period, as art went
through its phases. So, works of art may easily be taken to
imply a difference in the ships themselves, when the difference
is only in the mode of representing them.

The greatest caution is necessary in getting this evidence
at second hand from books. If a restorer has handled the
original relief or painting, his mistakes are sure to be em-
bodied in the copy; and generally some fresh mistakes are
introduced by draughtsmen and engravers and the people
who touch up photographs. The result is that very few of the
published copies are trustworthy in every detail, while many
of them might rank as caricatures: and yet those copies
are handed on from book to book, and quoted as authorities. But obviously the authors of these books have never
made a search for the originals, for then they would have
discovered that not a few of these supposed copies have
no originals at all[e].

---

[d] Plutarch, Lysander, 18. 2, τριήρης, διὰ χρυσοῦ πεποιημένη καὶ ἐλέφαντος, δυεῖν
πηχῶν.

The evidence from all sources falls short of what is needed for a complete description of the ships; for although our information on certain points is ample and conclusive, there are many points on which we have no information whatever. Practically, this is not a matter of importance, as nobody is likely to resuscitate the ancient style of shipbuilding in its entirety; and hitherto no attention has been given to devices that might still be serviceable. Thus, for example, the ancients saw their way to supplement a squaresail by a triangular topsail with its base along the yard and its apex at the top of the mast, so that no additional yard was needed; and to reinforce the ram by a series of auxiliary rams above, which not only increased the damage to an

---

e For example, in the last edition of Smith's *Dictionary of Greek and Roman Antiquities*, vol. ii, p. 218, there is a picture of an ancient anchor with flukes to its arms and no stock. A note says that the picture is taken from Baumeister. It occurs on p. 1614 in vol. iii of Baumeister's *Denkmäler des klassischen Altertums;* and there the statement is that the picture is taken from Kekulé, and that the original may be seen upon the balustrade round the temple of Athena Nike at Athens. But in Kekulé's *Reliefs an der Balustrade der Athena Nike* the picture is given on p. 12 among the *Ergänzungsskizzen,* merely as a suggestion of what might have filled a vacant place; and on the balustrade itself there is not the slightest trace of any anchor at all.—Again, in Smith's Dictionary, vol. i, p. 361, a picture of a boat, or coracle, is introduced with these remarks:—"The illustration, given both by Rich and Saglio, is taken from Scheffer, *De Militia Navali Veterum,* who describes it as from an ancient MS. of Vitruvius (Polenus, *Supplementum ad Grævium et Gronovium,* v. p. 831)." Saglio gives the picture on p. 915 of vol. i of Daremberg and Saglio's *Dictionnaire des Antiquités Grecques et Romaines,* saying that he took it from Scheffer, who took it from a MS. of Vitruvius, and that Rich had given it before. Rich gives it on p. 117 of his *Dictionary of Roman and Greek Antiquities,* third edition, saying that he took it from Scheffer, who took it from a MS. of Vitruvius. But Scheffer himself, p. 81— and Polenus reprints him rightly—says that he took it from a MS. of Vegetius. As a matter of fact, he did not take it from Vitruvius or Vegetius or from any MS. at all. An edition of Vegetius, *De Re Militari,* was printed at Paris in August, 1532. An edition of Robertus Valturius, *De Re Militari,* had been printed at the same press in July. And as the volumes were uniform, they generally were bound up together. Scheffer took the picture from an engraving on p. 316 of the treatise by Valturius. The engravings in this edition of Valturius are copied from the engravings in the original edition printed at Verona in 1472, and refer to matters of that period.—This sort of thing is not at all uncommon.

enemy, but also protected the stem from being crushed against her sides. Such devices as these, which proved of service in antiquity, would certainly be worth a trial on modern ships.

I must warn the reader that in the passages quoted in the notes I have silently omitted any subordinate clauses that do not bear upon the matter in hand. And also that I have made a rough use of round numbers in dating Egyptian monuments; my opinion being that the evidence does not justify the popular system of chronology.

The illustrations in plates 1 to 7 are by Mr J. A. Burt and those in 8 by Mr H. W. Bennett. I have never seen the originals of fgs. 10, 11, 29 to 31, and 40; but I can guarantee the accuracy of all the rest in every point on which I cite them as authorities. Unfortunately, the illustrations were arranged some while ago, before the book had assumed its present form; and they fall short of what would be desirable. But I hope that the complete work will contain a satisfactory copy of every monument that can elucidate the subject.

C. T.

TABLE OF CONTENTS.

ANCIENT SHIPS.

THE Mediterranean is a sea where a vessel with sails may lie becalmed for days together, while a vessel with oars could easily be traversing the smooth waters, with coasts and islands everywhere at hand to give her shelter in case of storm. In that sea, therefore, oars became the characteristic instruments of navigation; and the arrangement of oars, the chief problem in shipbuilding. And so long as the Mediterranean nations dominated Western Europe, vessels of the southern type were built upon the northern coasts, though there generally was wind enough here for sails and too much wave for oars. But afterwards the nations of Western Europe filled the Mediterranean with sailing-vessels of the types they had devised for voyages on the Ocean; and oars finally gave place to sails. Yet, only a few years before sails began in their turn to give place to steam, oars were still employed on vessels of considerable size that were intended for the Mediterranean alone; and probably would have been more generally employed there, had there still been an adequate supply of galley-slaves. In the ancient world, however, the rower was not usually a slave: and it is a strange fact that Athenian citizens in the age of Pericles, who were in no wise unconscious of their own transcendent gifts, willingly laboured at the oar to generate a mechanical force that was directed by the intelligence of others.

T.   *a*

The art of rowing can first be discerned upon the Nile. Boats with oars, as in fg. 2, are represented in the earliest pictorial monuments of Egypt, dating from about 2500 B.C.: and although some crews are paddling with their faces towards the bow, others are rowing with their faces towards the stern. The paddling is certainly the older practice; for the hieroglyph *chen* depicts two arms grasping an oar in the attitude of paddling, and the hieroglyphs were invented in the earliest ages. And that practice may really have ceased before 2500 B.C., despite the testimony of monuments of that date; for in monuments dating from about 1250 B.C. crews are represented unmistakably rowing with their faces towards the stern and yet grasping their oars in the attitude of paddling, as in fgs. 3 and 5, so that even then Egyptian artists mechanically followed the turn of the hieroglyph to which their hands were accustomed. In these reliefs there are twenty rowers on the boats on the Nile, as in fg. 3, and thirty on the ships on the Red Sea, as in fg. 5; but in the earliest reliefs, as in fg. 2, the number varies considerably and seems dependent on the amount of space at the sculptor's disposal. In the contemporary relief representing a battle fought in the Mediterranean about 1000 B.C. the Egyptian war-ships, as in fg. 6, have from twelve to twenty-two rowers apiece according to the requirements of the sculptor, while the Asiatic war-ships, as in fgs. 7 and 8, have not any rowers at all.

Among the Greeks the oars of a ship were collectively termed *tarsos*, and among the Hebrews ships of a certain type were known as ships of *taršiš*; and Tarsos and Taršiš

---

[1] Iliad, i. 308, 309, Ἀτρείδης δ' ἄρα νῆα θοὴν ἅλαδε προέρυσσεν, | ἐς δ' ἐρέτας ἔκρινεν ἐείκοσιν. xvi. 168—170, πεντήκοντ' ἦσαν νῆες θοαί, ᾗσιν Ἀχιλλεὺς | ἐς Τροίην ἡγεῖτο Διὶ φίλος· ἐν δ' ἄρ' ἑκάστῃ | πεντήκοντ' ἔσαν ἄνδρες ἐπὶ κληῖσιν ἑταῖροι. But this last line is clearly an interpolation: the κληῖδες are not mentioned elsewhere in the Iliad though often mentioned in the Odyssey— see note 110 on p. 46—and the number of rowers is unparalleled in the Iliad outside the Catalogue, while the number of the ships according to the Catalogue, ii. 685, would incite an interpolator to repetition.

[2] Iliad, i. 402—404, ὥχ' ἑκατόγχειρον καλέσασ' ἐς μακρὸν Ὄλυμπον, | ὃν Βριάρεων καλέουσι θεοί, ἄνδρες δέ τε πάντες | Αἰγαίωνα.

[3] The story of the Minyæ, for example, as narrated by Herodotos, iv. 148.

were the Greek and Hebrew names for Tarsus in Cilicia.
The coincidence suggests that this city was pre-eminent in
furthering the use of oars upon the Mediterranean. But of
this there are no records. The early progress of the Phœnicians and their neighbours must be divined from the progress
of their disciples, the Greeks. In the Iliad, apart from the
Catalogue, the Greeks have ships with twenty rowers[1] : but the
allusion to Briareos, the hundred-handed giant of the Ægean,
indicates some knowledge of the fifty-oared ship which forms
so essential a feature in legends of somewhat later date, such
as those of the fifty daughters of Danaos or the fifty comrades
of Jason[2]. The thirty-oared ship belongs to legends of far
later date[3]. In the Odyssey the Greeks still have ships with
twenty rowers, while the Phæacians at Corfu have a ship
with fifty[4]. An advance from twenty to fifty oars, without
intermediate steps, seems hardly possible unless a nation was
adopting the discoveries of another : and a greater advance,
again at a single step, may be traced in the Catalogue of the
Ships, which mentions ships with fifty rowers and ships with
a hundred and eighteen[5]. Ships could not be indefinitely
lengthened to accommodate an increasing number of rowers ;
and consequently the oars began to be arranged in two and
then in three banks one above another. These ships with a
hundred and eighteen rowers must have been two-banked
ships formed by inserting ports for eight and fifty oars in the
intervals between the tholes on ships of sixty oars. Yet the
Greeks never employed sixty-oared ships, and apparently
never knew that such existed, for they had no name for
them : so the invention was not theirs.

---

[4] Odyssey, i. 280, νῆ' ἄρσας ἐρέτῃσιν ἐείκοσιν. iv. 669, ἀλλ' ἄγε μοι δότε νῆα
θοὴν καὶ εἴκοσ' ἑταίρους. ix. 322, ὅσσον θ' ἱστὸν νηὸς ἐεικοσόροιο μελαίνης.
viii. 34—36, ἀλλ' ἄγε νῆα μέλαιναν ἐρύσσομεν εἰς ἅλα δῖαν | πρωτόπλοον, κούρω δὲ
δύω καὶ πεντήκοντα | κρινάσθων κατὰ δῆμον. These fifty-two men would include
κελευστής and κυβερνήτης, leaving fifty to row with one to mark time and one to
steer ; for they are described as κοῦροι, not ἐρέται or ἑταῖροι, as otherwise was
customary.

[5] Iliad, ii. 719, 720, ἑπτὰ νεῶν· ἐρέται δ' ἐν ἑκάστῃ πεντήκοντα | ἐμβέβασαν.
509, 510, τῶν μὲν πεντήκοντα νέες κίον· ἐν δὲ ἑκάστῃ | κοῦροι Βοιωτῶν ἑκατὸν καὶ
εἴκοσι βαῖνον. These hundred and twenty men, κοῦροι, would likewise include
κελευστής and κυβερνήτης.

There is nothing to shew when or where the ancients first built war-ships with a single bank of oars[6]. But two-banked war-ships were certainly in use in Phœnicia about 700 B.C., for Phœnician war-ships are represented with two banks of oars in Assyrian sculpture of that date, as in fgs. 10 and 11 : and if three-banked war-ships were built in Egypt about 600 B.C., as Herodotos relates, they probably were in use in Phœnicia at a somewhat earlier date[7]. According to Thucydides, the first ships that were built by the Greeks for use in warfare, were built about 700 B.C. at Corinth and at Samos ; and the first three-banked war-ships that were built for Greek fleets, were also built at Corinth ; but vessels of that type were not built in large numbers by the Greeks until a little before 500 B.C., and then chiefly in Sicily and Corfu[8].

[6] Various traditions about them are quoted, or misquoted, by Pliny, vii. 57, *longa nave Iasonem primum navigasse Philostephanus auctor est, Hegesias Paralum, Ctesias Semiramim, Archemachus Ægæonem ; biremem Damastes Erythræos fecisse, triremem Thucydides Aminoclem Corinthium, quadriremem Aristoteles Carthaginienses, quinqueremem Mnesigiton Salaminios, sex ordinum Xenagoras Syracusios, ab ea ad decemremem Mnesigiton Alexandrum Magnum, ad* XII *ordines Philostephanus Ptolemæum Soterem, ad* XV *Demetrium Antigoni, ad* XXX *Ptolemæum Philadelphum, ad* XL *Ptolemæum Philopatorem.*

[7] Herodotos, ii. 159, παυσάμενος δὲ τῆς διώρυχος ὁ Νεκὼς ἐτράπετο πρὸς στρατηίας, καὶ τριήρεες αἱ μὲν ἐπὶ τῇ βορηίῃ θαλάσσῃ ἐποιήθησαν, αἱ δ' ἐν τῷ Ἀραβίῳ κόλπῳ· καὶ ταύτῃσί τε ἐχρᾶτο ἐν τῷ δέοντι, κ.τ.λ. Nekau reigned from 610 to 594 B.C., or thereabouts. Clemens Alexandrinus, stromateis, i. 16. 76, τούς τε Σιδωνίους (πρώτους ἀκηκόαμεν) τρίκροτον ναῦν κατασκευάσαι.

[8] Thucydides, i. 13, ναυτικά τε ἐξηρτύετο ἡ Ἑλλὰς καὶ τῆς θαλάσσης μᾶλλον ἀντείχοντο. πρῶτοι δὲ Κορίνθιοι λέγονται ἐγγύτατα τοῦ νῦν τρόπου μεταχειρίσαι τὰ περὶ τὰς ναῦς, καὶ τριήρεις πρῶτον ἐν Κορίνθῳ τῆς Ἑλλάδος ναυπηγηθῆναι. φαίνεται δὲ καὶ Σαμίοις Ἀμεινοκλῆς Κορίνθιος ναυπηγὸς ναῦς ποιήσας τέσσαρας· ἔτη δ' ἐστὶ μάλιστα τριακόσια ἐς τὴν τελευτὴν τοῦδε τοῦ πολέμου ὅτε Ἀμεινοκλῆς Σαμίοις ἦλθεν. 14, ὀλίγον τε πρὸ τῶν Μηδικῶν καὶ τοῦ Δαρείου θανάτου τριήρεις περί τε Σικελίαν τοῖς τυράννοις ἐς πλῆθος ἐγένοντο καὶ Κερκυραίοις· ταῦτα γὰρ τελευταῖα πρὸ τῆς Ξέρξου στρατείας ναυτικὰ ἀξιόλογα ἐν τῇ Ἑλλάδι κατέστη. Αἰγινῆται γὰρ καὶ Ἀθηναῖοι καὶ εἴ τινες ἄλλοι βραχέα ἐκέκτηντο, καὶ τούτων τὰ πολλὰ πεντηκοντόρους. cf. Diodoros, xiv. 42, ἀκούων γὰρ ὁ Διονύσιος ἐν Κορίνθῳ ναυπηγηθῆναι τριήρη πρῶτον, κ.τ.λ. But while Diodoros says πρῶτον ἐν Κορίνθῳ, Thucydides takes care to say πρῶτον ἐν Κορίνθῳ τῆς Ἑλλάδος to save the priority of the Phœnicians. Thucydides can hardly mean that the Corinthians were building three-banked ships three centuries before the peace of 404 B.C. The allusion to their three-banked ships is parenthetical. His meaning must be that they were only then beginning to build war-ships of any sort. But, as to their priority in this, see Herodotos, i. 163, οἱ δὲ Φωκαιέες οὗτοι ναυτιλίῃσι μακρῇσι

For more than two hundred years the three-banked ships were the largest war-ships afloat: but at length the system of successive banks was tested thoroughly. The extant fragments of the inventories of the Athenian dockyards merely shew[9] that ships of four banks were first built there shortly before 330 B.C. and ships of five banks in 325 B.C. But according to Diodoros[10] ships of four and five banks were built for the Syracusan fleet in 398 B.C., five-banked ships being then built for the first time ; and according to Ælian[11] there were ships of five and six banks in that fleet forty years later. Pliny states that ships of four and five and six banks were first built at Chalcedon and Salamis and Syracuse respectively; and then Alexander the Great made the advance to ten banks[12]. A whole fleet of seven-banked ships was built by

πρῶτοι Ἑλλήνων ἐχρήσαντο, καὶ τόν τε Ἀδρίην καὶ τὴν Τυρσηνίην καὶ τὴν Ἰβηρίην καὶ τὸν Ταρτησὸν οὗτοι εἰσι οἱ καταδέξαντες· ἐναυτίλλοντο δὲ οὐ στρογγύλῃσι νηυσὶ ἀλλὰ πεντηκοντέροισι. Herodotos, however, may only mean that the Phocæans were the first Greeks to employ these war-ships on trading voyages and thus defy the piracy in the Western Mediterranean.

[9] Corp. Inscr. Attic. vol. ii, no. 807, col. b, ll. 76—79, τετρήρεις δ' ἐμ μὲν τοῖς νεωρίοις παρέδομεν ⌈lll, ἐμ πλῷ δὲ Δ—'Ἀριστοφῶντος ἄρχοντος, 330/329 B.C. : no. 809, col. d, ll. 87—91, τετρήρεις δ' ἐμ μὲν τοῖς νεωρίοις παρέδομεν ΔΔΔΔlll καὶ πεντήρεις ⌈ll, τετρήρεις δ' ἐμ πλῷ ⌈ll—'Ἀντικλέους ἄρχοντος, 325/324 B.C. Ships of four and five banks are not previously mentioned in these lists. There is a list for the year before 325/324, no. 808, col. d, ll. 22—39 ; but none at present for the years immediately before 330/329. The first eighteen four-banked ships probably were built in two or three years, as the next thirty-two were built in five years besides seven five-banked ships ; so the Athenians probably built their first four-banked ship in 331 or 332 B.C.

[10] Diodoros, xiv. 42, ἤρξατο δὲ (Διονύσιος) ναυπηγεῖσθαι τετρήρεις καὶ πεντηρικὰ σκάφη, πρῶτος ταύτην τὴν κατασκευὴν τῶν νεῶν ἐπινοήσας. cf. 41, διενοεῖτο γὰρ κατασκευάσαι ναῦς τετρήρεις καὶ πεντήρεις, οὐδέπω κατ' ἐκείνους τοὺς χρόνους σκάφους πεντηρικοῦ νεναυπηγημένου. 44, ἀπέστειλεν πεντήρη, πρῶτον νεναυπηγημένην.

[11] Ælian, variæ historiæ, vi. 12, ναῦς μὲν ἐκέκτητο (Διονύσιος ὁ δεύτερος) οὐκ ἐλάττους τῶν τετρακοσίων, ἐξήρεις καὶ πεντήρεις· πεζῶν δὲ δύναμιν εἰς δέκα μυριάδας, ἱππεῖς δὲ ἐννεακισχιλίους. Diodoros, xvi. 9, mentions these forces in narrating the events of 357 B.C., so Ælian is probably referring to that date : but Diodoros says nothing about the size of the ships.

[12] Pliny, vii. 57, already quoted in note 6. cf. Clemens Alexandrinus, stromateis, i. 16. 75, Καρχηδόνιοι δὲ πρῶτοι τετρήρη κατεσκεύασαν, ἐναυπήγησε δὲ αὐτὴν Βόσπορος, where the allusion to Bosporos shews that Chalcedon is meant, not Carchedon or Carthage. The common spelling, Calchedon for Chalcedon, would induce the error.

Alexander on the Euphrates in 323 B.C., according to Quintus Curtius: but the other biographers of Alexander nowhere mention ships of more than five banks[13]. According to Diodoros, there were ships of six and seven banks in the fleet of Demetrios Poliorcetes at the battle off Cyprus in 306 B.C., but none of more than five banks in the fleet of his opponent, Ptolemy Soter; while there had been a few ships of nine and ten banks in a fleet formed in 314 B.C. by Antigonos, the father of Demetrios, though apparently no other ships in that fleet were of more than five banks[14]. Pliny states that ships of twelve and fifteen banks were built by Ptolemy and Demetrios respectively: and a fifteen-banked ship is ascribed to Ptolemy by Pollux[15]. An eleven-banked

[13] Quintus Curtius, x. 1. 19, *igitur Mesopotamiæ prætoribus imperavit (Alexander) materia in Libano monte cæsa devectaque ad urbem Syriæ Thapsacum, septingentarum carinas navium ponere: septiremes omnes esse, deducique Babyloniam. Cypriorum regibus imperatum, ut æs stuppamque et vela præberent.* The statements of Aristobulos, who was present, are cited by Arrian, anabasis, vii. 19, κατέλαβε δὲ ('Αλέξανδρος) ἐν Βαβυλῶνι, ὡς λέγει 'Αριστόβουλος, καὶ τὸ ναυτικόν· τὸ μὲν κατὰ τὸν Εὐφράτην ποταμὸν ἀναπεπλευκὸς ἀπὸ θαλάσσης τῆς Περσικῆς· τὸ δὲ ἐκ Φοινίκης ἀνακεκομισμένον, πεντήρεις μὲν δύο τῶν ἐκ Φοινίκων, τετρήρεις δὲ τρεῖς, τριήρεις δὲ δώδεκα, τριακοντόρους δὲ ἐς τριάκοντα· ταύτας ξυντμηθείσας κομισθῆναι ἐπὶ τὸν Εὐφράτην ποταμὸν ἐκ Φοινίκης ἐς Θάψακον πόλιν, ἐκεῖ δὲ ξυμπηχθείσας αὖθις καταπλεῦσαι ἐς Βαβυλῶνα. λέγει δὲ ὅτι καὶ ἄλλος αὐτῷ ἐναυπηγεῖτο στόλος τέμνοντι τὰς κυπαρίσσους τὰς ἐν τῇ Βαβυλωνίᾳ. Also by Strabo, xvi. 1. 11, τὰ πλοῖα τὰ μὲν ἐν Φοινίκῃ τε καὶ Κύπρῳ ναυπηγησάμενον διάλυτά τε καὶ γομφωτά, ἃ κομισθέντα εἰς Θάψακον σταθμοῖς ἑπτὰ εἶτα τῷ ποταμῷ κατακομισθῆναι μέχρι Βαβυλῶνος, τὰ δ' ἐν τῇ Βαβυλωνίᾳ συμπηξάμενον τῶν ἐν τοῖς ἄλσεσι καὶ τοῖς παραδείσοις κυπαρίττων. And probably also by Plutarch, Alexander, 68, καὶ πλοῖα παντοδαπὰ περὶ Θάψακον ἐπήγνυντο. These statements shew that Curtius has confounded the ships that were built on the Euphrates with those other ships that were brought over in sections from Phœnicia; and sufficiently disprove his assertion that this fleet consisted entirely of seven-banked ships. But possibly the word *septiremes* stands for some word like *solutiles* denoting that the ships were in sections.

[14] Diodoros, xx. 49, εἶχε δὲ (Πτολεμαῖος) τὰς πάσας ναῦς μακρὰς ἑκατὸν καὶ τετταράκοντα· τούτων δ' ἦν ἡ μεγίστη πεντήρης, ἡ δ' ἐλαχίστη τετρήρης. 50, αὐτὸς δὲ (Δημήτριος) ἐκτάξας τὰς ναῦς ἀπήντα τοῖς πολεμίοις, ἔχων τὰς ἁπάσας ὀκτὼ πλείους τῶν ἑκατὸν σὺν ταῖς πληρωθείσαις ἐκ τῶν χωρίων τῶν ληφθέντων· τούτων δ' ἦσαν αἱ μέγισται μὲν ἑπτήρεις, αἱ πλεῖσται δὲ πεντήρεις. καὶ τὸ μὲν εὐώνυμον κέρας ἐπεῖχον ἑπτήρεις μὲν ἑπτὰ Φοινίκων, τετρήρεις δὲ τριάκοντα τῶν 'Αθηναίων· ἐπίπλους δὲ τούτοις ἔταξεν ἑξήρεις δέκα καὶ πεντήρεις ἄλλας τοσαύτας, κ.τ.λ. Speaking of the two hundred and forty war-ships collected by Antigonos, he says, xix. 62, τούτων δ' ἦσαν τετρήρεις μὲν ἐνενήκοντα, πεντήρεις δὲ δέκα, ἐννήρεις δὲ τρεῖς, δεκήρεις δὲ δέκα, ἄφρακτοι δὲ τριάκοντα. The rest presumably had the normal three banks.

ship unquestionably was built by Demetrios, for the fact is
mentioned by Theophrastos, a contemporary whose position
secured him most trustworthy information[16]. She was built
in Cyprus ; and therefore after the naval victory in 306 B.C.,
which made Demetrios master of the island and its timber.
According to Plutarch[17], Demetrios had a thirteen-banked
ship in 301 B.C., and built ships of fifteen and sixteen banks
in 288 B.C. And there certainly was a ship of sixteen banks
in the Macedonian fleet a century afterwards. She was
expressly mentioned in the treaty with the Romans in
197 B.C. : her arrival in the Tiber in 167 B.C. was a memor-
able event ; and she afterwards gave her name to one of the
docks at Rome[18].

[15] Pliny, vii. 57, already quoted in note 6.   Pollux, i. 83, καὶ Πτολεμαίου
ναῦς, πεντεκαιδεκήρης· καὶ Ἀντιγόνου, τριάρμενος.   For the meaning of τριάρμενος
see note 124 on p. 54.

[16] Theophrastos, historia plantarum, v. 8. 1, ἐν Κύπρῳ γοῦν οὐκ ἔτεμνον οἱ
βασιλεῖς (τὰ δένδρα) ἅμα μὲν τηροῦντες καὶ ταμιευόμενοι ἅμα δὲ καὶ διὰ τὸ
δυσκόμιστον εἶναι. μῆκος μὲν ἦν τῶν εἰς τὴν ἑνδεκήρη τὴν Δημητρίου τμηθέντων
τρισκαιδεκαόργυιον, αὐτὰ δὲ τὰ ξύλα τῷ μήκει θαυμαστὰ καὶ ἄοζα καὶ λεῖα. This is
repeated by Pliny, xvi. 76, with some exaggerations.

[17] Plutarch, Demetrius, 31, ὁ γοῦν Δημήτριος τότε προσέπεμψε τοῖς Ἀθηναίοις
ἐγκαλῶν μετρίως, ἀξιῶν δὲ τὰς ναῦς ἀπολαβεῖν, ἐν αἷς ἦν καὶ ἡ τρισκαιδεκήρης.   cf. 30,
καὶ γὰρ καὶ ναῦς ἐκεῖ καὶ χρήματα καὶ γυναῖκα ἐτύγχανε καταλελοιπώς.   32, πρότερον
μὲν Σέλευκος ἑστιάσας ἐπὶ σκηνῆς ἐν τῷ στρατοπέδῳ Δημήτριον, αὖθις δὲ Δημήτριος
ἐκεῖνον ἐν τῇ τρισκαιδεκήρει δεξάμενος.   43, στόλον δὲ νεῶν ἅμα πεντακοσίων κατα-
βαλλόμενος τὰς μὲν ἐν Πειραιεῖ τρόπεις ἔθετο, τὰς δὲ ἐν Κορίνθῳ, τὰς δὲ ἐν Χαλκίδι,
τὰς δὲ περὶ Πέλλαν, αὐτὸς ἐπιὼν ἑκασταχόσε καὶ διδάσκων ἃ χρὴ καὶ συντεχνώμενος,
ἐκπληττομένων ἁπάντων οὐ τὰ πλήθη μόνον ἀλλὰ καὶ τὰ μεγέθη τῶν ἔργων·   οὐδεὶς
γὰρ εἶδεν ἀνθρώπων οὔτε πεντεκαιδεκήρη ναῦν πρότερον οὔτε ἑκκαιδεκήρη.   cf.
20, καὶ τὰς μὲν ἑκκαιδεκήρεις αὐτοῦ καὶ τὰς πεντεκαιδεκήρεις ἐθαύμαζον ἑστῶτες οἱ
πολέμιοι παρὰ τὴν γῆν αὐτῶν πλεούσας, κ.τ.λ.

[18] This treaty is cited by Polybios, xviii. 27, τὰ δ' αἰχμάλωτα καὶ τοὺς αὐτομόλους
ἅπαντας ἀποκαταστῆσαι Φίλιππον Ῥωμαίοις ἐν τοῖς αὐτοῖς χρόνοις· ὁμοίως δὲ καὶ τὰς
καταφράκτους ναῦς, πλὴν πέντε σκαφῶν καὶ τῆς ἑκκαιδεκήρους, and by Livy, xxxiii.
30, *captivos transfugasque reddere Philippum Romanis, et naves omnes tectas
tradere præter quinque et regiam unam inhabilis prope magnitudinis, quam
sexdecim versus remorum agebant.*   The arrival in the Tiber is described by
Plutarch, Æmilius Paulus, 30, ἀνέπλει τὸν Θύβριν ποταμὸν ἐπὶ τῆς βασιλικῆς
ἑκκαιδεκήρους κατεσκευασμένης εἰς κόσμον ὅπλοις αἰχμαλώτοις καὶ φοινικίσι καὶ
πορφύραις, ὡς καὶ πανηγυρίζειν ἔξωθεν καθάπερ εἴς τινα θριαμβικῆς θέαν πομπῆς
καὶ προαπολαύειν τοὺς Ῥωμαίους τῷ ῥοθίῳ σχέδην ὑπάγοντι τὴν ναῦν ἀντιπαρεξά-
γοντας, and also by Livy, xlv. 35, *Paulus ipse post dies paucos regia nave
ingentis magnitudinis, quam sexdecim versus remorum agebant, ornata Mace-*

War-ships of still greater size are ascribed to Ptolemy Philadelphos and Ptolemy Philopator, who ruled Egypt from 285 to 247 B.C. and from 222 to 204 B.C. respectively. Athenæos states that, besides various ships of thirteen banks or less, Philadelphos had one ship of twenty banks and two of thirty banks, while Philopator built a ship of forty banks; and he quotes a long account of this ship from Callixenos of Rhodes[19]. Plutarch states that Philopator built a ship of forty banks, and then describes her in the phrases employed by Athenæos, so that he is also quoting from Callixenos[20]. Pliny states independently, on the authority of Philostephanos of Cyrene, that Philadelphos and Philopator built ships of thirty and forty banks respectively[21]. And these amazing statements have partly been confirmed by an inscription that was unearthed a few years ago in the temple of Aphrodite at Paphos in Cyprus, namely, a dedication by the reigning

donicis spoliis non insignium tantum armorum sed etiam regiorum textilium, adverso Tiberi ad urbem est subvectus, completis ripis obviam effusa multitudine, both authors doubtless copying the lost description by Polybios, who was in Rome soon afterwards and knew Paulus intimately. cf. Eutropius, iv. 8, *Romam cum ingenti pompa rediit (Paulus) in nave Persei, quæ inusitatæ magnitudinis fuisse traditur,* adeo ut sexdecim ordines dicatur habuisse remorum. The dock is mentioned by Polybios, xxxvi. 3, δι' οὗ παρακομισθέντες ἀσφαλῶς εἰς τὴν 'Ρώμην, σύνεκλείσθησαν ὁμοῦ πάντες εἰς τὸ τῆς ἐκκαιδεκήρους νεώριον.

[19] Athenæos, v. 36, πολλῶν δ' ὁ Φιλάδελφος βασιλέων πλούτῳ διέφερε, καὶ περὶ πάντα ἐσπουδάκει τὰ κατασκευάσματα φιλοτίμως, ὥστε καὶ πλοίων πλήθει πάντας ὑπερέβαλλε. τὰ γοῦν μέγιστα τῶν πλοίων ἦν παρ' αὐτῷ τριακοντήρεις δύο, εἰκοσήρης μία, τέσσαρες τρισκαιδεκήρεις, δωδεκήρεις δύο, ἑνδεκήρεις τεσσαρεσκαίδεκα, ἐννήρεις τριάκοντα, κ.τ.λ. 37, ἐπεὶ δὲ περὶ νεῶν κατασκευῆς εἰρήκαμεν, φέρ' εἴπωμεν καὶ τὰ ὑπὸ τοῦ Φιλοπάτορος βασιλέως κατεσκευασμένα σκάφη· περὶ ὧν ὁ αὐτὸς Καλλίξενος ἱστορεῖ ἐν τῷ πρώτῳ Περὶ 'Αλεξανδρείας οὑτωσὶ λέγων—τὴν τεσσαρακοντήρη ναῦν κατεσκεύασεν ὁ Φιλοπάτωρ, κ.τ.λ. The date of Callixenos cannot be fixed. A certain Callixenos held some high office at Rhodes about 100 B.C., for his name is found on Rhodian coins of that period : but there is nothing to shew that he was the historian.

[20] Plutarch, Demetrius, 43, ἀλλ' ὕστερον τεσσαρακοντήρη Πτολεμαῖος ὁ Φιλοπάτωρ ἐναυπηγήσατο, μῆκος διακοσίων ὀγδοήκοντα πηχῶν, ὕψος δὲ ἕως ἀκροστολίου πεντή-κοντα δυεῖν δεόντων, ναύταις δὲ χωρὶς ἐρετῶν ἐξηρτυμένην τετρακοσίοις, ἐρέταις δὲ τετρακισχιλίοις, χωρὶς δὲ τούτων ὁπλίτας δεχομένην ἐπί τε τῶν παρόδων καὶ τοῦ καταστρώματος ὀλίγῳ τρισχιλίων ἀποδέοντας. cf. Athenæos, v. 37, τὸ μῆκος ἔχουσαν διακοσίων ὀγδοήκοντα πηχῶν...ὕψος δὲ ἕως ἀκροστολίου τεσσαράκοντα ὀκτὼ πηχῶν... ἐδέξατο ἐρέτας πλείους τῶν τετρακισχιλίων, εἰς δὲ τὰς ὑπηρεσίας τετρακοσίους· εἰς δὲ τὸ κατάστρωμα ἐπιβάτας τρισχιλίους, ἀποδέοντας ἑκατὸν καὶ πεντήκοντα.

Ptolemy of the statue of a man who is there described as the architect of the thirty-banked ship[22]. There may have been a forty-banked ship: but Callixenos seems quite untrustworthy in his account of her. According to Diodoros[23], Sesostris built a sacred barge upon the Nile two hundred and eighty cubits in length: and numerous representations shew, as in fg. 3, that these sacred barges were vessels of light draught with curiously elevated stems and sterns. Now, according to Callixenos, the length of the forty-banked ship was two hundred and eighty cubits, the draught was under four cubits, and the height of the terminal ornaments at the stem and the stern was forty-eight and fifty-three cubits respectively[24]. These measurements must belong to one of those sacred barges, probably to the one mentioned by Diodoros: and such a barge could not possibly have forty banks of oars.

---

[21] Pliny, vii. 57, already quoted in note 6. Athenæos says that Philostephanos was a friend or follower of Callimachos, viii. 3, Καλλιμάχου δὲ γνώριμος, and Callimachos died about 240 B.C.

[22] This inscription is printed in the Journal of Hellenic Studies, vol. ix, p. 255:—B]ασιλεὺς Πτολεμαῖος | Πυργ]οτέλην Ζώητος ἀρχιτεκτονήσ[αντα | τὴν τριακοντήρη καὶ εἰκ[οσήρη. The term ἀρχιτέκτων was often applied to naval-architects: Aristotle, res publica Atheniensium, 46, χειροτονεῖ δ' ἀρχιτέκτονας ὁ δῆμος ἐπὶ τὰς ναῦς, cf. Athenæos, v. 40, Diodoros, iv. 41.

[23] Diodoros, i. 57, ἐναυπηγήσατο δὲ (Σεσόωσις) καὶ πλοῖον κέδρινον τὸ μὲν μῆκος πηχῶν διακοσίων καὶ ὀγδοήκοντα, τὴν δ' ἐπιφάνειαν ἔχον τὴν μὲν ἔξωθεν ἐπίχρυσον, τὴν δ' ἔνδοθεν κατηγυρωμένην· καὶ τοῦτο μὲν ἀνέθηκε τῷ θεῷ τῷ μάλιστα ἐν Θήβαις τιμωμένῳ, κ.τ.λ. This statement is not incredible. According to the Harris papyrus—plate 7, line 5, in Birch's facsimile—Ramessu III provided the great god at Thebes with a vessel of cedar-wood, decorated with bronze and gold, and a hundred and thirty cubits in length.

[24] Athenæos, v. 37, τὴν τεσσαρακοντήρη ναῦν κατεσκεύασεν ὁ Φιλοπάτωρ, τὸ μῆκος ἔχουσαν διακοσίων ὀγδοήκοντα πηχῶν, ὀκτὼ δὲ καὶ τριάκοντα ἀπὸ παρόδου ἐπὶ πάροδον, ὕψος δὲ ἕως ἀκροστολίου τεσσαράκοντα ὀκτὼ πηχῶν, ἀπὸ δὲ τῶν πρυμνητικῶν ἀφλάστων ἐπὶ τὸ πρὸς τῇ θαλάσσῃ μέρος αὐτῆς τρεῖς πρὸς τοῖς πεντήκοντα πήχεις......ὕστερον δὲ τῶν ἀπὸ Φοινίκης τις ἐπενόησε τὴν καθολκήν, τάφρον ὑποστησάμενος ἴσην τῇ νηὶ κατὰ μῆκος, ἣν πλησίον τοῦ λιμένος ὤρυξε. ταύτῃ δὲ τοὺς θεμελίους κατῳκοδόμησε λίθῳ στερεῷ πρὸς πέντε πήχεις τὸ βάθος, καὶ διὰ τούτων φάλαγγας ἐπικαρσίας κατὰ πλάτος τῆς τάφρου διώσας συνεχεῖς, τετράπηχυν εἰς βάθος τόπον ἀπολιπούσας. καὶ ποιήσας εἴσρουν ἀπὸ τῆς θαλάσσης ἐνέπλησεν αὐτῆς πάντα τὸν ὀρυχθέντα τόπον, εἰς ὃν ῥᾳδίως ἀπὸ τῶν τυχόντων ἀνδρῶν εἰσήγαγε τὴν ναῦν. As the ship was floated into the dock, and the dock was only four cubits in depth, the ship must have drawn less than four cubits of water.

According to Callixenos, the longest oars on the alleged forty-banked ship were thirty-eight cubits in length, the extreme breadth of the ship also being thirty-eight cubits, or fifty-seven feet. And he adds that they were weighted with lead inboard to balance the excessive length outboard : but this statement may safely be referred to the sacred barge from which he has evolved his ship, as some such weights are represented on the steering-oars of the sacred barge in fg. 3, and none are elsewhere ascribed to any ancient war-ship[25]. The oars of a three-banked ship must all have been of very moderate size and weight ; for a crew could make a forced march when each man was carrying his oar and its appurtenances[26]. In war-ships there were always as many rowers as oars : but in some smaller vessels the oars were light enough to be sculled in pairs[27].

Of the two hundred oars[28] which an Athenian three-banked ship carried for her crew of two hundred men, a hundred and seventy belonged to the three banks, while the remaining thirty were *perineōi*—a term which also denoted the men who did not row in the banks[29]. These thirty men must have worked these thirty oars from above the upper decking, for

[25] Athenæos, v. 37, πηδάλια δ' εἶχε τέτταρα τριακονταπήχη, κώπας δὲ θρανιτικὰς ὀκτὼ καὶ τριάκοντα πηχῶν τὰς μεγίστας, αἷ, διὰ τὸ μόλυβδον ἔχειν ἐν τοῖς ἐγχειριδίοις καὶ γεγονέναι λίαν εἴσω βαρεῖαι κατὰ τὴν ζύγωσιν, εὐήρεις ὑπῆρχον ἐπὶ τῆς χρείας. The extreme breadth of the ship is determined by the words already quoted in note 24, ὀκτὼ δὲ καὶ τριάκοντα (πηχῶν) ἀπὸ παρόδου ἐπὶ πάροδον.

[26] Thucydides, ii. 93, ἐδόκει δὲ λαβόντα τῶν ναυτῶν ἕκαστον τὴν κώπην καὶ τὸ ὑπηρέσιον καὶ τὸν τροπωτῆρα πεζῇ ἰέναι ἐκ Κορίνθου ἐπὶ τὴν πρὸς Ἀθήνας θάλασσαν, καὶ ἀφικομένους κατὰ τάχος ἐς Μέγαρα, καθελκύσαντας ἐκ Νισαίας τοῦ νεωρίου αὐτῶν τεσσαράκοντα ναῦς αἳ ἔτυχον αὐτόθι οὖσαι, πλεῦσαι εὐθὺς ἐπὶ τὸν Πειραιᾶ.

[27] Thucydides, iv. 67, ἀκάτιον ἀμφηρικὸν ὡς λῃσταὶ εἰώθεσαν ἐπὶ ἁμάξῃ διὰ τῆς τάφρου κατακομίζειν τῆς νυκτὸς ἐπὶ τὴν θάλασσαν καὶ ἐκπλεῖν, cf. Leonidas of Tarentum, in the Anthology, vi. 4. 6, καὶ τοὺς ἐξ ἀκάτων διχθαδίους ἐρέτας. Lucian, Charon, 1, ἐγὼ δὲ πρεσβύτης ὢν τὴν δικωπίαν ἐρέττω μόνος. Aristophanes, ecclesiazusæ, 1091, πῶς οὖν δικωπεῖν ἀμφοτέρας δυνήσομαι; Synesios, epistolæ, p. 165, ἧκεν ἐπὶ κελητίου δισκάλμου. Cicero, de oratore, i. 38, *citius hercule is, qui duorum scalmorum naviculam in portu everterit, in Euxino ponto Argonautarum navem gubernarit.* Livy, xxiv. 40, *legati venerunt nuntiantes Philippum primum Apolloniam tentasse, lembis biremibus centum viginti flumine adverso subvectum, deinde etc.,* cf. Virgil, georgics, i. 201, 202, *qui adverso vix flumine lembum | remigiis subigit.*

there certainly was not any space for them below. As for the other hundred and seventy oars, sixty-two of these belonged to the upper bank, and fifty-four to each of the lower banks: yet fifty-eight, as the mean between fifty-four and sixty-two, would naturally be the number of oars for the middle bank. In the earliest two-banked ships with a hundred and eighteen rowers[30] there clearly were fifty-eight in the lower bank and sixty in the upper bank, the lower oars being inserted in the spaces between the tholes on a sixty-oared ship. Apparently two oars were added, whereby the upper bank obtained four oars more than the bank below, and then a third bank was added with four oars less than the bank above; a three-banked ship therefore requiring a hundred and seventy-four rowers. And the Athenians perhaps found afterwards that more hands were needed for other purposes, and diminished the number of rowers rather than increase the crew and thereby complicate their estimates for pay; for with a crew of exactly two hundred men a talent a month a ship gave a drachm a day a man, thirty mnas a month a ship gave three obols a day a man, and so forth[31].

---

[28] Corp. Inscr. Attic. vol. ii, no. 797, col. a, ll. 17—24, col. b, ll. 6—13, 24—31, col. c, ll. 39—46, no. 798, col. a, ll. 10—17, 27—34, col. b, ll. 18—25, no. 800, col. a, ll. 52—59, giving a total of two hundred oars in the last seven instances, κῶπαι θρανίτιδες 𐊠ΔΙΙ, ζύγιαι 𐊠ΙΙΙΙ, θαλάμιαι 𐊠ΙΙΙΙ, περίνεῳ ΔΔΔ, and doubtless in the first instance also, although the mason has there cut 𐊠ΔΙΙΙΙ for 𐊠ΔΙΙ, presumably by repetition of the ΙΙΙΙ from the ends of the adjacent lines. The full numbers occur elsewhere in the extant fragments of the inventories, but not in groups that give a total. Lower numbers often occur, as many oars were missing.

[29] Thucydides, i. 10, αὐτερέται δὲ ὅτι ἦσαν καὶ μάχιμοι πάντες, ἐν ταῖς Φιλοκτήτου ναυσὶ ("Ομηρος) δεδήλωκεν · τοξότας γὰρ πάντας πεποίηκε τοὺς προσκώπους. περίνεως δὲ οὐκ εἰκὸς πολλοὺς ξυμπλεῖν ἔξω τῶν βασιλέων καὶ τῶν μάλιστα ἐν τέλει. cf. Procopios, de bello Vandalico, i. 11, quoted in note 45 on p. 17. Dion Cassius, xlix. 1, καὶ τοὺς δούλους τοὺς τριηρίτας ἠλευθέρωσε, τούς τε περίνεως ἐς τὸ τοῦ Ἀντωνίου ναυτικὸν ὀλιγανδροῦν κατέταξεν.

[30] Iliad, ii. 509, 510, already quoted in note 5 on p. 3.

[31] Thucydides, vi. 31, τοῦ μὲν δημοσίου δραχμὴν τῆς ἡμέρας τῷ ναύτῃ ἑκάστῳ διδόντος καὶ ναῦς παρασχόντος καινὰς ἑξήκοντα μὲν ταχείας τεσσαράκοντα δὲ ὁπλιτα-γωγούς, cf. 8, ἑξήκοντα τάλαντα ἀσήμου ἀργυρίου ὡς ἐς ἑξήκοντα ναῦς μηνὸς μισθόν. Xenophon, Hellenica, i. 5. 5—7, ὁ δὲ (Κῦρος) καλῶς μὲν ἔφη αὐτοὺς λέγειν, οὐ δυνατὸν δ' εἶναι παρ' ἃ βασιλεὺς ἐπέστειλεν αὐτῷ ἄλλα ποιεῖν. εἶναι δὲ καὶ τὰς

The number of oars in the four-banked ships is nowhere recorded: but in the inventories of the Athenian dockyards a complete set is valued at six hundred and sixty-five drachms. If every bank was intended to contain four oars more than the bank below, a four-banked ship could carry sixty-six oars in her upper bank; and, including thirty *perineōi*, would thus have two hundred and sixty-six altogether. This number gives exactly two drachms and a half for each oar, while the neighbouring numbers give improbably complicated prices: and that price seems highly probable, for condemned oars were then being sold for two drachms apiece, and timbers bought for three drachms apiece to make new oars[32]. The five-banked ships in the Roman and Carthaginian fleets in 256 B.C. each carried three hundred rowers besides the combatants[33]. With fifty-four oars in the lowest bank and four more in each succeeding bank, a five-banked ship would have three hundred and ten oars in the banks, and therefore three hundred rowers approximately—or perhaps exactly, if here

συνθήκας οὕτως ἐχούσας, τριάκοντα μνᾶς ἑκάστῃ νηὶ τοῦ μηνὸς διδόναι, ὁπόσας ἂν βούλωνται τρέφειν Λακεδαιμόνιοι. ὁ δὲ Λύσανδρος τότε μὲν ἐσιώπησε· μετὰ δὲ τὸ δεῖπνον, ἐπεὶ αὐτῷ προπιὼν ὁ Κῦρος ἤρετο τί ἂν μάλιστα χαρίζοιτο ποιῶν, εἶπεν ὅτι Εἰ πρὸς τὸν μισθὸν ἑκάστῳ ναύτῃ ὀβολὸν προσθείης. ἐκ δὲ τούτου τέτταρες ὀβολοὶ ἦν ὁ μισθός, πρότερον δὲ τριώβολον.

[32] Corp. Inscr. Attic. vol. ii, no. 809, col. c, ll. 210—214, παρὰ Νεοπτολέμου Δεκελέως ταρροῦ τετρηριτικοῦ ἀπελάβομεν ⌐ΗΑ̣ΔΓ, ὃν ἔλαβεν ἐπὶ τὴν Σειρῆνα, Ἀριστοκράτους ἔργον, ll. 215—225, παρὰ Λυσανίου Σουνιέως...ταρροῦ ἀργοῦ, ὃν οὐκ ἀνεγέγραπτο ἔχων, ὃν εἶχεν ὧν Δημάδης εἰσεπρίατο, ἀπελάβομεν ΗΗΗΗΔΓ, cf. col. b, ll. 115, 116, ταρροὺς ἐπὶ τετρήρεις, οὓς Δημάδης εἰσεπρίατο. The first payment is apparently in full; but the second must be merely on account, the round sum of 250 drachms remaining due, for the oars would be worth more than 415 drachms, even when condemned. Corp. Inscr. Attic. vol. ii, no. 803, col. c, ll. 129—139, Εὔθυνος Λαμπτρεύς, ταμίας γενόμενος τριηροποικῶν ἐπὶ Ἀρχίου ἄρχοντος, ΧΧΧ⌐ΡΗ, ἀπολαβὼν κώπας παρ' ἡμῶν ἐκ τοῦ νεωρίου τῶν παραδοθεισῶν, ὧν αὐτὸς εἰσήνεγκεν, ἀδοκίμους χιλίας ὀκτακοσίας, no. 811, col. c, ll. 122—128, τοὺς τῶν νεωρίων ἐπιμελητὰς τοὺς ἐφ' Ἡγησίου ἄρχοντος ἀναγράψαι Σώπολιν ἀποδεδωκότα τῶν κωπέων ἑκάστου ΗΗΗ δραχμὰς τῶν εἰσενηνεγμένων αὐτῷ εἰς τὸ νεώριον. These κωπεῖς were κώπαι in the rough.

[33] Polybios states that 330 Roman ships fought 350 Carthaginian ships at the battle of Ecnomos in 256 B.C., and that these were five-banked ships, i. 25, Ῥωμαῖοι μὲν τριάκοντα καὶ τριακοσίαις μακραῖς ναυσὶ καταφράκτοις, Καρχη-

again some of the banks were not fully manned. Subsequently the rowers in such five-banked ships were reckoned roughly at four hundred[34]. And an increase in the number of oars was certainly to be expected : for under that system of constructing every bank for four oars more than the bank below, the lower banks would prove disproportionately short in ships of ten or sixteen banks; so that some new system would be devised for these larger ships, and then applied in course of time to the five-banked ships and possibly to the three-banked ships themselves. Nothing is known for certain about the number or arrangement of the oars in ships of more than five banks. It is said that as early as 280 B.C. there was an eight-banked ship in the fleet of Heracleia on the Black Sea with a hundred rowers in each file, and consequently eight hundred on each side, or sixteen hundred altogether. Thus, at least, Photios transcribes Memnon : but the multiplication of the numbers reads like a gloss of his own ; and these files must be the banks themselves, not the lines of

δόνιοι δὲ πεντήκοντα καὶ τριακοσίαις ναυσὶ καταφράκτοις, i. 63, μικρῷ λείπουσιν ἑπτακοσίοις σκάφεσι πεντηρικοῖς ἐναυμάχησαν πρὸς ἀλλήλους. He calculates that the Romans had about 140,000 men afloat, reckoning 300 rowers and 120 combatants for each ship, i. 26, καὶ τὸ μὲν σύμπαν ἦν στράτευμα τούτων τῆς ναυτικῆς δυνάμεως περὶ τέτταρας καὶ δέκα μυριάδας· ὡς ἂν ἑκάστης ἰδίᾳ νεὼς λαμβανούσης ἐρέτας μὲν τριακοσίους, ἐπιβάτας δὲ ἑκατὸν εἴκοσι. And he estimates that the Carthaginians had over 150,000 men afloat, judging by the number of their ships, i. 26, τό γε μὴν πλῆθος αὐτῶν ἦν ὑπὲρ πεντεκαίδεκα μυριάδας, κατὰ τὸν τῶν νεῶν λόγον. He therefore reckons a Carthaginian crew at practically the same figure as a Roman crew.

34 Pliny, xxxii. 1, *cum e tota classe quinqueremis sola non proficeret, exsilientibus protinus qui quærerent circa navem, invenere (auspicalem pisciculum) adhærentem gubernaculo, ostenderuntque Gaio, indignanti hoc fuisse quod se revocaret, quadringentorumque remigum obsequio contra se intercederet.* cf. Silius Italicus, xiv. 384—388, *medias inter sublimior ibat | terribilis visu puppis, qua nulla per omne | egressa est Libycis maior navalibus ævum : | nam quater hæc centum numeroso remige pontum | pulsabat tonsis.* Silius and Pliny were contemporary : but Pliny is speaking of a ship of 40 A.D., and Silius of a ship of 212 B.C. The Romans captured a seven-banked ship from the Carthaginians at the battle of Mylæ in 260 B.C. ; and Silius must have known this, for the capture is recorded on the Columna Rostrata of Duilius : see Corp. Inscr. Latin. vol. i, no. 195. Silius is therefore allowing 400 rowers for a ship of seven banks at least : and this allowance seems too small, seeing that there were then 300 rowers on a ship of five banks.

rowers, for a bank of two hundred oars is beyond belief[35]. On the forty-banked ship, if Callixenos may be believed, there were about four thousand rowers ; and therefore upon the average a hundred rowers for every bank of oars[36]. In both these cases the total seems to be deduced from a statement that there were a hundred oars in every bank : and such statements might not be strictly true, for ships of a single bank were sometimes said grandiloquently to have a hundred oars, although they never had more than fifty or sixty[37].

The two hundred oars of an Athenian three-banked ship were reduced to sixty when she was employed as a transport for cavalry. She then carried thirty horses; or a horse for each of the thirty spaces between the tholes of the upper bank[38]. The hold being now required for the horses, the oars in the banks could not be worked for want of space, and the oars above the upper decking would alone be avail-

[35] Memnon, Fr. 13, apud Photium, p. 226, ἦσαν δ' ἐν αὐταῖς ἄλλαι τε καὶ τῆς Ηρακλείας αἱ μετάπεμπτοι, ἐξήρεις τε καὶ πεντήρεις καὶ ἄφρακτοι, καὶ ὀκτήρης μία ἡ Λεοντοφόρος καλουμένη, μεγέθους ἕνεκα καὶ κάλλους ἥκουσα εἰς θαῦμα· ἐν ταύτῃ γὰρ ἑκατὸν μὲν ἄνδρες ἕκαστον στοῖχον ἤρεττον, ὡς ὀκτακοσίους ἐκ θατέρου μέρους γενέσθαι, ἐξ ἑκατέρων δὲ χιλίους καὶ ἑξακοσίους, οἱ δὲ ἀπὸ τῶν καταστρωμάτων μαχησόμενοι χίλιοι καὶ διακόσιοι, καὶ κυβερνῆται δύο. The sixteenth book of Memnon's history ended with 46 B.C., and that book was not the last, cf. Photios, pp. 239, 240 ; so he probably lived some generations later. Photios made his transcript about 850 A.D. He clearly takes στοῖχος to mean a line of rowers ; but in the passage quoted in note 43 on p. 16, Aristeides uses στοῖχος to denote a bank of oars, and he was probably a contemporary of Memnon. The credibility of the figures is not enhanced by the statement about the combatants. A ship of eight banks would hardly carry 1200 at a time when ships of five banks carried only 120: see note 33.

[36] Athenæos, v. 37, and Plutarch, Demetrius, 43, both quoted already in note 20 on p. 8.

[37] Pollux, i. 82, ἑκατόντορος, πεντηκόντορος, τριακόντορος, εἰκόσορος. The term ἑκατόντορος must refer, like the rest, to ships of a single bank: but there is no ground for thinking that such ships ever had an hundred oars.

[38] Thucydides, vi. 43, καὶ ἱππαγωγῷ μιᾷ τριάκοντα ἀγούσῃ ἱππέας. This was in 415 B.C. The same arrangement may perhaps be traced in the navy of the kings of Pergamos in 168 B.C. Livy, xliv. 28, mentions *quinque et triginta naves, quas hippagogos vocant, cum equitibus Gallis equisque*, and then says *octingenti ferme Gallorum occisi, ducenti vivi capti*, clearly meaning that they were all killed or captured. He therefore reckons them roughly as a thousand : and they would have numbered a thousand and fifty, if those thirty-five ships carried thirty apiece.

able : so the *perineōi* oars must have been doubled in number, while the rest were withdrawn[39]. Superannuated three-banked ships were first utilized as cavalry-transports at Athens in 430 B.C.; transports having previously been expressly built for cavalry[40].

Some anomalous ships termed *hemioliai* and *triemioliai* are first mentioned about 350 B.C., and thereafter frequently. These would technically be ships of a bank and a half, but must really be two-banked ships of an abnormal type. In the contemporary three-banked ships the men described as *perineōi* rowed an additional half-bank of oars from above the upper decking, and could presumably do likewise in two-banked ships of the same build: but if the build made this impossible, they would have to man half an ordinary bank ; and their oars would not count in numbering the banks, since they were *perineōi*. Thus, as three practically meant three and a half, one and a half would practically mean two[41].

[39] Corp. Inscr. Attic. vol. ii, no. 807, col. b, ll. 42—66, τριήρεις τάσδε ἱππηγούς,... Γνώμη—κώπας 𐌈Δ,...Ἀσκληπιάς—κώπας 𐌈Δ,... Καλλιξένα—κώπας 𐌈Δ, no. 808, col. b, ll. 8, 9, καὶ ἱππηγῶν τριῶν ταρρούς, κώπας ἑκάστης 𐌈Δ.

[40] Thucydides, ii. 56, ἦγε δὲ (Περικλῆς) ἐπὶ τῶν νεῶν ὁπλίτας Ἀθηναίων τετρακισχιλίους, καὶ ἱππέας τριακοσίους ἐν ναυσὶν ἱππαγωγοῖς πρῶτον τότε ἐκ τῶν παλαιῶν νεῶν ποιηθείσαις. Herodotos, vi. 95, παρεγένοντο δὲ καὶ αἱ ἱππαγωγοὶ νέες, τὰς τῷ προτέρῳ ἔτει προεῖπε τοῖσι ἑωυτοῦ δασμοφόροισι Δαρεῖος ἑτοιμάζειν, cf. 48, κελεύων νέας τε μακρὰς καὶ ἱππαγωγὰ πλοῖα ποιέεσθαι.

[41] Theophrastos, characteres, 25. 1; Arrian, anabasis, iii. 2. 4, vi. 1. 1, 18. 3; Diodoros, xvi. 61. 4, xix. 65. 2, xx. 93. 3; Polybios, v. 101. 2, xvi. 2. 10, 3. 4, 3. 14, 7. 1, 7. 3; Appian, de rebus Punicis, 75, de bello Mithridatico, 92; etc. The term ἡμιολία rightly describes one and a half as a whole and a half: but the term τριημιολία seems formed on false analogy with words like τριημιπόδιον, which describe one and a half as three halves, the ὁλ in τριημιολία being thus ignored. The form τριηρημιολίας occurs in Athenæos, v. 36, τὰ δ' ἀπὸ τετρήρους μέχρι τριηρημιολίας, but is plainly a corruption from τριήρεις and ἡμιολίας which occur in the parallel passage, Appian, præfatio, 10, τριήρεις δ' ἀπὸ ἡμιολίας μέχρι πεντήρους, where τριήρεις is used as a generic term for war-ships. The existence of three banks of oars on the τριημιολίαι is not to be inferred from Polybios, xvi. 3, ὑποπεσούσης γὰρ αὐτῇ (τῇ δεκήρει) τριημιολίας, ταύτῃ δοῦσα πληγὴν βιαίαν κατὰ μέσον τὸ κῦτος ὑπὸ τὸν θρανίτην σκαλμόν, ἐδέθη, τοῦ κυβερνήτου τὴν ὁρμὴν τῆς νεὼς οὐκέτι δυνηθέντος ἀναλαβεῖν. The expression θρανίτης σκαλμός would certainly refer to the upper bank on a three-banked ship: but it would also refer to the upper bank in any ship with more than one. Thus Athenæos speaks of the longest oars in the forty-banked ship as κώπας θρανιτικάς, v. 37.

The Liburnians used to build very handy two-banked ships for their irregular warfare in the Adriatic; and soon after 50 B.C. the Romans took these as models for their own two-banked ships[42]. This type may perhaps be recognized in the Roman two-banked ship in fg. 25. The Greeks had made *trieres*, a three-banked ship, a generic term for war-ships[43], though some had more banks than three and some had less. And in course of time the Romans made *liburna*, a two-banked ship, a similar generic term; applying it indiscriminately about 400 A.D. to war-ships of every rate from those of one bank to those of five banks—for apparently they still had such ships in the West, though in the East their largest war-ships were merely of two banks[44]. But about 500 A.D. the Byzan-

---

[42] Appian, de rebus Illyricis, 3, καὶ ναυτικοὶ μὲν ἐπὶ τοῖς ᾿Αρδιαίοις ἐγένοντο Λιβυρνοί, γένος ἕτερον ᾿Ιλλυριῶν, οἳ τὸν ᾿Ιόνιον καὶ τὰς νήσους ἐλῄστευον ναυσὶν ὠκείαις τε καὶ κούφαις. ὅθεν ἔτι νῦν ῾Ρωμαῖοι τὰ κοῦφα καὶ ὀξέα δίκροτα Λιβυρνίδας προσαγορεύουσιν. See also note on *lembi* on p. 115 as to the style of shipbuilding adopted in Illyria. The employment of Liburnian ships in Roman fleets is mentioned by Cæsar, de bello civili, iii. 5, 9, in 48 B.C. and by Horace, epodes, i. 1, in 31 B.C.; and subsequently by Lucan, iii. 534, with reference to 49 B.C. These ships never had ten banks of oars: the reading *deceris* is merely a foolish emendation for *de cedris* in Suetonius, Caligula, 37, *fabricavit et de cedris Liburnicas gemmatis puppibus, versicoloribus velis, etc.* There were only two banks, Lucan, iii. 529—536, *cornua Romanæ classis, validæque triremes, | quasque quater surgens exstructi remigis ordo | commovet, et plures quæ mergunt æquore pinus, | multiplices cinxere rates. hoc robur aperto | oppositum pelago. lunata fronte recedunt | ordine contentæ gemino crevisse Liburnæ. | celsior at cunctis Bruti prætoria puppis | verberibus senis agitur.* Thus in inscriptions the Romans described ships as six-banked, five-banked, four-banked, three-banked, and Liburnian: see Corp. Inscr. Latin. vol. x, index, p. 1128, *naves*.

[43] Appian, præfatio, 10, τριήρεις δὲ ἀπὸ ἡμιολίας μέχρι πεντήρους. Ælius Aristeides, Rhodiaca, p. 341, τριήρεις δ᾿ ἐπὶ τούτοις ὑπῆρχεν ἰδεῖν δικρότους καὶ τρικρότους καὶ εἰς ἑπτὰ καὶ εἰς ἐννέα στοίχους.

[44] Vegetius, iv. 37, *quod ad magnitudinem pertinet, minimæ liburnæ remorum habent singulos ordines, paulo maiores binos, idoneæ mensuræ ternos vel quaternos interdum quinos sortiuntur remigio gradus. nec hoc cuiquam enorme videatur, cum in Actiaco prælio longe maiora referantur concurrisse navigia, ut senorum etiam vel ultra ordinum fuerint.* But this usage is not adopted by his contemporary, Zosimos, v. 20, ἐπεμελεῖτο δὲ (Φραουῖτος) καὶ τοῦ ναυτικοῦ· πλοῖα γὰρ ἦν αὐτῷ πρὸς ναυμαχίαν ἀρκοῦντα, Λίβερνα ταῦτα καλούμενα, ἀπό τινος πόλεως ἐν ᾿Ιταλίᾳ κειμένης ὀνομασθέντα, καθ᾿ ἣν ἐξ ἀρχῆς τούτων τῶν πλοίων τὸ εἶδος ἐναυπηγήθη. δοκοῦσι δέ πως τὰ πλοῖα ταῦτα ταχυναυτεῖσθαι πεντηκοντόρων οὐχ ἧττον, κατὰ πολὺ τῶν τριηρικῶν ἐλαττούμενα, πλείστοις ἔτεσι τῆς τούτων ἐκλιπούσης

tines introduced *dromon* as a generic term for war-ships, calling them racers in allusion to their superiority to merchant-ships in speed. In the Byzantine fleet at this time they were ships of a single bank, but those built in Italy for the fleet at Ravenna were three-banked ships[45]. Unfortunately, the contemporary mosaic at Ravenna in fg. 39 represents the fleet in the harbour there very unintelligently.

The arrangement of the oars in Byzantine war-ships is clearly described in a treatise attributed by tradition to Leo VI., but apparently reduced to its present form during the reign of his son and successor Constantine VII. No ship had more than two banks of oars. Every two-banked ship had at least twenty-five oars on each side of each bank, or a hundred

δημιουργίας, εἰ καὶ Πολύβιος ὁ συγγραφεὺς ἐκτίθεσθαί πως ἔδοξε τῶν ἑξηρικῶν πλοίων τὰ μέτρα, οἷς φαίνονται πολλάκις Ῥωμαῖοι καὶ Καρχηδόνιοι πολεμήσαντες πρὸς ἀλλήλους. Zosimos obviously is describing two-banked ships as πλοῖα Λίβερνα, just as he describes three-banked ships as πλοῖα τριηρικά and ships of a single bank as πεντηκόντοροι, his notion being simply that ships of two banks are superior to ships of one bank but inferior to ships of three banks. The vague usage is sanctioned by Tacitus, Germania, 9, *signum ipsum in modum liburnæ figuratum*, i.e. *Isidis navigium*. And by Pliny, ix. 5, *ceu liburnicarum rostris fodiunt*, ix. 47, *liburnicarum ludens imagine*, x. 32, *liburnicarum modo, rostrato impetu feruntur*, xvi. 17, *liburnicarum ad usus*. Tacitus and Pliny clearly are treating the Liburnians as a representative class of ships; for in these comparisons nothing turns on any peculiarity in the build.

[45] Procopios, de bello Vandalico, i. 11, ἦσαν δὲ αὐτοῖς καὶ πλοῖα μακρά, ὡς ἐς ναυμαχίαν παρεσκευασμένα, ἐνενήκοντα δύο, μονήρη μέντοι καὶ ὀροφὰς ὕπερθεν ἔχοντα, ὅπως οἱ ταῦτα ἐρέσσοντες πρὸς τῶν πολεμίων ὡς ἥκιστα βάλλοιντο. δρόμωνας καλοῦσι τὰ πλοῖα ταῦτα οἱ νῦν ἄνθρωποι· πλεῖν γὰρ κατὰ τάχος δύνανται μάλιστα. ἐν τούτοις δὴ Βυζάντιοι δισχίλιοι ἔπλεον, αὐτερέται πάντες· περίνεως γὰρ ἦν ἐν τούτοις οὐδείς. This certainly does not imply that these ninety-two ships carried only two thousand rowers altogether, or hardly more than twenty rowers apiece. The point is that the two thousand Byzantines helped to row the ships, though normally exempted from this drudgery as combatants. Leo, tactica, xix. 1, ἐπὶ θαλάσσης μάχεσθαι διὰ τῶν ποτε λεγομένων τριήρων, νῦν δὲ δρομώνων καλουμένων. Cassiodorus, epistolæ variæ, v. 16, *cum nostrum igitur animum frequens cura pulsaret naves Italiam non habere, decrevimus mille interim dromones fabricandos assumere.* 17, *renuntias illico completum quod vix credi poterat inchoatum. obtulisti oculis nostris subito classeam silvam hominum, domos aquatiles, exercituales pedes: trireme vehiculum, remorum tantum numerum prodens sed hominum facies diligenter abscondens—hoc primum instituisse legimus Argonautas...ad urbem Ravennatam congregatio navium cuncta conveniat.* Both those despatches are from Theodoric to Abundantius. For the expression *trireme vehiculum*, cf. Paulinus Nolanus, poemata, xxiv. 72, *quadriremis machina.*

T.   *b*

altogether; and each oar was worked by one man. The two-banked ships were of two sizes. The smaller carried at least a hundred men for rowing and fighting. The larger carried at least two hundred men; and in action fifty rowed in the lower bank, while a hundred and fifty fought above[46]. Ships of this type were employed by Constantine VII. for an attack on Crete in 949 A.D. The smaller had a company of a hundred and eight or ten men; and the larger had a double company of two hundred and twenty men with one hundred and twenty oars. But ships of another type were also employed: the smaller carrying a hundred and twenty men, and the larger a hundred and fifty[47]. As a hundred men sufficed for two banks of oars, these ships presumably were also of two banks. Ten men more were carried on the ships of this type that were employed by Leo VI. for an attack on Crete about 906 A.D.; or a hundred and thirty in the smaller, and a hundred and sixty in the larger. The larger ships of the other type were also employed, but not the smaller. They also carried ten men more at that time, or two hundred and

---

[46] Leo, tactica, xix. 7, ἕκαστος δὲ τῶν δρομώνων εὐμήκης ἔστω καὶ σύμμετρος, ἔχων μὲν τὰς λεγομένας ἐλασίας δύο, τήν τε κάτω καὶ τὴν ἄνω. 8, ἑκάστη δὲ ἐχέτω ζυγοὺς τὸ ἐλάχιστον πέντε καὶ εἴκοσιν, ἐν οἷς οἱ κωπηλάται καθεσθήσονται. ὡς εἶναι ζυγοὺς τοὺς ἅπαντας κάτω μὲν εἴκοσι καὶ πέντε, ἄνω δὲ ὁμοίως εἴκοσι καὶ πέντε, ὁμοῦ πεντήκοντα· καθ' ἕνα δὲ αὐτῶν δύο καθεξέσθωσαν οἱ κωπηλατοῦντες, εἷς μὲν δεξιά, εἷς δὲ ἀριστερά. ὡς εἶναι τοὺς ἅπαντας κωπηλάτας ὁμοῦ (καὶ τοὺς αὐτοὺς καὶ στρατιώτας) τούς τε ἄνω καὶ τοὺς κάτω ἄνδρας ἑκατόν. 9, καὶ ἕτεροι δὲ δρόμωνες κατασκευαζέσθωσάν σοι τούτων μείζονες, ἀπὸ διακοσίων χωροῦντες ἀνδρῶν (ἢ πλείω τούτων ἢ ἐλάττω κατὰ τὴν χρείαν τὴν δέουσαν ἐπὶ καιροῦ κατὰ τῶν ἐναντίων) ὧν οἱ μὲν πεντήκοντα τὴν κάτω ἐλασίαν ὑπουργήσουσιν, οἱ δὲ ἑκατὸν πεντήκοντα ἄνω ἑστῶτες ἅπαντες ἔνοπλοι μαχήσονται τοῖς πολεμίοις.

[47] Porphyrogenitos, de cærimoniis, ii. 45, p. 384, ὁ στρατηγὸς τοῦ Αἰγαίου πελάγους μετὰ χελανδίων παμφύλων ϛ´ ἀνὰ ἀνδρῶν ρκ´ καὶ χελανδίων οὐσιακῶν δ´ ἀνὰ ἀνδρῶν ρη´· κατελείφθη δὲ καὶ μία οὐσία εἰς τὸ κόψαι τὴν τῆς ὀγδόης ἰνδικτίονος ξυλήν. ὁ στρατηγὸς τῆς Σάμου μετὰ χελανδίων παμφύλων ϛ´ ἀνὰ ἀνδρῶν ρν´ καὶ χελανδίων οὐσιακῶν ϛ´ ἀνὰ ἀνδρῶν ρη´· ἀπεστάλησαν δὲ μετὰ τοῦ πρωτοσπαθαρίου Ἰωάννου καὶ ἀσηκρήτης ἐν Ἀφρικῇ χελάνδια γ´ καὶ δρόμωνες δ´ ἀνὰ ἀνδρῶν σκ´. ὁ στρατηγὸς τῶν Κιβυρραιωτῶν μετὰ χελανδίων παμφύλων ϛ´ ἀνὰ ἀνδρῶν ρν´ καὶ χελανδίων οὐσιακῶν ϛ´ ἀνὰ ἀνδρῶν ρι´· κατελείφθη δὲ καὶ εἰς φύλαξιν τοῦ θέματος πάμφυλοι β´, οὐσιακὰ δ´· κατελείφθη δὲ καὶ εἰς τὸ κόψαι τὴν τῆς ὀγδόης ἰνδικτίονος ξυλὴν οὐσίαι β´· κατελείφθη δὲ καὶ εἰς φύλαξιν τοῦ κυροῦ Στεφάνου τοῦ γυναικαδελφοῦ τοῦ βασιλέως ἐν Ῥόδῳ οὐσία α´ καὶ δρομώνων δ´ ἀνὰ ἀνδρῶν σκ´. An οὐσία was a company, and the χελάνδια οὐσιακά were ships carrying a company apiece. They carried 108 or 110

thirty, besides seventy others for fighting only and not for rowing; and therefore carried three hundred altogether[48]. As there were more rowers than oars in many of these ships, though every oar was managed by one man, these rowers must have worked by turns.

Thus, after a lapse of sixteen centuries, the system of successive banks was again restricted to two-banked ships with a hundred and twenty oars at most; and soon afterwards it was abandoned. The term *galea* was already applied to war-ships of a single bank[49]: but those new systems were not yet devised, which made the single bank of the mediæval galleys as effective as the numerous banks of the ancient war-ships. One of these new systems increased the number of oars by placing them at shorter intervals along the bank, and making them of several different lengths inboard, the rowers being arranged in several lines along the deck; while the other maintained the number of oars at fifty or sixty, but increased their size and strength, several rowers working together at every oar[50].

men; so the eight dromons, which each carried 220 men, each carried two companies. Twenty other dromons are explicitly credited with two companies apiece, p. 384, δρόμονες κ′ ἀνὰ οὐσιῶν β′· οὐσίαι μ′. Each therefore carried 220 men: yet only 120 oars, p. 388, εἰς ἐξόπλισιν τῶν κ′ δρομονίων—κωπία ἀνὰ ρκ′· ὁμοῦ ,βυ′.

[48] Porphyrogenitos, de cærimoniis, ii. 44, p. 377, διὰ τοῦ θέματος τοῦ Αἰγαίου πελάγους. δρόμονες ϛ′ ἔχοντες ἀνὰ ἀνδρῶν κωπηλατῶν σλ′ καὶ ἀνὰ πολεμιστῶν ο′· ὁμοῦ ,βρ′. πάμφυλοι ϛ′ ἔχοντες οἱ μὲν γ′ ἀνὰ ἀνδρῶν ρξ′, οἱ δὲ ἕτεροι δ′ ἀνὰ ἀνδρῶν ρλ′· ὁμοῦ ,α. ὁμοῦ τὸ πᾶν διὰ τοῦ θέματος τοῦ Αἰγαίου πελάγους ,γρ′. cf. ii. 45, p. 387, ὁ δρόμων ὀφείλει ἔχειν ἄνδρας τ′, οἱ μὲν σλ′ πλόϊμοι κωπηλάται ἤτοι καὶ πολεμισταί, καὶ οἱ ἕτεροι ο′ ἄνδρες πολεμισταί. That refers to 949 A.D.: but the ἐξόπλισις δρόμονος α′, pp. 386, 387, differs materially from the ἐξόπλισις τῶν κ′ δρομονίων, pp. 387, 388, so this dromon had now become anomalous.

[49] Leo, tactica, xix. 10, καὶ ἔτι δὲ κατασκευάσεις δρόμωνας ἐλάττους δρομικωτάτους, οἱονεὶ γαλαίας ἢ μονήρεις λεγομένους. The forms γαλαίαι and γαλέαι were used indifferently at this period.

[50] According to Pantero Pantera, armata navale, i. 15, the big oars were known as *remi di scaloccio*, and were worked by two or three men apiece on the *galeotte*, by three or four and sometimes by five or six on the *galee*, and by as many as eight or even more on the *galeazze*. The big oars were superseding the small oars. These were known as *remi à zenzile*, and had usually been worked in groups of three or four or five, with one man for every oar. Pantera was captain of the Papal galleys, and published his work at Rome in 1614.

b 2

Merchant-ships were generally too bulky to be propelled by oars. Nevertheless they carried a few, very often twenty[51]: and these probably sufficed for bringing the ship's head round and other such purposes, though hardly numerous enough for driving the ship along. Thus, a merchant-ship trying to make some headway with her oars is compared by Aristotle to an insect feebly buzzing along on wings too small for its body, after the manner of cockchafers and bees: whereas a war-ship under way, rhythmically dipping her vast mass of oars, was commonly compared to a bird upon its flight[52].

The banks of oars were so arranged that the largest war-ships were of no great height. To shew the size of the great ships in Antony's fleet at the battle of Actium in 31 B.C., Orosius remarks that they actually were ten feet in height above the

---

[51] Odyssey, ix. 322—324, ὅσσον θ' ἱστὸν νηὸς ἐεικοσόροιο μελαίνης, | φορτίδος, εὐρείης, ἥτ' ἐκπεράᾳ μέγα λαῖτμα· | τόσσον ἔην μῆκος, τόσσον πάχος εἰσοράασθαι. Demosthenes, in Lacritum, 18, τὰ δὲ τρισχίλια κεράμια ἄγεσθαι ταῦτα εἰς τὸν Πόντον ἐν τῇ εἰκοσόρῳ ἣν Ὑβλήσιος ἐναυκλήρει. Athenæos, v. 41, ἦν δ' ἡ ναῦς τῇ μὲν κατασκευῇ εἰκόσορος, κ.τ.λ., cf. 40, πλοῖα σιτηγὰ κατασκευαζόμενος, ὧν ἑνὸς τῆς κατασκευῆς μνησθήσομαι.

[52] Aristotle, de animalium incessu, 10, βραδεῖα δ' ἡ πτῆσις τῶν ὁλοπτέρων ἐστὶ καὶ ἀσθενὴς διὰ τὸ μὴ κατὰ λόγον ἔχειν τὴν τῶν πτερῶν φύσιν πρὸς τὸ τοῦ σώματος βάρος, ἀλλὰ τὸ μὲν πολύ, τὰ δὲ μικρὰ καὶ ἀσθενῆ· ὥσπερ ἂν οὖν εἰ ὁλκαδικὸν πλοῖον ἐπιχειροίη κώπαις ποιεῖσθαι τὸν πλοῦν, οὕτω ταῦτα τῇ πτήσει χρῆται. ὑπεναντίως δ' ἔχουσιν οἱ ὄρνιθες τοῖς ὁλοπτέροις τὴν τῶν πτερῶν φύσιν, κ.τ.λ.   The metaphor about the birds occurs frequently. Odyssey, xi. 124, 125, οὐδ' ἄρα τοίγ' ἴσασι νέας φοινικο-παρῄους, | οὐδ' εὐήρε' ἐρετμά, τάτε πτερὰ νηυσὶ πέλονται. Euripides, Troades, 1085, 1086, ἐμὲ δὲ πόντιον σκάφος | ἀΐσσον πτεροῖσι πορεύσει. Æschylos, Agamemnon, 52, πτερύγων ἐρετμοῖσιν ἐρεσσόμενοι, sc. αἰγύπιοι. Polybios, i. 46, αἱ δὲ νῆες ἐπεῖχον, ἐπτερωκυῖαι πρὸς τὴν ἐμβολήν. Plutarch, Antonius, 63, τοὺς δὲ ταρσοὺς τῶν νεῶν ἐγείρας καὶ πτερώσας ἑκατέρωθεν. Moschos, ii. 59, 60, ὄρνις, ἀγαλλόμενος πτερύγων πολυανθέι χροιῇ, | ταρσὰ δ' ἀναπλώσας, ὡσεί τέ τις ὠκύαλος νηῦς.   Also in Latin.   Virgil, Æneid, i. 300, 301, volat ille per aera magnum | remigio alarum. Propertius, iv. 6. 47, 48, nec te, quod classis centenis remigat alis, | terreat.   But this does not please Quintilian, viii. 6. 18.

[53] Orosius, vi. 19, classis Antonii centum septuaginta navium fuit, quantum numero cedens tantum magnitudine præcellens, nam decem pedum altitudine a mari aberant.   This definite statement deserves more attention than the grotesque exaggerations of Virgil, Æneid, viii. 691, 692, pelago credas innare revulsas | Cycladas, aut montes concurrere montibus altos.   The notion of an encounter with islands is neatly parodied by Lucian, veræ historiæ, i. 40—42; but is adopted with some apology by Dion Cassius, l. 33, εἴκασεν ἄν τις ἰδὼν τὰ γιγνόμενα, ὡς μικρὰ μεγάλοις ὁμοιῶσαι, τείχεσί τισιν ἢ καὶ νήσοις πολλαῖς καὶ πυκναῖς ἐκ θαλάσσης

water-line[53] : and these great ships were of ten banks[54]. He therefore allows a foot of freeboard for each bank of oars ; and thus would make a sixteen-banked ship only sixteen feet in height above the water-line. And practically there never were more than sixteen banks on a sea-going ship.

A ship of a single bank, which was preserved at Rome as a relic of Æneas, was a hundred and twenty feet in length[55]: and as she probably was a fifty-oared ship, there probably were twenty-five oars on each side, and therefore twenty-four spaces between the tholes, or one such space for every five feet of her length. And this relation would not be fortuitous; for in ancient ships all the dimensions were related to the interval between the tholes[56]. A thirty-oared ship, with fourteen such spaces, would thus be seventy feet in length;

πολιορκουμέναις. The tamer notion of an encounter with forts seems due to Plutarch, Antonius, 66, where he compares the battle to a τειχομαχία, apparently in imitation of the common-place in Latin that war-ships were like walled towns. Thus, the expression *urbis instar* is applied to a four-banked ship by Cicero, in Verrem, ii. v. 34, and the expression *urbis opus* to a three-banked ship by Virgil, Æneid, v. 119.

[54] Plutarch, Antonius, 64, ὡς δὲ ναυμαχεῖν ἐδέδοκτο, τὰς μὲν ἄλλας ἐνέπρησε ναῦς—πλὴν ἐξήκοντα τῶν Αἰγυπτίων—τὰς δὲ ἀρίστας καὶ μεγίστας ἀπὸ τριήρους μέχρι δεκήρους ἐπλήρου. Dion Cassius, l. 23, τριήρεις μὲν γὰρ ὀλίγας, τετρήρεις δὲ καὶ δεκήρεις καὶ τὰ λοιπὰ τὰ διὰ μέσου πάντα ἐξεποίησεν. Strabo, vii. 7. 6, ἀνέθηκε Καῖσαρ τὴν δεκαναίαν ἀκροθίνιον ἀπὸ μονοκρότου μέχρι δεκήρους.

[55] Procopios, de bello Gothico, iv. 22, ἔτι μέντοι καὶ ὅσα μνημεῖα τοῦ γένους ἐλέλειπτο ἔτι, ἐν τοῖς καὶ ἡ ναῦς Αἰνείου, τοῦ τῆς πόλεως οἰκιστοῦ, καὶ εἰς τόδε κεῖται, θέαμα παντελῶς ἄπιστον. νεώσοικον γὰρ ποιησάμενοι ἐν μέσῃ τῇ πόλει παρὰ τὴν τοῦ Τιβέριδος ὄχθην, ἐνταῦθά τε αὐτὴν καταθέμενοι, ἐξ ἐκείνου τηροῦσιν. ἥπερ ὁποία ποτέ ἐστιν αὐτὸς θεασάμενος ἐρῶν ἔρχομαι. μονήρης δὲ ἡ ναῦς ἥδε καὶ περιμήκης ἄγαν τυγχάνει οὖσα, μῆκος μὲν ποδῶν εἴκοσι καὶ ἑκατόν, εὖρος δὲ πέντε καὶ εἴκοσι, τὸ δέ γε ὕψος τοσαύτη ἐστὶν ὅσον αὐτὴν ἐρέσσεσθαι μὴ ἀδύνατα εἶναι.

[56] Vitruvius, i. 2. 4, *uti in hominis corpore e cubito pede palmo digito ceterisque particulis symmetros est eurythmiæ qualitas, sic est in operum perfectionibus: et primum in ædibus sacris aut e columnarum crassitudinibus aut triglypho aut etiam embate, sed et ballistæ e foramine, quod Græci* PERITRETON *vocitant, navis interscalmio, quod* DIPHECIACA *dicitur, item ceterorum operum e membris invenitur symmetriarum ratiocinatio.* The letters DIPHECIACA seem intended for some Greek word ; and the word διπηχαική has been invented for the occasion. If this word had any meaning, it would mean that the interval between the tholes amounted to two cubits, and was therefore a fixed distance : but the distance certainly was variable, since it formed the unit for calculating the dimensions of a ship, and all ships were not alike.

and a three-banked ship, with thirty such spaces in the upper
bank, a hundred and fifty feet in length. These dimensions
certainly appear excessive. Yet the oars could hardly have
been worked, had the interval between the tholes been less
than three feet; so the distance from the first thole to the
last must have been at least forty-two feet on a thirty-oared
ship, seventy-two feet on a fifty-oared ship, and ninety feet
on a three-banked ship: and this distance seems little more
than three-fifths of the extreme length in most of the ships
depicted by the ancients. Moreover, these ships look as
though they were clear of the water for fully a fifth of their
length by reason of the overhanging stern and the elevated
ram. The ship of Æneas was twenty-five feet broad, or more
than a fifth of her length in beam: but the Greek war-ships
were considerably narrower. The remains of the Athenian
docks in the harbour of Zea shew that originally they were
quite a hundred and fifty feet in length but only twenty feet in

[57] Plans and measurements of the docks at Zea in the Πρακτικὰ τῆς ἐν᾿Αθήναις
ἀρχαιολογικῆς ἑταιρίας for 1885, plates 2 and 3, cf. pp. 63—71. The docks
themselves are about 19 ft. 5 in. in breadth, or twenty feet by ancient Greek
measurement; and they are divided by partitions which are about 1 ft. 11 in. in
breadth, so that the distance from centre to centre is about 21 ft. 4 in. In the
ruins of the docks at Munychia this distance is about 10 in. less: but possibly the
partitions were narrower. All the docks at Zea are in ruins at the lower end:
yet some of them are still 144 ft. in length. They certainly were not meant
to take two ships apiece, one behind another: there never were double docks,
νεώρια, though sometimes there were double sheds above the docks, νεωσοίκοι.
Diodoros, xiv. 42, ᾠκοδόμει δὲ (Διονύσιος) καὶ νεωσοίκους πολυτελεῖς ἑκατὸν ἑξήκοντα,
τοὺς πλείστους δύο ναῦς δεχομένους, Plato, Critias, p. 116, τέμνοντες δὲ ἅμα ἀπειργά-
ζοντο νεωσοίκους κοίλους διπλοῦς ἐντός, κατηρεφεῖς αὐτῇ τῇ πέτρᾳ. There are lines
of columns between the docks at Zea; and these columns are spaced differently in
alternate lines, as if to carry different weights. So these docks undoubtedly were
roofed in pairs: but in no other sense were they double.

[58] Athenæos, v. 37, already quoted in note 24 on p. 9. A ship of this length
would have 170 oars in the uppermost bank, with 84 spaces between the tholes on
either side, if she had one such space for every five feet of her length : and if each
bank held four oars more than the bank below, and there were 54 in the lowest
bank—see pp. 11 ff.—there would be 170 in the uppermost bank on a ship of
thirty banks. The coincidence is curious.

[59] This usage of μακρά and longa occurs frequently, e.g. Polybios, xxii. 26, ἀποδότω
δὲ καὶ τὰς ναῦς τὰς μακρὰς καὶ τὰ ἐκ τούτων ἄρμενα καὶ τὰ σκεύη = Livy, xxxviii. 38,
tradito et naves longas armamentaque earum, both authors quoting from the treaty
under which Antiochos surrendered his navy to the Romans in 189 B.C. There

breadth[57]. These docks presumably were not much longer than the ships for which they were designed, and the ships certainly were not broader than the docks; so these ships could hardly have exceeded two-fifteenths of their length in beam. And this is approximately the ratio of length to breadth which Callixenos ascribes to the alleged forty-banked ship, the length being four hundred and twenty feet and the breadth fifty-seven[58].

The regular war-ships differed so strikingly from merchant-ships in their proportions that they were generally known as the long ships, while these were known as the round ships[59]. But ships sometimes were constructed on an intermediate system of proportion, and consequently could not thus be classed as long or round[60]. And the round ships were themselves of several different types; while a multitude of types prevailed among the vessels that were not large enough to rank as ships[61].

was a corresponding usage of στρογγύλη. Athenæos, viii. 42, ἐρωτηθεὶς δὲ (Στρατό-νικος) ὑπό τινος, τίνα τῶν πλοίων ἀσφαλέστατα ἐστί ; τὰ μακρά, ἢ τὰ στρογγύλα ; τὰ νενεωλκημένα, εἶπεν. Theophrastos, historia plantarum, v. 7. 1, τὰς μὲν γὰρ τριήρεις καὶ τὰ μακρὰ πλοῖα ἐλάτινα ποιοῦσι διὰ κουφότητα, τὰ δὲ στρογγύλα πεύκινα διὰ τὸ ἀσαπές. Xenophon, Hellenica, v. 1. 21, καὶ καταδύειν μὲν οὐκ εἴα στρογγύλον πλοῖον οὐδὲ λυμαίνεσθαι ταῖς ἑαυτῶν ναυσίν · εἰ δέ που τριήρη ἴδοιεν ὁρμοῦσαν, ταύτην πειρᾶσθαι ἄπλουν ποιεῖν. cf. Herodotos, i. 163, already quoted in note 8 on p. 4. But this usage was not adopted in Latin; and navis longa is opposed to navis oneraria, just as ναῦς μακρά is sometimes opposed to ὁλκάς. Cæsar, de bello Gallico, iv. 22, navibus circiter octoginta onerariis coactis contractisque, quot satis esse ad duas transportandas legiones existimabat, quicquid præterea navium longarum habebat, quæstori legatis præfectisque distribuit. Appian, de bellis civilibus, ii. 54, καὶ δύο τελῶν ἄλλων ἐπελθόντων, ὅδε καὶ τάδε προσλαβὼν ἀνήγετο χειμῶνος ἐπὶ ὁλκάδων · αἱ γὰρ ἦσαν αὐτῷ νῆες ὀλίγαι μακραί, Σαρδὼ καὶ Σικελίαν ἐφρούρουν.

[60] Athenæos, v. 38, quoting Callixenos, τὸ δὲ σχῆμ' αὐτῆς οὔτε ταῖς μακραῖς ναυσὶν οὔτε ταῖς στρογγύλαις ἐοικός, ἀλλὰ παρηλλαγμένον τε καὶ πρὸς τὴν χρείαν τοῦ ποταμοῦ τὸ βάθος. Arrian, Fr. 19, apud Suidam, s. v. ναῦς :—εἶχε δὲ ἡ ναῦς μῆκος μὲν κατὰ τριήρη μάλιστα, εὖρος δὲ καὶ βάθος καθ' ὁλκάδα, ὅσον μεγίστη Νικομηδὶς ἢ Αἰγυπτία. Both these vessels were designed for rivers ; the former for the Nile under Ptolemy Philopator, the latter apparently for the Tigris under Trajan. Appian, de bellis civilibus, v. 95, ἐδωρήσατο δὲ καὶ Ὀκταουία τὸν ἀδελφόν, αἰτήσασα παρ' Ἀντωνίου, δέκα φασήλοις τριηρετικοῖς, ἐπιμίκτοις ἔκ τε φορτίδων νεῶν καὶ μακρῶν. See note on μυοπάρωνες on p. 108 for a further account of these ships.

[61] See note on actuariæ on p. 105, and subsequent notes in the Appendix. The 'round' class would include the γαῦλοι and the ἵπποι, the corbitæ and the cybææ, and perhaps the κάνθαροι and the κύκνοι and also the pontones.

The dimensions of one of the great merchant-ships employed in carrying corn from Egypt to Italy about 150 A.D. have fortunately been put on record. According to Lucian, her length was a hundred and eighty feet, while her breadth was slightly more than a fourth of her length, and her depth was forty-three feet and a half, reckoning from the upper deck to the bottom of the hold; so that, including the keel, her depth must have been about the same as her breadth[62].

The well-known dimensions in the Hebrew version of the legend of the Flood, four hundred and fifty feet of length, seventy-five feet of breadth, and forty-five feet of depth, apparently belong to the ark that has been introduced there under Egyptian influence, and not to the ship that has been implicitly retained there with other features of the Babylonian versions. The earlier Babylonian version in the inscriptions states that the depth of the ship was the same as the breadth, but is illegible in its statement of the measurements[63]. The extant copies of the later Babylonian version recorded by Berosos state that the length of the ship was either five or fifteen stades, and the breadth two stades[64]. In this equality

---

[62] Lucian, navigium, 1, τί γὰρ ἔδει καὶ ποιεῖν, ὦ Λυκῖνε, σχολὴν ἄγοντα, πυθόμενον οὕτως ὑπερμεγέθη ναῦν καὶ πέρα τοῦ μέτρου εἰς τὸν Πειραιᾶ καταπεπλευκέναι μίαν τῶν ἀπ' Αἰγύπτου εἰς Ἰταλίαν σιταγωγῶν ; 5, ἀλλὰ μεταξὺ λόγων, ἡλίκη ναῦς, εἴκοσι καὶ ἑκατὸν πήχεων ἔλεγε τὸ μῆκος ὁ ναυπηγός, εὖρος δὲ ὑπὲρ τὸ τέταρτον μάλιστα τούτου, καὶ ἀπὸ τοῦ καταστρώματος ἐς τὸν πυθμένα, ᾗ βαθύτατον κατὰ τὸν ἄντλον, ἐννέα πρὸς τοῖς εἴκοσι.

[63] Rawlinson, Cuneiform Inscriptions of Western Asia, vol. iv, pl. 50, col. 1, ll. 25, 26=pl. 43, col. 1, ll. 27, 28, in the new edition. I am indebted to Dr Budge, of the British Museum, for verifying the statement in the text.

[64] Berosos, Fr. 7, apud Syncellum, p. 30, σκάφος, τὸ μὲν μῆκος σταδίων πέντε, τὸ δὲ πλάτος σταδίων δύο, but the length is estimated at fifteen stades instead of five in the corresponding extract from Berosos in the first book of the Chronica of Eusebios, as retranslated from the Armenian edition. If these were common stades of a hundred fathoms each, the length of the ship would be either 3000 ft. or 9000 ft., and the breadth 1200 ft.: so the reading must be corrupt.

[65] Genesis, vi. 15, καὶ οὕτω ποιήσεις τὴν κιβωτόν· τριακοσίων πήχεων τὸ μῆκος τῆς κιβωτοῦ, καὶ πεντήκοντα πήχεων τὸ πλάτος, καὶ τριάκοντα πήχεων τὸ ὕψος αὐτῆς. The word seems to have puzzled Philo Judæus, for he speaks vaguely of a wooden structure without a hint about its shape, vita Moysis, ii. 11, ξύλινον δημιουργήσας ἔργον μέγιστον εἰς πήχεις τριακοσίους μῆκος, κ.τ.λ. cf. 12, πρόεισιν ἐκ τοῦ ξυλίνου κατασκευάσματος. In the Greek version of the legend, with Deucalion as hero, the vessel is termed a box, λάρναξ.

of breadth and depth the legendary vessel resembles the merchant-ship just mentioned; and in a possible ratio of breadth to length she resembles the war-ships for which the docks at Zea were constructed: but in none of her proportions does she resemble the ark. The authors of the Septuagint had every means of ascertaining the exact sense of the word *têbâh*, or *ark*, since it was of Egyptian origin; and they translated it by the word *kibotos*, or *chest*. This was an epithet of Apameia in Phrygia: and upon coins of that city the ark of Noah is represented as a rectangular chest[65].

The tonnage of ancient ships cannot safely be deduced from their dimensions, as so little is known about their form. But the amount of cargo carried by various merchant-ships is here and there recorded, this amount being generally computed by the talent or the amphora, which each weighed about a fortieth part of a ton[66]. And the largest merchant-ships are always described as carrying ten thousand talents, or 250 tons, though they may really have carried rather more, ten thousand being a round number of the vaguest sort[67]. The tonnage of such ships would be roughly 150, register.

[66] Herodotos, i. 194, ποιέεται δὲ καὶ κάρτα μεγάλα ταῦτα τὰ πλοῖα καὶ ἐλάσσω· τὰ δὲ μέγιστα αὐτῶν καὶ πεντακισχιλίων ταλάντων γόμον ἔχει, ii. 96, ἔστι δέ σφι τὰ πλοῖα ταῦτα πλήθεϊ πολλά, καὶ ἄγει ἔνια πολλὰς χιλιάδας ταλάντων, the former on the Euphrates and the latter on the Nile. Athenæos, v. 43, κέρκουρος, τρισχίλια τάλαντα δέχεσθαι δυνάμενος. Livy, xxi. 63, citing a law enacted at Rome shortly before 220 B.C., *ne quis senator, cuive senatorius pater fuisset, maritimam navem, quæ plus quam trecentarum amphorarum esset, haberet: id satis habitum ad fructus ex agris vectandos: quæstus omnis Patribus indecorus visus est.* Cicero, ad familiares, xii. 15. 2, *naves onerarias, quarum minor nulla erat duum millium amphorum.* Pliny, vi. 24, *magnitudo (navium) ad terna millia amphorum.* As the talent and the amphora each represented a cubic foot of water, and a Greek or Roman foot measured about ·97 of an English foot, the talent and the amphora each weighed very nearly 57 lbs.

[67] Ctesias, Fr. 57. 6, apud Photium, p. 45, τὸ δὲ ὕψος, ὅσον μυριοφόρου νεὼς ἱστός. Thucydides, vii. 25, προσαγαγόντες γὰρ ναῦν μυριοφόρον, κ.τ.λ. Pollux, iv. 165, μυριοφόρος, ὡς Θουκυδίδης· ὡς δὲ Δείναρχος, μυριαγωγοῦσα. cf. Philo Judæus, de plantatione Noe, 6, μυριαγωγὰ σκάφη, de incorruptibilitate mundi, 26, μυριοφόροις ναυσίν. Strabo, iii. 3. 1, ὁ δὲ Τάγος καὶ τὸ πλάτος ἔχει τοῦ στόματος εἴκοσί που σταδίων καὶ τὸ βάθος μέγα, ὥστε μυριαγωγοῖς ἀναπλεῖσθαι, xvii. 1. 26, πλάτος δ' ἔχει πηχῶν ἑκατὸν ἡ διῶρυξ, βάθος δ' ὅσον ἀρκεῖν μυριοφόρῳ νηί. Heliodoros, Æthiopica, iv. 16, ἔλεγον δὴ οὖν εἶναι Φοίνικες Τύριοι, τέχνην δ' ἔμποροι, πλεῖν δ' ἐπὶ Καρχηδόνα τὴν Λιβύων, ὁλκάδα μυριοφόρον Ἰνδικῶν τε καὶ Αἰθιοπικῶν καὶ τῶν

Larger ships were built for special purposes. About 40 A.D. the Vatican obelisk and its pedestal were brought from Egypt to Italy in a ship which Pliny describes as the most wonderful vessel that ever was beheld upon the sea; evidently meaning that she was the largest, for he comments on her length and her capacity and the size of her mast, but says nothing about any peculiarity in design. The obelisk and pedestal together weigh between 496 and 497 tons; and about 800 tons of lentils were stowed on board to keep them steady[68]. Therefore, unless there is some error about the quantity of lentils, the ship carried fully 1,300 tons, or more than five times the load of the largest merchant-ships afloat. This ship was

ἐκ Φοινίκης ἀγωγίμων φέροντες. Themistios, oratio xvi, p. 212, καὶ νῦν καθέστηκε μὲν ἄπασα ἤπειρος, γῇ δὲ καὶ θάλαττα τοὺς προστάτας στεφανοῦσιν, ἡ δὲ ἀρχὴ καθάπερ ναῦς μυριοφόρος πολλὰ δὴ πονηθεῖσα ὑπὸ χειμῶνος καὶ τρικυμίας ἀναλαμβάνει καὶ ὀχυροῦται. Himerios, oratio xiv, p. 622, πλεῖ ποτὲ καὶ μυριόφορτος ὁλκάς, πολὺν μὲν χρόνον χερσεύουσα, ὅτι μὴ πέλαγος τοσοῦτον εὕρισκε βαθύτητι, ὥστε καὶ λῦσαι τὰ πείσματα. Automedon, in the Anthology, x. 23. 5, ναῦς ἅτε μυριόφορτος. Manasses, 4886, 4887, καὶ ταῦτ᾽ εἰπὼν ἐκέλευσε γνάθοις πυρὸς παμφάγου | τὴν ναῦν τὴν μυριό-φορτον αὐτόφορτον βρωθῆναι.

[68] Pliny, xvi. 76, *abies admirationis præcipuæ visa est in nave, quæ ex Ægypto Gaii principis iussu obeliscum in Vaticano Circo statutum quattuorque truncos lapidis eiusdem ad sustinendum eum adduxit, qua nave nihil admirabilius visum in mari certum est.* CXX M *modiorum lentis pro saburra ei fuere. longitudo spatium obtinuit magna ex parte Ostiensis portus latere lævo : ibi namque demersa est a Claudio principe cum tribus molibus turrium altitudine in ea exædificatis obiter Puteolano pulvere advectisque. arboris eius crassitudo quattuor hominum ulnas complectentium implebat.* A modius was equivalent to the third part of a cubic foot, so that 120,000 modii would occupy a space of 40,000 cubic feet : and the weight would be nearly 46 lbs. for every cubic foot, as Egyptian lentils weigh about 50 lbs. per cubic English foot, when closely packed. According to Fontana, Della trasportation dell' obelisco Vaticano, pp. 9, 23, the obelisk itself weighs 963,537 lbs., while the four blocks of the pedestal weigh 165,464 and 67,510 and 179,826 and 110,778 lbs. respectively : and a ton contains about 2,996 lbs. of this measure. Fontana replaced the obelisk upon the original pedestal after its removal from the Circus in 1586.

[69] Pliny, xxxvi. 1, *navesque marmorum causa fiunt, ac per fluctus, sævissimam rerum naturæ partem, huc illuc portantur iuga.*

[70] Pliny, xxxvi. 14, *super omnia accessit difficultas mari Romam (obeliscos) devehendi, spectatis admodum navibus. divus Augustus priorem advexerat, mira-culique gratia Puteolis navalibus perpetuis dicaverat ; sed incendio consumpta est. divus Claudius aliquot per annos asservatam, quam Gaius Cæsar importaverat, omnibus quae unquam in mari visa sunt mirabiliorem, in ipsa turribus Puteolis e pulvere exædificatis, perductam Ostiam portus gratia mersit.*

doubtless of the class that the Romans built expressly for transporting marble[69]. Pliny says plainly that she was larger than the ship which had performed the somewhat easier task of carrying the Flaminian obelisk from Egypt to Italy fifty years before[70] : yet that ship was afterwards reputed to have carried 2,700 tons of corn, a quantity of pepper and linen and paper and glass, and also fourteen hundred men, besides the obelisk and its pedestal[71]. The tale is absurd : and so also is the tale that 2,400 tons of corn, 250 tons of salted fish, 500 tons of wool, and 500 tons of miscellaneous cargo were put on board a ship that Hieron built at Syracuse and afterwards gave to Ptolemy on finding her too large for use[72]. Athenæos

[71] Cedren, p. 172, ἐπὶ δὲ τῆς βασιλείας Αὐγούστου Καίσαρος εἰσῆλθε πλοῖον ἀπὸ Ἀλεξανδρείας εἰς τὴν πόρταν Ῥώμης, ἐπιφερόμενον σίτου μοδίων χιλιάδας υ΄, ἐπιβάτας ,ασ΄, ναύτας σ΄, πέπερι, ὀθόνας, χάρτην, ὑέλια, καὶ τὸν μέγαν ὀβελίσκον μετὰ τοῦ βασιλέως, αὐτόν τε ἐστῶτα ἐν τῷ μεγάλῳ ἱππικῷ, ἔχοντα ὕψος πόδας πζ΄ ἥμισυν. For τοῦ βασιλέως read τῆς βάσεως. Another version is printed by Mommsen, Ueber den Chronographen vom Jahre 354, at p. 646, *hoc imp. navis Alexandrina primum in portu Romano introivit nomine Acatus, qui attulit frumenti modios* CCCC, *vectores* MCC, *piper, linteamen, carta, vitria, et opoliscum cum sua sibi base, qui est in Circo Maximo altum pedes* LXXXVIIS. A modius being equivalent to the third part of a cubic foot, 400,000 modii would occupy a space of 133,333 cubic feet : and the weight would be about 45 lbs. for every cubic foot, since corn weighs rather more than 49 lbs. per cubic English foot. According to Fontana, *l. c.*, p. 75, the Flaminian obelisk weighs 702,276 lbs. and its pedestal 497,187 lbs.; or altogether 287,652 lbs. less than the Vatican obelisk and pedestal.

[72] Athenæos, v. 40, περὶ δὲ τῆς ὑπὸ Ἱέρωνος τοῦ Συρακοσίου κατασκευασθείσης νεώς, ἧς καὶ Ἀρχιμήδης ἦν ὁ γεωμέτρης ἐπόπτης, οὐκ ἄξιον εἶναι κρίνω σιωπῆσαι, σύγγραμμα ἐκδόντος Μοσχίωνος τινός, ᾧ οὐ παρέργως ἐνέτυχον ὑπογυίως. γράφει οὖν ὁ Μοσχίων οὕτως, κ.τ.λ. 44, σίτου δὲ ἐνεβάλλοντο εἰς τὴν ναῦν μυριάδες ἕξ, ταρίχων δὲ Σικελικῶν κεράμια μύρια, ἐρεῶν τάλαντα δισμύρια, καὶ ἕτερα δὲ φορτία δισμύρια. χωρὶς δὲ τούτων ὁ ἐπισιτισμὸς ἦν τῶν ἐμπλεόντων. ὁ δ᾽ Ἱέρων, ἐπεὶ πάντας τοὺς λιμένας ἤκουε, τοὺς μὲν ὡς οὐ δύνατοί εἰσι τὴν ναῦν δέχεσθαι, τοὺς δὲ καὶ ἐπικινδύνους ὑπάρχειν, διέγνω δῶρον αὐτὴν ἀποστεῖλαι Πτολεμαίῳ τῷ βασιλεῖ εἰς Ἀλεξάνδρειαν· καὶ γὰρ ἦν σπάνις σίτου κατὰ τὴν Αἴγυπτον. καὶ οὕτως ἐποίησε· καὶ ἡ ναῦς κατήχθη εἰς τὴν Ἀλεξάνδρειαν, ἔνθα καὶ ἐνεωλκήθη. ὁ δ᾽ Ἱέρων καὶ Ἀρχίμηλον, τὸν τῶν ἐπιγραμμάτων ποιητήν, γράψαντα εἰς τὴν ναῦν ἐπίγραμμα, χιλίοις πυρῶν μεδίμνοις, οὓς καὶ παρέπεμψεν ἰδίοις δαπανήμασιν εἰς τὸν Πειραιᾶ, ἐτίμησεν. The corn would all be measured by the medimnos, as was customary : and a medimnos was equivalent to two cubic feet. So the 60,000 measures of corn would occupy a space of 120,000 cubic feet. A κεράμιον was presumably an amphora ; and a φορτίον the equivalent of a talent or an amphora, as that meaning is implied in μυριόφορτος : see note 67. It is clear that nothing was known of Moschion even then, else Athenæos would not speak of him as Μοσχίωνος τινός.

quotes this tale from Moschion, and Moschion cites an epigram by Archimelos : but nothing whatever is known of Archimelos or of Moschion ; and Athenæos did not write until 200 A.D., while Hieron died before 200 B.C. The epigram celebrates a ship that brought some gifts of corn from Hieron to the Greeks, and declares her size by saying that the hull rivalled Etna in its bulk, the mast touched the stars, and so forth[73] : but such language seems hardly more appropriate if the ship carried 3,650 tons, than if she carried a half or a quarter or an eighth of that load ; and a ship might fairly be deemed a monster, if she carried even 500 tons at a time when others could not carry more than 250. In his narrative Moschion says that Archimedes succeeded in launching this huge ship by means of some mechanical contrivance of his own invention : yet Plutarch tells substantially the same story about Archimedes without a hint

[73] Athenæos, v. 44, ἔχει δ' οὕτως τὸ ἐπίγραμμα :—τίς τόδε σέλμα πέλωρον ἐπὶ χθονὸς εἵσατο ; ποῖος | κοίρανος ἀκαμάτοις πείσμασιν ἠγάγετο ; | πῶς δὲ κατὰ δρυόχων ἐπάγη σανίς ; ἢ τίνι γόμφοι | τμηθέντες πελέκει τοῦτ' ἔκαμον τὸ κύτος, | ἢ κορυφαῖς Αἴτνας παρισούμενον, ἤ τινι νάσων, | ἃς Αἰγαῖον ὕδωρ Κυκλάδας ἐνδέδεται, | τοίχοις ἀμφοτέρωθεν ἰσοπλατές ; ἢ ῥα Γίγαντες | τοῦτο πρὸς οὐρανίας ἔξεσαν ἀτραπιτούς. | ἄστρων γὰρ ψαύει καρχήσια, καὶ τριελίκτους | θώρακας μεγάλων ἐντὸς ἔχει νεφέων. | πείσμασιν ἀγκύρας ἀπερείδεται, οἷσιν Ἀβύδου | Ξέρξης καὶ Σηστοῦ δισσὸν ἔδησε πόρον. | μανύει στιβαρᾶς κατ' ἐπωμίδος ἀρτιχάρακτον | γράμμα, τίς ἐκ χέρσου τάνδ' ἐκύλισε τρόπιν · | φατὶ γὰρ ὡς "Ἱέρων Ἱεροκλέος Ἑλλάδι πάσᾳ | καὶ νάσοις καρπῶν πίονα δωροφόρον | Σικελίας σκαπτοῦχος ὁ Δωρικός." ἀλλά, Πόσειδον, | σῶζε κατὰ γλαυκῶν σέλμα τόδε ῥοθίων. A certain Archimedes is the author of the epigram in the Anthology, vii. 50, the manuscript distinctly naming Ἀρχιμήδους, though editors have printed this as Ἀρχιμήλου to match the name in Athenæos. Nothing is known of this Archimelos.

[74] Athenæos, v. 40, ὡς δὲ περὶ τὸν καθελκυσμὸν αὐτοῦ τὸν εἰς τὴν θάλασσαν πολλὴ ζήτησις ἦν, Ἀρχιμήδης ὁ μηχανικὸς μόνος αὐτὸ κατήγαγε δι' ὀλίγων σωμάτων. κατασκευάσας γὰρ ἕλικα, τὸ τηλικοῦτον σκάφος εἰς τὴν θάλασσαν κατήγαγε. πρῶτος δ' Ἀρχιμήδης εὗρε τὴν τῆς ἕλικος κατασκευήν. Plutarch, Marcellus, 14, θαυμάσαντος δὲ τοῦ Ἱέρωνος καὶ δεηθέντος εἰς ἔργον ἐξαγαγεῖν τὸ πρόβλημα καὶ δεῖξαί τι τῶν μεγάλων κινούμενον ὑπὸ σμικρᾶς δυνάμεως, ὁλκάδα τριάρμενον τῶν βασιλικῶν πόνῳ μεγάλῳ καὶ χειρὶ πολλῇ νεωλκηθεῖσαν, ἐμβαλὼν (Ἀρχιμήδης) ἀνθρώπους τε πολλοὺς καὶ τὸν συνήθη φόρτον, αὐτὸς ἄπωθεν καθήμενος, οὐ μετὰ σπουδῆς ἀλλὰ ἠρέμα τῇ χειρὶ σείων ἀρχήν τινα πολυσπάστου, προσηγάγετο λείως καὶ ἀπταίστως καὶ ὥσπερ διὰ θαλάττης ἐπιθέουσαν. ἐκπλαγεὶς οὖν ὁ βασιλεύς, κ.τ.λ. For the meaning of τριάρμενος, see note 124 on p. 54. The term πολύσπαστον denotes a combination of ropes and pulleys, cf. Vitruvius, x. 2. 10 : and the term ἕλιξ may well denote the same machine, for it conveys the notion of some sort of twisting, and the ropes

that the ship was of abnormal size[74]. And then Moschion
dilates upon the luxury of the cabins and the baths and the
covered walks on deck, shaded by vines and whole gardens of
plants in pots; while Suetonius describes the very same
display of luxury on board Caligula's yachts: and Caligula
was the emperor who built the great ship for the obelisk[75].
Thus, in all probability, Moschion has blended some of the
characteristics of that great ship and those luxurious yachts
in a vessel of ideal size and splendour; and then endeavoured
to give reality to his idea by associating it with some vessel
that Hieron sent to Ptolemy.

Caligula perhaps was rivalled or surpassed in shipbuilding by some of his successors: but there is no proof of this.
A great ship was built by Constantine for the Lateran
obelisk, which is the largest obelisk of all, and weighs between
441 and 442 tons[76]: but the Vatican obelisk came over with

here twisted round the pulleys.   Archimedes' screw was termed κοχλίας, and
obviously has nothing to do with this ἕλιξ.   The story is subsequently told by
Proclos, in Euclidem, p. 18, οἷον δὴ καὶ Ἱέρων ὁ Συρακούσιος εἰπεῖν λέγεται περὶ
Ἀρχιμήδους; ὅτε τὴν τριάρμενον κατεσκεύασε ναῦν, ἣν παρεσκευάζετο πέμπειν Πτολεμαίῳ τῷ βασιλεῖ τῷ Αἰγυπτίῳ.   πάντων γὰρ ἅμα Συρακουσίων ἑλκύσαι τὴν ναῦν
οὐ δυναμένων, Ἀρχιμήδης τὸν Ἱέρωνα μόνον αὐτὴν καταγαγεῖν ἐποίησεν.   καταπλαγεὶς
δὲ ἐκεῖνος, κ.τ.λ.   And again by Tzetzes, chiliades, ii. 103—108, ὁ Ἀρχιμήδης ὁ
σοφός, μηχανητὴς ἐκεῖνος, | τῷ γένει Συρακούσιος ἦν, γέρων γεωμέτρης, | χρόνους τε
ἑβδομήκοντα καὶ πέντε παρελαύνων, | ὅστις εἰργάσατο πολλὰς μηχανικὰς δυνάμεις, |
καὶ τῇ τρισπάστῳ μηχανῇ χειρὶ λαιᾷ καὶ μόνῃ | πεντεμυριομέδιμνον καθείλκυσεν
ὁλκάδα.   There is a variant ἑπταμυριομέδιμνον for πεντεμυριομέδιμνον in the last
line.

[75] Suetonius, Caligula, 37, and Athenæos, v. 41, 42, both quoted in note 133 on
pp. 58, 59.

[76] Ammianus, xvii. 4. 13, quo (obelisco) convecto per alveum Nili, proiectoque
Alexandriæ, navis amplitudinis antehac inusitatæ ædificata est, sub trecentis re-
migibus agitanda.   14, quibus ita provisis, digressoque vita principe memorato
(sc. Constantino), urgens effectus intepuit: tandemque sero impositus navi per
maria fluentaque Tybridis, velut paventis ne quod pæne ignotus miserat Nilus,
ipse parum sub meatus sui discrimine mœnibus alumnis inferret, defertur in vicum
Alexandri, tertio lapide ab urbe seiunctum ; unde chamulcis impositus, tractusque
lenius, per Ostiensem portam piscinamque publicam Circo illatus est Maximo.
The oars must have been auxiliary—see p. 20—for three hundred rowers would
have been of little service in propelling a ship of that size.   According to Fontana,
Della trasportatione dell' obelisco Vaticano, p. 70, the Lateran obelisk weighs
1,322,938 lbs.: and a ton contains about 2,996 lbs. of this measure.   The existing
pedestal was constructed by Fontana in 1588.

its pedestal, whereas this had none; and Caligula's ship thus took a heavier load than Constantine's. The merchant-ships employed as transports with Justinian's fleet in 533 A.D. must have carried from 120 to 200 tons apiece, and not from 120 to 2,000, as stated in the current reading of Procopios. There were five hundred of them; and if they carried 160 tons upon the average, they carried 80,000 tons altogether, and thus afforded ample transport for an army of only sixteen thousand men: whereas the army would have had far more transport than it needed, if the largest of the ships had carried 2,000 tons apiece[77].

War-ships were relatively of very little burden; for they were not meant to keep the sea, and consequently had hardly anything to carry except their crew. Thus the Tiber was still navigable as far as Rome for ten-banked war-ships at a time when any merchant-ship carrying more than three thousand talents was compelled to anchor at the mouth[78]. Therefore, unless war-ships were relatively of lighter draught than

[77] Procopios, de bello Vandalico, i. 11, ἤδη δὲ ξὺν αὐτοῖς καὶ τὴν ἐς Καρχηδόνα στρατείαν ἐν παρασκευῇ εἶχε, πεζοὺς μὲν στρατιώτας μυρίους, ἱππέας δὲ πεντακισχιλίους ἔκ τε στρατιωτῶν καὶ φοιδεράτων ξυνειλεγμένους...εἵποντο δὲ αὐτοῖς Ἔρουλοι τετρακόσιοι, καὶ ξύμμαχοι βάρβαροι ἑξακόσιοι μάλιστα ἐκ τοῦ Μασσαγετῶν ἔθνους, ἱπποτοξόται πάντες...ναῦς δὲ ἡ ξύμπασα στρατιὰ πεντακοσίας ἦγε, καὶ αὐτῶν οὐδεμία πλέον ἢ κατὰ μυριάδας πέντε μεδίμνων φέρειν οἷα τε ἦν, οὐ μὴν οὐδὲ ἔλασσον ἢ κατὰ τρισχιλίους. ναῦται δὲ δισμύριοι ἐπέπλεον ἁπάσαις. A great number of these sailors must have been employed as rowers on the war-ships: see note 45 on p. 17. As the medimnos was primarily a measure for corn, the load was probably about 90 lbs. for every medimnos: for a medimnos was equivalent to two cubic feet, and the weight would be about 45 lbs. for every cubic foot, since corn weighs rather more than 49 lbs. per cubic English foot. The emendation is necessarily χιλιάδας for μυριάδας.

[78] Dionysios of Halicarnassos, iii. 44, αἱ μὲν οὖν ἐπίκωποι νῆες ὁπηλίκαι ποτ' ἂν οὖσαι τύχωσι, καὶ τῶν ὁλκάδων αἱ μέχρι τρισχιλιοφόρων, εἰσάγουσί τε διὰ τοῦ στόματος αὐτοῦ καὶ μέχρι τῆς Ῥώμης εἰρεσίᾳ καὶ ῥύμασι παρελκόμεναι κομίζονται· αἱ δὲ μείζους πρὸ τοῦ στόματος ἐπ' ἀγκυρῶν σαλεύουσαι ταῖς ποταμηγοῖς ἀπογεμίζονταί τε καὶ ἀντιφορτίζονται σκάφαις. Dionysios was at Rome from 30 to 8 B.C., working at his history; and ten-banked ships presumably were the largest war-ships then afloat, as they were the largest that fought at Actium in 31 B.C.: see note 54 on p. 21.

[79] Thucydides, iv. 118, citing the treaty of 423 B.C., Λακεδαιμονίους καὶ τοὺς ξυμμάχους πλεῖν μὴ μακρᾷ νηί, ἄλλῳ δὲ κωπήρει πλοίῳ ἐς πεντακόσια τάλαντα ἄγοντι μέτρα.

merchant-ships on account of some difference in design, a war-ship of ten banks did not carry more than three thousand talents, or 75 tons ; and that would be the weight of a crew of a thousand men, weighing twelve stone apiece upon the average. At this rate a war-ship of three banks, with a crew of two hundred men, carried only six hundred talents, or 15 tons : and in a treaty concluded at a time when war-ships were normally of three banks, a prohibition against war-ships is backed by a prohibition against any other ships propelled by oars, if they carried more than five hundred talents ; apparently, just to preclude the construction of vessels that could be converted into war-ships on emergency[79].

The hull, as a whole, generally was built of pine on merchant-ships and fir on war-ships; though pine and cypress and cedar were also used for war-ships, the practice varying in different districts according to the nature of the timber that they produced[80]. The timber for the keels was selected with especial care[81]. All the larger merchant-ships had keels

---

[80] Theophrastos, historia plantarum, v. 7. 1, ἐλάτη μὲν οὖν καὶ πεύκη καὶ κέδρος, ὡς ἁπλῶς εἰπεῖν, ναυπηγήσιμα. τὰς μὲν γὰρ τριήρεις καὶ τὰ μακρὰ πλοῖα ἐλάτινα ποιοῦσι διὰ κουφότητα, τὰ δὲ στρογγύλα πεύκινα διὰ τὸ ἀσαπές· ἔνιοι δὲ καὶ τὰς τριήρεις διὰ τὸ μὴ εὐπορεῖν ἐλάτης. οἱ δὲ κατὰ Συρίαν καὶ Φοινίκην ἐκ κέδρου· σπανίζουσι γὰρ καὶ πεύκης. οἱ δ' ἐν Κύπρῳ πίτυος· ταύτην γὰρ ἡ νῆσος ἔχει, καὶ δοκεῖ κρείττων εἶναι τῆς πεύκης. Plutarch, quæstiones convivales, v. 3. 1, οὐ μὴν ἀλλὰ κατ' ἰδίαν τῷ Ποσειδῶνι φαίη τις ἂν τὴν πίτυν προσήκειν διὰ τὰς ναυπηγίας μάλιστα. καὶ γὰρ αὐτὴ καὶ τὰ ἀδελφὰ δένδρα, πεῦκαι καὶ στρόβιλοι, τῶν τε ξύλων παρέχει τὰ πλοιμώτατα, κ.τ.λ. This στρόβιλος is presumably the tibulus which Pliny mentions as a species of the pinus silvestris growing in Italy, and used there for shipbuilding, xvi. 17, liburnicarum ad usus. Plato, leges, p. 705 C, τί δὲ δή; ναυπηγησίμης ὕλης ὁ τόπος ἡμῖν τῆς χώρας πῶς ἔχει ;—οὐκ ἔστιν οὔτε τις ἐλάτη λόγου ἀξία οὔτ' αὖ πεύκη, κυπάριττός τε οὐ πολλή. Vegetius, iv. 34, ex cupresso igitur et pinu domestica sive silvestri et abiete præcipue liburna contexitur.

[81] Theophrastos, historia plantarum, v. 7. 2, τὴν δὲ τρόπιν τριήρει μὲν δρυΐνην (ποιοῦσι) ἵνα ἀντέχῃ πρὸς τὰς νεωλκίας, ταῖς δὲ ὁλκάσι πευκίνην—ὑποτιθέασι δ' ἔτι καὶ δρυΐνην ἐπὰν νεωλκῶσι—ταῖς δὲ ἐλάττοσιν ὀξυΐνην· καὶ ὅλως ἐκ τούτου τὸ χέλυσμα. cf. v. 8. 3, ἡ δὲ τῶν Λατίνων ἔφυδρος πᾶσα· καὶ ἡ μὲν πεδεινὴ δάφνην ἔχει καὶ μυρρίνους καὶ ὀξύην θαυμαστήν, τηλικαῦτα γὰρ τὰ μήκη τέμνουσι ὥστ' εἶναι διηνεκῶς τῶν Τυρρηνίδων ὑπὸ τὴν τρόπιν· ἡ δὲ ὀρεινὴ πεύκην καὶ ἐλάτην. In the former passage Theophrastos says that the χέλυσμα was usually of beech, and in the latter he speaks of beech-wood ὑπὸ τὴν τρόπιν : so these passages may justify the assertion of Pollux, i. 86, τὸ δ' ὑπὸ τὴν τρόπιν τελευταῖον προσηλούμενον, τοῦ μὴ τρίβεσθαι τὴν τρόπιν, χέλυσμα καλεῖται.

of pine, but were provided with false-keels of oak, if they were going to be hauled up ashore or set upon one of those ship-tramways which ran from sea to sea at Corinth and some other places; and the war-ships always had keels of oak, as they used to be hauled up ashore almost every day. Ships of any size generally had false-keels of beech; and the keel itself was made of beech in smaller vessels. Pine

[82] Theophrastos, historia plantarum, v. 7. 3, ἡ δὲ τορνεία τοῖς μὲν πλοίοις γίνεται συκαμίνου, μελίας, πτελέας, πλατάνου· γλισχρότητα γὰρ ἔχειν δεῖ καὶ ἰσχύν. χειρίστη δὲ ἡ τῆς πλατάνου· ταχὺ γὰρ σήπεται. ταῖς δὲ τριήρεσιν ἔνιοι καὶ πιτυίνας ποιοῦσι διὰ τὸ ἐλαφρόν. τὸ δὲ στερέωμα, πρὸς ᾧ τὸ χέλυσμα καὶ τὰς ἐπωτίδας, μελίας καὶ συκαμίνου καὶ πτελέας· ἰσχυρὰ γὰρ δεῖ ταῦτ' εἶναι. v. 7. 5, φίλυρα δὲ πρὸς τὰ σανιδώματα τῶν μακρῶν πλοίων. See last note for χέλυσμα, and note 141 on p. 62 for ἐπωτίδες. The σανίδωμα must be some sort of planking, and the στερέωμα some sort of backing. The τορνεία would be timber cut to shape by carpenters; but possibly ἡ δὲ τορνεία should be read ἡ δ' ἐντερόνεια, cf. Aristophanes, equites, 1185, εἰς τὰς τριήρεις ἐντερόνεια, Livy xxviii. 45, interamenta navium. Plato, leges, p. 705 C, πίτυν τ' αὖ καὶ πλάτανον ὀλίγην ἂν εὕροι τις, οἷς δὴ πρὸς τὰ ἐντὸς τῶν πλοίων μέρη ἀναγκαῖον τοῖς ναυπηγοῖς χρῆσθαι ἑκάστοτε. Theophrastos, historia plantarum, iv. 2. 8, καὶ ἐν ταῖς ναυπηγίαις χρῶνται πρὸς τὰ ἐγκοίλια αὐτῇ, sc. ἀκάνθῃ. Theophrastos is describing the Egyptian acacia, or mimosa: and Herodotos, ii. 96, remarks that the trading-vessels on the Nile were built entirely of this. For ἐγκοίλια see note 95 on p. 39.

[83] Iliad, xvi. 482—484, ἤριπε δ', ὡς ὅτε τις δρῦς ἤριπεν, ἢ ἀχερωΐς, | ἠὲ πίτυς βλωθρή, τήν τ' οὔρεσι τέκτονες ἄνδρες | ἐξέταμον πελέκεσσι νεήκεσι, νήϊον εἶναι. Odyssey, v. 239, 240, κλήθρη τ' αἴγειρός τ', ἐλάτη τ' ἦν οὐρανομήκης, | αὖα πάλαι, περίκηλα, τά οἱ πλώοιεν ἐλαφρῶς. Thus, besides pine and fir, there are here two kinds of poplar, ἀχερωΐς and αἴγειρος, and also oak and alder. Alder was so generally employed for shipbuilding in Italy that the Roman poets use alnus like abies and pinus to denote a ship. Virgil, georgics, i. 136, tunc alnos primum fluvii sensere cavatas, ii. 451, torrentem undam levis innatat alnus, cf. Æneid, viii. 91, abies, x. 206, pinus. Lucan, iii. 520, emeritas repetunt navalibus alnos. Silius, xii. 522, transmittunt alno vada. But they do not use quercus in this sense. Valerius Flaccus, v. 66, is referring to the piece of Dodona oak in the bows of the Argo. Theophrastos, historia plantarum, v. 4. 3, δοκεῖ γὰρ (δρῦς) ὅλως ἀσαπὲς εἶναι· δι' ὃ καὶ εἰς τοὺς ποταμοὺς καὶ εἰς τὰς λίμνας ἐκ τούτων ναυπηγοῦσιν· ἐν δὲ τῇ θαλάττῃ σήπεται. But sea-going ships are described by Cæsar, de bello Gallico, iii. 13, naves totæ factæ ex robore ad quamvis vim et contumeliam perferendam: and Strabo here translates ex robore by δρυΐνης ὕλης, iv. 4. 1. These ships, however, were peculiar to the Bay of Biscay. Claudian names beech with alder as a wood for shipbuilding, de raptu Proserpinæ, iii. 365, fagos metitur et alnos: but the beech, like the oak, probably was wanted for the keel. Theophrastos, historia plantarum, iv. 2. 6, ξύλον δὲ (βαλάνου) ἰσχυρὸν καὶ εἰς ἄλλα τε χρήσιμον καὶ εἰς τὰς ναυπηγίας. Theophrastos is describing the Egyptian moringa, the tree that produces oil of ben.

and plane, elm and ash, mulberry and lime and acacia, were all employed in the interior of the hull[82]. And alder and poplar and the timber of a balsam-tree are also named among the kinds of wood in use in shipbuilding[83]. But in some outlandish districts the sides of the ships were formed of leather instead of wood[84]. The masts and yards were made of fir, or else of pine; and so also were the oars[85].

[84] Cæsar, de bello civili, i. 54, *imperat militibus Cæsar ut naves faciant, cuius generis eum superioribus annis usus Britanniæ docuerat. carinæ primum ac statumina levi materia fiebant: reliquum corpus navium viminibus contextum coriis integebatur.* Lucan, iv. 131—135, *primum cana salix madefacto vimine parvam | texitur in puppim, cæsoque inducta iuvenco | vectoris patiens tumidum superenatat amnem. | sic Venetus stagnante Pado, fusoque Britannus | navigat oceano.* Pliny, vii. 57, *etiam nunc in Britannico oceano (naves) vitiles corio circumsutæ fiunt.* Dion Cassius, xlviii. 18, δερμάτινα πλοῖα κατὰ τοὺς ἐν τῷ ὠκεανῷ πλέοντας ἐκποιῆσαι ἐπεχείρησεν, ἔνδοθεν μὲν ῥάβδοις αὐτὰ κούφαις διαλαμβάνων, ἔξωθεν δὲ βοὸς δέρμα ὠμὸν ἐς ἀσπίδος κυκλοτεροῦς τρόπον περιτείνων. cf. 19, πλοιάρια βύρσινα. Antiphilos, in the Anthology, ix. 306, ὑλοτόμοι παύσασθε νεῶν χάριν. οὐκέτι πεύκη | κύματος, ἀλλ' ἤδη ῥινὸς ἐπιτροχάει. Strabo speaks of similar vessels on the north coast of Spain, iii. 3. 7, διφθερίνοις πλοίοις, and also in the Red Sea, xvi. 4. 19, δερματίνοις πλοίοις. Herodotos describes the practice in Assyria, i. 194, ἐπεὰν γὰρ νομέας ἰτέης ταμόμενοι ποιήσωνται, περιτείνουσι τούτοισι διφθέρας στεγαστρίδας ἔξωθεν ἐδάφεος τρόπον, οὔτε πρύμνην ἀποκρίνοντες οὔτε πρώρην συνάγοντες, ἀλλ' ἀσπίδος τρόπον κυκλοτερέα ποιήσαντες, κ.τ.λ. According to Zosimos, iii. 13, five hundred vessels of this sort were built for Julian's campaign there in 363 A.D.

[85] Iliad, vii. 5, 6, ἐπὴν κεκάμωσιν εὐξέστῃς ἐλάτῃσιν | πόντον ἐλαύνοντες. Odyssey, xii. 171, 172, οἱ δ' ἐπ' ἐρετμὰ | ἑζόμενοι λεύκαινον ὕδωρ ξεστῇς ἐλάτῃσιν. Theophrastos, historia plantarum, v. 1. 6, ἔστι δὲ καὶ πολύλοπον ἡ ἐλάτη καθάπερ καὶ τὸ κρόμυον· ἀεὶ γὰρ ἔχει τινὰ ὑποκάτω τοῦ φαινομένου καὶ ἐκ τοιούτων ἡ ὅλη. δι' ὃ καὶ τὰς κώπας ξύοντες ἀφαιρεῖν πειρῶνται καθ' ἕνα καὶ ὁμαλῶς· ἐὰν γὰρ οὕτως ἀφαιρῶσιν, ἰσχυρὸς ὁ κωπεών, ἐὰν δὲ παραλλάξωσι καὶ μὴ κατασπῶσιν ὁμοίως, ἀσθενής· πληγὴ γὰρ οὕτως, ἐκείνως δ' ἀφαίρεσις. ἔστι δὲ καὶ μακρότατον ἡ ἐλάτη καὶ ὀρθοφυέστατον. δι' ὃ καὶ τὰς κεραίας καὶ τοὺς ἱστοὺς ἐκ ταύτης ποιοῦσιν. Pliny, xvi. 76, *hæ omnium arborum altissimæ ac rectissimæ,* sc. *larix et abies. navium malis antennisque propter levitatem præfertur abies.* See also the passage quoted from Pliny in note 68 on p. 26. Odyssey, xv. 289, 290, ἱστὸν δ' εἰλάτινον κοίλης ἔντοσθε μεσόδμης | στῆσαν ἀείραντες. Apuleius, metamorphoses, xi. 16, *iam malus insurgit, pinus rotunda.* Lucan, ii. 695, 696, *dum iuga curvantur mali, dumque ardua pinus | erigitur.* iii. 529—531, *validæque triremes, | quasque quater surgens exstructi remigis ordo | commovet, et plures quæ mergunt æquore pinus.* According to Theophrastos, historia plantarum, iv. 1. 2, 4, wood from chilly places was reckoned the best for yards and oars, but not for masts. See also Claudian, de raptu Proserpinæ, iii. 367—369, *quæ longa est, tumidis præbebit cornua velis: | quæ fortis, malo potior: quæ lenta, favebit | remigio.*

T.   c

The timber for ships never was seasoned thoroughly, as it then became too stiff to bend into the needful shapes : but, as a rule, it was allowed some while for drying after it was felled, and then for settling after it was built into a ship ; for otherwise the seams were likely to expand considerably and admit the water[86]. The seams were calked by filling them with tow and other packing[87], and fixing this with wax or tar : and the whole of the outer planking was protected with a coat of tar

[86] Theophrastos, historia plantarum, v. 7. 4, τεκτονικῇ μὲν οὖν ἡ παλαιοτάτη (ὕλη) κρατίστη, ἐὰν ᾖ ἀσαπής· εὐθετεῖ γὰρ ὡς εἰπεῖν πᾶσι χρῆσθαι. ναυπηγικῇ δὲ διὰ τὴν κάμψιν ἐνικμοτέρᾳ ἀναγκαῖον· ἐπεὶ πρός γε τὴν κόλλησιν ἡ ξηροτέρα συμφέρει. ἵσταται γὰρ καινὰ τὰ ναυπηγούμενα καὶ ὅταν συμπαγῇ καθελκυσθέντα συμμύει καὶ στέγει πλὴν ἐὰν μὴ παντάπασιν ἐξικμασθῇ· τότε δὲ οὐ δέχεται κόλλησιν ἢ οὐχ ὁμοίως. Plutarch, de fortuna Romanorum, 9, γενομένην δὲ (ναῦν) στῆναι δεῖ καὶ παγῆναι σύμμετρον χρόνον, ἕως οἵ τε δεσμοὶ κάτοχοι γένωνται καὶ συνήθειαν οἱ γόμφοι λάβωσιν· ἐὰν δὲ ὑγροῖς ἔτι καὶ περιολισθαίνουσι τοῖς ἁρμοῖς κατασπασθῇ, πάντα χαλάσει διατιναχθέντα καὶ δέξεται τὴν θάλατταν. Vegetius, iv. 36, illud etiam cavendum ne continuo, ut deiectæ fuerint, trabes secentur vel statim, ut sectæ fuerint, mittantur in navem; siquidem et adhuc solidæ arbores et iam divisæ per tabulas duplices ad maiorem siccitatem mereantur indutias. nam quæ virides compinguntur, cum nativum umorem exudaverint, contrahuntur et rimas faciunt latiores. Thus, the notion was that the timber ought to be moderately dry, ἐνικμοτέρα, ξηροτέρα, ad maiorem siccitatem, but not completely dry, μὴ παντάπασιν ἐξικμασθῇ.

[87] Iliad, ii. 135, καὶ δὴ δοῦρα σέσηπε νεῶν καὶ σπάρτα λέλυνται. This line is noticed by Pliny, xxiv. 40, nondum enim fuisse Africanum vel Hispanum spartum in usu, certum est: et cum sutiles fierent naves, lino tamen non sparto unquam sutas. And also by Varro, apud Aulum Gellium, xvii. 3, in Græcia sparti copia modo cœpit esse ex Hispania: neque ea ipsa facultate usi Liburni, set hi plerasque naves loris suebant, Græci magis cannabo et stuppa ceterisque sativis rebus, a quibus σπάρτα appellabant. At Portus near the mouth of the Tiber there was a guild of calkers entitled splendidissimum corpus stuppatorum: see Corp. Inscr. Latin. vol. xiv, no. 44. Herodotos, ii. 96, ἔσωθεν δὲ τὰς ἁρμονίας ἐν ὦν ἐπάκτωσαν τῇ βύβλῳ, sc. οἱ Αἰγύπτιοι. Pliny, xvi. 64, ubi lignosiore callo (arundo) induruit, sicut in Belgis, contusa et interiecta navium commissuris ferruminat textus, glutino tenacior, rimisque explendis fidelior pice. Strabo, iv. 4. 1, οὐ συνάγουσι τὰς ἁρμονίας τῶν σανίδων, ἀλλ' ἀραιώματα καταλείπουσι· ταῦτα δὲ βρύοις διανάττουσι. This refers to the ships in the Bay of Biscay.

[88] Genesis, vi. 14, καὶ ἀσφαλτώσεις αὐτὴν (τὴν κιβωτὸν) ἔσωθεν καὶ ἔξωθεν τῇ ἀσφάλτῳ. Hipponax, Fr. 50, apud Harpocrationem, s. v. μάλθη:—ἔπειτα μάλθη τὴν τρόπιν παραχρίσας, cf. Virgil, Æneid, iv. 398, uncta carina. This μάλθη was asphalte: see Pliny, ii. 108, in Commagenes urbe Samosatis stagnum est, emittens limum (maltham vocant) flagrantem. Pliny, xvi. 21, pix liquida in Europa e tæda coquitur navalibus muniendis, 23, non omittendum, apud eosdem zopissam vocari derasam navibus maritimis picem cum cera. cf. Arrian, periplus, 5, καὶ ὁ κηρὸς

or wax or both together[88].   The wax had to be melted over
a fire until it was soft enough to be laid on with a brush;
and usually some paint was melted with the wax, so that the
ship received a coat of colour in encaustic.   Pliny states that
seven kinds of paint were used in this way, a purple, a violet,
a blue, two whites, a yellow and a green ; and at a later date
there was a paint which matched the colour of the waves[89].
This was selected for vessels employed in reconnoitring or

ἀπεξύσθη. Valerius Flaccus, i. 478—480, *sors tibi, ne qua | parte trahat tacitum
puppis mare, fissaque fluctu | vel pice vel molli conducere vulnera cera.* Ovid,
metamorphoses, xi. 514, 515, *spoliataque tegmine ceræ | rima patet, præbetque
viam letalibus undis.* Lucian, dialogi mortuorum, 4, καὶ κηρόν, ὡς ἐπιπλάσαι τοῦ
σκαφιδίου τὰ ἀνεῳγότα. Plutarch, quæstiones convivales, v. 3. 1, πίττης τε καὶ
ῥητίνης ἀλοιφήν, ἧς ἄνευ τῶν συμπαγέντων ὄφελος οὐδὲν ἐν τῇ θαλάττῃ. Vegetius,
iv. 44, *unctasque cera et pice et resina tabulas,* sc. *navium.* Porphyrogenitos, de cærimoniis, ii. 45, ἐδόθη ὑπὲρ καλαφατήσεως τῶν αὐτῶν ιά καραβίων· λγ́, cf. Zonaras,
xvii. 18, τῶν γὰρ τὰς νῆας καταπιττούντων ἦν αὐτῷ ὁ πατήρ, sc. ὁ Καλαφάτης.

[89] Pliny, xxxv. 41, *encausto pingendi duo fuisse antiquitus genera constat,
donec classes pingi cæpere: hoc tertium accessit, resolutis igni ceris penicillo utendi,
quæ pictura in navibus nec sole nec sale ventisque corrumpitur.* This must mean
that the new process was introduced when encaustic was first employed in painting
ships—not when ships first were painted, for that was in the earliest times.
Pliny, xxxv. 31, *ceræ tinguntur iisdem his coloribus ad eas picturas quæ inuruntur,
alieno parietibus genere sed classibus familiari, iam vero et onerariis navibus,* these
colours being *purpurissum, indicum, cæruleum, melinum, auripigmentum, appianum* and *cerussa.* The *purpurissum* was a shade of purple, and the *cæruleum* was
blue; while the *indicum* was some colour between blue and purple, xxxv. 27, *in
diluendo mixturam purpuræ cæruleique mirabilem reddit.* The *melinum* is described as *candidum* in xxxv. 19, and classed as *album* in xxxv. 32; so this was
white. The *auripigmentum* was presumably a shade of orange. The *appianum*
was a shade of green, xxxv. 29, *viride quod appianum vocatur.* The *cerussa* was
white-lead, xxxv. 19, *est et colos tertius e candidis, cerussæ, cuius rationem in
plumbi metallis diximus. fuit et terra per se in Theodoti fundo inventa Smyrnæ,
qua veteres ad navium picturas utebantur. nunc omnis ex plumbo et aceto fit, ut
diximus.* But Vitruvius, vii. 7. 4, says that this *terra* was *creta viridis,* and was
known as *theodotium,* while Pliny, xxxv. 29, says that *creta viridis* was used for
appianum. Vegetius, iv. 37, *ne tamen exploratoriæ naves candore prodantur,
colore veneto, qui marinis est fluctibus similis, vela tinguntur et funes; cera etiam,
qua ungere solent naves, inficitur.* cf. Philostratos, imagines, i. 18, γλαυκοῖς μὲν
γέγραπται χρώμασι, sc. ναῦς λῃστρική. Corp. Inscr. Attic. vol. ii, no. 807, col. b,
ll. 114—118, ὑπαλοιφὴ ἐμ φιδακνίῳ μέλαινα· ἑτέρα ἐν ἀμφορεῖ μέλαινα· ἑτέρα λευκὴ
ἐμ φιδακνίῳ· ἐν ἀμφορεῦσι δυοῖν λευκή. These paints were for the ships: see no.
803, col. e, l. 156, col. f, l. 4. Polyænos, v. 34, Νίκων Σάμιος κυβερνήτης,
πλησίον τριήρων πολεμίων ὁρμουσῶν, βουλόμενος παραπλεύσας λαθεῖν, τὴν ἀλοιφὴν τῆς
αὐτοῦ νεὼς ὁμοίαν καταχρίσας ταῖς πολεμίαις τριήρεσι, ἔπλει κ.τ.λ.

piracy, to keep them out of sight.   But the encaustic was often put to a better use than merely giving the ship a coat of colour; and elaborate designs were painted all along the sides, with great groups of figures at the ends, especially at the stern[90].   Such groups may be seen on the sterns of the Greek ships of about 200 B.C. in fg. 24 and the Roman ship of about 200 A.D. in fg. 29.   The earliest Greek ships had only patches of colour on the bows, blue or purple or ver-

[90] Athenæos, v. 37, ζῷα μὲν γὰρ εἶχεν (ἡ ναῦς) οὐκ ἐλάττω δώδεκα πηχῶν κατὰ πρύμναν τε καὶ πρῴραν, καὶ πᾶς τόπος αὐτῆς κηρογραφίᾳ κατεπεποίκιλτο, τὸ δ' ἔγκωπον ἅπαν μέχρι τῆς τρόπεως κισσίνην φυλλάδα καὶ θύρσους εἶχε πέριξ.   42, ἡ δὲ ναῦς πᾶσα οἰκείαις γραφαῖς ἐπεπόνητο, where οἰκείαις denotes encaustic, the genus classibus familiare of Pliny, xxxv. 31 : see last note.   Valerius Flaccus, i. 127 ff, constitit ut longo moles non pervia ponto | puppis, et ut tenues subiere latentia ceræ | lumina, picturæ varios superaddit honores. | hic..., 140, parte alia......, describing in detail two large groups.   On one side, Thetis is riding on a dolphin towards the home of Peleus.   Three of the Nereids are following her; and Galatea, the last of these, is beckoned back to Sicily by Polyphemos.   In front of Thetis is the home of Peleus, where she is seen again at a banquet of the sea-gods. The centaur Cheiron is playing to them on the lyre.   On the other side, the centaurs have broken loose at the marriage-feast of Hippodameia.   Peleus and his comrades keep them off with sword and spear.   The monsters wield fire-brands and use their hoofs; but one is still in his cups and another is galloping away. Horace, odes, i. 14. 14, 15, nil pictis timidus navita puppibus | fidit.   Ovid, fasti, iv. 275, 276, picta coloribus ustis | cœlestum matrem concava puppis habet, heroides, 16. 112—114, accipit et pictos puppis adunca deos. | qua tamen ipse vehor, comitata Cupidine parvo | sponsor coniugii stat dea picta sui, tristia, i. 4. 7, 8, monte nec inferior proræ puppique recurvæ | insilit, et pictos verberat unda deos.   Persius, vi. 30, ingentes de puppe dei.   Propertius, iv. 6. 49, vehunt proræ Centauros saxa minantes.   Lucian, navigium, 5, τὴν ἐπώνυμον τῆς νεὼς θεὸν ἔχουσα τὴν *Ἰσιν ἑκατέρωθεν, sc. ἡ πρῷρα.   These last passages, however, may perhaps refer to carvings: see note 148 on p. 65.   On the other hand, several of the passages quoted in that note probably refer to paintings.   Aristophanes, ranæ, 932, Διόνυσος:— τὸν ξουθὸν ἱππαλεκτρυόνα ζητῶν, τίς ἐστιν ὄρνις. 933, Αἰσχύλος:—σημεῖον ἐν ταῖς ναυσίν, ὠμαθέστατ', ἐνεγέγραπτο.   The allusion is to the verses quoted from Æschylos by the scholiast, in pacem, 1177, ἀπὸ δ' αὖτε ξουθὸς ἱππαλεκτρυῶν | στάζει κηρόθεν τῶν φαρμάκων πολὺς πόνος.   The reading is corrupt: but κηρόθεν suggests a word akin to κηρός, and the sense is obviously that the picture melted off in drops while the vessel was burning.   That seems to be the earliest record of encaustic on a ship.   Hipponax, Fr. 49, apud Tzetzen, in Lycophronem, 424, μιμνῆ κακομήχανε, μηκέτι γράψῃς | ὄφιν τριήρευς ἐν πολυζύγῳ τοίχῳ | ἀπ' ἐμβόλου φεύγοντα πρὸς κυβερνήτην.   The point of this appears to be that the painter meant to put a horizontal band of colour round the ship, but drew it so unsteadily that it twisted about like a snake.   According to Pliny, xxxv. 36, there was a tale that Protogenes was once a painter of ships; but the phrase naves pinxisse is ambiguous,

milion, the rest of the hull being black with tar; and possibly the painting on the bows was not in wax[91]. Occasionally, the coats of wax or tar were replaced by a sheathing of lead outside the outer planking, some layers of tarred sail-cloth being interposed between the metal and the wood[92]. The timbers of a ship were held together by wooden pegs and metal nails; and bronze was preferred to iron for the nails, as it was better able to resist the action of the water[93]. When

and may refer to pictures on ships or pictures of ships. It was said that he introduced ships in the background in two of his masterpieces, *ut appareret a quibus initiis ad arcem ostentationis opera sua pervenissent:* and this suggests that he had begun life as a painter of rough pictures of ships. Such pictures were presumably in great demand at a large sea-port like Rhodes, where Protogenes resided, for it was then the custom to dedicate pictures as thank-offerings for escape from storm and shipwreck: see Cicero, de natura deorum, iii. 37.

[91] Herodotos, iii. 58, τὸ δὲ παλαιὸν ἅπασαι αἱ νέες ἔσαν μιλτηλιφέες. The epithet μιλτοπάρῃος occurs once in the Iliad, ii. 637, that is to say, in the Catalogue, and once in the Odyssey, ix. 125; and the epithet φοινικοπάρῃος occurs twice in the Odyssey, xi. 124, xxiii. 271: but μέλαινα and κυανόπρῳρος are the normal epithets in both the poems, so that τὸ παλαιόν cannot include the earliest times. The colour must have been confined to patches on the bows, for in the Odyssey, xiv. 308, 311, a ship is first described as μέλαινα and then as κυανόπρῳρος, and the παρήϊα would not be far from the ὀφθαλμοί and σίμωμα, as to which see note 147 on p. 65 and note 153 on p. 69.

[92] Athenæos, v. 40, τὸ μὲν οὖν ἥμισυ τοῦ παντὸς τῆς νεὼς ἐν μησὶν ἓξ εἰργάσατο, καὶ ταῖς ἐκ μολίβου ποιηθείσαις κεραμίσιν ἀεὶ καθ᾽ ὃ ναυπηγηθείη μέρος περιελαμβάνετο......ὡς δὲ καὶ τὰ λοιπὰ μέρη τῆς νεὼς ἐν ἄλλοις ἓξ μησὶ κατεσκευάσθη, καὶ τοῖς χαλκοῖς ἥλοις πᾶσα περιελήφθη, ὧν οἱ πολλοὶ δεκάμνοοι ἦσαν, οἱ δ᾽ ἄλλοι τούτων ἡμιόλιοι· διὰ τρυπάνων δ᾽ ἦσαν οὗτοι ἡρμοσμένοι, τοὺς σταμῖνας συνέχοντες· μολυβδίναις δὲ κεραμίσιν ἀπεστεγανοῦντο πρὸς τὸ ξύλον, ὑποτιθεμένων ὀθονίων μετὰ πίττης. Although Athenæos asserts here that sheathing was used on a ship belonging to Hieron, he may really be describing a practice of Caligula's time or afterwards: see pp. 27—29. L. B. Alberti, de re ædificatoria, v. 12, *ex navi Traiani per hos dies dum quæ scripsimus commentarer ex lacu Nemorensi eruta (quo loci annos plus* MCCC *demersa et destituta iacuerat) adverti pinum materiam et cupressum egregie durasse: in ea tabulis extrinsecus duplicem superextensam et pice atra perfusam telam ex lino adglutinarant supraque id chartam plumbeam claviculis eneis coadfirmarant.* This was written in 1485 A.D.

[93] Odyssey, v. 248, γόμφοισιν δ᾽ ἄρα τήν γε καὶ ἁρμονίῃσιν ἄρασσεν. 361, ὄφρ᾽ ἂν μέν κεν δούρατ᾽ ἐν ἁρμονίῃσιν ἀρήρῃ. Apollonios Rhodios, i. 369, 370, ἵν᾽ εὖ ἀραροίατο γόμφοις | δούρατα. ii. 79—81, ὡς δ᾽ ὅτε νήϊα δοῦρα θοοῖς ἀντίξοα γόμφοις | ἀνέρες ὑληουργοί, ἐπιβλήδην ἐλάοντες, | θείνωσι σφύρῃσιν. Plutarch, de fortuna Romanorum, 9, ὥσπερ γὰρ ὁλκὰς ἢ τριήρης ναυπηγεῖται μὲν ὑπὸ πληγῶν καὶ βίας πολλῆς, σφύραις καὶ ἥλοις ἀρασσομένη καὶ γομφώμασι καὶ πρίοσι καὶ πελέκεσι, γενομένην δὲ στῆναι δεῖ καὶ παγῆναι σύμμετρον χρόνον, ἕως οἵ τε δεσμοὶ κάτοχοι

necessary, these fastenings were arranged in such a way that
the ship could easily be divided into sections for transport
overland; and war-ships of three and four and five banks
were thus conveyed to distant waters, presumably in thirty or
forty sections apiece, since those of thirty oars used to be
divided into three[94].

γένωνται καὶ συνήθειαν οἱ γόμφοι λάβωσιν. cf. Æschylos, supplices, 846, γομφοδέτῳ
δόρει. Thus, while the δεσμοί are coupled with the γόμφοι by Plutarch, the
ἁρμονίαι are coupled with the γόμφοι in the Odyssey, so the ἁρμονίαι and the
δεσμοί may be the same things under different names : cf. Odyssey, v. 33, σχεδίης
πολυδέσμου. And as the γόμφοι certainly were pegs, the δεσμοί or ἁρμονίαι would
naturally be the sockets for those pegs. Apparently γομφώμασι is equivalent to
γόμφοις in the passage just quoted from Plutarch, and ἁρμοσμάτων to ἁρμονιῶν in
Euripides, Helena, 411, τρόπις δ' ἐλείφθη ποικίλων ἁρμοσμάτων. In that passage
Plutarch mentions ἧλοι as well as γόμφοι, and these were usually of metal : see
Athenæos, v. 40, quoted in the last note, χαλκοῖ ἧλοι. Cæsar, de bello Gallico,
iii. 13, *transtra pedalibus in latitudinem trabibus confixa clavis ferreis digiti pollicis
crassitudine.* Vegetius, iv. 34, *utilius (liburna) æreis clavis quam ferreis confin-
genda ; quamlibet enim gravior aliquanto videatur expensa ; tamen, quia amplius
durat, lucrum probatur afferre : nam ferreos clavos tepore et umore celeriter robigo
consumit, ærei autem etiam in fluctibus propriam substantiam servant.* See also
Procopios, de bello Gothico, iv. 22, quoted in note 97 on p. 40, and Tacitus,
historiæ, iii. 47, quoted in the note on *camaræ* on p. 107.

94 Arrian, anabasis, v. 8, ταῦτα ὡς ἔγνω Ἀλέξανδρος, Κοῖνον μὲν τὸν Πολεμο-
κράτους πέμψας ὀπίσω ἐπὶ τὸν Ἰνδὸν ποταμόν, τὰ πλοῖα ὅσα παρεσκεύαστο αὐτῷ ἐπὶ
τοῦ πόρου τοῦ Ἰνδοῦ ξυντεμόντα κελεύει φέρειν ὡς ἐπὶ τὸν Ὑδάσπην ποταμόν. καὶ
ξυνετμήθη τε τὰ πλοῖα καὶ ἐκομίσθη αὐτῷ, ὅσα μὲν βραχύτερα διχῇ διατμηθέντα, αἱ
τριακόντεροι δὲ τριχῇ ἐτμήθησαν, καὶ τὰ τμήματα ἐπὶ ζευγῶν διεκομίσθη ἔστε ἐπὶ τὴν
ὄχθην τοῦ Ὑδάσπου· κἀκεῖ ξυμπηχθὲν τὸ ναυτικὸν αὖθις δὴ ὁμοῦ ὤφθη ἐν τῷ Ὑδάσπῃ.
According to Arrian, anabasis, vii. 19, already quoted in note 13 on p. 6, ships
of three and four and five banks were afterwards brought over from the Mediterranean to the Euphrates for Alexander's fleet. See also Strabo, xvi. i. 11, and
Quintus Curtius, x. 1. 19, already quoted in that same note. The vessels on the
Indus are mentioned by Curtius, viii. 10. 2, *iussitque ad flumen Indum procedere
et navigia facere, quis in ulteriora transportari posset exercitus. illi, quia plura
flumina superanda erant, sic iunxere naves ut solutæ plaustris vehi possent rursusque
coniungi.* All these devices are attributed to Semiramis by Diodoros, ii. 16,
μετεπέμψατο δὲ καὶ ναυπηγοὺς ἔκ τε Φοινίκης καὶ Συρίας καὶ Κύπρου καὶ τῆς ἄλλης τῆς
παραθαλαττίου χώρας, οἷς ἄφθονον ὕλην μεταγαγοῦσα διεκελεύσατο κατασκευάζειν
ποτάμια πλοῖα διαιρετά. 17, ναῦς δὲ ποταμίας κατεσκεύασε διαιρετὰς δισχιλίας, αἷς
παρεσκευάσατο καμήλους τὰς πεζῇ παρακομιζούσας τὰ σκάφη. Diodoros is quoting
from Ctesias, and Ctesias lived before the time of Alexander; so these devices
were customary in those regions. It is said that Nero tried to drown Agrippina by
putting her on board a vessel that was to come to pieces on the voyage : Suetonius,
Nero, 34, *solutilem navem.* But the project miscarried : Tacitus, annales, xiv. 5,
nec dissolutio navigii sequebatur.

The outer framework of the hull consisted of a keel and ribs[95]. There was not any stern-post; nor was there a stem-post, unless the ship was built to carry a ram. And thus in war-ships and merchant-ships alike the after part of the keel curved slowly upwards till it reached the level of the deck; while in the merchant-ships the fore part made a similar curve

[95] Ovid, heroides, 16. 109, 110, *fundatura citas flectuntur robora naves, | texitur et costis panda carina suis.* Procopĭos, de bello Gothico, iv. 22, ἥ τε γὰρ τρόπις μονοφυὴς οὖσα ἐκ πρύμνης ἄκρας ἄχρι ἐς τὴν πρῷραν᾿ διήκει, κατὰ βραχὺ μὲν θαυμασίως ἐπὶ τὸ κοῖλον ὑποχωροῦσα, καὶ αὖ πάλιν ἐνθένδε κατὰ λόγον εὖ μάλα ἐπὶ τὸ ὀρθόν τε καὶ διατεταμένον ἐπανιοῦσα. τά τε παχέα ξύμπαντα ξύλα ἐς τὴν τρόπιν ἐναρμοσθέντα—ἅπερ οἱ μὲν ποιηταὶ δρυόχους καλοῦσιν, ἕτεροι δὲ νομέας—ἐκ τοίχου μὲν ἕκαστον θατέρου ἄχρι ἐς τῆς νεὼς διήκει τὸν ἕτερον τοῖχον. This ship was preserved at Rome as a relic of Æneas: see note 55 on p. 21. The term δρύοχοι occurs in the Odyssey, xix. 574, where the axes are set up in a long row like the ribs of a ship, δρυόχους ὥς. Also in Polybios, i. 38, αὖθις ἔγνωσαν ἐκ τῶν δρυόχων εἴκοσι καὶ διακόσια ναυπηγεῖσθαι σκάφη, in Plato, Timæos, p. 81 B, οἷον ἐκ δρυόχων, and in similar passages; the notion being that a ship was altogether new, if the ribs were new, as they formed the best part of the framework. The term νομέες is employed by Herodotos, ii. 96, περὶ γόμφους πυκνοὺς καὶ μακροὺς περιείρουσι τὰ διπήχεα ξύλα· ἐπεὰν δὲ τῷ τρόπῳ τούτῳ ναυπηγήσωνται, ζυγὰ ἐπιπολῆς τείνουσι αὐτῶν· νομεῦσι δὲ οὐδὲν χρέονται. This seems to mean that the ribs (νομέες) were replaced by trenails (γόμφοι) in these trading-vessels on the Nile, *i.e.* the timbers of the side were not nailed to vertical supports behind them, but were held together by vertical supports which ran right through them. The term νομέες is again applied to the ribs in the passage quoted from Herodotos in note 84 on p. 33; and in the passage quoted from Cæsar in that note the ribs are termed *statumina,* which answers to σταμίνες in Greek. Odyssey, v. 252, 253, ἴκρια δὲ στήσας, ἀραρὼν θαμέσι σταμίνεσσι, | ποίει· ἀτὰρ μακρῇσιν ἐπηγκενίδεσσι τελεύτα. These σταμίνες must be the ribs, which stand behind the timbers of the side, ἐπηγκενίδες, and support the upper decking, ἴκρια. And in the passage quoted in note 92 on p. 37 Athenæos says incidentally that the skin and sheathing of the ship were nailed to the σταμίνες. Athenæos classes the σταμίνες with ἐγκοίλια and γόμφοι—cf. v. 40, γόμφους τε καὶ ἐγκοίλια καὶ σταμίνας—and these γόμφοι may be the trenails which Herodotos describes as substitutes for ribs. In translating from Theophrastos, historia plantarum, iv. 2. 8, Pliny renders ἐγκοίλια by *costæ,* xiii. 19. And the *costæ* were the ribs, this metaphor surviving from those times: but the ἐγκοίλια were metaphorically the guts—ἐντερόνεια, *interamenta,* see note 82 on p. 32. They are mentioned again by Strabo, xv. 1. 15, κατεσκευασμένας δὲ (ναῦς) ἀμφοτέρωθεν ἐγκοιλίοις μητρῶν χωρίς. In the mediæval galleys every pair of ribs was in three sections, the *matere* in the middle and the *stamenali* at each end; and these terms must be survivals of μῆτραι and σταμίνες. So, if a vessel had σταμίνες or ἐγκοίλια without μῆτραι, each pair of ribs made an acute angle at the keel. Leo, tactica, xix. 5, ἐχέτω δὲ καὶ ἐκ περισσοῦ ξύλα τινὰ ἐγκοίλια καὶ σανίδας καὶ στυππία καὶ πίσσαν καὶ ὑγρόπισσον. These things apparently were meant for stopping up holes in the ship's side, the ἐγκοίλια being a makeshift for ribs to put behind the planks.

towards the bows[96]. The skin of the ships was formed of planking laid upon the ribs, and fastened through them to the beams[97]. This planking was seldom of any great thickness : sometimes three inches, sometimes only two and a quarter, and rarely more than five and a quarter[98]. But outside the planking there usually were several waling-pieces, that is to say, long strips of timber running horizontally round the ship in the manner shewn in fgs. 20 to 23, 26 and 29, and known accordingly as *zosteres*, or belts[99].

[96] The contour of the earliest Greek ships is indicated by the epithets in the Iliad, xviii. 3, νεῶν ὀρθοκραιράων, 338, νηυσὶ κορωνίσι, 573, βοῶν ὀρθοκραιράων, cf. Theocritos, xxv. 151, βουσὶ κορωνίσι. And if the ships curved upwards at the ends like a bull's horns, the στείρη was simply the fore part of the keel, not a separate stem-post. Iliad, i. 481, 482, ἀμφὶ δὲ κῦμα | στείρῃ πορφύρεον μεγάλ' ἴαχε νηὸς ἰούσης. Apollonios Rhodios, i. 525—527, Πηλιὰς ἴαχεν Ἀργώ.........ἐν γάρ οἱ δόρυ θεῖον ἐλήλατο, τό ῥ' ἀνὰ μέσσην | στεῖραν Ἀθηναίη Δωδωνίδος ἥρμοσε φηγοῦ. Thus when Lucian says ἡ τῆς Ἀργοῦς τρόπις ἐλάλησεν, somnium, 2, and speaks of τὴν Ἀργώ, τὴν λάλον αὐτῆς τρόπιν, de saltatione, 52, he implies that the keel curved upwards till it ended in the figure-head. Lucian, navigium, 5, ὡς δὲ ἡ πρύμνα μὲν ἐπανέστηκεν ἠρέμα καμπύλη χρυσοῦν χηνίσκον ἐπικειμένη, καταντικρὺ δὲ ἀνάλογον ἡ πρῷρα ὑπερβέβηκεν ἐς τὸ πρόσω ἀπομηκυνομένη. That refers to a merchant-ship of about 150 A.D. : and the contour seems there to be the same as in the earliest Greek ships. Hence that curvature of the keels which is noted by Ovid and Procopios in the passages quoted at the beginning of the last note.

[97] Bianor, in the Anthology, xi. 248, ἤδη γάρ μιν ἅπασαν ἐπὶ ζυγὰ γομφωθεῖσαν | ἤλειφον πεύκης τῇ λιπαρῇ νοτίδι. It was clearly the skin that was bolted to the beams, as it was the skin that received the coat of tar. Procopios, de bello Gothico, iv. 22, σανίς τε πρὸς ἐπὶ τούτοις ἑκάστη ἐκ πρύμνης ἄκρας ἐς τῆς νηὸς ἐξικνεῖται τὴν ἑτέραν ἀρχήν, μηνοειδὴς οὖσα καὶ κέντρα σιδηρᾶ τούτου ἕνεκα προσλαβοῦσα μόνον, ὅπως δὴ ταῖς δοκοῖς ἐναρμοσθεῖσα τὸν τοῖχον ποιεῖ. These δοκοί are presumably the beams, though possibly they are the παχέα ξύλα which Procopios has just defined —see note 95—as δρύοχοι, or ribs: cf. Athenæos, v. 44, πῶς δὲ κατὰ δρυόχων ἐπάγη σανίς; Cæsar, de bello Gallico, iii. 13, *transtra pedalibus in latitudinem trabibus confixa clavis ferreis*. These *trabes* appear to be the timbers of the side.

[98] Diogenes Laertios, i. 103, μαθὼν (Ἀνάχαρσις) τέτταρας δακτύλους εἶναι τὸ πάχος τῆς νεώς, τοσοῦτον ἔφη τοῦ θανάτου τοὺς πλέοντας ἀπέχειν. cf. Juvenal, xii. 58, 59, *digitis a morte remotus | quattuor, aut septem, si sit latissima tæda*. Dion Chrysostom, oratio 64, p. 594, οὐδὲ γὰρ πίττῃ τὴν ψυχὴν οὔτε σχοινίοις ἐπιτρέπουσιν, οὔτε τριδάκτυλον αὐτοὺς σώζει ξύλον πεύκινον.

[99] Heliodoros, Æthiopica, i. 1, ὁλκὰς ἀπὸ πρυμνησίων ὥρμει, τῶν μὲν ἐμπλεόντων χηρεύουσα, φόρτου δὲ πλήθουσα· καὶ τοῦτο γὰρ ἦν συμβαλεῖν καὶ τοῖς πόρρωθεν· τὸ γὰρ ἄχθος ἄχρι καὶ ἐπὶ τρίτου ζωστῆρος τῆς νεὼς τὸ ὕδωρ ἀνέθλιβεν. These ζωστῆρες can only be the waling-pieces which figure so prominently on the merchant-ships of that period in plate 6. There does not appear to be any earlier instance of this use of the term. Later instances are plentiful. Manasses, 4876,

On the war-ships the hull was strengthened externally by a set of cables.   These were known as *hypozomata*, or girdles, and used to be fastened round the ship horizontally ; the two ends of each cable being joined together, so as to make it a complete girdle extending from stem to stern along the starboard side and back from stern to stem along the port side[100].   On the Egyptian ships of about 1250 B.C., as in fgs. 4 and 5, similar cables were stretched from stem to stern over posts amidship[101]: but these clearly were intended to

[4877], ἐπὶ γὰρ τρίτον τῆς νηὸς τῆς φορτηγοῦ ζωστῆρα | τὴν θάλασσαν ἀνέθλιβε τῶν ἀγωγίμων βάρος, where Zonaras says, xv. 25, φορτὶς βάρει τῶν ἀγωγίμων πεφορτισμένη, καὶ τούτῳ μέχρις ἐσχάτου ζωστῆρος καταβεβαπτισμένη.   Theodoros Prodromos, Rhodanthe et Dosicles, v. 444, 445, ἐκ δευτέρου ζωστῆρος ἄχρι καὶ τρίτου | πίλοις κατεσκέπαστο ναστοῖς παχέσιν.   Unlike the others, these were war-ships, cf. 439, 462 : and the padding was meant to turn off missiles.   Anna Comnena, vi. 5, αὗται δὲ (αἱ νῆες) τῇ κουφότητι ἐπεπόλαζον οἷον τοῖς ὕδασιν ἀνεχόμεναι, ὡς μηδ' ἄχρι δευτέρου ζωστῆρος τοῦ ὕδατος φθάνοντος.   The waling-pieces had perhaps been known as σέλματα in earlier times.   Euripides, Cyclops, 503—506, πλέως μὲν οἴνου, | γάνυμαι δὲ δαιτὸς ἥβῃ, | σκάφος, ὁλκὰς ὥς, γεμισθεὶς | ποτὶ σέλμα γαστρὸς ἄκρας.

[100] Athenæos, v. 37, τὴν τεσσαρακοντήρη ναῦν κατεσκεύασεν ὁ Φιλοπάτωρ, τὸ μῆκος ἔχουσαν διακοσίων ὀγδοήκοντα πηχῶν, ὀκτὼ δὲ καὶ τριάκοντα ἀπὸ παρόδου ἐπὶ πάροδον, ὕψος δὲ κ.τ.λ.......ὑποζώματα δὲ ἐλάμβανε δώδεκα· ἐξακοσίων δ' ἦν ἕκαστον πηχῶν.   Each of these cables being 600 cubits in length, while the ship was 280 in length and 38 in breadth, each one would just be long enough to pass once round the ship from stem to stern.   These measurements may all be fictitious, for Athenæos is quoting from Callixenos : but Callixenos presumably took the trouble to see that his measurements were consistent with each other, so the statement is admissible as evidence that the girding-cables would have been of this length on a ship of these dimensions.   Some similar cables on a battering-ram are mentioned by the other Athenæos, mechanica, p. 6, ὑποζώννυται δὲ ὅλος ὁ κριὸς ὅπλοις ὀκταδακτύλοις τρισί, καὶ διαλαμβάνεται κατὰ μέσον ἐκ τριῶν διαλειμμάτων ἁλύσεσι πηχυαίαις : and these statements are repeated by Vitruvius, x. 15. 6, *a capite autem ad imam calcem tigni contenti fuerunt funes* IIII *crassitudine digitorum* VIII, *ita religati quemadmodum navis a puppi ad proram continetur; eiusque præcincturæ funes transversis erant ligati, habentes inter se palmipedalia spatia.*   This shews that the girding-cables went from the stem of a ship to the stern.   Plato, civitas, p. 616 C, οἷον τὰ ὑποζώματα τῶν τριήρων, οὕτω πᾶσαν συνέχον τὴν περιφοράν.   This shews that these cables went right round a ship externally.   Throughout the inventories of the Athenian dockyards the ὑποζώματα are named among the σκεύη κρεμαστά, which are distinguished from the σκεύη ξύλινα—see, for example, the passages cited in note 103—and this excludes the notion that they were made of wood.

[101] The ends of these cables seem to be coiled round the stem and the stern : but those coils may belong to smaller cables for strengthening these parts, as similar coils are represented at the stern of one of the Greek war-ships of about 200 B.C. in the so-called Telephos frieze from Pergamos.

prevent the ship from hogging, and would have been super-
fluous on Greek or Roman war-ships, which had decking
enough to hold the stem and stern together.   The girding-
cables proved of service to the war-ships in keeping the
timbers firm when the ship was labouring in a seaway, or
forcing them back into position afterwards if any of them
had been started[102]: yet these cables must primarily have
been intended to prevent the ship from going to pieces under
the heavy shocks from ramming and the constant strain from
the working of so many oars, for otherwise they would have
been employed on merchant-ships also.   In the Athenian
navy a set of girding-cables was provided for every ship of
three or four banks, though possibly the set did not consist of
more than two[103]; and occasionally this provision was increased.   Thus in 324 B.C., when a squadron was leaving for
the Adriatic, every ship of three or four banks was supplied

---

[102] Apollonios Rhodios, i. 367—370, νῆα δ' ἐπικρατέως Ἀργου ὑποθημοσύνῃσιν |
ἔζωσαν πάμπρωτον ἐυστρεφεῖ ἔνδοθεν ὅπλῳ | τεινάμενοι ἑκάτερθεν, ἵν' εὖ ἀραροίατο
γόμφοις | δούρατα, καὶ ῥοθίοιο βίην ἔχοι ἀντιόωσαν. cf. Horace, odes, i. 14. 6—9, *ac
sine funibus | vix durare carinæ | possint imperiosius | æquor.* Appian, de bellis
civilibus, v. 91, ὁ δὲ (Πομπήιος) οὔτε περὶ τῆς γῆς ἐνενόησεν, οὔτε τοῖς λειψάνοις τοῦ
ναυαγίου παροῦσιν ἢ ἀπιοῦσι, καταστάντος τοῦ κλύδωνος, ἐπεχείρησεν · ἀλλ' ὑπερεῖδεν
ἐκ τῶν δυνατῶν διαζωννυμένους τὰ σκάφη, καὶ ἀνέμῳ διαπλέοντας ἐς τὸ Ἱππώνειον.
The διά in διαζωννυμένους is perhaps a corruption of ὑπό resulting from a repetition
of the διά in διαπλέοντας. Acts, xxvii. 17, βοηθείαις ἐχρῶντο, ὑποζωννύντες τὸ
πλοῖον. This obscure statement seems to mean that they used expedients which
answered the purpose of the girding-cables. They would not find any of these
cables on board, for they were on a merchant-ship, and these were used for war-
ships: nor could they fix them on a ship during a storm at sea, for even in a
dockyard this was a long and troublesome process. cf. Polybios, xxvii. 3, καὶ
τεσσαράκοντα ναῦς συμβουλεύσας τοῖς Ῥοδίοις ὑποζωννύειν, ἵνα, ἐάν τις ἐκ τῶν καιρῶν
γένηται χρεία, μὴ τότε παρασκευάζωνται πρὸς τὸ παρακαλούμενον, ἀλλ' ἑτοίμως
διακείμενοι πράττωσι τὸ κριθὲν ἐξαυτῆς. The phrase βοηθείαις ἐχρῶντο ὑποζωννύντες
matches Appian's phrase ἐκ τῶν δυνατῶν διαζωννυμένους: but Appian is speaking
of war-ships already provided with ὑποζώματα. Apollonios indeed refers to
ὑποζώματα on the Argo, which was hardly a war-ship: yet he is justified in
treating her as such, since he takes her for a ship of fifty oars.

[103] Corp. Inscr. Attic. vol. ii, no. 807, col. c, ll. 66—102, no. 808, col. d,
ll. 119—151, no. 809, col. e, ll. 75—110, no. 811, col. c, ll. 11—32. These are
the lists of the entire gear (ἐντελῆ σκεύη) supplied to ships of three and four
banks in 330/329 B.C. and following years; and in every case they mention
ὑποζώματα in the plural, but without any further indication of the number allowed
for each ship. The opinion that there were more than three is founded on a

with two girding-cables in addition to the usual set; while
every cavalry-transport was supplied with four, and every
ship of thirty oars with two, borrowed from the stock of
girding-cables intended for the three-banked ships[104]. Such
cables would fit the cavalry-transports, as these were old
three-banked ships; but would be far too long for the thirty-
oared ships, unless each cable made two girdles: in which
case a ship of three banks must have been fully twice as long
as a ship of thirty oars[105].

The sides of a war-ship had to be pierced with a row of
port-holes for each bank of oars below the first; so that
a ship of several banks was almost honey-combed. On the
Athenian ships these openings were closed against the water
by leathern bags termed *askomata*, which could cling round
the oars without much hindrance to their motion[106]; and some
protection here was indispensable, as the gap generally was

restoration of no. 809, col. b, l. 131.   The words ὑποζώματα ἐπὶ ναῦς HHΔΔI
are followed by καὶ τὸν III on the margin of the stone, and this has been restored
as καὶ (ὑπο)[ζώμ](ατα) III, the TON being changed to IΩM : but such a
restoration seems unwarrantable.

[104] Corp. Inscr. Attic. vol. ii, no. 809, col. a, ll. 1—63, ships of three banks:
in each case σκεύη ἔχουσιν ξύλινα ἐντελῆ, κρεμαστὰ ἐντελῆ, καὶ ἔτερα ὑποζώματα
ἔλαβον τῶν ἐγλυθέντων δύο κατὰ ψήφισμα δήμου, ὃ εἶπεν Ἀγνωνίδης Περγασῆθεν,
ll. 64—90, cavalry-transports: in each case σκεύη ἔχουσιν ξύλινα ἐντελῆ, κρεμαστὰ
ἐντελῆ, ὑποζώματα δὲ IIII τριηριτικῶν, or τῶν ἐγλυ(θέντων) τριηρ(ιτικῶν), ll. 91—
164, ships of thirty oars: in each case—disregarding minor differences—σκεύη
ἔχει ξύλινα ἐντελῆ, κρεμαστά, ὑποζώματα τριηριτικὰ τῶν ἐγλυθέντων δύο ἔλαβεν κατὰ
ψήφισμα δήμου, ὃ εἶπεν Ἀγνωνίδης Περγασῆθεν, col. b, ll. 40—45, a ship of four
banks: σκεύη ἔχει κρεμαστὰ ἐντελῆ καὶ ὑποζώματα II τῶν ἐγλυθέντων κατὰ ψήφισμα
δήμου, ὃ εἶπεν Ἀγνωνίδης Περγ(ασῆθεν).

[105] See pp. 21, 22, as to the grounds for thinking that the lengths were 70 ft.
and 150 ft. respectively.

[106] Corp. Inscr. Attic. vol. ii, no. 791 : some of the ships are marked ἤσκωται,
others are marked ἀσκωμάτων ἡ ἀρχὴ ἔχει ΔΔΔΔHHII usually abbreviated
into ἀσκω. ἡ ἀρχὴ ἔχει ΔΔΔΔHHII, while others are marked ἀσκώματα
τριήραρχος always abbreviated into ἀσκώ. τριήραρχος or ἀσκώ. τριή. The term
ἄσκωμα must denote a leathern bag of some sort: the cost of a set, 43 drachms
2 obols, shews that each ship had a great many: the expression ἤσκωται shews
that they were fixtures: and a joke by Aristophanes indicates that they were fixed
on the ports, Acharnenses, 97, ἄσκωμ' ἔχεις που περὶ τὸν ὀφθαλμὸν κάτω.

large enough for a man to put his head through[107]. In the Roman ship of about 50 A.D. in fg. 25 similar bags may be observed around the oars just outside the ports. Curiously, the edges of the ports were not utilized as rowlocks; and the oars of all the lower banks were worked against tholes to which they were fastened by leathern loops, just like the oars above the gunwale[108].

In the Phœnician two-banked ships of about 700 B.C. in fgs. 10 and 11, and also in the Athenian two-banked ship of about 500 B.C. in fg. 17, the oars of the first bank pass over the gunwale, and the ports of the second bank lie midway between the tholes of the first and somewhat lower down. The ports of the third bank in a three-banked ship would then be placed midway between the ports of the second and somewhat lower down ; so that these ports of the third bank would lie vertically below the tholes of the first, while the ports of the second would lie diagonally between : and in the Athenian three-banked ship of about 400 B.C. in fg. 21 the ports of the third bank are approximately in this position[109]. The ports of the fourth bank would then be placed vertically below the ports of the second, the ports of the fifth bank vertically below the ports of the third, and so on, the ports

---

[107] Herodotos, v. 33, ὁ δὲ δεινόν τι ποιησάμενος ἐκέλευσε τοὺς δορυφόρους ἐξευρόντας τὸν ἄρχοντα ταύτης τῆς νεός, τῷ οὔνομα ἦν Σκύλαξ, τοῦτον δῆσαι διὰ θαλαμίης διελόντας τῆς νεὸς κατὰ τοῦτο, ἔξω μὲν κεφαλὴν ποιεῦντας, ἔσω δὲ τὸ σῶμα. With ports of this size there necessarily was some leakage in rough weather in spite of the ἀσκώματα. Arrian, periplus ponti Euxini, 3, κοίλην μὲν γὰρ δι᾽ ὀλίγου τὴν θάλατταν (τὸ πνεῦμα) ἐποίησεν, ὡς μὴ κατὰ τὰς κώπας μόνον, ἀλλὰ καὶ ὑπὲρ τὰς παρεξειρεσίας ἐπεισρεῖν ἡμῖν ἐκατέρωθεν ἀφθόνως τοῦ ὕδατος. Lucilius, in the Anthology, xi. 245, οἱ τοῖχοι, Διόφαντε, τὰ κύματα πάντα δέχονται, | καὶ διὰ τῶν θυρίδων Ὠκεανὸς φέρεται.

[108] Odyssey, viii. 53, ἠρτύναντο δ᾽ ἐρετμὰ τροποῖς ἐν δερματίνοισι. Æschylos, Persæ, 375, 376, ναυβάτης τ᾽ ἀνὴρ | τροποῦτο κώπην σκαλμὸν ἀμφ᾽ εὐήρετμον. Aristophanes, Acharnenses, 553, θαλαμῶν τροπουμένων. Vitruvius, x. 3. 6, etiam remi circa scalmos struppis religati cum manibus impelluntur et reducuntur. Æschylos and Vitruvius are both speaking of oars generally, not merely of oars above the gunwale, and Aristophanes refers explicitly to a lower bank; so that all the oars must have had these tholes and loops. The loops were known as κωπητῆρες or τροπωτῆρες as well as τροποί : see note 114 on p. 47. It is clear that the oars were worked against the tholes, and not against the loops : see Aristotle, mechanica, 5, quoted in note 115 on p. 48.

being thus kept clear of the ship's ribs : but there is no direct evidence that this system was pursued. If the rowers in fg. 21 are men of ordinary stature, the gunwale of this three-banked ship must be rather more than three feet above the water-line, and the tholes of the first bank rather more than two feet above the ports of the third : yet clearly there cannot be space enough for the rowers of the first bank to sit vertically above the rowers of the third, or for the rowers of the second bank to sit diagonally between. The three lines of rowers on either side of a three-banked ship would naturally be ranged along three tiers of seats ascending from the centre of the ship like steps, so that each rower in the lower banks could get free play for his oar beneath the legs of a rower in the next bank above. But there are no materials for rigidly determining the relative positions of the lines of rowers in these three-banked ships, or in the larger war-ships.

In the earliest Greek ships the beams formed the upper limit of the hold, and above them were the thwarts for the rowers of the single bank ; these thwarts doubtless being placed in the intervals between the beams, so that the rowers might plant their feet against the beams, and make them

---

[109] The first two horizontal bands above the water-line seem to be waling-pieces, and the next is unquestionably the gunwale with tholes above for the first bank of oars. The ports of the third bank are just above the lower waling-piece, and almost vertically below the tholes of the first bank. But the ports of the second bank are hard to find. Three sets of bands run downwards from the gunwale, the first to the upper waling-piece, the second to the lower waling-piece, and the third to the water-line ; and these all look like portions of the hull. But apparently the bands that reach the water-line were intended for the oars of the second bank, and should have ended in ports just above the upper waling-piece, though the sculptor has carelessly prolonged them to the gunwale like their neighbours.—These waling-pieces appear again upon the three-banked ship represented in relief on Trajan's Column ; and here the ports of the third bank are between the waling-pieces, and the ports of the second bank unmistakably between the upper waling-piece and the gunwale. The ports of the second bank are probably meant to lie diagonally between the tholes of the first and the ports of the third ; though in that case an oar has been omitted in the third bank, either to avoid confusion, or from mere carelessness. In the first bank the oars are hopelessly entangled in a railing above the gunwale : and altogether the design makes little pretension to accuracy of detail.

serve as stretchers[110]. A second bank of oars could thus be
added to a ship without any alteration in her build, simply
by seating rowers on the beams and piercing port-holes for
their oars[111]; and with a slight increase in her freeboard, a
third bank could be added by putting rowers in the hold just
underneath the rowers of the first bank. But if the rowers
of the first bank sat on thwarts, the rowers of the third bank
must have been seated so much lower down that these thwarts
were clear of their heads: and the thwarts may have therefore
been replaced by planks that did not reach across the ship,
so that the rowers of the third bank might be nearly on a
level with the rowers of the first, if only they were seated a
little further inboard[112]. The beams must then have been

[110] Odyssey, ix. 98, 99, τοὺς μὲν ἐγὼν ἐπὶ νῆας ἄγον κλαίοντας ἀνάγκῃ, | νηυσὶ
δ᾽ ἐνὶ γλαφυρῇσιν ὑπὸ ζυγὰ δῆσα ἐρύσσας. xiii. 20—22, καὶ τὰ μὲν εὖ κατέθηχ᾽
ἱερὸν μένος Ἀλκινόοιο, | αὐτὸς ἰὼν διὰ νηὸς ὑπὸ ζυγά, μή τιν᾽ ἑταίρων | βλάπτοι
ἐλαυνόντων, ὁπότε σπερχοίατ᾽ ἐρετμοῖς. cf. Theognis, 513, 514, νηός τοι πλευρῇσιν
ὑπὸ ζυγὰ θήσομεν ἡμεῖς, | Κλεάρισθ᾽, οἳ᾽ ἔχομεν χοῖα διδοῦσι θεοί. The ζυγά are
not mentioned in the Iliad; but the compounds πολύζυγος and ἑκατόζυγος occur
there, ii. 293, xx. 247. These beams are not to be confounded with the seats.
Iliad, xv. 728, 729, ἀλλ᾽ ἀνεχάζετο τυτθόν, διόμενος θανέεσθαι, | θρῆνυν ἐφ᾽ ἑπταπόδην,
λίπε δ᾽ ἴκρια νηὸς ἐΐσης. This name θρῆνυς is preserved in θρανίτης, which denoted
a rower of the first bank in ships with more than one bank, while ζυγίτης denoted
a rower of the second bank. But the name is changed to κληίς in the Odyssey,
ii. 419, ἂν δὲ καὶ αὐτοὶ βάντες ἐπὶ κληῖσι κάθιζον, viii. 37, 38, δησάμενοι δ᾽ εὖ πάντες
ἐπὶ κληῖσιν ἐρετμὰ | ἔκβην᾽, xii. 214, 215, ὑμεῖς μὲν κώπῃσιν ἁλὸς ῥηγμῖνα βαθεῖαν |
τύπτετε κληίδεσσιν ἐφήμενοι, xiii. 76, 77, τοὶ δὲ κάθιζον ἐπὶ κληῖσιν ἕκαστοι | κόσμῳ,
cf. iv. 579, ix. 103, 179, 471, 563, xi. 638, xii. 146, xv. 221, 549. The κληῖδες are
mentioned only once in the Iliad, and then in a questionable line, xvi. 170—see
note 1 on p. 2—but the compound πολυκληΐς occurs several times in the Iliad as
well as the Odyssey. Apollonios Rhodios, i. 395, 396, κληΐδας μὲν πρῶτα πάλῳ
διεμοιρήσαντο, | ἄνδρ᾽ ἐντυναμένω δοιὼ μίαν. Apollonios therefore supposed that
the κληῖδες reached right across the ship and seated two rowers apiece: but the
expression in the Odyssey, xiii. 76, ἐπὶ κληῖσιν ἕκαστοι, suggests that each rower
was on a separate seat. The expression in the Iliad, xv. 729, θρῆνυν ἐφ᾽ ἑπταπόδην,
makes it clear that the θρῆνυες reached right across the ship. This θρῆνυς was
apparently the nearest to the stern, so the width thereabouts would thus be seven
feet internally: and that is likely enough, as three-banked ships were nowhere
more than twenty feet in width: see note 57 on p. 22.

[111] Arrian, anabasis, vi. 5, ὅσαι τε δίκροτοι αὐτῶν τὰς κάτω κώπας οὐκ ἐπὶ πολὺ
ἔξω ἔχουσαι τοῦ ὕδατος. Arrian is contrasting the war-ships of two banks with
those of a single bank, for there were not any ships of more than two banks in the
fleet: so the ships of two banks must have carried oars at a lower level than the
ships of one bank.

displaced, if a fourth bank was to be appended to the second as the third was to the first: but there is nothing to shew whereabouts the beams were placed in any of the larger war-ships, or where space was found in three-banked ships for the additional beams that sometimes were inserted to make them seaworthy[113]. To mitigate the roughness of the beams or other seats, every rower was provided with a cushion which he carried about with him from ship to ship[114].

Ships normally attain their greatest width in the middle and their greatest height at the ends, curving outward and downward from the ends towards the middle. And, according to Aristotle, the nearer amidship a rower sat, the greater was his leverage on his oar, as he had a greater length of oar

[112] Euripides, Helena, 1531—1533, Σιδωνίαν ναῦν πρωτόπλουν καθείλκομεν, | ζυγῶν τε πεντήκοντα κἀρετμῶν μέτρα | ἔχουσαν. There are here as many ζυγά as oars: and when Theocritos says τριακοντάζυγον ᾿Αργώ, xiii. 74, he seems to be giving the legendary ship thirty oars instead of fifty, for ships of sixty oars do not appear in legend. This indicates that the rowers now had separate seats, the term ζυγά being applied to seats in any of the banks. Sophocles, Ajax, 249, 250, ἣ θοὸν εἰρεσίας ζυγὸν ἐζόμενον | ποντοπόρῳ ναὶ μεθεῖναι. Latin authors use *transtra* in this sense. Virgil, Æneid, iv. 573, *considete transtris*, v. 136, *considunt transtris, intentaque brachia remis, etc.* cf. Cicero, in Verrem, ii. v. 51, quoted in note 129 on p. 56. Virgil and Cicero include ships of three and four banks in these allusions; and such ships could hardly have a tier of beams for every bank of oars. The two-banked ships of the Byzantines certainly had two tiers of beams, ζυγοί, with two rowers on each beam—see note 46 on p. 18—but these were ships of quite another type.

[113] Thucydides, i. 29, καὶ τὰς ναῦς ἅμα ἐπλήρουν, ζεύξαντές τε τὰς παλαιὰς ὥστε πλοίμους εἶναι καὶ τὰς ἄλλας ἐπισκευάσαντες. Ships in this condition are marked διάζυξ in the inventories of the Athenian dockyards: see Corp. Inscr. Attic. vol. ii, no. 809, col. b, l. 45, no. 811, col. b, l. 144, no. 812, col. a, l. 144, and also no. 808, col. a, l. 20, with the fragment in the appendix at p. 515.

[114] Thucydides, ii. 93, ἐδόκει δὲ λαβόντα τῶν ναυτῶν ἕκαστον τὴν κώπην καὶ τὸ ὑπηρέσιον καὶ τὸν τροπωτῆρα πεζῇ ἰέναι κ.τ.λ. Plutarch, Themistocles, 4, τὸ δόρυ καὶ τὴν ἀσπίδα τῶν πολιτῶν παρελόμενος, εἰς ὑπηρέσιον καὶ κώπην συνέστειλε τὸν τῶν ᾿Αθηναίων δῆμον. The term ὑπηρέσιον was applied to saddles for horses, cf. Diodoros, xx. 4. 1; so it must here denote some similar covering for the thwarts. Pollux, x. 40, τὸ ναυτικὸν ὑπηρέσιον ἰδίως ἐν ταῖς ῟Ωραις Κρατῖνος προσκεφάλαιον, cf. Hesychios, s.v. πανικτόν:—῾Ερμιππος ἐν Στρατιώταις, Α. ὥρα τοίνυν μετ᾿ ἐμοῦ χωρεῖν ἐπὶ κωπητῆρα, λαβόντα | καὶ προσκεφάλαιον, ἵν᾿ ἐς τὴν ναῦν ἐμπηδήσας ῥοθιάζῃς. | Β. ἀλλ᾿ οὐ δέομαι, πανικτὸν ἔχων τὸν πρωκτόν. Cratinos and Hermippos were both contemporary with Thucydides. The τροποί mentioned in the Odyssey, viii. 53—see note 108 on p. 44—are here styled τροπωτῆρες by Thucydides and κωπητῆρες by Hermippos.

inboard by reason of the greater width of the ship[115]. So the lines of rowers did not follow the ship's curve outward. The oars may have increased in length towards the middle of each bank[116] : yet the increase inboard must have been relatively greater than the increase outboard, for otherwise the leverage would have remained the same. So the lines of rowers could not have followed the ship's curve downward, as the oars amidship would then have lost their hold upon the water. And if the lines of rowers did not follow the ship's curve outward or downward, they presumably were straight. The rowers would consequently be seated in a rectangular structure within the ship ; and as every rower must have been seated some way inboard to give him the necessary leverage on his oar, this structure would nowhere occupy the whole width of the ship.

[115] Aristotle, mechanica, 5, διὰ τί οἱ μεσόνεοι μάλιστα τὴν ναῦν κινοῦσιν; ἢ διότι ἡ κώπη μοχλός ἐστιν; ὑπομόχλιον μὲν γὰρ ὁ σκαλμὸς γίνεται—μένει γὰρ δὴ τοῦτο· τὸ δὲ βάρος ἡ θάλαττα, ἣν ἀπωθεῖ ἡ κώπη· ὁ δὲ κινῶν τὸν μοχλὸν ὁ ναύτης ἐστίν. ἀεὶ δὲ πλέον βάρος κινεῖ, ὅσῳ ἂν πλέον ἀφεστήκῃ τοῦ ὑπομοχλίου ὁ κινῶν τὸ βάρος. ἐν μέσῃ δὲ τῇ νηὶ πλεῖστον τῆς κώπης ἐντός ἐστιν· καὶ γὰρ ἡ ναῦς ταύτῃ εὐρυτάτη ἐστίν, ὥστε πλεῖον ἐπ' ἀμφότερα ἐνδέχεσθαι μέρος τῆς κώπης ἑκατέρου τοίχου ἐντὸς εἶναι τῆς νεώς.

[116] Aristotle, de partibus animalium, iv. 10, καὶ ὁ ἔσχατος δὲ (τῶν δακτύλων) μικρὸς ὀρθῶς, καὶ ὁ μέσος μακρός, ὥσπερ κώπη μέσον νεώς· μάλιστα γὰρ τὸ λαμβανόμενον ἀνάγκη περιλαμβάνεσθαι κύκλῳ κατὰ τὸ μέσον πρὸς τὰς ἐργασίας. Galen, de usu partium, i. 24, διὰ τί δὲ ἄνισοι πάντες ἐγένοντο (οἱ δάκτυλοι) καὶ μακρότατος ὁ μέσος; ἢ ὅτι τὰς κορυφὰς αὐτῶν ἐπὶ ἴσον ἐξικνεῖσθαι βέλτιον ἦν ἐν τῷ περιλαμβάνειν ὄγκους τινὰς μεγάλους ἐν κύκλῳ;......καθάπερ, οἶμαι, κἂν ταῖς τριήρεσι τὰ πέρατα τῶν κωπῶν εἰς ἴσον ἐξικνεῖται, καίτοι γ' οὐκ ἴσων ἁπασῶν οὐσῶν· καὶ γὰρ οὖν κἀκεῖ τὰς μέσας μεγίστας ἀπεργάζονται διὰ τὴν αὐτὴν αἰτίαν. Aristotle and Galen are apparently asserting here that the oars amidship were longer than the rest. But in the inventories of the Athenian dockyards the oars of a bank are always classed together as though they were all exactly alike. So these assertions may only apply to the aspect of the oars inside the ship. When Galen adds that the ends of the oars all reached equally far, he probably means that the inner ends reached a line parallel to the ship's keel, the oars being of unequal length inboard—he could hardly mean that they reached a curve parallel to the ship's side, the oars being of equal length inboard, for then he would be contradicting Aristotle, mechanica, 5 : but possibly he means that the outer ends reached a line parallel to the ship's keel, the oars being of equal length altogether but unequal outboard and unequal inboard also, or that they reached a curve parallel to the ship's side, the oars being of unequal length altogether but equal outboard and unequal inboard only.

A heavy superstructure is represented on the Phœnician ships of about 700 B.C. in fgs. 10 and 11 and on the Greek ships of about 550 B.C. in fgs. 15 and 16 and also on the Athenian ship of about 400 B.C. in fg. 21. At the top there is a deck like the hurricane-deck on modern ships. That deck must be the *katastroma*: for these representations tally with the statements of ancient authors that this was the post of the combatants on board Greek ships when in action, while in Phœnician ships it was of larger build, and was occupied by dignitaries during voyages, the space below being fully occupied by rowers[117]. If the rowers in fg. 21 are men of ordinary stature, that hurricane-deck stands about four feet above the gunwale; and about a foot above the gunwale there is another piece of planking. This must be the starboard gangway: for there was a *parodos*, or gangway, on

---

117 Thucydides, i. 49, συμμίξαντες δὲ ἐναυμάχουν, πολλοὺς μὲν ὁπλίτας ἔχοντες ἀμφότεροι ἐπὶ τῶν καταστρωμάτων, πολλοὺς δὲ τοξότας τε καὶ ἀκοντιστάς, τῷ παλαιῷ τρόπῳ ἀπειρότερον ἔτι παρεσκευασμένοι. Plutarch, Themistocles, 14, τὰς μὲν Ἑλληνικὰς οὐκ ἔβλαπτε ναῦς (τὸ κῦμα) ἁλιτενεῖς οὔσας καὶ ταπεινοτέρας, τὰς δὲ βαρβαρικὰς ταῖς τε πρύμναις ἀνεστώσας καὶ τοῖς καταστρώμασιν ὑψορόφους καὶ βαρείας ἐπιφερομένας ἔσφαλλε προσπῖπτον καὶ παρεδίδου πλαγίας τοῖς Ἕλλησιν. Herodotos, viii. 118, αὐτὸς δὲ (Ξέρξης) ἐπὶ νεὸς Φοινίσσης ἐπιβὰς ἐκομίζετο ἐς τὴν Ἀσίην. πλώοντα δέ μιν ἄνεμον Στρυμονίην ὑπολαβέειν μέγαν καὶ κυματίην. καὶ δὴ μᾶλλον γάρ τι χειμαίνεσθαι γεμούσης τῆς νεὸς ὥστε ἐπὶ τοῦ καταστρώματος ἐπεόντων συχνῶν Περσέων τῶν σὺν Ξέρξῃ κομιζομένων, ἐνθαῦτα ἐς δεῖμα πεσόντα τὸν βασιλέα εἴρεσθαι βώσαντα τὸν κυβερνήτεα εἴ τις ἔστι σφι σωτηρίη, καὶ τὸν εἶπαι—δέσποτα, οὐκ ἔστι οὐδεμία, εἰ μὴ τούτων ἀπαλλαγή τις γένηται τῶν πολλῶν ἐπιβατέων. 119, εἰ γὰρ δὴ ταῦτα οὕτω εἱρέθη ἐκ τοῦ κυβερνήτεω πρὸς Ξέρξεα, ἐν μυρίῃσι γνώμῃσι μίαν οὐκ ἔχω ἀντίξοον μὴ οὐκ ἂν ποιῆσαι βασιλέα τοιόνδε, τοὺς μὲν ἐκ τοῦ καταστρώματος καταβιβάσαι ἐς κοίλην νέα ἐόντας Πέρσας καὶ Περσέων τοὺς πρώτους, τῶν δ' ἐρετέων ἐόντων Φοινίκων ὅκως οὐκ ἂν ἴσον πλῆθος τοῖσι Πέρσῃσι ἐξέβαλε ἐς τὴν θάλασσαν. The term κατάστρωμα was habitually applied to the deck for combatants on war-ships: but it also was applied to the upper deck on merchant-ships. Thus the depth of a merchant-ship is reckoned by Lucian, navigium, 5, ἀπὸ τοῦ καταστρώματος ἐς τὸν πυθμένα, ᾗ βαθύτατον κατὰ τὸν ἄντλον. cf. Demosthenes, in Phormionem, 10, γεγεμισμένης γὰρ ἤδη τῆς νεώς, ὡς ἀκούομεν, μᾶλλον τοῦ δέοντος, προσανέλαβεν ἐπὶ τὸ κατάστρωμα χιλίας βύρσας, ὅθεν καὶ ἡ διαφθορὰ τῇ νηὶ συνέβη, Synesios, epistolæ, p. 178, πλείτω δὲ δεδεμένος ἐπὶ τοῦ καταστρώματος· μὴ γὰρ εἰς κοίλην ναῦν καταβαίη, ἐπεὶ μὴ θαυμάσῃς εἰ συχνὰ τῶν κεραμίων ἡμιδεῆ σοι ποιήσει. Indeed, the term was not reserved exclusively for the decks of ships. Athenæos applies it to the flooring or roofing of a battery erected on an armed merchant-ship, v. 43, τεῖχος δέ, ἐπάλξεις ἔχον καὶ καταστρώματα, διὰ νεὼς ἐπὶ κιλλιβάντων κατεσκεύαστο· ἐφ' οὗ λιθοβόλος ἐφειστήκει.

T.   *d*

either side of a Greek war-ship; and as combatants were posted on the gangways as well as on the hurricane-deck, these gangways formed part of the upper decking[118]. Thus the upper decking of a Greek war-ship must have consisted of a hurricane-deck, which did not extend from side to side, and two gangways, which were placed a few feet lower down and occupied the remaining width. And the superstructure between the gangways, comprising the hurricane-deck and its vertical supports on either side, would naturally correspond to the rectangular structure below for the rowers, and hence would form the top of that structure.

This hurricane-deck was apparently the only place available for working the supplementary oars known as *perineōi*. The length of these oars on the Athenian three-banked ships was nine cubits or nine and a half, that is to say, thirteen feet and a half or fourteen and a quarter[119]; some change occurring soon after 400 B.C. In the Athenian three-banked ship of this date in fg. 21 the hurricane-deck must be about five cubits above the water-line, and the gangway about two cubits below the hurricane-deck, if those rowers of the

---

[118] Athenæos, v. 37, τὸ μῆκος ἔχουσαν (τὴν ναῦν) διακοσίων ὀγδοήκοντα πηχῶν, ὀκτὼ δὲ καὶ τριάκοντα ἀπὸ παρόδου ἐπὶ πάροδον, ὕψος δὲ κ.τ.λ. The measurement from πάροδος to πάροδος is clearly intended for the breadth, so the πάροδοι were at the sides; and their name implies that they were gangways. Athenæos is indeed quoting from Callixenos, so the measurement may be false, or the ship imaginary: yet the statement proves that measurement from πάροδος to πάροδος was a recognized mode of reckoning the breadth of a war-ship. Plutarch, Demetrius, 43, ὁπλίτας δεχομένην (τὴν ναῦν) ἐπί τε τῶν παρόδων καὶ τοῦ καταστρώματος ὀλίγῳ τρισχιλίων ἀποδέοντας. Plutarch is likewise quoting from Callixenos: but the statement proves that combatants were normally posted on the πάροδοι of a war-ship. In the passage already quoted in note 35 on p. 14 Memnon speaks of the combatants as οἱ ἀπὸ τῶν καταστρωμάτων μαχησόμενοι, and the πάροδοι and κατάστρωμα may here be classed together as καταστρώματα : but apparently the plural was treated as equivalent to the singular, cf. Pausanias, i. 29, πλοῖον καθῆκον ἐς ἐννέα ἐρέτας ἀπὸ τῶν καταστρωμάτων. According to the present reading, Thucydides says καὶ αὗται οὔπω εἶχον διὰ πάσης καταστρώματα, i. 14, in speaking of the ships built by the Athenians under Themistocles, as though their ships afterwards had καταστρώματα διὰ πάσης νεώς, which might mean that these hurricane-decks reached right across the ship and left no space for gangways. But the words διὰ πάσης must be a corruption of some word connected with διάβασις. cf. Plutarch, Cimon, 12, ὥρμησεν (Κίμων) ἄρας ἀπὸ Κνίδου καὶ Τριοπίου διακοσίαις τριήρεσι. πρὸς μὲν τάχος ἀπ' ἀρχῆς καὶ περιαγωγὴν ὑπὸ Θεμιστοκλέους ἄριστα

upper bank are men of ordinary stature: and as the gangway would hardly be more than a cubit in width, an oar of nine cubits and a half might dip quite a cubit and a half in the water, if worked from the hurricane-deck with seven cubits and a half outboard and two cubits inboard. Some oars are certainly being worked from the hurricane-deck in the Athenian ship of about 600 B.C. in fg. 14: and these presumably are *perineōi*, since they are not in the banks. And if half a bank was allotted to these supplementary oars in the ships termed *triemioliai*, this may have been because there was not any hurricane-deck[120].

War-ships generally were classed by the Greeks as *kataphraktoi* or *aphraktoi*, that is to say, completely fenced or unfenced: and these terms would well denote the presence or absence of a line of screens on either side to close the open space between the hurricane-deck and the gangway, and thus protect the rowers of the upper bank from missiles[121]. In the Egyptian ships of about 1000 B.C., as in fg. 6, the rowers on either side were protected by a long screen above the gunwale; and similar screens are mentioned in the Odyssey,

κατεσκευασμέναις, ἐκεῖνος δὲ τότε καὶ πλατυτέρας ἐποίησεν αὐτὰς καὶ διάβασιν τοῖς καταστρώμασιν ἔδωκεν. In this context διάβασις would mean *breadth*, as in Hippocrates, epistolæ, 14, οἶδα παρὰ σοὶ γενόμενος ἐν ᾿Ρόδῳ, Δαμάγητε, τὴν ναῦν ἐκείνην— ᾿Αλίας ἐπιγραφὴ ἦν αὐτῇ—πάγκαλόν τινα καὶ εὔπρυμνον, ἱκανῶς τε τετροπισμένην, καὶ διάβασιν εἶχε πολλήν. Thus, as the ships were themselves made broader, the hurricane-decks could also be made broader without encroaching on the space required for the gangways.

119 Corp. Inscr. Attic. vol. ii, no. 789, col. a, l. 14, περίνεως (ἔχει) ΔΔΓΙΙΙΙ, ἀδόκιμον Ι, ἐννεαπήχεις καὶ σπιθαμι(αίας), l. 51, περίνεῳ ἐννέα πήχεων καὶ σπιθαμῆς. The length of the other oars is never stated, so the length of these would not be stated unless it varied: and the words αὗται ἐννεαπήχεις and τούτων ἐννεαπήχεις Γ occur in ll. 22, 55, where they must refer to the περίνεῳ. The inscription belongs to the archonship of Asteios, 373/2 B.C.

120 See p. 15 as to these ships and their oars.

121 The words φράσσειν and φραγμός or φράγμα properly refer to fences; and the κατά in κατάφρακτος clearly means that the ship was fenced completely, not that she was fenced down or decked, for then κατάφρακτος would be opposed to ἀκατάφρακτος instead of ἄφρακτος. cf. Arrian, anabasis, vii. 16, ναυπηγεῖσθαι ναῦς μακράς, ἀφράκτους τε καὶ πεφραγμένας. Apparently the κατά in κατάστρωμα also indicates completeness, like the *con* in *constratum*, the στρῶμα and *stratum* indicating sufficiently that the deck was laid down. Cicero opposes *constratus* to

but only as bulwarks for the water[122]. Screens for missiles, however, were probably in use on the Phœnician war-ships of about 700 B.C. : for there are certain square objects upon the superstructure of the ship in fg. 10, which has a ram and must therefore be a war-ship ; and these are absent from the ship in fg. 11, which has no ram and therefore cannot be a war-ship ; so they certainly served some purpose in warfare, yet seem unserviceable unless they could be lowered to protect the rowers. Had there been such screens on the Athenian war-ship of about 400 B.C. in fg. 21, they would doubtless have fitted into the gaps between the supports of the hurricane-deck. In the Athenian war-ships the rowers were also protected against sun and spray by awnings termed *pararrhymata* or *parablemata*, which were spread along each side to cover the open space below the hurricane-deck. Every

apertus in describing ships with and without a κατάστρωμα, in Verrem, ii. v. 40, *poterone in eos esse vehemens, qui naves non modo inanes habuerunt sed etiam apertas : in eum dissolutus, qui solus habuerit constratam navem et minus exinanitam?* cf. Aulus Hirtius, de bello Alexandrino, 11, *quattuor constratæ naves et complures apertæ.* But he simply transliterates ἄφρακτος, ad Atticum, v. 13. 1, *navigavimus sine timore et sine nausea : sed tardius, propter aphractorum Rhodiorum imbecillitatem*, cf. v. 11. 4, 12. 1, vi. 8. 4. And Livy says *naves tectas*, xxxiii. 30, where Polybios says καταφράκτους ναῦς, xviii. 27, in citing the same document. Now, if these screens closed the open space below the hurricane-deck, a ship could not be κατάφρακτος unless she had a κατάστρωμα, so that every *navis tecta* would be *constrata* but no *navis aperta* would be *tecta*. Thus Livy uses the terms indifferently, xxxvi. 42, *C. Livius, præfectus Romanæ classis, cum quinquaginta navibus tectis profectus,...quum sex Punicas naves ad auxilium missas accepisset,...Piræum ad veterem classem pervenit.* a *Piræo A. Atilius, traditis successori quinque et viginti navibus tectis, Romam est profectus: Livius una et octoginta constratis navibus Delum traiecit.* 43, *Eumenes cum quattuor et viginti navibus tectis, apertis pluribus paullo, ad Romanos rediit. inde centum quinque navibus tectis, etc.* cf. Appian, de rebus Syriacis, 22, καὶ τὸν ὑπ' Ἀτιλίῳ στόλον παραλαβών, ἔπλει (Λίβιος) καταφράκτοις ὀγδοήκοντα καὶ μιᾷ, ἑπομένου καὶ Εὐμενοῦς πεντήκοντα ἰδίαις· καὶ ἦν κατάφρακτον καὶ τῶνδε τὸ ἥμισυ. The decked and undecked merchant-ships were distinguished in Greek by other terms. Antiphon, de cæde Herodis, 22, ἐν ᾧ μὲν γὰρ ἐπλέομεν, ἀστέγαστον ἦν τὸ πλοῖον, εἰς ὃ δὲ μετέβημεν, ἐστεγασμένον· τοῦ δὲ ὑετοῦ ἕνεκα ταῦτ' ἦν. See also note 126 on p. 55 for this use of στέγη and *stega*.

[122] Odyssey, v. 256, 257, φράξε δέ μιν ῥίπεσσι διαμπερὲς οἰσυΐνῃσι | κύματος εἶλαρ ἔμεν. Bulwarks of this rough sort were sometimes made to serve as a defence against missiles. Cæsar, de bello civili, iii. 24, *virtute militum confisus, scaphas navium magnarum circiter sexaginta cratibus pluteisque contexit, eoque milites delectos imposuit, etc.*

ship carried two pairs of these, one pair of sail-cloth and the other of horse-hair or possibly of hide. Two other awnings were carried on these ships to cover some other spaces, a *katablema* for above and a *hypoblema* for below: but the exact position of these is doubtful[123].

A later arrangement of the upper decking may be seen in the Roman two-banked ship of about 50 A.D. in fg. 25. The oars of the upper bank here pass through ports, instead of passing over the gunwale: and as the rowers of the upper bank are therefore lower down in the ship, the deck above their heads is also lower; so that this deck for combatants no longer forms a hurricane-deck, but now stands between bulwarks which represent the former lines of screens, whilst the gangways retain their place outside.

[123] Corp. Inscr. Attic. vol. ii, no. 809, col. e, ll. 75—110, no. 811, col. c, ll. 11—32 : these are the lists of gear for three-banked ships and four-banked ships in 325/4 B.C. and 323/2 B.C.—at present there is no list for 324/3 B.C. Both lists include καταβλήματα and παραρρύματα λευκά and παραρρύματα τρίχινα for three-banked ships and for four-banked ships : but the earlier list includes ὑποβλήματα for three-banked ships only, and the later list does not include them at all. These discrepancies indicate that the ὑποβλήματα were discarded about that date upon the three-banked ships, and never came into use upon the four-banked ships : cf. no. 807, col. c, ll. 66—102, no. 808, col. d, ll. 119—151. A list of gear in store in 357/6 B.C. shews that each three-banked ship used to have a pair of παραρρύματα of each sort, but only one κατάβλημα and one ὑπόβλημα, no. 793, col. e, ll. 6—21. A list of ships some twenty years before incidentally mentions παραβλήματα, no. 791, l. 31. Two instances of the use of παραρρύματα and παραβλήματα in 406 and 405 B.C. are mentioned by Xenophon, Hellenica, i. 6. 19, τοὺς ἐπιβάτας εἰς κοίλην ναῦν μεταβιβάσας καὶ τὰ παραρρύματα παραβαλών, ii. 1. 22, πάντα δὲ παρασκευασάμενος ὡς εἰς ναυμαχίαν καὶ τὰ παραβλήματα παραβαλών. In both instances a fight was expected; yet the παραρρύματα and παραβλήματα were not spread to protect the crew, but to conceal the crew for a surprise : so they were spread over the open spaces below the hurricane-deck, for here alone would the crew be visible. Thus the παραβλήματα may merely be the παραρρύματα under another name, which ranges better with καταβλήματα and ὑποβλήματα. In the arsenal the παραρρύματα λευκά were stored in the same chests with the sails, and so were probably of similar material. Corp. Inscr. Attic. vol. ii, no. 1054, ll. 85—87, ποιήσει δὲ καὶ κιβωτοὺς τοῖς ἱστίοις καὶ τοῖς παραρρύμασιν τοῖς λευκοῖς, ἀριθμὸν ἑκατὸν τριάκοντα τέτταρας. The other παραρρύματα were perhaps of horse-hair, for that seems the likeliest meaning of τρίχινα, but were possibly of hide. cf. Cæsar, de bello civili, iii. 15, *pellibus, quibus erant tectæ naves*. The καταβλήματα and ὑποβλήματα were presumably of some similar material ; and certainly were not of timber, for in the lists they are classed with the παραρρύματα amongst the σκεύη κρεμαστά, which are distinguished from the σκεύη ξύλινα.

The three-banked ships were termed *triremes* in Latin and *triereis* in Greek: but while the Latin term implies a triple arrangement for the oars, the Greek term implies a triple arrangement of some undetermined sort; and the cognate adjective *triarmenoi* was applied to large sailing-ships, which had not any banks of oars[124]. These sailing-ships, however, used often to have three decks.

Thus, while Plutarch and Proclos describe a ship as *triarmenos,* Athenæos describes her as *triparodos,* that is to say, with three gangways; and states that these gangways stood one above another, and gave access to cabins along the sides and at the ends: so that this clearly was a three-decked ship, though apparently the planking of the decks did not extend over the whole

[124] The older form of *triremis* was *triresmus,* cf. Corp. Inscr. Latin. vol. i, no. 195, l. 12, *triresmosque naveis:* and both these forms are connected with ἐρετμός and ἐρέσσειν, whereas τριήρης is connected with ἄρειν, and thus with ἄρμενος. The term τριάρμενος was introduced about 100 A.D.; but not to designate a novel type of ship, for it is applied to ships of earlier times by Pollux, i. 83, καὶ Πτολεμαίου ναῦς, πεντεκαιδεκήρης· καὶ Ἀντιγόνου, τριάρμενος, and by Plutarch and Proclos in the passages quoted in note 74 on p. 28. The term is employed by Lucian, navigium, 14, πέντε γάρ, εἰ βούλει, καλλίω καὶ μείζω τοῦ Αἰγυπτίου πλοίου ἤδη ἔχε, καὶ τὸ μέγιστον οὐδὲ καταδῦναι δυνάμενα,......ὃς γὰρ ἔτι ἑνὸς πλοίου τουτουὶ δεσπότης ὢν παρήκουες βοώντων, εἰ πέντε κτήσαιο πρὸς τούτῳ τριάρμενα πάντα καὶ ἀνώλεθρα, οὐδὲ ὄψει δηλαδὴ τοὺς φίλους. Again by Lucian, Lexiphanes, 15, ὁλκάδα τριάρμενον ἐν οὐρίῳ πλέουσαν, ἐμπεπνευματωμένου τοῦ ἀκατείου, εὐφορούσάν τε καὶ ἀκροκυματοῦσαν, cf. pseudologistes, 27, μικροῦ γοῦν φασιν ἀποπνιγῆναί σε ναύτῃ τινὶ τῶν τριαρμένων ἐντυχόντα, ὃς ἐμπεσὼν ἀπέφραξέ σοι τὸ στόμα. Also by Philostratos, vita Apollonii, iv. 9, καὶ ἅμα διιὼν ταῦτα ναῦν εἶδε τῶν τριαρμένων ἐκπλέουσαν καὶ τοὺς ναύτας ἄλλον ἄλλως ἐς τὸ ἀνάγεσθαι αὐτὴν πράττοντας. cf. Synesios, epistolæ, p. 161, ταχὺ μὲν τὴν γῆν ἀπεκρύπτομεν, ταχὺ δὲ μετὰ τῶν ὁλκάδων ἦμεν τῶν διαρμένων.

[125] Athenæos, v. 41, ἦν δ᾿ ἡ ναῦς τῇ μὲν κατασκευῇ εἰκόσορος, τριπάροδος δέ, τὴν μὲν κατωτάτω ἔχουσα ἐπὶ τὸν γόμον, ἐφ᾿ ἣν διὰ κλιμάκων πυκνῶν ἡ κατάβασις ἐγίνετο· ἡ δ᾿ ἑτέρα τοῖς εἰς τὰς διαίτας βουλομένοις εἰσιέναι μεμηχάνητο· μεθ᾿ ἣν ἡ τελευταία τοῖς ἐν τοῖς ὅπλοις τεταγμένοις. ἦσαν δὲ τῆς μέσης παρόδου παρ᾿ ἑκάτερον τῶν τοίχων δίαιται τετράκλινοι τοῖς ἀνδράσι, τριάκοντα τὸ πλῆθος. ἡ δὲ ναυκληρικὴ δίαιτα κλινῶν μὲν ἦν πεντεκαίδεκα, θαλάμους δὲ τρεῖς εἶχε τρικλίνους, ὧν ἦν τὸ κατὰ τὴν πρύμναν ὀπτάνιον. κατὰ δὲ τὴν ἀνωτάτω πάροδον γυμνάσιον ἦν, καὶ περίπατοι, κ.τ.λ. For a further account of the structures on the upper πάροδος, see note 133 on p. 58. The ship here described as τριπάροδος is described as τριάρμενος by Plutarch and by Proclos in the passages quoted in note 74 on p. 28. Athenæos is quoting here from Moschion, and applies the term πάροδοι to the three decks of the ship; whereas in quoting from Callixenos—see note 118 on p. 50—he applies the term to a pair of gangways along the two sides of the ship: but Moschion seems to be

ship, but left the centre open[125]. And the term *triereis* was itself applied by certain authors to three-decked ships, and even to three-storied buildings[126]; while in the Septuagint the Ark is described as *triorophos*, that is to say, with three stories, though in the original its triple arrangement is of an undetermined sort[127]. The three-banked war-ships may therefore have inherited the name *triereis* from three-decked ships of earlier date : but they never had three decks themselves. The rowers of the lower bank were indeed styled *thalamitai*, as if they had originally sat in a *thalamos*, or chamber: but the rowers of the middle bank were styled *zygitai*, as if they had originally sat upon the *zyga*, or beams; and if the beams served as seats, they could not carry a deck,

reckoning each pair of gangways as a single structure, for he states explicitly that the middle πάροδος had cabins on each side of the ship. Possibly the open space between the gangways was covered over by a deck corresponding to the κατάστρωμα on a war-ship, so that the ships described as τριπάροδοι or τριάρμενοι really had four decks altogether. Thus, Lucian reckons the depth of a merchant-ship ἀπὸ τοῦ καταστρώματος, navigium, 5, and she was one of the πλοῖα τριάρμενα, navigium, 14. Cabins at the stern are mentioned by Lucian, navigium, 5, αἱ κατὰ τὴν πρύμναν οἰκήσεις—cf. Lucan, ix. 110, 111, *puppisque cavernis | delituit*—and these probably answer to Moschion's ναυκληρικὴ δίαιτα and its θάλαμοι, the *diæta magistri* of Petronius, satiræ, 115.

[126] Etymologicum Magnum, s. v. διήρης :—'Ἀπολλώνιος δὲ καὶ τὰς ναῦς τὰς ἐχούσας δύο ἢ καὶ τρεῖς στέγας διήρεις καὶ τριήρεις λέγει. This obviously does not imply that the three-banked ships had three decks themselves : it merely shews that this author applied the name for three-banked ships to three-decked ships also. The author may be either Apollonios or Apollodoros, as the reading is doubtful. For this sense of στέγη, cf. Plautus, Bacchides, ii. 3. 44, Stichus, iii. 1. 12, *in stega*. Ælius Aristeides, panegyrica in Cyzico, p. 420, ἀντὶ γὰρ τῶν οἰκιῶν τῶν τριωρόφων καὶ τῶν τριήρων πάρεστιν ὁρᾶν νεὼν τὸν μέγιστον, τῶν μὲν ἄλλων πολλαπλασίονα, αὐτὸν δὲ τριπλοῦν τῇ φύσει. τὰ μὲν γὰρ αὐτοῦ κατάγειός ἐστι θέα, τὰ δ' ὑπερῷος, μέση δὲ ἡ νενομισμένη. δρόμοι δὲ ὑπὸ γῆν τε καὶ κρεμαστοὶ δι' αὐτοῦ διήκοντες κύκλῳ, ὥσπερ οὐκ ἐν προσθήκης μέρει, ἀλλ' ἐξεπίτηδες εἶναι δρόμοι πεποιημένοι. The interior of this temple thus bore some resemblance to the interior of a three-decked ship, as described by Athenæos in the passage quoted in the last note : and this resemblance may have led Aristeides to use the term τριήρης in his comparison. See also Athenæos, ii. 5, as to a dwelling-house known as τριήρης at Agrigentum : he quotes the story from Timæos.

[127] Genesis, vi. 15, καὶ οὕτω ποιήσεις τὴν κιβωτόν, 16, κατάγαια, διώροφα καὶ τριώροφα ποιήσεις αὐτήν. A fourth deck is mentioned by Philo Judæus, vita Moysis, ii. 11, καὶ συνεχῆ κατασκευασάμενος ἔνδον οἰκήματα, ἐπίπεδα καὶ ὑπερῷα, τριώροφα καὶ τετρώροφα. And also by Josephus, de antiquitatibus Judaicis, i. 3. 2, λάρνακα τετράστεγον κατασκευάσας.

and the space below could only figuratively be termed a chamber. Moreover, there is a characteristic little jest of Aristophanes to prove that in his day the rowers of the middle and lower banks had no deck between them[128]. And Xenophon speaks as though the rowers of all three banks had to pull together to avoid collision with each other[129].

The earliest Greek ships had little decks at stem and stern, somewhat above the level of the beams[130]; and similar decks are represented on Egyptian and Asiátic ships of still earlier date, as in fgs. 4 to 8, the bulwarks marking their extent. But on Greek ships of about 500 B.C., as in fgs. 17 and 19, the forecastle appears without the poop; and

---

[128] Aristophanes, ranæ, 1074, καὶ προσπαρδεῖν γ᾽ εἰς τὸ στόμα τῷ θαλάμακι. But see Appian, de bellis civilibus, v. 107, ὁ δὲ Ἀγρίππας ἵετο μάλιστα εὐθὺ τοῦ Παπίου, καὶ αὐτῷ κατὰ τὴν ἐπωτίδα ἐμπεσὼν κατέσεισε τὴν ναῦν καὶ ἐς τὰ κοῖλα ἀνέρρηξεν· ἡ δὲ τούς τε ἐν τοῖς πύργοις ἀπεσείσατο, καὶ τὴν θάλασσαν ἀθρόως ἐδέχετο· καὶ τῶν ἐρετῶν οἱ μὲν θαλαμίαι πάντες ἀπελήφθησαν, οἱ δ᾽ ἕτεροι τὸ κατά-στρωμα ἀναρρήξαντες ἐξενήχοντο. This was in an action off Mylæ in 36 B.C. The incident rather suggests that there was a deck just above the rowers of the lower bank, since they were all drowned, while the rest escaped. But as the survivors had to make their escape by breaking through the upper decking, the rowers of the lower bank may have been delayed until too late by the crowd above. See also Silius Italicus, xiv. 424—426, *trepidatur omisso | summis remigio : sed enim tam rebus in arctis | fama mali nondum tanti penetrarat ad imos.* But this cannot reasonably be taken to imply a deck between the banks.

[129] Xenophon, economica, 8. 8, καὶ τριήρης δέ τοι ἡ σεσαγμένη ἀνθρώπων διὰ τί ἄλλο φοβερόν ἐστι πολεμίοις ἢ φίλοις ἀξιοθέατον ἢ ὅτι ταχὺ πλεῖ; διὰ τί δὲ ἄλλο ἄλυποι ἀλλήλοις εἰσὶν οἱ ἐμπλέοντες ἢ διότι ἐν τάξει μὲν κάθηνται, ἐν τάξει δὲ προνεύουσιν, ἐν τάξει δ᾽ ἀναπίπτουσιν, ἐν τάξει δ᾽ ἐμβαίνουσι καὶ ἐκβαίνουσι; But although they had thus to pull together when they were all at work, one set could go on working while another stopped. Thucydides, iii. 49, οἱ μὲν ὕπνον ᾑροῦντο κατὰ μέρος, οἱ δὲ ἤλαυνον. Xenophon, Hellenica, vi. 2. 29, εἰ μὲν αὖρα φέροι, θέοντες ἅμα ἀνεπαύοντο· εἰ δὲ ἐλαύνειν δέοι, κατὰ μέρος τοὺς ναύτας ἀνέπαυεν. Polyænos, v. 22. 4, τοῖς δὲ ἐρέταις (παραγγείλας) ἀνὰ μέρος ὁτὲ μὲν τὰς θαλαμίας, ὁτὲ δὲ τὰς ζυγίας, ὁτὲ δὲ τὰς θρανίτιδας κώπας ἀναφέρειν. The stratagem here was to make the enemy believe that the ships were fully manned, when there really were only hands enough for one bank of oars : but the enemy would not have been deceived, unless the three banks were often worked separately. Of course, there was space enough in the hold for the combatants as well as the rowers : Xenophon, Hellenica, i. 6. 19, τοὺς ἐπιβάτας εἰς κοίλην ναῦν μεταβιβάσας. But there was no space to spare : Cicero, in Verrem, ii. v. 51, *ea est enim ratio instructarum ornatarumque navium, ut non modo plures, sed ne singuli quidem possint accedere...classem instructam atque ornatam fuisse, nullum propugnatorem abfuisse, nullum vacuum transtrum fuisse.*

on Greek ships of somewhat later date, as in fg. 23, and even on the ship of earlier date in fg. 15, the bulwarks of this forecastle are represented as supporting the fore part of a hurricane-deck and enclosing a cabin underneath. Some such forecastle was wanted on the war-ships, as their bows sloped down to meet the ram : but the merchant-ships had clipper bows high out of water; and by about 500 B.C. the forecastle had already been deprived of bulwarks on vessels of that class, as may be seen from fg. 18, and apparently was on a level with the ordinary deck amidship. The stern now held a tier of seats for the steerer and others in command; but this did not necessitate a separate deck there[131].

[130] Odyssey, v. 163, 164, ἀτὰρ ἴκρια πῆξαι ἐπ' αὐτῆς | ὑψοῦ, ὥς σε φέρῃσιν ἐπ' ἠεροειδέα πόντον, 252, 253, ἴκρια δὲ στήσας, ἀραρὼν θαμέσι σταμίνεσσι, | ποίει. xii. 229, 230, εἰς ἴκρια νηὸς ἔβαινον | πρῴρης, 411—414, ὁ δ' ἄρα πρύμνῃ ἐνὶ νηὶ | πλῆξε κυβερνήτεω κεφαλήν, σὺν δ' ὀστέ' ἄραξεν | πάντ' ἄμυδις κεφαλῆς· ὁ δ' ἄρ' ἀρνευτῆρι ἐοικὼς | κάππεσ' ἀπ' ἰκριόφιν. xiii. 73—75, κὰδ δ' ἄρ' Ὀδυσσῆι στόρεσαν ῥῆγός τε λίνον τε | νηὸς ἐπ' ἰκριόφιν γλαφυρῆς, ἵνα νήγρετον εὕδοι, | πρύμνης. cf. iii. 353, xv. 283, 552 ; also Iliad, xv. 685, 729. The term is used in prose by Synesios, epistolæ, p. 161, ἐπὶ τῶν ἰκρίων ἑστώς, and also by Heliodoros, Æthiopica, v. 24, τῶν μὲν εἰς τὰ κοῖλα τῆς νεὼς καταδυομένων, τῶν δὲ πρὸς μάχην ἐπὶ τῶν ἰκρίων ἀλλήλοις παρακελευομένων.   Pliny, vii. 57, tectas longas (naves invenere) Thasii : antea ex prora tantum et puppi pugnabatur.   This probably answers to the statement in Thucydides, i. 10, οὐδ' αὖ τὰ πλοῖα κατάφρακτα ἔχοντας, ἀλλὰ τῷ παλαιῷ τρόπῳ λῃστικώτερον παρεσκευασμένα.   As to the statement in Thucydides, i. 14, καὶ αὗται οὔπω εἶχον διὰ πάσης καταστρώματα, see note 118 on p. 50.   And see note 121 on p. 51 for the meaning of tectas and κατάφρακτα.

[131] Ptolemy, Almagest, viii. 1, Ἀργοῦς ἀστερισμός, employs the phrase ἐν τῷ καταστρώματι τῆς πρύμνης : but this does not imply that the ship had a separate deck at the stern, any more than his phrase ἐν τῇ τρόπει τῆς πρύμνης implies that she had a separate keel there.   So also Petronius employs the phrase supra constratum puppis, satiræ, 100 ; the construction being determined by the context ut supra constratum navis occuparemus secretissimum locum.   The same interpretation must be placed upon the phrase in Aulus Gellius, xvi. 19, stansque in summæ puppis foro.   This is a translation from Herodotos, i. 24, who speaks of Arion στάντα ἐν τοῖσι ἑδωλίοισι while the robbers ἀναχωρῆσαι ἐκ τῆς πρύμνης ἐς μέσην νέα.   cf. Euripides, Helena, 1571, Ἑλένη καθέζετ' ἐν μέσοις ἑδωλίοις, 1602, 1603, παρακέλευσμα δ' ἦν | πρύμνηθεν Ἑλένης.   These ἑδώλια at the stern were presumably a set of seats, the term ἑδώλια being equivalent to sedilia in Latin. Virgil, Æneid, v. 837, sub remis fusi per dura sedilia nautæ.   For the other ἑδώλιον that held the mast, see note 196 on p. 91.   Apparently, the term ζυγόν served also to denote some bench at the stern.   Æschylos, Agamemnon, 1617, 1618, σὺ ταῦτα φωνεῖς, νερτέρα προσήμενος | κώπῃ, κρατούντων τῶν ἐπὶ ζυγῷ δορός ; cf. Euripides, Cyclops, 14, 15, ἐν πρύμνῃ δ' ἄκρᾳ | αὐτὸς λαβὼν εὔθυνον

Ships generally had a deck-house at the stern for the commander and his friends, sometimes constructed solidly, but oftener of wicker-work or merely of awnings[132]. The heavier type is represented on the Roman merchant-ship in fg. 29, and the lighter type on the Roman war-ship in fg. 35. Some ships had deck-houses all along the upper decking; and these were fitted with every luxury, baths of bronze and marble in the bath-room, paintings and statues and mosaics in the principal saloons, and even a library of books. And alongside these deck-houses there were covered walks with rows of vines and fruit-trees planted in flower-pots[133].

ἀμφῆρες δόρυ. This ζυγόν may answer to the *iuga longa* of Virgil, Æneid, vi. 411, 412, *inde alias animas, quæ per iuga longa sedebant,* | *deturbat, laxatque foros :* for the ghosts here were not on board as rowers, so these *iuga* would not be the rowers' seats, nor could those seats be described as *longa.*—In this passage Virgil calls the deck *fori*, whereas Aulus Gellius calls it *forus :* but singular and plural were used indifferently.   Sallust, apud Nonium, p. 206, *illum nautis forum.* Cicero, de senectute, 6, *alii per foros cursent.*   Lucan, iii. 630, *ad summos repleta foros, desedit in undas,* sc. *navis.*   Ennius, apud Isidorum, origines, xix. 2. 4, *multa foro ponit et agea longa repletur,* where *agea* or ἀγυιά is probably a synonym for πάροδος.   These terms *forus* and *fori* must convey the notion of an open space, like *Forum* ; and hence denote a deck.   Ammianus, xxvii. 5. 2, *ponteque contabulato supra navium foros flumen transgressus est Histrum.*

132 Herodotos, vii. 100, ὡς δὲ ταῦτα οἱ ἐπεποίητο, τῶν νεῶν κατελκυσθεισέων ἐς θάλασσαν, ἐνθαῦτα ὁ Ξέρξης μετεκβὰς ἐκ τοῦ ἄρματος ἐς νέα Σιδωνίην ἵζετο ὑπὸ σκηνῇ χρυσέῃ καὶ παρέπλωε παρὰ τὰς πρώρας τῶν νεῶν.   Arrian, anabasis, vi. 13, καὶ πλέων κατὰ τὸν ποταμόν, ὡς ἐπέλαξεν ἡ ναῦς ἤδη τῷ στρατοπέδῳ τὸν βασιλέα φέρουσα, κελεύει δὴ (Ἀλέξανδρος) ἀφελεῖν τὴν σκηνὴν ἀπὸ τῆς πρύμνης, ὡς καταφανὴς εἶναι πᾶσιν.   Chariton, viii. 6, εἰσέπλευσεν οὖν τριήρης ἡ Χαιρέου πρώτη.   εἶχε δ' ἐπάνω σκηνὴν συγκεκαλυμμένην Βαβυλωνίοις περιπετάσμασιν...αἰφνίδιον εἱλκύσθη τὰ παραπετάσματα, καὶ ὤφθη Καλλιρρόη, κ.τ.λ.   Tacitus, annales, xiv. 5, *Crepereius Gallus haud procul gubernaculis adstabat, cum dato signo ruere tectum loci multo plumbo grave; pressusque Crepereius et statim exanimatus est.* cf. Suetonius, Nero, 34, *cameræ ruina.*   Sidonius, epistolæ, viii. 12, *hic, superflexa crate paradarum, sereni brumalis infida vitabis.*   Ausonius, epistolæ, 5. 28, 29, *Medullini te feret ora noti* | *expositum subter paradas.*

133 Athenæos, v. 41, κατὰ δὲ τὴν ἀνωτάτω πάροδον γυμνάσιον ἦν, καὶ περίπατοι, σύμμετρον ἔχοντες τὴν κατασκευὴν τῷ τοῦ πλοίου μεγέθει, ἐν οἷς κῆποι παντοῖοι θαυμασίως ἦσαν περιβάλλοντες ταῖς φυτείαις, διὰ κεραμίδων μολυβδίνων κατεστεγανωμένοι.   ἔτι δὲ σκηναὶ κιττοῦ λευκοῦ καὶ ἀμπέλων, ὧν αἱ ῥίζαι τὴν τροφὴν ἐν πίθοις εἶχον γῆς πεπληρωμένοις, τὴν αὐτὴν ἄρδευσιν λαμβάνουσαι καθάπερ καὶ οἱ κῆποι.   αὗται δὲ αἱ σκηναὶ συνεσκίαζον τοὺς περιπάτους.   ἑξῆς δὲ τούτων Ἀφροδίσιον κατεσκεύαστο τρίκλινον, δάπεδον ἔχον ἐκ λίθων ἀχατῶν τε καὶ ἄλλων χαριεστάτων, ὅσοι κατὰ τὴν νῆσον ἦσαν · τοὺς τοίχους δ' εἶχε καὶ τὴν ὀροφὴν κυπαρίττου, τὰς δὲ θύρας

Ships also carried turrets on the upper decking to enable their crews to shoot down missiles on an enemy[134]; and merchant-ships carried them as much as war-ships, since they had often to encounter pirates. These turrets could easily be set up and taken down again, their foundations alone being fixtures in the hull: and apparently those foundations sometimes projected overboard, as though the turrets reached right across the ship or else were placed in pairs on either side. A merchant-ship might carry as many as eight, two in the bows, two near the stern, and four amidship; and such turrets might contain three stories each, and thus be fully twenty feet in

ἐλέφαντος καὶ θύου· γραφαῖς δὲ καὶ ἀγάλμασιν ἔτι δὲ ποτηρίων κατασκευαῖς ὑπερβαλλόντως κατεσκεύαστο. 42, τούτου δ᾽ ἐφεξῆς σχολαστήριον ὑπῆρχε πεντάκλινον, ἐκ πύξου τοὺς τοίχους· καὶ τὰ θυρώματα κατεσκευασμένον, βιβλιοθήκην ἔχον ἐν αὐτῷ, κατὰ δὲ τὴν ὀροφὴν πόλον, ἐκ τοῦ κατὰ τὴν Ἀχραδίνην ἀπομεμιμημένον ἡλιοτροπίου. ἦν δὲ καὶ βαλανεῖον τρίκλινον, πυρίας χαλκᾶς ἔχον τρεῖς καὶ λουτῆρα πέντε μετρητὰς δεχόμενον, ποικίλον τοῦ Ταυρομενίτου λίθου. κατεσκεύαστο δὲ καὶ οἰκήματα, κ.τ.λ. Athenæos ascribes this ship to Hieron, but the description seems to be inspired by ships of later date: see pp. 27—29. Suetonius, Caligula, 37, *fabricavit et de cedris Liburnicas gemmatis puppibus, versicoloribus velis, magna thermarum et porticuum et tricliniorum laxitate, magnaque etiam vitium et pomiferarum arborum varietate; quibus discumbens de die inter choros ac symphonias litora Campaniæ peragraret.* Maximus Tyrius, i. 3, λέγω δὲ οὐ μῦθον πλάττων, ἀλλὰ οὐ πολὺς χρόνος ὅτε ἐξ Αἰγύπτου ἐς Τύρον ἔπλει βασιλεὺς τῶν ὑπὲρ Φοινίκης βαρβάρων ἐκείνων τῶν ἀνδρῶν, οἳ "οὐκ ἴσασι θάλατταν, οὐδὲ ἀλέγουσι τοῦ Αἰγιόχου Διὸς οὐδὲ θεῶν μακάρων." παρεσκευάσατο δὴ μέλλων πλεῖν ὁ ἄθεος οὗτος καὶ ἀθάλαττος βασιλεὺς μεγάλην καὶ εὐρύχωρον ναῦν, ἵνα αὐτῷ πᾶσαι αἱ ἡδοναὶ συμπλέωσι· τὸ μὲν γὰρ αὐτῆς βασίλεια ἦν οἷα κάλλιστα, παστάδες, καὶ εὐναί, καὶ δρόμοι· "ἔκτοσθεν δ᾽ αὐλῆς μέγας ὄρχατος ἄγχι θυράων τετράγυος," καὶ δένδρα ἐμπεφύκεσαν, ῥοιαί, καὶ ὄγχναι, καὶ μηλέαι, καὶ ἄμπελοι· τὸ δὲ αὐτῆς λουτρὸν ἦν, καὶ γυμνάσιον· τὸ δὲ ὀψοποιοῖς χώρα· τὸ δὲ θάλαμοι παλλακίσιν· τὸ δὲ συμπόσιον· τὸ δὲ ἄλλο τι μέρος τρυφώσης πόλεως. This would naturally refer to some king of the Nabatæans; but in the context his name is given as Æetes, and that does not suit any king in history. Plutarch, Lucullus, 7, ἔτι δὲ ναῦς οὐ χρυσορόφοις σκηνίσιν οὐδὲ λουτροῖς παλλακίδων καὶ γυναικωνίτισι τρυφώσαις ἠσκημένας, ἀλλ᾽ ὅπλων καὶ βελῶν καὶ χρημάτων γεμούσας παραρτυσάμενος, sc. Μιθριδάτης.

[134] Pliny, xxxii. 1, *sed armatæ classes imponunt sibi turrium propugnacula, ut in mari quoque pugnetur velut e muris.* Vegetius, iv. 44, *in maioribus etiam liburnis propugnacula turresque constituunt, ut tamquam de muro ita de excelsioribus tabulatis facilius vulnerent vel perimant inimicos.* Horace, epodes, i. 1, 2, *ibis liburnis inter alta navium, | amice, propugnacula.* The term *liburni* is used strictly by Horace, but loosely by Vegetius—see p. 16 and notes 42, 44—so their statements are not contradictory. Lucan, iv. 226, *turrigeras classis pelago sparsura carinas,* cf. iii. 514. Virgil, Æneid, viii. 693, *turritis puppibus.*

height[135]. A little turret is represented in the bows of the Roman war-ship of about 50 A.D. in fig. 25. On such ships the turrets were painted; and their colouring served to distinguish one squadron from another[136]. To counterbalançe these encumbrances upon the upper decking, quantities of ballast would be required at the bottom of the hold; and some gravel or sand or stone always was carried there for steadying the ship[137]. And this ballast could

[135] Thucydides, vii. 25, προσαγαγόντες γὰρ ναῦν μυριοφόρον αὐτοῖς οἱ Ἀθηναῖοι, πύργους τε ξυλίνους ἔχουσαν καὶ παραφράγματα, κ.τ.λ. Appian, de bellis civilibus, v. 106, καὶ πύργους ἐπὶ τῶν νεῶν εἶχον κατά τε πρῷραν καὶ κατὰ πρύμναν. Athenæos, v. 43, πύργοι τε ἦσαν ἐν αὐτῇ ὀκτώ, σύμμετροι τὸ μέγεθος τοῖς τῆς νεὼς ὄγκοις· δύο μὲν κατὰ πρύμναν, οἱ δ' ἴσοι κατὰ πρῷραν, οἱ λοιποὶ δὲ κατὰ μέσην ναῦν. cf. 42, ἄτλαντές τε περιέτρεχον τὴν ναῦν ἐκτὸς ἐξαπήχεις, οἳ τοὺς ὄγκους ὑπειλήφεσαν τοὺς ἀνωτάτω. These ὄγκοι are presumably the πυργοῦχοι of Polybios, xvi. 3, παραπεσὼν δὲ τοῖς πολεμίοις, ἀπέβαλε τὸν δεξιὸν ταρσὸν τῆς νεώς, ὁμοῦ συρραγέντων καὶ τῶν πυργούχων. Thus the ὄγκοι or πυργοῦχοι would be beams or platforms projecting from the ship, and serving as foundations for the turrets. Dion Cassius, l. 33, οἱ μὲν τὰ ἱστία ἤγειρον, οἱ δὲ τούς τε πύργους καὶ τὰ ἔπιπλα εἰς τὴν θάλασσαν ἐρρίπτουν, ὅπως κουφίσαντες διαφύγωσι. Appian, de bellis civilibus, iv. 72, ἐλπίζων γάρ τι τοιοῦτον, ἐπεφέρετο (Κάσσιος) πύργους ἐπτυγμένους, οἳ τότε ἀνίσταντο. Cæsar, de bello Gallico, iii. 14, turribus excitatis, de bello civili, i. 26, turres cum ternis tabulatis erigebat. The reference is here to merchant-ships; and so also in the passages quoted above from Athenæos and Thucydides. Although the statements of Athenæos are questionable, since they are borrowed from Moschion—see pp. 27 to 29—they probably are based on fact.

[136] Appian, de bellis civilibus, v. 121, μόλις δέ ποτε ταῖς χροιαῖς τῶν πύργων, αἷς δὴ μόναις διέφερον ἀλλήλων, ὁ Ἀγρίππας συνεὶς πλέονας ἀπολωλέναι τοῦ Πομπηίου ναῦς, ἐθάρρυνε τοὺς συνόντας, κ.τ.λ. See also Polyænos, v. 34, already quoted at the end of note 89 on p. 35, as to uniformity of colouring in a fleet.

[137] Odyssey, v. 257, πολλὴν δ' ἐπεχεύατο ὕλην. Lycophron, 618, τὸν ἑρματίτην νηὸς ἐκβαλὼν πέτρον. Plato, Theætetos, p. 144 A, καὶ ἅττοντες φέρονται ὥσπερ τὰ ἀνερμάτιστα πλοῖα. Plutarch, animi et corporis affectiones, 4, ἀκυβέρνητος καὶ ἀνερμάτιστος εἴς τι ναυάγιον φοβερὸν ἐξέπεσε, ad principem ineruditum, 5, ἕρματος πολλοῦ καὶ κυβερνήτου μεγάλου δεόμενον. Livy, xxxvii. 14, onerarias multa saburra gravatas. Pliny, xvi. 76, CXX M modiorum lentis pro saburra ei fuere. See also Aristotle, historia animalium, viii. 12. 5, ix. 40. 21; Pliny, x. 30, xviii. 87; Aristophanes, aves, 1428, 1429; Virgil, georgics, iv. 194—196; Plutarch, de solertia animalium, 10. 10, 28. 2. At Portus, near the mouth of the Tiber, the ballast-heavers formed a guild, corpus saburrariorum: Corp. Inscr. Latin. vol. xiv, no. 102.

[138] Arrian, anabasis, ii. 19, ἕρματά τε ἐς τὴν πρύμναν ἐνέθεσαν, τοῦ ἐξᾶραι εἰς ὕψος τὴν πρῷραν πιεζομένης κατὰ πρύμναν τῆς νεώς. Polybios, xvi. 4, αὐτοὶ μὲν γὰρ ἔμπρωρα τὰ σκάφη ποιοῦντες, ἐξάλους ἐλάμβανον τὰς πληγάς· τοῖς δὲ πολεμίοις ὕφαλα τὰ τραύματα διδόντες, ἀβοηθήτους ἐσκεύαζον τὰς πληγάς.

easily be shifted fore or aft to depress or elevate the bows, as need arose for ramming or manœuvring[138]. At the bottom of the hold there was also a mass of bilge-water, which needed constant baling out by buckets or else by a machine consisting of an Archimedean screw worked by some sort of treadmill[139]. And probably the cisterns for the drinking-water were also down below, serving like the bilge to increase the weight of ballast[140].

[139] Odyssey, xii. 410, 411, ἱστὸς δ᾽ ὀπίσω πέσεν, ὅπλα τε πάντα | εἰς ἄντλον κατέχυντο. xv. 479, ἄντλῳ δ᾽ ἐνδούπησε πεσοῦσ᾽, ὡς εἰναλίη κήξ. Sophocles, Philoctetes, 481, 482, ἐμβαλοῦ μ᾽ ὅπη θέλεις ἄγων, | εἰς ἀντλίαν, ἐς πρῷραν, ἐς πρύμνην. Cicero, ad familiares, ix. 15. 3, sedebamus enim in puppi et clavum tenebamus: nunc autem vix est in sentina locus. Sallust, Catilina, 37, Romam, sicut in sentinam, confluxerant. These terms ἄντλος or ἀντλία and sentina, which thus denoted the bilge of a ship, also denoted the bilge-water. Æschylos, septem adversus Thebas, 795, 796, καὶ κλυδωνίου | πολλαῖσι πληγαῖς ἄντλον οὐκ ἐδέξατο. Seneca, epistolæ, 30, quemadmodum in nave, quæ sentinam trahit, uni rimæ aut alteri obsistitur, ubi plurimis locis laxari cœpit et cedere, succurri non potest navigio dehiscenti. Euripides, Troades, 685, 686, ὁ μὲν παρ᾽ οἴαχ᾽, ὁ δ᾽ ἐπὶ λαίφεσιν βεβώς, | ὁ δ᾽ ἄντλον εἴργων ναός. Cicero, de senectute, 6, alii malos scandant, alii per foros cursent, alii sentinam exhauriant. The buckets for the baling were known as ἀντλητήρια or sentinacula. Dion Cassius, l. 34, οὔτε γὰρ πολλὰ ἢ καὶ μεγάλα τὰ ἀντλητήρια εἶχον, καὶ ἡμιδεᾶ αὐτὰ ἅτε ταραττόμενοι ἀνέφερον. Paulinus Nolanus, epistolæ, 49. 3, et post unum vel alterum brevis sentinaculi haustum humore destricto siccataque navi, etc. The pump is mentioned by Athenæos, v. 43, ἡ δὲ ἀντλία, καίπερ βάθος ὑπερβάλλον ἔχουσα, δι᾽ ἑνὸς ἀνδρὸς ἐξηντλεῖτο διὰ κοχλίου, Ἀρχιμήδους ἐξευρόντος. cf. Vitruvius, x. 6. 3, cochlea hominibus calcantibus facit versationes. Artemidoros, oneirocritica, i. 48, οἶδα δέ τινα, ὃς ἔδοξε τοῦ παντὸς σώματος ἀτρέμα μένοντος τοὺς πόδας αὐτοῦ μόνους βαδίζειν, καὶ προβαίνειν μὲν μηδὲ βραχύ, ὅμως δὲ κινεῖσθαι. συνέβη αὐτῷ εἰς ἀντλίαν καταδικασθῆναι. καὶ γὰρ ἐκεῖ τοῖς ἀντλοῦσι συμβέβηκε διαβαίνειν μὲν ὡς βαδίζουσιν, ἀεὶ δὲ μένειν ἐν τῷ αὐτῷ τόπῳ. For the phrase εἰς ἀντλίαν καταδικασθῆναι, cf. Suetonius, Tiberius, 51, in antliam condemnato. In the context Artemidoros says that a man was set to bale ὄντι πανούργῳ, and Lucian reckons it fit work for the ἀργὸν καὶ ἄτεχνον καὶ ἄτολμον, Jupiter tragœdus, 48. See also Paulinus Nolanus, epistolæ, 49. 12, seni persona sentinatoris, et in nautis vilissima.

[140] Lucian, veræ historiæ, i. 5, πάμπολλα μὲν σιτία ἐνεβαλόμην, ἱκανὸν δὲ καὶ ὕδωρ ἐνεθέμην, κ.τ.λ. ii. 1, τὴν ναῦν ἐπεσκευάζομεν, ὕδωρ τε ὡς ἔνι πλεῖστον ἐμβαλλόμενοι καὶ τὰ ἄλλα ἐπιτήδεια. Dion Cassius, l. 34, τὸ μὲν πρῶτον τῷ ποτίμῳ ὕδατι ᾧ ἐπεφέροντο ἐχρῶντο, καί τινα κατέσβεσαν· ἐπεὶ δὲ ἐκεῖνο καταναλώθη, ἤντλουν τὸ θαλάττιον. Athenæos, v. 42, ἦν δὲ καὶ ὑδροθήκη κατὰ τὴν πρῷραν κλειστή, δισχιλίους μετρητὰς δεχομένη, ἐκ σανίδων καὶ πίττης καὶ ὀθονίων κατεσκευασμένη. As a μετρητής was equivalent to a cubic foot and a half, this cistern would contain 3000 cubic feet of water; and that would weigh about 75 tons. The statement is open to suspicion as it comes from Moschion: see pp. 27—29.

In the fore part of the war-ships everything was constructed with a view to ramming. The catheads were massive, and stood out far enough to tear away the upper works of a hostile ship, while the ram was piercing her below; for which purpose they occasionally were strengthened at the ends by timbers springing from the hull some way behind[141]. And they must also have served in ramming to protect the oars from damage by the enemy. Their position and design may be observed in the Greek war-ships of about 300 B.C. in fgs. 22 and 23. Here the catheads are on a level with the gunwale and the gangway, which both finish at this point, while the waling-pieces run onward to the stem. Right forward the keel and stem-post and the lower pair of waling-pieces converge to hold the ram; and higher up the stem-

---

[141] Thucydides, vii. 34, τῶν δ' Ἀθηναίων κατέδυ μὲν οὐδεμία ἁπλῶς, ἑπτὰ δέ τινες ἄπλοι ἐγένοντο ἀντίπρῳροι ἐμβαλλόμεναι καὶ ἀναρραγεῖσαι τὰς παρεξειρεσίας ὑπὸ τῶν Κορινθίων νεῶν ἐπ' αὐτὸ τοῦτο παχυτέρας τὰς ἐπωτίδας ἐχουσῶν. 36, καὶ τὰς πρῴρας τῶν νεῶν ξυντεμόντες (οἱ Συρακόσιοι) ἐς ἔλασσον στεριφωτέρας ἐποίησαν, καὶ τὰς ἐπωτίδας ἐπέθεσαν ταῖς πρῴραις παχείας, καὶ ἀντηρίδας ἀπ' αὐτῶν ὑπέτειναν πρὸς τοὺς τοίχους ὡς ἐπὶ ἓξ πήχεις ἐντός τε καὶ ἔξωθεν, ᾧπερ τρόπῳ καὶ οἱ Κορίνθιοι πρὸς τὰς ἐν τῇ Ναυπάκτῳ ναῦς ἐπισκευασάμενοι πρῴραθεν ἐναυμάχουν. 40, οἱ δὲ Συρακόσιοι δεξάμενοι καὶ ταῖς τε ναυσὶν ἀντιπρῴροις χρώμενοι, ὥσπερ διενοήθησαν, τῶν ἐμβόλων τῇ παρασκευῇ ἀνερρήγνυσαν τὰς τῶν Ἀθηναίων ναῦς ἐπὶ πολὺ τῆς παρεξειρεσίας, κ.τ.λ. cf. 36, ἀντίπρῳροι γὰρ (ἐνόμισαν) ταῖς ἐμβολαῖς χρώμενοι ἀναρρήξειν τὰ πρῴραθεν αὐτοῖς. In these passages the term παρεξειρεσία denotes the bows; but its meaning is merely that the place was out beyond the oars, and sometimes it denotes the quarters or the stern, as in the passages quoted from Polyænos in note 170 on p. 75 and from Thucydides and Plutarch in note 223 on p. 102. In saying that the bows were made shorter, Thucydides may only mean that the distance between the ram and the catheads was reduced by carrying the catheads further forward. Diodoros says that the bows were also made lower, xiii. 10, but that was merely a matter of ballasting: see note 138 on p. 60. The ἀντηρίδες were clearly a pair of props sloping upwards and forwards from some point in the keel to the extremities of the catheads, and thus passing through the ship's sides a little ahead of the oars of the lower banks. The term ἀντηρίδες is employed by Polybios to denote the props for a gangway, viii. 6. 6. Dion Cassius, xlix. 3, καὶ τοῖς μὲν τό τε ὕψος τῶν σκαφῶν καὶ τὸ πάχος τῶν ἐπωτίδων οἵ τε πύργοι συνῆροντο, τοὺς δ' ἑτέρους οἵ τε διέκπλοι ἀνέφερον, κ.τ.λ. This refers to the action off Mylæ in 36 B.C. between the fleets of Augustus Cæsar and Sextus Pompeius. As a rule, the ἐπωτίδες had a backing of the strongest timber. Theophrastos, historia plantarum, v. 7. 3, τὸ δὲ στερέωμα, πρὸς ᾧ τὸ χέλυσμα καὶ τὰς ἐπωτίδας, μελίας καὶ συκαμίνου καὶ πτελέας· ἰσχυρὰ γὰρ δεῖ ταῦτ' εἶναι. For the use of the ἐπωτίδες as catheads for the anchors, see note 154 on p. 69.

post a smaller ram is fixed upon the junction of the upper
pair of waling-pieces. In ships of more than three banks
there was presumably an extra ram for every extra pair of
waling-pieces; and here some rams are fixed upon false
waling-pieces on a level with the catheads[142]. All these
auxiliary rams would extend the wound inflicted by the
principal ram, and thus cut an enemy open from the gunwale
to the water-line; while they would also protect the stem-post
underneath them from being shattered by contact with her
sides.

The rams usually were made of bronze[143]. On the
Athenian three-banked ships the principal ram did not weigh
more than three talents or thereabouts, that is to say, 170 lbs.;
so the metal could only have formed a sheathing round a

---

[142] Athenæos, v. 37, καὶ ἔμβολα εἶχεν ἑπτά· τούτων ἐν μὲν ἡγούμενον, τὰ δ'
ὑποστέλλοντα· τινὰ δὲ κατὰ τὰς ἐπωτίδας. This refers to the alleged ship of forty
banks. Apparently, the meaning of the last words is that she had some auxiliary
rams on a level with the catheads in addition to the other six. Æschylos applied
the epithet δεκέμβολος to Nestor's ship in the 'Myrmidons', according to the
scholiast on Aristophanes, aves, 1256, οὕτω γέρων ὢν στύομαι τριέμβολον. cf.
Fr. 301, apud Athenæum, i. 52, ἐπεγερεῖ τὸν ἔμβολον. But clearly the meaning
was that a good ship could go on ramming time after time; not that ten rams were
carried, or even three. Corp. Inscr. Attic. vol. ii, no. 795, col. d, ll. 3—7,
Νικηφόρος, Θεοδώρου ἔργον, ἐπισκευῆς δεομένη, προεμβόλιον οὐκ ἔχουσα, cf. col. e,
ll. 28—32, no. 796, col. a, ll. 38—41, col. e, ll. 4—7. These entries refer to ships
of three banks; and indicate that such ships had only one προεμβόλιον, or auxiliary
ἔμβολος.

[143] Æschylos, Persæ, 408, 409, ναῦς ἐν νηὶ χαλκήρη στόλον | ἔπαισεν, 415, 416,
ἐμβολαῖς χαλκοστόμοις | παίοντο. Plutarch, Antonius, 67, πλὴν οὐκ ἐνέβαλεν εἰς
τὴν 'Αντωνίου ναῦν, ἀλλὰ τὴν ἑτέραν τῶν ναυαρχίδων τῷ χαλκώματι πατάξας
περιερρόμβησε, Sulla, 22, ναῦς χαλκήρεις, Pompeius, 28, ναῦς χαλκεμβόλους. cf.
Euripides, Iphigeneia in Aulide, 1319, ναῶν χαλκεμβολάδων, Electra, 436, πρῴραις
κυανεμβόλοισιν. Philippos, in the Anthology, vi. 236, ἔμβολα χαλκογένεια,
φιλόπλοα τεύχεα νηῶν. Petronius, satiræ, 30, embolum navis æneum. Statius,
Thebais, v. 335, ærata dispellens æquora prora. Virgil, Æneid, i. 35, spumas
salis ære ruebant, viii. 675, classes æratas. Cæsar, de bello civili, ii. 3, cum classe
navium sexdecim, in quibus paucæ erant æratæ. Horace, odes, ii. 16. 21, 22,
scandit æratas vitiosa naves | cura, iii. 1. 39, decedit ærata triremi. Iron is
mentioned by Pliny, xxxii. 1, rostra illa, ære ferroque ad ictus armata, and by
Vitruvius, x. 15. 6, is autem aries habuerat de ferro duro rostrum, ita uti naves
longæ solent habere. But see Tibullus, iv. 1. 173, ferro tellus, pontus conscinditur
ære. Corp. Inscr. Attic. vol. ii, no. 789 b, ll. 27, 32, 89, 90, τὸ χάλκωμα τὸ ἄνω.
This was presumably the προεμβόλιον.

core of timber[144]. And thus the ram was often a treacherous weapon in warfare, inasmuch as it was slender enough to be wrenched off the ship in delivering its blow, and started her timbers as it broke away[145]. As a rule, it had three teeth; so that it looked like a trident, when viewed from the side[146]. These teeth are conspicuous in the Greek ship of about 300 B.C. in fg. 23; but in the Greek ship of about 600 B.C. in fg. 13, and also in the Phœnician ship of about 700 B.C. in fg. 10, the ram has only a single tooth: and here the ram curves slightly upward, whereas the trident ram curves down, as though it was intended to heel an enemy over. This downward curve appears again in one of the Greek ships of about 550 B.C. in fgs. 15 and 16, while the curve points upward in the other; so both the forms were then in use concurrently. And apparently the earlier form was developing the curious type depicted in the Athenian ships of

---

144 Corp. Inscr. Attic. vol. ii, no. 809, col. e, ll. 169—172, ἔ[μβολοι] τ[έ]τ[ταρ]ες, σταθμ[ὸν] ΤΤΤ μναῖ Δ[Δ]ΔΓ, τιμὴ ΓΔΔꟾꟾꟾ....cf. no. 811, col. c, l. 87, [ἐμ]βόλους Γ, σταθμὸν....l. 88, ΔΔΔΓ, τιμὴ.... These are entries of delivery and receipt, and ought therefore to correspond. The word τέτταρες has been defaced by the mason; so it was inserted by mistake, the number really being five. There probably were other figures in the gap between σταθμ and ΤΤΤ, perhaps ΔΤ, or even ΔΓ, for the price is a trifle under 525 drachms, and this would represent about fifteen talents of metal for the five rams, as bronze was selling for 35 drachms a talent at that period: see Corp. Inscr. Attic. vol. i, no. 319, ll. 2—4, χαλκὸς ἐωνήθ[η...τάλαντα...]καίδεκα καὶ μναῖ δέκ[α]. τι[μ]ὴ [τοῦ ταλάντου τρι]άκοντα πέντε δραχμαί. These restorations are considerable; but they are justified by what follows. cf. ll. 5—8, καττίτερος ἐωνήθη...τὸ τάλαντον διακοσίων τρ[ιάκ]οντα δραχμῶν τιμή.

145 Herodotos, i. 166, αἱ μὲν γὰρ τεσσεράκοντά σφισι νέες διεφθάρησαν, αἱ δὲ εἴκοσι αἱ περιεοῦσαι ἔσαν ἄχρηστοι· ἀπεστράφατο γὰρ τοὺς ἐμβόλους. Dion Cassius, xlix. 1, πρός τε τὰς ἐμβολὰς τῶν ἐναντίων ἀντέχειν, καὶ τοὺς ἐμβόλους αὐτῶν ἀποστρέφειν. Plutarch, Antonius, 66, ἀπεθραύοντο γὰρ τὰ ἔμβολα ῥαδίως. Polybios, xvi. 5, ταύτης γὰρ (ἦν ἐκυβέρνα Αὐτόλυκος) ἐμβαλούσης εἰς πολεμίαν ναῦν, καὶ καταλιπούσης ἐν τῷ σκάφει τὸν ἔμβολον, συνέβη δή, τὴν μὲν πληγεῖσαν αὔτανδρον καταδῦναι, τοὺς δὲ περὶ τὸν Αὐτόλυκον, εἰσρεούσης εἰς τὴν ναῦν τῆς θαλάσσης διὰ τῆς πρῴρας, κ.τ.λ....τὴν μὲν ναῦν οὐκ ἠδυνήθη σῶσαι, διὰ τὸ πλήρη θαλάττης εἶναι, κ.τ.λ. Aulus Hirtius, de bello Alexandrino, 46, itaque primus (Vatinius) sua quinqueremi in quadriremem ipsius Octavi impetum fecit. celerrime fortissimeque contra illo remigante, naves adversæ rostris concurrerunt adeo vehementer ut navis Octaviana, rostro discusso, ligno contineretur...deprimitur ipsius Octavi quadriremis. cf. Cæsar, de bello civili, ii. 6, præfracto rostro.

about 500 B.C. in fgs. 17 and 19, where the ram assumes the shape of a boar's head. This type was characteristic of Samian ships in the days of Polycrates[147], who ruled there from 532 to 522 B.C.; but it afterwards came into use on ships of other states. And in later times, when the principal ram was usually a trident, the boar's head was retained for a smaller ram above, as in the Leucadian ship of about 150 B.C. in fg. 42. Some of these smaller heads are extant; and one of them is drawn to scale in fg. 43. They probably belonged to Roman ships.

Before the introduction of the ram, animals had been carved upon the prow for figure-heads, as in the Egyptian war-ship of about 1000 B.C. in fg. 6. And generally there was either a figure-head, or else a painting or relief on both the bows; the subject corresponding to the name of the ship, and serving to distinguish her from others[148]. Such paintings

---

146 Virgil, Æneid, v. 142, 143, *infindunt pariter sulcos, totumque dehiscit | convulsum remis rostrisque tridentibus æquor*, cf. viii. 689, 690. Valerius Flaccus, i. 687, 688, *volat immissis cava pinus habenis | infinditque salum, et spumas vomit ære tridenti.*

147 Herodotos, iii. 59, ἔκτῳ δὲ ἔτει Αἰγινῆται αὐτοὺς (Σαμίους) ναυμαχίῃ νικήσαντες ἠνδραποδίσαντο μετὰ Κρητῶν, καὶ τῶν νεῶν καπρίους ἐχουσέων τὰς πρῴρας ἠκρωτηρίασαν καὶ ἀνέθεσαν ἐς τὸ ἱρὸν τῆς Ἀθηναίης ἐν Αἰγίνῃ. Anonymus, apud Hesychium, s. v. Σαμακὸς τρόπος:—ναῦς δέ τις ὠκύπορος Σαμία ὑὸς εἶδος ἔχουσα. Plutarch, Pericles, 26, ἡ δὲ Σάμαινα ναῦς ἐστιν ὑπόπρωρος μὲν τὸ σίμωμα, κοιλοτέρα δὲ καὶ γαστροειδής, ὥστε καὶ φορτοφορεῖν καὶ ταχυναυτεῖν. οὕτω δ' ὠνομάσθη διὰ τὸ πρῶτον ἐν Σάμῳ φανῆναι, Πολυκράτους τυράννου κατασκευάσαντος. cf. Alexis Samios, apud Athenæum, xii. 57, πρῶτος δὲ ὁ Πολυκράτης καὶ ναῦς πήξας ἀπὸ τῆς πατρίδος Σαμίας ἐκάλεσε. For σίμωμα, cf. Thucydides, iv. 25, ἀποσιμωσάντων καὶ προεμβαλόντων, Appian, de bellis civilibus, iv. 71, ἐμβολαὶ καὶ ἀποσιμώσεις, Aristotle, problemata, xxiii. 5, ἀνάσιμα τὰ πλοῖα ποιοῦνται. Thus the stem was styled the nose, just as the bows were styled the cheeks and the hawse-holes the eyes : see note 91 on p. 37 and note 153 on p. 69.

148 Diodoros, iv. 47, διαπλεῦσαι γὰρ αὐτὸν (Φρίξον) φασὶν οἱ μὲν ἐπὶ νεὼς προτομὴν ἐπὶ τῆς πρῴρας ἐχούσης κριοῦ, κ.τ.λ. Apollodoros, Fr. 105, apud Stephanum, s. v. Ταυρέεις:—ταυροφόρος ἦν ἡ ναῦς ἡ διακομίσασα τοὺς τὴν πόλιν κτίσαντας,...ἀπὸ τοῦ ἐπισήμου τῆς νεὼς τὴν πόλιν ὠνόμασαν. A λεοντοφόρος is mentioned in the passage quoted from Memnon in note 35 on p. 14. Plutarch, de mulierum virtutibus, 9, ἔπλει δὲ (Χίμαρρος) πλοίῳ λέοντα μὲν ἔχοντι πρῴραθεν ἐπίσημον, ἐκ δὲ πρύμνης δράκοντα. Strabo, ii. 3. 4, εὑρόντα δ' ἀκρόπρῳρον ξύλινον ἐκ ναυαγίου, ἵππον ἔχον ἐγγεγλυμμένον, δεικνύναι τοῖς ναυκλήροις, γνῶναι δὲ Γαδειριτῶν ὄν· τούτων γὰρ τοὺς μὲν ἐμπόρους μεγάλα στέλλειν πλοῖα, τοὺς δὲ πένητας μικρά, ἃ καλεῖν ἵππους ἀπὸ τῶν ἐν ταῖς πρῴραις ἐπισήμων. Hippocrates, epistolæ, 17, ἐξέπεμψας δέ μοι, φιλότης,

T.   e

or reliefs may be seen upon the Roman ships of about
200 A.D. in fgs. 29 and 31, and a figure-head upon the Roman
ship of about 50 A.D. in fg. 26. The only figure-head now
extant is drawn to scale in fg. 41. This was found off
Actium, and probably dates from the time of the battle. On
ships of that period it was customary to add some carved or
painted figures as supporters; so that if a ship were called
the Ida and had a personification of the mountain on her
prow, she would have a pair of Phrygian lions down below,
as in the Roman war-ship of about 50 A.D. in fg. 25, where
the crocodiles indicate that the ship was called the Nile[149].
All these figures on the stem were intended to distinguish
ship from ship, and had nothing to do with the statues of the

ὡς ἀληθέως Ἀσκληπιάδα νῆα, ᾗ πρόσθες μετὰ τοῦ Ἀλίου ἐπίσημον καὶ Ὑγιείην. But
while animals would be suitable for figure-heads, this group of Helios and Hygieia
suggests a relief or painting on the bows: cf. Lucian, navigium, 5, τὴν ἐπώνυμον
τῆς νεὼς θεὸν ἔχουσα τὴν Ἶσιν ἑκατέρωθεν, sc. ἡ πρῷρα. Strictly a figure-head
would be an ἐπίσημον, while such a painting or relief would be a παράσημον.
Acts, xxviii. 11, ἐν πλοίῳ Ἀλεξανδρινῷ, παρασήμῳ Διοσκούροις. Plutarch, Themistocles, 15, πρῶτος μὲν οὖν λαμβάνει ναῦν Λυκομήδης, ἀνὴρ Ἀθηναῖος, τριηραρχῶν, ἧς
τὰ παράσημα περικόψας ἀνέθηκεν Ἀπόλλωνι δαφνηφόρῳ, the plural indicating that
the παράσημον was repeated on each bow of the ship. Plutarch, septem sapientium
convivium, 18, πυθόμενον τοῦ τε ναυκλήρου τοὔνομα καὶ τοῦ κυβερνήτου καὶ τῆς νεὼς
τὸ παράσημον. cf. Herodotos, viii. 88, σαφέως τὸ ἐπίσημον τῆς νεὸς ἐπισταμένους.
Thus the terms παράσημον and ἐπίσημον were used indifferently to denote the
badges which distinguished one ship from another. But where Diodoros says
τοῖς ἐπὶ ταῖς πρώραις ἐπισήμασι, xiii. 3, Thucydides merely says σημείοις, vi. 31;
and the wider term is approved by Aristophanes, ranæ, 932, Διόνυσος:—τὸν
ξουθὸν ἱππαλεκτρυόνα ζητῶν, τίς ἐστιν ὄρνις. 933, Αἰσχύλος:—σημεῖον ἐν ταῖς
ναυσίν, ὠμαθέστατ', ἐνεγέγραπτο. The term insigne was employed in Latin.
Tacitus, annales, vi. 34, navis insigne fuit, sc. aries. Propertius, iv. 6. 49, vehunt
proræ Centauros saxa minantes. Virgil, Æneid, x. 195—197, ingentem remis
Centaurum promovet: ille | instat aquæ, saxumque undis immane minatur |
arduus, et longa sulcat maria alta carina, cf. 156—158, 209—212. Silius Italicus
enumerates a whole fleet of ships and their badges, xiv. 567 ff:—Europa on the
bull, a Nereid on a dolphin, Pegasus, a Siren, a Triton, sundry deities, mount
Etna personified, and so also Sidon, Libya, etc.

[149] Virgil, Æneid, x. 156—158, Æneia puppis | prima tenet, rostro Phrygios
subiuncta leones : | imminet Ida super, profugis gratissima Teucris. Inscription in
the Bulletin épigraphique de la Gaule, vol. ii, p. 139, Ti(berio) Claudio, Aug(usti)
lib(erto), Eroti, trierarcho liburnæ Nili. This must date from the middle of the
First Century, the deceased being a freedman of Claudius or Nero; so the Roman
fleet contained a two-banked ship called the Nile about the time when the two-
banked ship with the crocodiles was being carved in that relief.

gods by which the ships belonging to one state were distinguished from the ships belonging to another; every Athenian ship carrying a statue of Pallas Athene, every Carthaginian ship a statue of Ammon, and so forth. On the Roman ship of about 200 A.D. in fg. 29 one of these statues may perhaps be seen at the far end of the stern, which was the usual place for them[150]. The stern here is prolonged into a kind of gallery, while its true contour is marked by the swan's neck that rises in a curve within; and in the Roman ship of about 50 A.D. in fg. 26 the structure is the same, the swan or goose being a recognized feature in ships of that period[151]. Very often the goose was gilded; and so also were the statues of the gods.

[150] Euripides, Iphigeneia in Aulide, 239—241, χρυσέαις δ' εἰκόσιν | κατ' ἄκρα Νηρῇδες ἔστασαν θεαὶ | πρύμναις, σῆμ' Ἀχιλλείου στρατοῦ, 246—258, Ἀτθίδος δ' ἄγων | ἑξήκοντα ναῦς ὁ Θησέως | παῖς ἑξῆς ἐναυλόχει, θεὰν | Παλλάδ' ἐν μωνύχοις | ἔχων πτερωτοῖσιν ἅρμασιν θετόν, | εὔσημόν γε φάσμα ναυβάταις. | τῶν Βοιωτῶν δ' ὅπλισμα, ποντίας | πεντήκοντα νῆας εἰδόμαν | σημείοισιν ἐστολισμένας· | τοῖς δὲ Κάδμος ἦν | χρύσεον δράκοντ' ἔχων | ἀμφὶ ναῶν κόρυμβα. 273—276, ἐκ Πύλου δὲ Νέστορος | Γερηνίου κατειδόμαν | πρύμνας σῆμα ταυρόπουν ὁρᾶν | τὸν πάροικον Ἀλφεόν. Aristophanes, Acharnenses, 544—547, καὶ κάρτα μεντᾶν εὐθέως καθείλκετε | τριακοσίας ναῦς, ἦν δ' ἂν ἡ πόλις πλέα | θορύβου στρατιωτῶν, περὶ τριηράρχου βοῆς, | μισθοῦ διδομένου, Παλλαδίων χρυσουμένων, κ.τ.λ. Virgil, Æneid, x. 170, 171, una torvus Abas: huic totum insignibus armis | agmen, et aurato fulgebat Apolline puppis. Silius Italicus, xiv. 408—410, irrumpit Cumana ratis,...numen erat celsæ puppis vicina Dione, 438, 439, Ammon numen erat Libycæ gentile carinæ, | cornigeraque sedens spectabat cœrula fronte. Ovid, tristia, i. 10. 12, Palladio numine tuta fuit; sc. navis, cf. 1, flavæ tutela Minervæ. Valerius Flaccus, viii. 202, 203, puppe procul summa vigilis post terga magistri | hæserat auratæ genibus Medea Minervæ, cf. i. 301, fulgens tutela carinæ. Seneca, epistolæ, 76. 13, tutela (navis) ebore cœlata est. The distinction between the tutela and the insigne is obvious in Ovid, tristia, i. 10. 1, 2, est mihi, sitque precor, flavæ tutela Minervæ | navis, et a picta casside nomen habet. There is presumably an error, πρῴρῃσι for πρύμνῃσι, in the current reading of Herodotos, iii. 37, ἔστι γὰρ τοῦ Ἡφαίστου τώγαλμα τοῖσι Φοινικηίοισι Παταικοῖσι ἐμφερέστατον, τοὺς οἱ Φοίνικες ἐν τῇσι πρῴρῃσι τῶν τριηρέων περιάγουσι. ὃς δὲ τούτους μὴ ὄπωπε, ἐγὼ δέ οἱ σημανέω· πυγμαίου ἀνδρὸς μίμησίς ἐστι.

[151] Lucian, navigium, 5, ἡ πρύμνα μὲν ἐπανέστηκεν ἠρέμα καμπύλη χρυσοῦν χηνίσκον ἐπικειμένη, cf. Jupiter tragœdus, 47, quoted in note 158 on p. 71. Apuleius, metamorphoses, xi. 16, puppis intorta chenisco bracteis aureis vestito fulgebat. Lucian, veræ historiæ, ii. 41, ὅ τε γὰρ ἐν τῇ πρύμνῃ χηνίσκος ἄφνω ἐπτερύξατο καὶ ἀνεβόησε, καὶ ὁ κυβερνήτης φαλακρὸς ἤδη ὢν ἀνεκόμησε, κ.τ.λ. This passage is obviously a skit on the Homeric hymn to Dionysos. The χηνίσκος is mentioned again by Ptolemy, Almagest, viii. 1, Ἀργοῦς ἀστερισμός.

The stern used generally to be surmounted by an ornament, which may originally have been an imitation of the bud
or flower of the lotos, as in the Egyptian ships of about
1250 B.C. in fgs. 3 to 5; but this developed into something
like a plume or fan, that always looks rather massive in reliefs,
as in fg. 24, but light and feathery in paintings, as in fgs. 17
to 19, 35 and 36. This ornament was taken as a trophy,
whenever a ship was captured[152]. Another such ornament
used sometimes to surmount the stem in default of a figure-
head, as in the Greek and Roman war-ships in fgs. 23 and 25.
The type depicted in fg. 23 and previously in fg. 13 can be
traced to its origin in fg. 3, an old Egyptian form of bow surviving in this useless ornament above the ram. And the type

---

[152] Iliad, ix. 241, 242, στεῦται γὰρ νηῶν ἀποκόψειν ἄκρα κόρυμβα, | αὐτάς τ'
ἐμπρήσειν μαλεροῦ πυρός. Apollonios Rhodios, ii. 601, ἔμπης δ' ἀφλάστοιο παρέ-
θρισαν ἄκρα κόρυμβα = Valerius Flaccus, iv. 691, extremis tamen increpuere corymbis.
Here the κόρυμβα must be the aftermost piece of the ship, as the legend was that
the Symplegades did not snap at the Argo till she was all but clear of them; and
they are reckoned as part of the ἄφλαστον, which was certainly at the stern. Iliad,
xv. 716, 717, Ἕκτωρ δὲ πρύμνηθεν ἐπεὶ λάβεν, οὐχὶ μεθίει, | ἄφλαστον μετὰ χερσὶν
ἔχων, cf. Lucan, iii. 586, Graiumque audax aplustre retentat.   Lucretius, iv. 437,
438, at maris ignaris in portu clauda videntur | navigia aplustris fractis obnitier
undæ.   This shews that the aplustre reached down below the water-line, for
Lucretius is speaking of the refraction through the water; so the aplustre or
ἄφλαστον was presumably the after part of the keel, answering to the στεῖρα at the
other end, as to which see note 96 on p. 40.   But in Juvenal, x. 135, 136,
victæque triremis | aplustre, the name aplustre seems to be transferred from the
ἄφλαστον as a whole to the part that formed the trophy, the ἄκρα κόρυμβα.   Many
authors speak of ἀκροστόλια as trophies: Diodoros, xviii. 75, xx. 87; Strabo, iii.
4. 3; Plutarch, Alcibiades, 32; Appian, de bello Mithridatico, 25; Polyænos, iv.
6. 9.   But authors of earlier date, and others who quote from them, prefer the
term ἀκρωτήρια: Herodotos, iii. 59, viii. 121; Xenophon, Hellenica, ii. 3. 8, vi. 2.
36; Polyænos, v. 41; Athenæos, xii. 49.   In the former passage Herodotos refers
to ἀκρωτήρια at the bows—see note 147 on p. 65—but in the latter he describes a
statue holding an ἀκρωτήριον in its hand; and when such figures appear on coins,
the trophy in their hands is always the ornament from the stern. cf. Hymnus in
Dioscuros, 10, 11, ἐπ' ἀκρωτήρια βάντες | πρύμνης.   Again, in the passage quoted
from Athenæos in note 24 on p. 9, Callixenos assigns the ἀκροστόλιον to the bows,
contrasting it with the ἄφλαστον or ἄφλαστα at the stern; while in the Almagest,
viii. 1, Ἀργοῦς ἀστερισμός, Ptolemy places a pair of stars ἐν τῷ ἀκροστολίῳ, and the
constellation shewed only the after part of the ship.   Thus ἀκρωτήριον and
ἀκροστόλιον appear to be general terms for ornaments at either extremity of a ship,
though oftenest applied to the ornament at the stern, as that was the more
conspicuous.   There is no warrant for the notion that the stem-post was called the

depicted in fg. 25 preserves the normal contour of the bow in merchant-ships. On the Roman merchant-ship in fg. 26 there is a gallery round the stem as well as round the stern ; and both these galleries appear again in the ships of later date in fgs. 37 and 40.

On each bow of a ship there generally was a huge eye, as in fgs. 12, 13, 15, 19 and 40; and sometimes more than one, as in fg. 23. These pairs of eyes doubtless owed their origin to the sentiment that a ship is a living thing and must see her way : but in course of time they probably were turned to account as hawse-holes for the anchor-cables[153]. The anchors used to be suspended from the catheads a little way abaft of these hawse-holes[154].

στόλος, and that the ἀκροστόλιον was the top of this ; for in Æschylos, Persæ, 408, 409, εὐθὺς δὲ ναῦς ἐν νηὶ χαλκήρη στόλον | ἔπαισεν, the term στόλος can hardly mean more than structure — cf. 416, ἔθραυον πάντα κωπήρη στόλον — and in Euripides, Iphigeneia in Tauris, 1135, the meaning seems to be just as vague : see note 202 on p. 94. All these terms are avoided by Pausanias, v. 11. 5, καὶ Σαλαμὶς ἔχουσα ἐν τῇ χειρὶ τὸν ἐπὶ ταῖς ναυσὶν ἄκραις ποιούμενον κόσμον, x. 11. 6, ἀνάκειται δὲ καὶ πλοίων τὰ ἄκρα κοσμήματα.

[153] Æschylos, supplices, 716, καὶ πρῷρα πρόσθεν ὄμμασι βλέπουσ᾽ ὁδόν, 743, 744, δορυπαγεῖς δ᾽ ἔχοντες κυανώπιδας | νῆας ἔπλευσαν, cf. Persæ, 559, 560, κυανώπιδες | νᾶες. Philostratos, imagines, i. 18, γλαυκοῖς μὲν (ἡ ναῦς) γέγραπται χρώμασι, βλοσυροῖς δὲ κατὰ πρῷραν ὀφθαλμοῖς οἶον βλέπει. Corp. Inscr. Attic. vol. ii, no. 789, col. a, l. 24, αὕτη σκεῦος ἔχει οὐθέν, οὔθ᾽ οἱ ὀφθαλμοὶ ἔνεισιν, no. 791, l. 68, ὀφθαλμὸς κατέαγεν, cf. ll. 41, 75. These entries shew that the eyes were not mere ornaments painted on the ship, but served some useful purpose : and they could hardly be used for anything but hawse-holes. The epithet κυανῶπις suggests that they were made of bronze, like the ram : cf. Aristophanes, equites, 554, 555, κυανέμβολοι | τριήρεις, ranæ, 1318, πρῴραις κυανεμβόλοις. See note 147 on p. 65 as to the nose of a ship, and note 91 on p. 37 as to the cheeks.

[154] Euripides, Iphigeneia in Tauris, 1350, 1351, οἱ δ᾽ ἐπωτίδων | ἀγκύρας ἐξανῆπτον, cf. Pindar, Pythia, iv. 191, 192, ἐπεὶ δ᾽ ἐμβόλου | κρέμασαν ἀγκύρας ὕπερθεν. There are two slits in the side of each cathead on the ship of about 300 B.C., which is viewed from the front in fg. 22. Each slit is horizontal, and is crossed by a vertical pin in the middle : and abaft of the pin the depth decreases gradually in a slope up to the outer surface of the cathead. On each cathead one of the slits stands a little above and abaft of the other. These slits seem to be intended for a loop of rope to hold the anchor; the two ends of the rope entering the slits from behind and passing out again in front of the pins to form the loop. An elaborate theory has been based upon the supposition that these two slits are the port-holes for the bow oars of an upper and a lower bank, the cathead being merely the front of a long structure serving as an outrigger. There is not any evidence of that.

The genuine anchor with a pair of arms was reckoned among the inventions of Anacharsis[155]; and he was in his prime about 600 B.C. In earlier times the anchors had been made of stone[156]. At first the metal anchors were made of iron; and these were singularly light, an anchor of less than half a hundred-weight being in use in the Athenian navy. But all such anchors had a mass of stone and lead fixed on to them by means of iron clamps, and thus acquired what weight they wanted[157]. Apparently, this ballast was fastened to the anchor near the bottom of the shank, and filled up

[155] Strabo, vii. 3. 9, καὶ τὸν Ἀνάχαρσιν δὲ σοφὸν καλῶν ὁ Ἔφορος τούτου τοῦ γένους (Σκυθῶν) φησὶν εἶναι· νομισθῆναι δὲ καὶ ἑπτὰ σοφῶν ἕνα τελείᾳ σωφροσύνῃ καὶ συνέσει· εὑρήματά τε αὐτοῦ λέγει τά τε ζώπυρα καὶ τὴν ἀμφίβολον ἄγκυραν καὶ τὸν κεραμικὸν τροχόν. Some sort of anchor had already been invented by Midas, according to Pausanias, i. 4. 5, ἄγκυρα δέ, ἣν ὁ Μίδας ἀνεῦρεν, ἦν ἔτι καὶ ἐς ἐμὲ ἐν ἱερῷ Διός. cf. Pliny, vii. 57, ancoram (invenit) Eupalamus; eandem bidentem Anacharsis. Latin writers often termed the arm of the anchor its tooth, and spoke of its bite: Livy, xxxvii. 30, ancora unco dente alligavit, Virgil, Æneid, i. 169, unco non alligat ancora morsu, vi. 3, 4, dente tenaci | ancora fundabat naves. And Greek writers also: Lycophron, 99, 100, καμπύλους σχάσας | πεύκης ὀδόντας, ἕκτορας πλημμυρίδος, Lucian, Lexiphanes, 15, ἕκτορας ἀμφιστόμους. But see Plutarch, de mulierum virtutibus, 8, ἅμα δὲ ὁ Πόλλις κατέμαθε τῇ ἀγκύρᾳ τὸν ὄνυχα μὴ προσόντα· βίᾳ γὰρ ἑλκομένης, ὡς ἔοικεν, ἐν τόποις ὑποπέτροις ἀποσπασθεὶς ἔλαθε. Here the arm is termed the talon: and possibly uncus should be read unguis in Lucan, ii. 694, and Valerius Flaccus, ii. 428. The name ἄγκυρα appears for the first time in Alcæos, Fr. 18, apud Heracleitum, allegoriæ, 5, χόλαισι δ᾽ ἄγκυραι, and then in Theognis, 459, οὐδ᾽ ἄγκυραι ἔχουσιν.

[156] Arrian, periplus, 9, ἐνταῦθα καὶ ἡ ἄγκυρα δείκνυται τῆς Ἀργοῦς. καὶ ἡ μὲν σιδηρᾶ οὐκ ἔδοξέ μοι εἶναι παλαιά. λιθίνης δέ τινος ἄλλης θραύσματα ἐδείκνυτο παλαιά, ὡς ταῦτα μᾶλλον εἰκάσαι ἐκεῖνα εἶναι τὰ λείψανα τῆς ἀγκύρας τῆς Ἀργοῦς. Apollonios Rhodios, i. 955—958, κεῖσε καὶ εὐναίης ὀλίγον λίθον ἐκλύσαντες | Τίφυος ἐννεσίῃσιν ὑπὸ κρήνῃ ἐλίποντο, | κρήνῃ ὑπ᾽ Ἀρτακίῃ· ἕτερον δ᾽ ἕλον, ὅστις ἀρήρει, | βριθύν. These stone anchors are termed εὐναί in the Homeric poems. Iliad, i. 436, ἐκ δ᾽ εὐνὰς ἔβαλον, κατὰ δὲ πρυμνῇσι᾽ ἔδησαν, xiv. 77, ὕψι δ᾽ ἐπ᾽ εὐνάων ὁρμίσσομεν. Odyssey, ix. 137, οὔτ᾽ εὐνὰς βαλέειν οὔτε πρυμνῇσι᾽ ἀνάψαι, cf. xv. 498. The form εὐναῖαι occurs again in Apollonios Rhodios, i. 1277, ii. 1282, iv. 888; but gives place to εὐναί at iv. 1713. See also Oppian, de piscatione, iii. 373, νέρθεν ἀναψάμενοι τρητὸν λίθον εὐναστῆρα. This refers to a plummet for a weel. In the Odyssey, xiii. 77, πεῖσμα δ᾽ ἔλυσαν ἀπὸ τρητοῖο λίθοιο, the stone is clearly a fixture on the shore, with a hole through it for a ship's cable; but according to Herodotos, ii. 96, vessels coming down the Nile used to tow a λίθος τετρημένος astern to steady them against the current. In mooring vessels for floating-bridges the Romans made use of conical baskets filled with stones. Arrian, anabasis, v. 7, καὶ ἐνταῦθα ἤδη καθίεται πλέγματα ἐκ λύγου πυραμοειδῆ πλήρη λίθων λογάδων ἀπὸ πρῴρας ἑκάστης νεώς, τοῦ ἀνέχειν τὴν ναῦν πρὸς τὸν ῥοῦν.

all the space between the arms, as shewn on the coin of about 350 B.C. in fg. 44. At a later date the anchors were made of lead, and perhaps of other metals[158]. The remains of an anchor of this class, lately recovered near Cyrene, are drawn to scale in fgs. 45 to 47. One piece seems to be the stock, and the other two the arms; and these are all of lead, without any alloy[159]. The shank was probably of wood, as that has perished. The three surviving pieces weigh 372 lbs. and 472 and 473 lbs. respectively, or 1317 lbs. altogether; and a wooden shank would increase the weight to more

[157] Corp. Inscr. Attic. vol. ii, no. 807, col. b, ll. 83—88, ἀγκύρας σιδηρ[ᾶς, σ]ταθμὸν μναῖ ΔΔ . . , δεσμὰ σιδηρᾶ δόκιμ[α τὰ] ἐκ τῶν λίθων ἐγλυθέν[τα] σὺν τῷ μολύβδῳ, ἀρι[θμὸς] ΗΗΗΔΔΔΓ. This inscription dates from 329 B.C. Inscription from Delos in the Bulletin de Correspondance Hellénique, vol. vi, p. 47, l. 171, ἄγκυρα σιδηρᾶ, λίθον οὐκ ἔχουσα, cf. l. 168, ἄγκυρα σιδηρᾶ, καὶ λίθος μολυβδοῦς. This inscription dates from 180 B.C. Diodoros, v. 35, ἐπὶ τοσοῦτο δέ (φασι) τοὺς ἐμπόρους διατεῖναι τῆς φιλοκερδίας ὥστε, ἐπειδὰν καταγόμων ὄντων τῶν πλοίων περιττεύῃ πολὺς ἄργυρος, ἐκκόπτειν τὸν ἐν ταῖς ἀγκύραις μόλιβδον καὶ ἐκ τοῦ ἀργύρου τὴν ἐκ τοῦ μολίβδου χρείαν ἀλλάττεσθαι. In the Athenian inscription the first numeral would be Ͱ in place of Δ, if the weight had exceeded 50 mnas; and 50 mnas are rather less than 50 lbs.

[158] Lucian, Jupiter tragœdus, 47, ἀλλ' ὁ μὲν πρότονος, εἰ τύχοι, ἐς τὴν πρύμναν ἀποτέταται, οἱ πόδες δὲ ἐς τὴν πρῶραν ἀμφότεροι· καὶ χρυσαῖ μὲν αἱ ἄγκυραι ἐνίοτε, ὁ χηνίσκος δὲ μολυβδοῦς, καὶ τὰ μὲν ὕφαλα κατάγραφα, τὰ δ' ἔξαλα τῆς νεὼς ἄμορφα. This implies that the anchors used generally to be made of lead at that period, the χηνίσκος being gilt: see note 151 on p. 67. According to the present reading, wooden anchors are mentioned by Moschion, apud Athenæum, v. 43, ἄγκυραι δὲ ἦσαν ξύλιναι μὲν τέτταρες, σιδηραῖ δὲ ὀκτώ. But they are not mentioned by any other ancient author: so the reading is probably corrupt. For ξύλιναι read ὑάλιναι. cf. Lucian, veræ historiæ, i. 42, καὶ γὰρ ἀγκύραις ἐχρῶντο μεγάλαις, ὑαλίναις, καρτεραῖς. Apparently, some metal was known as ὕαλος, for ὑάλινος cannot here refer to glass; and this metal may be intended in the story of the ποτήριον ὑαλοῦν in Dion Cassius, lvii. 21, Petronius, 51, Pliny, xxxvi. 66, and Isidore, origines, xvi. 16. 6. It is obviously the ship, not the anchor, that Lycophron describes as πεύκη in the passage quoted in note 155: cf. Euripides, Phœnissæ, 209, ἐλάτᾳ πλεύσασα, Alcestis, 444, ἐλάτᾳ δικώπῳ.

[159] The components of a sample were lead 98·65 per cent, iron ·55, tin ·12, silver ·011, and gold ·0005. Some oxygen was present also. I am indebted to Mr Roberts Austen of the Royal Mint for making the analysis. To judge by look, the material is just the same in a similar arm recovered near Syme and now in the collection of the Archæological Society at Athens. This arm retains a portion of a bar corresponding to the bar that runs across the opening in the stock in fg. 45; and there are traces of another such bar in both the arms belonging to that stock.

than 1400 lbs., or twelve and a half hundred-weight, which is now the allowance for the best bower on a sailing-ship of 250 tons. But this anchor could never have held so firmly as a modern anchor of equal weight; so its ship was probably of lower tonnage. The ship's name, Zeus Hypatos, is inscribed in relief upon the arms[160]. In the Athenian navy the war-ships carried two anchors apiece[161]: but large merchant-ships carried more, and sometimes had three or four anchors out at once; the anchor that was let go last of all—the sheet-anchor now—passing among sailors as the holy anchor[162]. Cork floats were kept for marking the position of

---

[160] This inscription reads ΣΕΥΕ ΥΠΑΤΟΕ. The words are not repeated; but Ζεύς is on the right arm facing one way, and ὕπατος on the right arm facing the other way. The word ΑϞꓫϟΤꓠꕬ is inscribed upon the arm at Athens. The form of the lettering in these inscriptions dates them near the beginning of the Christian Era.

[161] Corp. Inscr. Attic. vol. ii, no. 807, col. c, ll. 66—102, no. 808, col. d, ll. 119—151, no. 809, col. e, ll. 75—110, no. 811, col. c, ll. 11—32. These are the lists of the entire gear (ἐντελῆ σκεύη) supplied to ships of three and four banks in 330/329 B.C. and following years; and in every case they mention ἀγκύρας σιδηρᾶς δύο, or simply ἀγκύρας δύο: cf. no. 793, col. f, ll. 6—8, ἀγκυρῶν ἀριθ[μὸς] ΔΠΙΙΙ· αὗται γίγ[νονται] ἐπὶ ναῦς ΠΙΙΙΙ ἐ[ντελεῖς. In one instance there are four anchors, no. 803, col. c, ll. 54—72: but this is a list of gear supplied to a ship during the term of a command, and consequently does not show that she had all the four at once.

[162] Plutarch, Solon, 19, τὴν δ' ἄνω βουλὴν ἐκάθισεν, οἰόμενος ἐπὶ δυσὶ βουλαῖς ὥσπερ ἀγκύραις ὁρμοῦσαν ἧττον ἐν σάλῳ τὴν πόλιν ἔσεσθαι, cf. Demosthenes, in Dionysodorum, 44, ἐπὶ δυοῖν ἀγκύραιν ὁρμεῖν. Synesios, epistolæ, p. 164, ἡ μὲν οὖν ναῦς ἐσάλευεν ἐπ' ἀγκύρας μιᾶς, ἡ ἑτέρα γὰρ ἀπημπόλητο, τρίτην δὲ ἄγκυραν Ἀμάραντος οὐκ ἐκτήσατο. Euripides, Phaethon, Fr. 7, apud Stobæum, xliii. 3, ναῦν τοι μί' ἄγκυρ' οὐδαμοῦ σώζειν φιλεῖ, | ὡς τρεῖς ἀφέντι. Acts, xxvii. 29, ἐκ πρύμνης ῥίψαντες ἀγκύρας τέσσαρας. Lucian, fugitivi, 13, ἔδοξε δὴ σκοπουμένοις τὴν ὑστάτην ἄγκυραν, ἣν ἱερὰν οἱ ναυτιλλόμενοί φασι, καθιέναι, cf. Jupiter tragœdus, 51. Plutarch, præcepta gerendæ rei publicæ, 15. 15, μηδὲ (δεῖ) ὥσπερ ἐν πλοίῳ σκεῦος ἱερὸν ἀποκεῖσθαι, τὰς ἐσχάτας περιμένοντα χρείας, 19. 8, ὥσπερ ἄγκυραν ἱερὰν ἀράμενον ἐπὶ τοῖς μεγίστοις, cf. Coriolanus, 32.

[163] Pausanias, viii. 12. 1, Ἀρκάδων δὲ ἐν τοῖς δρυμοῖς εἰσιν αἱ δρῦς διάφοροι, καὶ τὰς μὲν πλατυφύλλους αὐτῶν, τὰς δὲ φηγοὺς καλοῦσιν· αἱ τρίται δὲ ἀραιὸν τὸν φλοιὸν καὶ οὕτω δή τι παρέχοντα κοῦφον ὥστε ἀπ' αὐτοῦ καὶ ἐν θαλάσσῃ ποιοῦνται σημεῖα ἀγκύραις καὶ δικτύοις. cf. Theophrastos, historia plantarum, iii. 16. 3, ὃ δὲ καλοῦσιν οἱ Ἀρκάδες φελλόδρυν. Pliny, xvi. 13, *suberi minima arbor, glans pessima, rara: cortex tantum in fructu, præcrassus ac renascens, atque etiam in denos pedes undique explanatus. usus eius ancoralibus maxime navium piscantiumque tragulis.*

the anchors, when that was necessary[163]; and these did duty as life-buoys, if anybody fell overboard[164]. The cables were sometimes made of chain, but usually of rope: and a thicker rope was needed for large merchant-ships than for the war-ships[165]. Rope-cables of two sizes were in use in the Athenian navy, one described as six-inch and the other as four-inch and a half: but unfortunately there is nothing to shew whether these measurements refer to the circumference or the diameter[166]. Four cables of each sort were carried by each ship, one set to serve the two anchors at the bows, and the other for making the ship fast to the shore by her stern:

[164] Lucian, Toxaris, 20, φελλούς τε γὰρ πολλοὺς ἀφεῖναι αὐτοῖς καὶ τῶν κοντῶν τινας, ὡς ἐπὶ τούτων ἀπονήξαιντο, εἴ τινι αὐτῶν περιτύχοιεν, καὶ τέλος καὶ τὴν ἀποβάθραν αὐτὴν οὐ μικρὰν οὖσαν. 21, τὸ μὲν γὰρ πρῶτον φελλοῖς τισι περιπεσόντας ἀνέχειν ἐπὶ τούτων ἑαυτοὺς καὶ ἀπονήχεσθαι πονήρως, ὕστερον δὲ τὴν ἀποβάθραν ἰδόντας, κ.τ.λ.

[165] Aristophanes, pax, 36, 37, ὥσπερ οἱ τὰ σχοινία | τὰ παχέα συμβάλλοντες εἰς τὰς ὁλκάδας. Arrian, anabasis, ii. 21, ἀλύσεσιν εἰς τὰς ἀγκύρας ἀντὶ σχοινίων χρώμενοι, cf. Herodotos, ix. 74, χαλκέῃ ἁλύσι δεδεμένην ἄγκυραν σιδηρέην. Cæsar, de bello Gallico, iii. 13, ancoræ, pro funibus, ferreis catenis revinctæ.

[166] Corp. Inscr. Attic. vol. ii, no. 807, col. c, ll. 66—102, no. 808, col. d, ll. 119—151, no. 809, col. e, ll. 75—110, no. 811, col. c, ll. 11—32. These are the lists of the entire gear (ἐντελῆ σκεύη) supplied to ships of three and four banks in 330/329 B.C. and following years; and in every case they mention σχοινία, ὀκτωδάκτυλα ||||, ἑξδάκτυλα ||||. These cables were described as ἐπίγυα and ἀγκύρεια a few years earlier. Corp. Inscr. Attic. vol. ii, no. 793, col. e, ll. 22—26, σχοινία· Ἀκροτέρᾳ ἐπίγυα |||, Ἡδίστῃ ἐπίγυα ||, Ναυκράτιδι ἐπίγυα ||||,Ἔνη ἐπίγυα ||, col. h, ll. 19, 20, [ἐπὶ] τὴν Ἡδίστην [σχ]οινία ἀγκύρεια ||||, no. 794, col. b, ll. 33—35, σχοινίων ἀριθ(μὸς) ἐντελῆ ἐπὶ να(ῦς) Ⅎ ΔΔΓ|| καὶ ἐπίγυ(α) ΔΔΔ||| καὶ ἀγκυρείων ἔν. These inscriptions of 357/6 and 356/5 indicate that only two sorts of σχοινία were then in use, and that four of each sort made a complete set: so the change was merely in the names. For the name ἐπίγυα see Polybios, iii. 46, τὴν δ' ἀπὸ τοῦ ρεύματος πλευρὰν ἠσφαλίζοντο τοῖς ἐκ τῆς γῆς ἐπιγύοις, εἰς τὰ περὶ τὸ χεῖλος πεφυκότα τῶν δένδρων ἐνάπτοντες, xxxiii. 7, τἀπόγαια καὶ τὰς ἀγκύρας, Lucian, veræ historiæ, i. 42, ἐξάψαντες αὐτοῦ τὰ ἀπόγεια, καὶ ἐπ' ἀγκυρῶν πλησίον ὁρμισάμενοι, Aristophanes, apud Harpocrationem, s.v. ἐπιβάτης:—εὖ γ' ἐξεκολύμβησ' οὐπιβάτης, ὡς ἐξοίσων ἐπίγειον, and Leonidas of Tarentum, in the Anthology, x. i. 5, ἀγκύρας ἀνέλοιο καὶ ἐκλύσαιο γύαια: also Quintilian, iv. 2. 41, sublatæ sunt ancoræ, solvimus oram, and Livy, xxii. 19, resolutis oris, in ancoras evehuntur, xxviii. 36, orasque et ancoras, ne in moliendo mora esset, præcidunt. These shore-cables seem to be the same as the stern-cables, πρυμνήσια, which were likewise named apart from the anchor-cables; and also the same as the mooring-cables, πείσματα, which were likewise made fast to the shore. Odyssey, xv. 498, ἐκ δ' εὐνὰς ἔβαλον, κατὰ δὲ

and ships everywhere carried some shore-cables at the stern in addition to the anchor-cables at the bows. Ships being thus fitted for cables at each end, anchors could easily be put out astern, if needed there for any manœuvre or to help the ship ride out a gale[167].

The ships used to be steered with a pair of very large oars at the stern, one on either side[168]. In vessels built for rowing either way, and therefore shaped alike at stem and stern, a pair was carried at each end[169]. And occasionally a second

πρυμνῆσι' ἔδησαν, x. 96, πέτρης ἐκ πείσματα δήσας, xiii. 77, πεῖσμα δ' ἔλυσαν ἀπὸ τρητοῖο λίθοιο, xv. 286, τοὶ δὲ πρυμνῆσι' ἔλυσαν, cf. Apollonios Rhodios, i. 912, 913, πρυμνήσια δὲ σφίσιν Ἄργος | λῦσεν ὑπὲκ πέτρης ἁλιμυρέος. Athenæos, xv. 12, λυσαμένους δ' αὐτοὺς τὰ πρυμνήσια καὶ τὰς ἀγκύρας ἀνελομένους. Polyænos, iv. 6. 8, ἄλλοι μὲν ἀνέσπων τὰ πρυμνήσια, ἄλλοι δὲ ἀγκύρας ἀνιμῶντο. Philostratos, vita Apollonii, iii. 56, πεῖσμα ἐκ τῆς νήσου βάλλεσθαι, vi. 12, βάλλεσθαι τινὰ ἄγκυραν ἢ πεῖσμα. The πρυμνήσια and the πείσματα are mentioned together in Odyssey, ix. 136, 137, ἐν δὲ λιμὴν εὔορμος, ἵν' οὐ χρεὼ πείσματός ἐστιν, | οὔτ' εὐνὰς βαλέειν οὔτε πρυμνῆσι' ἀνάψαι. But that is mere tautology; and the passage is translated accordingly by Virgil, Æneid, i. 168, 169, hic fessas non vincula naves | ulla tenent, unco non alligat ancora morsu. Here πείσματα is rendered by vincula, as in Pliny, xxxii. 1, non vincula ulla, non ancoræ: but elsewhere by retinacula. Ovid, metamorphoses, xv. 696, solvunt retinacula puppis, cf. xiv. 547.

167 Polyænos, iii. 9. 63, Ἰφικράτης περὶ Φοινίκην καταπλέων ἑκατὸν τριακοντόροις, ἔνθα τεναγώδης αἰγιαλὸς ἦν, παρήγγειλεν, ὅταν τὸ σημεῖον ἀναδειχθῇ, τοῖς μὲν κυβερνήταις ἄγκυραν ἀφιέναι κατὰ πρύμναν καὶ τὴν καταγωγὴν ἐν τάξει ποιεῖσθαι, τοῖς δὲ στρατιώταις, κ.τ.λ.......ὡς δὲ ἤδη σύμμετρον ὑπέλαβεν εἶναι τὸ τῆς θαλάσσης βάθος, ἀνέτεινε τὸ σημεῖον τῆς ἐκβάσεως. αἱ τριακόντοροι μὲν ἐν τάξει κατήγοντο διὰ τῶν ἀγκυρῶν, οἱ δὲ ἄνδρες, κ.τ.λ. This happened about 375 B.C. Appian, de rebus Punicis, 123, Ῥωμαίοις δὲ ὁ μὲν ἐπίπλους ἦν ῥᾴδιος, καὶ τὸ μάχεσθαι ναυσὶν ἑστώσαις εὐμαρές· αἱ δ' ἀναχωρήσεις δι' ἀναστροφὴν τῶν νεῶν, μακρῶν οὐσῶν, βραδεῖαί τε καὶ δυσχερεῖς ἐπεγίγνοντο· ὅθεν ἀντέπασχον ἐν τῷδε τὰ ὅμοια, ὅτε γὰρ ἐπιστρέφοιντο, ἐπλήσσοντο ὑπὸ τῶν Καρχηδονίων ἐπιπλεόντων. μέχρι νῆες Σιδητῶν πέντε, αἳ φιλίᾳ Σκιπίωνος εἵποντο, τὰς μὲν ἀγκύρας καθῆκαν ἐκ πολλοῦ διαστήματος ἐς τὸ πέλαγος, ἁψάμεναι δ' ἀπ' αὐτῶν κάλους μακρούς, εἰρεσίᾳ τοῖς Καρχηδονίοις ἐπέπλεον, καὶ ὅτε ἐγχρίμψειαν, ὑπεχώρουν, τοὺς κάλους ἐπισπώμεναι κατὰ πρύμναν· αὖθίς τε ῥοθίῳ καταπλέουσαι, πάλιν ἀνήγοντο κατὰ πρύμναν. This happened in 147 B.C. Appian, de bellis civilibus, v. 89, τὰς ναῦς ἑκατέρωθεν ἀγκύραις ἔκ τε τοῦ πελάγους καὶ ἀπὸ τῆς γῆς διεκράτουν. This was in a gale in 38 B.C. Acts, xxvii. 29, ἐκ πρύμνης ῥίψαντες ἀγκύρας τέσσαρας. This was also in a gale. An anchor is represented at the stern of one of the ships on Trajan's Column, where the fleet appears to be going down a river.

168 Corp. Inscr. Attic. vol. ii, no. 793, col. a, ll. 23—27, [π]ηδαλίων ἀριθμὸς ΗΗΗΗⳆ𐅄ΔΓΙΙΙΙ · ταῦτα γίγνεται ἐπὶ ναῦς ΗΗΔΔΔΙΙΙΙ καὶ ἐν πηδάλιον. cf. Heliodoros, Æthiopica, v. 22, τῶν πηδαλίων θάτερον ἀποβαλόντες, Apuleius,

pair was carried near the stern in vessels of ordinary build ; so that if the ship was pitching heavily enough for the usual steering-oars to come out of the water at every plunge, the steering could be managed with another pair placed a little further forward[170]. The steering-oars were fastened to the sides of a ship just below the gunwale, either by passing the loom of the oar through some sort of loop or ring, or else by tying it between a pair of pegs[171]: and these fastenings may be noticed on the ships in fgs. 3 to 5, 17, 18 and 40. The

metamorphoses, ii. 14, *utroque regimine amisso.* Herodotos, ii. 96, πηδάλιον δὲ ἐν ποιεῦνται, καὶ τοῦτο διὰ τῆς τρόπιος διαβύνεται. Herodotos is speaking of vessels on the Nile ; and his emphasis shews how unusual it was for a vessel to have only a single steering-oar. In these Egyptian vessels the steering-oar must have passed through the after end of the keel, where it curved upwards in place of a stern-post : see p. 39 and notes 95, 96.

[169] Athenæos, v. 37, πηδάλια δ' εἶχε τέτταρα,....δίπρῳρος δ' ἐγεγόνει καὶ δίπρυμνος. Dion Cassius, lxxiv. 11, καί τινα αὐτῶν ἑκατέρωθεν καὶ ἐκ τῆς πρύμνης καὶ ἐκ τῆς πρῴρας πηδαλίοις ἤσκετο. Tacitus, annales, ii. 6, *appositis utrimque gubernaculis, converso ut repente remigio hinc vel illinc appellerent.*

[170] Polyænos, iii. 11. 14, Χαβρίας πρὸς τοὺς πελαγίους πλοῦς καὶ τοὺς ἐν τῇ θαλάττῃ χειμῶνας κατεσκεύαζεν ἑκάστῃ τῶν νηῶν δισσὰ πηδάλια. καὶ τοῖς μὲν ὑπάρχουσιν ἐν ταῖς εὐδίαις ἐχρῆτο· εἰ δὲ ἡ θάλασσα κοίλη γένοιτο, θάτερα διὰ τῆς παρεξειρεσίας κατὰ τὰς θρανίτιδας κώπας παρετίθει, τοὺς αὐχένας ἔχοντα καὶ τοὺς οἴακας ὑπὲρ τοῦ καταστρώματος, ὥστε ἐξαιρομένης τῆς πρύμνης τούτοις τὴν ναῦν κατευθύνεσθαι. Here αὐχήν must mean the loom of the oar, the handle being known as οἴαξ : but it afterwards came to mean the oar itself. Leo, tactica, xix. 8, καὶ τοὺς δύο κυβερνήτας τῶν τοῦ δρόμωνος αὐχένων. See note 172 as to the meanings of οἴαξ. The παρεξειρεσία is here the space between the rowers and the stern, as also in Polyænos, iii. 11. 13, Χαβρίας πρὸς τὰς ἐπιβολὰς τῶν κυμάτων ὑπὲρ τὴν παρεξειρεσίαν ἑκατέρου τοίχου δέρρεις παρέβαλεν, καὶ κατηλώσας ἀρτίως τῷ καταστρώματι κατὰ τὸ ὕψος φράγμα κατελάμβανεν αὐτὸ πρὸς τὰς παρεξειρεσίας. τοῦτο δὲ ἐκώλυε τὴν ναῦν ὑποβρύχιον φέρεσθαι καὶ τοὺς ναύτας ὑπὸ τῶν κυμάτων βρέχεσθαι· καὶ τὰ ἐπιφερόμενα κύματα οὐχ ὁρῶντες διὰ τὴν τοῦ φράγματος πρόσθεσιν οὐκ ἐξανίσταντο διὰ τὸν φόβον οὐδὲ τὴν ναῦν ἔσφαλλον. See note 141 on p. 62 for another meaning of παρεξειρεσία.

[171] Euripides, Helena, 1536, πηδάλιά τε ζεύγλαισι παρακαθίετο. Acts, xxvii. 40, ἀνέντες τὰς ζευκτηρίας τῶν πηδαλίων. cf. Aristotle, mechanica, 6, ᾗ μὲν δὴ τὸ πηδάλιον προσέζευκται, δεῖ οἷόν τι τοῦ κινουμένου μέσον νοεῖν, καὶ ὥσπερ ὁ σκαλμὸς τῇ κώπῃ. The term ζύγωσις is used by Callixenos in speaking of oars for rowing, when he may really be referring to the steering-oars : see p. 10 and note 25. Orpheus, Argonautica, 278, 279, ἔπι δ' αὖτ' οἴηκας ἔδησαν, | πρυμνόθεν ἀρτήσαντες, ἐπεσφίγξαντο δ' ἱμᾶσιν. The term οἴαξ must here denote the entire steering-oar : see next note. Vegetius, iv. 46, *per has (bipennes) in medio ardore pugnandi peritissimi nautæ vel milites cum minoribus scaphulis secreto incidunt funes, quibus adversariorum ligata sunt gubernacula.*

steering-oars could thus be worked like oars for rowing ; and
while the rowers drove the ship ahead and astern by pulling
their oars forward or pushing them aft, the steerer drove her
to port and starboard by pulling his oar inboard or pushing it
outboard, if he steered with one, and moving the other in the
same direction, if he steered with two[172]. But this method was
impracticable when the steering-oars were big and heavy ;
and they used then to be worked by turning them round a
little way. So long as the blades were parallel to the ship's
keel, the ship went straight ahead : but if the oars were

[172] Aristotle, mechanica, 6, διὰ τί τὸ πηδάλιον, μικρὸν ὂν καὶ ἐπ' ἐσχάτῳ
τῷ πλοίῳ, τοσαύτην δύναμιν ἔχει ὥσθ' ὑπὸ μικροῦ οἴακος καὶ ἑνὸς ἀνθρώπου δυνάμεως,
καὶ ταύτης ἠρεμαίας, μεγάλα κινεῖσθαι μεγέθη πλοίων ; ἢ διότι καὶ τὸ πηδάλιόν ἐστι
μοχλός, καὶ μοχλεύει ὁ κυβερνήτης ; ἢ μὲν οὖν προσήρμοσται τῷ πλοίῳ, γίνεται
ὑπομόχλιον, τὸ δ' ὅλον πηδάλιον ὁ μοχλός, τὸ δὲ βάρος ἡ θάλασσα, ὁ δὲ κυβερνήτης
ὁ κινῶν......ἡ μὲν οὖν κώπη κατὰ πλάτος τὸ βάρος ὠθοῦσα καὶ ὑπ' ἐκείνου ἀντωθουμένη
εἰς τὸ εὐθὺ προάγει· τὸ δὲ πηδάλιον, ὥσπερ κάθηται πλάγιον, τὴν εἰς τὸ πλάγιον
ἢ δεῦρο ἢ ἐκεῖ ποιεῖ κίνησιν......ἧ μὲν δὴ τὸ πηδάλιον προσέζευκται, δεῖ οἷόν τι τοῦ
κινουμένου μέσον νοεῖν, καὶ ὥσπερ ὁ σκαλμὸς τῇ κώπῃ· τὸ δὲ μέσον ὑποχωρεῖ ἧ ὁ οἴαξ
μετακινεῖται. ἐὰν μὲν εἴσω ἄγῃ, καὶ ἡ πρύμνα δεῦρο μεθέστηκεν, ἡ δὲ πρῷρα εἰς
τοὐναντίον νεύει. cf. Plato, Alcibiades, p. 117 C, τί δ' εἰ ἐν νηὶ πλέοις, ἆρα δοξάζοις
ἄν, πότερον χρὴ τὸν οἴακα εἴσω ἄγειν ἢ ἔξω ; Aristotle is followed by Vitruvius, x.
3. 5, quemadmodum etiam navis onerariæ maximæ gubernator, ansam gubernaculi
tenens, qui oïax a Græcis appellatur, una manu, momento per centri librationem
pressionibus artis agitans, versat eam amplissimis et immanibus mercis et penus
ponderibus oneratam, reading librationem for rationem—cf. 4, per scapi librationem
—and assuming that artis comes from artus. The term οἴαξ is here applied to the
handle of the steering-oar ; and so also in Polyænos, iii. 11. 14—see note 170—
and in Plutarch, Lysander, 12, ἦσαν δέ τινες οἱ τοὺς Διοσκόρους ἐπὶ τῆς Λυσάνδρου
νεὼς ἑκατέρωθεν ἄστρα τοῖς οἴαξιν ἐπιλάμψαι λέγοντες. But it used also to be
applied to the entire steering-oar, as in Orpheus, Argonautica, 278—see last note
—and in Euripides, Iphigeneia in Tauris, 1356, 1357, καὶ διευθυντηρίας | οἴακας
ἐξῃροῦμεν εὐπρύμνου νεώς. This can only mean that they took away the steering-
oars, which was then the ordinary way of disabling a ship : cf. Herodotos, iii. 136 ;
Athenæos, viii. 61 ; Xenophon, anabasis, v. 1. 11. The cognate term οἰήιον
denotes the entire steering-oar in Odyssey, ix. 539, 540, κὰδ δ' ἔβαλεν μετόπισθε
νεὸς κυανοπρῴροιο | τυτθόν, ἐδεύησεν δ' οἰήιον ἄκρον ἱκέσθαι. This term occurs again
in Odyssey, xii. 218, ἐπεὶ νηὸς γλαφυρῆς οἰήια νωμᾷς, and in Iliad, xix. 43, καὶ ἔχον
οἰήια νηῶν, but without anything to shew whether it denotes the whole of the oar
or only the handle. Apparently οἴαξ was synonymous with πλῆκτρον. Herodotos,
i. 194, ἰθύνεται δὲ ὑπό τε δύο πλήκτρων καὶ δύο ἀνδρῶν ὀρθῶν ἐστεώτων, καὶ ὁ μὲν
ἔσω ἕλκει τὸ πλῆκτρον, ὁ δὲ ἔξω ὠθέει. Sophocles, Fr. 151, apud Pollucem, x. 133,
πλήκτροις ἀπευθύνουσιν οὐρίαν τρόπιν. Silius Italicus, xiv. 401, 402, residentis
puppe magistri | affixit plectro dextram, sc. telum.

turned to bring the fore part of each blade to starboard and the after part to port, the action of the water on the oars was enough to thrust the ship's stern to starboard and thus send her head to port; and, conversely, if the oars were turned to bring the fore part of each blade to port and the after part to starboard, the ship's head went to starboard. There was probably a tiller in the loom or handle of each steering-oar and a piece of gear to join these tillers; so that the steerer could turn both oars at once[173]. In the Egyptian ships of early date, as in fgs. 3 to 5, the steering-oars appear to be

[173] Plutarch, de fortuna Romanorum, 4, οὐ μὲν γὰρ ἀπειθής, κατὰ Πίνδαρον, οὐδὲ δίδυμον στρέφουσα πηδάλιον, sc. ἡ Τύχη. Lucian, navigium, 6, κἀκεῖνα πάντα μικρός τις ἀνθρωπίσκος γέρων ἤδη ἔσω ζεν ὑπὸ λεπτῇ κάμακι τὰ τηλικαῦτα πηδάλια περιστρέφων. The equivalent of κάμαξ was adminiculum. Pliny, vii. 57, adminicula gubernandi (addidit) Tiphys. In the passage just quoted from Lucian the term κάμαξ is used in the singular with πηδάλια in the plural, and so also is οἴαξ in Plato, politicus, p. 272 E, πηδαλίων οἴακος ἀφέμενος, sc. ὁ κυβερνήτης, and likewise clavus with gubernacula in Cicero, pro Sestio, 9, clavum tanti imperii tenere et gubernacula rei publicæ tractare. These passages imply that the two steering-oars were controlled by a single piece of gear, and that this used sometimes to be termed οἴαξ and clavus as well as κάμαξ and adminiculum; and various other passages imply that ships were steered by turning the clavus or οἴαξ. Quintilian, ii. 17. 24, dum clavum rectum teneam. Virgil, Æneid, v. 177, clavumque ad litora torquet. Euripides, Helena, 1590, 1591, πάλιν πλέωμεν, ναυβάταν. κέλευε σύ· | σὺ δὲ στρέφ' οἴακα. Æschylos, septem adversus Thebas, 62, ὥστε ναὸς κεδνὸς οἰακοστρόφος. Pindar, Isthmia, iii. 89, κυβερνατῆρος οἰακοστρόφου. The expression χαλινὰ οἰήκων is merely a pleonasm of Oppian, de piscatione, i. 189—192, ἕσπονται πομπῆες ὁμόστολοι, ἄλλοθεν ἄλλος, | ἀμφιπερισκαίροντες εὔζυγον ἄρμα θαλάσσης, | τοίχους τ' ἀμφοτέρους, περί τε πρυμναῖα χαλινὰ | οἰήκων· ἄλλοι δὲ περὶ πρῴρην ἀγέρονται. For the converse metaphor, see Oppian, de venatione, i. 96, ἵππων κυβερνητῆρα χαλινόν, and Æschylos, septem adversus Thebas, 206, ἱππικῶν πηδαλίων. A similar pleonasm is introduced by Statius, Thebais, x. 182—185, non secus, amisso medium cum præside puppis | fregit iter, subit ad vidui moderamina clavi | aut laterum custos, aut quem penes obvia ponto | prora fuit. The term moderamen was used by itself, like regimen, to denote a steering-oar. Ovid, metamorphoses, iii. 644, capiatque alius moderamina, dixi, xv. 726, innixus moderamine navis, iii. 593, 594, addidici regimen, dextra moderante, carinæ | flectere, xi. 552, frangitur et regimen; Apuleius, metamorphoses, ii. 14, utroque regimine amisso. The πτέρυξ was presumably the blade of the steering-oar. Corp. Inscr. Attic. vol. ii, no. 790, col. b, ll. 44—46, ἔχει πη[δ]άλια δύο, τοῦ ἑ[τέρου] ἡ πτέρυξ ἀδόκιμος [π]α[ράκει]ται. Apollonios Rhodios, iv. 931, ἡ δ' ὄπιθεν πτέρυγος θίγε πηδαλίοιο. Apollonios is narrating how a goddess rose from the deep and laid her hand upon the steering-oar; so the πτέρυξ was necessarily at the lower end.

attached to a pair of posts upon the deck besides the rings underneath, as though their function was simply to turn upon their axis : and in the Roman ships of about 200 A.D., as in fg. 29, the motion of the steering-oars seems to be restricted to the same extent by ropes fastened through the blades. In these Roman ships both the oars were sheltered from the impact of the waves by a prolongation of the upper waling-pieces, or something of the sort, as may be seen in fgs. 26, 28, 29, 36 and 38. Curiously, the steering-gear was used to keep the ship on either tack, when the wind was light, the yard being left amidship ; though in a stronger wind the yard was properly braced round and the square-sail trimmed accordingly[174].

In every age and every district of the ancient world the method of rigging ships was substantially the same : and this method is first depicted by the Egyptians. Their ships on the Red Sea about 1250 B.C., as in fgs. 4 and 5, had one mast with two yards, and carried one large square-sail. The mast was secured to a prop at its foot to keep it steady, and was held by two fore-stays and one back-stay ; the two halyards of the upper yard being carried down to the quarters, so that the strain on these relieved the back-stay and partially obviated the need for shrouds. It is strange that the mast had no shrouds at all : but a curious double mast, like a pair of sheer-legs, had formerly been carried by vessels on the Nile, as in fg. 1, which mast was always set athwartship, so that no shrouds were needed on these vessels ; and possibly mere force of habit kept the Egyptians from fitting shrouds to the single mast of later times. Each yard was formed of two spars lashed together, so as to avoid the waste of timber in tapering the thicker end of a single spar to balance with the thinner end : and this device was adopted by the Greeks and Romans, as may be seen from the Athenian ships of about 500 B.C. in fg. 19 and the Pompeian ship of about 50 A.D. in fg. 26, and was thus transmitted to the modern world[175]. The yards were each worked by two braces ; and there were numerous lifts to support the lower-yard at all

---

[174] Aristotle, mechanica, 8, quoted in note 206 on p. 96.

times and the upper-yard when lowered. The other ropes were brails for taking in the sail. In the great relief representing the battle in the Mediterranean about 1000 B.C. the rigging is indicated very roughly both in the victorious Egyptian ships, as in fg. 6, and in the defeated Asiatic ships, as in fgs. 7 and 8 : but two things at least are clear. The lower-yard had been discarded ; so that the lower corners of the sail must now have been controlled by sheets. And the sail was no longer taken in by brails stretching down obliquely from the centre of the upper-yard, but by brailing-ropes stretching vertically down from several points along the yard. A figure of a square-sail on a mast with two yards forms the hieroglyph *nef*, and forms part of the hieroglyph *chont*, which represents a boat: so the unnecessary lower-yard had been in use from very early times. But now it was discarded finally. In the vase-paintings of about 600 B.C. in fgs. 12 and 13, which come from Etruria and Attica respectively, the ships certainly look as though they had this yard. But in the former the painter has simply reproduced the hieroglyph *chont*; as was perhaps to be expected, for the vase was made by some Greek settler in the Delta of the Nile, and thence exported to Etruria. And in the latter the absurdly straight sides to the sail shew that its straight base is solely due to the painter's methods.

The Phœnician ships of about 700 B.C., as in fg. 10, had one mast with one yard, and carried a square-sail. They are sometimes represented with two fore-stays and a back-stay, sometimes with two back-stays and a fore-stay; and always with four other ropes, which seem to be sheets and braces : but no further details can be traced. These ships, then, were rigged like the ships that fought in the Mediterranean three centuries before: so this scheme of rigging had probably been long in use among the Phœnicians; and thus came to be adopted by the Greeks, when they began seafaring.

[175] This explains why the Greeks and Romans usually spoke of the yard in the plural as κεραῖαι or *antennæ*. The Greeks should strictly have used the dual : but the plural does not imply that there were more than two spars. Corp. Inscr. Attic. vol. ii, no. 802, col. a, ll. 4, 5, κεραῖαι μεγάλαι· ἡ ἑτέρα ἀδόκιμος.

The Homeric poems shew clearly enough how the earliest
Greeks rigged their ships. There was the *histos* or mast,
supported at its foot by a prop termed *histopede*, and held by
two *protonoi* or fore-stays and an *epitonos* or back-stay.
When the mast was not in use, it lay aft in a rest termed
histodoke; being raised thence and lowered thither again by
means of the fore-stays[176]. Upon the mast was the *epikrion* or
yard; and upon this was the sail. The sail is styled indifferently *speiron* and *histion* and *histia*; the plural perhaps
denoting that it was formed of many pieces, as in the
Athenian ship of about 600 B.C. in fg. 13: and its whiteness
is emphasized. Ropes termed *hyperai* and *kaloi* and *podes*
are mentioned, but without any indication of their nature:
and the presence of halyards and brailing-ropes is implied[177].
The *hyperai* and *podes*, that is to say, the upper ropes and the

---

[176] Odyssey, xii. 178, 179, οἱ δ' ἐν νηί μ' ἔδησαν ὁμοῦ χεῖράς τε πόδας τε | ὀρθὸν ἐν
ἱστοπέδῃ, ἐκ δ' αὐτοῦ πείρατ' ἀνῆπτον, where αὐτοῦ must refer to ἱστοῦ. cf. Alcæos,
Fr. 18, apud Heracleitum, allegoriæ, 5, περ μὲν γὰρ ἄντλος ἱστοπέδαν ἔχει. Odyssey,
xii. 409—412, ἱστοῦ δὲ προτόνους ἔρρηξ' ἀνέμοιο θύελλα | ἀμφοτέρους· ἱστὸς δ' ὀπίσω
πέσεν, ὅπλα τε πάντα | εἰς ἄντλον κατέχυνθ'· ὁ δ' ἄρα πρύμνῃ ἐνὶ νηί | πλῆξε κυβερ-
νήτεω κεφαλήν. These verses are imitated by Apollonios Rhodios, i. 1203, 1204,
ὑψόθεν ἐμπλήξασα θοὴ ἀνέμοιο κατάιξ | αὐτοῖσι σφήνεσσιν ὑπὲκ προτόνων ἐρύσηται.
The σφῆνες are probably the παραστάται which replaced the ἱστοπέδη: see note
181. Odyssey, xii. 422, 423, ἐκ δέ οἱ ἱστὸν ἄραξε ποτὶ τρόπιν· αὐτὰρ ἐπ' αὐτῷ | ἐπί-
τονος βέβλητο, βοὸς ῥινοῖο τετευχώς. There is no direct proof that ἐπίτονος means
back-stay; but as πρότονος means fore-stay, there is not much room for doubt. Iliad,
i. 434, ἱστὸν δ' ἱστοδόκῃ πέλασαν, προτόνοισιν ὑφέντες. Odyssey, ii. 424, 425, ἱστὸν δ'
εἰλάτινον κοίλης ἔντοσθε μεσόδμης | στῆσαν ἀείραντες, κατὰ δὲ προτόνοισιν ἔδησαν.
These verses are imitated by Apollonios Rhodios, i. 563, 564, δή ῥα τότε μέγαν
ἱστὸν ἐνεστήσαντο μεσόδμῃ, | δῆσαν δὲ προτόνοισι τανυσσάμενοι ἑκάτερθεν. In his
opinion, then, the fore-stays were made fast on either side of the bow, not right
forward. See also Lucian, amores, 6, τὸν ἱστὸν ἐκ τῶν μεσοκοίλων ἄραντες, where
μεσοκοίλων seems intended to convey the sense of κοίλης μεσόδμης, and clearly is
equivalent to κοίλης ἱστοδόκης in Apollonios Rhodios, ii. 1262—1264, αὐτίκα δ' ἱστία
μὲν καὶ ἐπίκριον ἔνδοθι κοίλης | ἱστοδόκης στείλαντες ἐκόσμεον· ἐν δὲ καὶ αὐτὸν | ἱστὸν
ἄφαρ χαλάσαντο παρακλιδόν. Apparently ἔντοσθε means *from within* and goes
with ἀείραντες in the Odyssey, though Apollonios thinks it means *within* and goes
with στῆσαν: so the μεσόδμη was probably the ἱστοδόκη under another name, or else
the hold containing the ἱστοδόκη. Thus the μεσόδμαι are contrasted with the decks
at stem and stern by Lycophron, 751, 752, αὐταῖς μεσόδμαις καὶ σὺν ἰκρίοις βαλεῖ |
πρὸς κῦμα δύπτην. The ἱστοδόκη is mentioned by Ptolemy, Almagest, viii. 1,
'Αργοῦς ἀστερισμός: but the measurements are too corrupt for fixing its position
accurately, though they indicate a place towards the stern.

foot ropes, are presumably braces and sheets; while the
kaloi are certainly the brailing-ropes, for Herodotos employs
this name for them in noting the perversity of the Egyptians
in putting the brailing-rings on the after side of the sail[177].
The Greek ships represented in vase-paintings invariably
have one mast with one yard, and carry a square-sail; and
probably they are all intended to have the same sorts of
ropes, though these are always sketched carelessly. The
Athenian ships of about 500 B.C. in fgs. 17 to 19 have
numerous brailing-ropes; and in the merchant-ship, which
presumably was rigged on a larger scale than the war-ships,
each brailing-rope makes several loops round the sail. In
these ships, and also in the earlier Athenian ship in fg. 13,
the halyards are carried down to the waist, and thus take
the place of shrouds in supporting the mast.

177 Odyssey, v. 254, ἐν δ' ἱστὸν ποίει καὶ ἐπίκριον ἄρμενον αὐτῷ, 260, ἐν δ' ὑπέρας
τε κάλους τε πόδας τ' ἐνέδησεν ἐν αὐτῇ. 316—318, μέσον δέ οἱ ἱστὸν ἔαξε | δεινὴ
μισγομένων ἀνέμων ἐλθοῦσα θύελλα, | τηλοῦ δὲ σπεῖρον καὶ ἐπίκριον ἔμπεσε πόντῳ.
Iliad, i. 480, 481, οἱ δ' ἱστὸν στήσαντ', ἀνά θ' ἱστία λευκὰ πέτασσαν· | ἐν δ' ἄνεμος
πρῆσεν μέσον ἱστίον. Odyssey, ii. 426, 427, ἕλκον δ' ἱστία λευκὰ ἐυστρέπτοισι
βοεῦσιν· | ἔμπρησεν δ' ἄνεμος μέσον ἱστίον. iii. 10, 11, οἱ δ' ἰθὺς κατάγοντο, ἱδ' ἱστία
νηὸς ἐίσης | στεῖλαν ἀείραντες, τὴν δ' ὥρμισαν, ἐκ δ' ἔβαν αὐτοί. xii. 170, 171,
ἀνστάντες δ' ἕταροι νεὸς ἱστία μηρύσαντο, | καὶ τὰ μὲν ἐν νηὶ γλαφυρῇ θέσαν, οἱ δ' ἐπ'
ἐρετμά, κ.τ.λ. These last verses shew that there were halyards for hoisting sail;
and also brailing-ropes of some sort, as the crew took in the sail by pulling it up,
στεῖλαν ἀείραντες, μηρύσαντο. For the latter term, see Sophocles, Fr. 699, apud
Athenæum, iii. 55, ναῦται δὲ μηρύσαντο νηὸς ἰσχάδα, and Oppian, de venatione,
i. 50, ἰχθὺν ἀσπαίροντα βυθῶν ἀπομηρύσασθαι. The meaning was apparently to
coil up cords or cables, and so haul up things attached to them.
178 Herodotos, ii. 36, τῶν ἱστίων τοὺς κρίκους καὶ κάλους οἱ μὲν ἄλλοι ἔξωθεν
προσδέουσι, Αἰγύπτιοι δὲ ἔσωθεν. The brailing-ropes, and the rings to keep them
in their place, may be seen upon the fore side of the sail on the Roman ship in
fg. 29: and these clearly are the ropes and rings intended by Herodotos. Moreover, the word κάλος or κάλως occurs in various phrases where it can hardly refer
to any ropes but these. Plato, Protagoras, p. 338, μήτ' αὖ Πρωταγόραν (συμβου-
λεύω) πάντα κάλων ἐκτείναντα, οὐρίᾳ ἐφέντα, φεύγειν εἰς τὸ πέλαγος τῶν λόγων, cf.
Sisyphos, p. 389, τὸ λεγόμενόν γε, πάντα κάλον ἐφέντες. Aristophanes, equites, 756,
νῦν δή σε πάντα δεῖ κάλων ἐξιέναι σεαυτοῦ. Euripides, Medea, 278, ἐχθροὶ γὰρ
ἐξιᾶσι πάντα δὴ κάλων, Troades, 94, ὅταν στράτευμ' Ἀργεῖον ἐξίῃ κάλως. To let out
the brailing-ropes was to let out the sail; and to let these ropes out altogether was
to let the sail out to the full, and hence by metaphor, to make every effort.
Oppian, de piscatione, ii. 223, γαστρὶ δὲ πάντας ἐπιτρωπῶσι κάλωας, where he
alludes to gluttons; while now-a-days a sail is said to belly.

T.   f

The inventories of the Athenian dockyards shew that in 330 B.C. the rigging for the war-ships of three and four banks consisted of the *histos* or mast, the *keraiai* or yard, the *histion* or sail, and the *topeia* or ropes ; and that in four-banked ships the *topeia* consisted of eighteen loops of *kalodia*, two *himantes*, a double *agkoina*, two *podes*, two *hyperai*, and a *chalinos*[179]. The distinction between these six sorts of ropes is not indicated by the inscriptions ; nor can it safely be inferred from the language of ancient authors, since technical terms were often used very loosely : the term *topeia*, for example, which here denotes the ropes collectively, being popularly employed to denote the halyards alone. But probably there were

[179] Corp. Inscr. Attic. vol. ii, no. 807, col. c, ll. 66—102, no. 808, col. d, ll. 119—151, no. 809, col. e, ll. 75—110, no. 811, col. c, ll. 11—32. These are the lists of the entire gear (ἐντελῆ σκεύη) supplied to ships of three and four banks in 330/329 B.C. and following years; and the only items of rigging included therein are ἱστός, κεραῖαι, ἱστίον, τοπεῖα. In no. 809 the word τοπεῖα is missing: but line 106 of col. e may be restored as κατάβλημ[α, τοπεῖ]α to match line 30 of col. c in no. 811. The suggested restoration καταβλήμ[ατ]α seems too short. For τοπεῖα see no. 807, col. a, ll. 141—146, 153, 159—163, 178—183, no. 808, col. b, ll. 189—193, no. 809, col. b, ll. 222—227, τοπεῖα τετρήρων, or τοπεῖα ἐπὶ τετρήρεις, ἑκάστης καλῳδίων μηρύματα Δ𝚪|||, ἱμάντες ||, ἄγκοινα διπλῆ, πόδες ||, ὑπέραι ||, χαλινὸς |. See also no. 807, col. a, ll. 62—64, 73—75, no. 808, col. b, ll. 110, 111, 115—118, no. 809, col. b, ll. 145—147, 150—152, τοπεῖα ἐπὶ ναῦς ⊦⊦⊦Ⅎ△△|, πλὴν μηρυμάτων καλῳδίων |||, which shews that there were μηρύματα καλῳδίων among the τοπεῖα for three-banked ships, but unfortunately gives no further information. The κάλοι or κάλως had probably been replaced by these καλῳδια of smaller size, when the brailing-ropes began to be looped round the sail instead of merely passing down the front ; and the loops might well be termed μηρύματα. If so, there were not eighteen separate brailing-ropes, but six with three loops each, or nine with two loops.

[180] Strattis, Macedones, Fr. 1, τὸν πέπλον δὲ τοῦτον | ἕλκουσιν ὀνεύοντες τοπείοις ἄνδρες ἀναρίθμητοι | εἰς ἄκρον, ὥσπερ ἱστίον, τὸν ἱστόν. Archippos, asini umbra, Fr. 1, τροχιλίαισι ταῦτα καὶ τοπείοις | ἱστᾶσιν οὐκ ἄνευ πόνου. Both quoted by Harpocration, s.v. τοπεῖον. The plays were produced at Athens about 400 B.C.: so this popular usage of the term τοπεῖα was concurrent with the technical usage. Assuming that the καλῳδια and πόδες and ὑπέραι were brailing-ropes and sheets and braces, the ἱμάντες and ἄγκοινα and χαλινὸς would naturally be halyards and fore-stay and back-stay. The halyards are termed ἱμάντες by Apollonios Rhodios, iv. 889, 890, ὕψι δὲ λαῖφος | εἴρυσσαν τανύσαντες ἐν ἱμάντεσσι κεραίης, this τανύσαντες ἐν representing ἐντανύσαντες. cf. Heliodoros, Æthiopica, v. 27, τὰ ἱστία ἀνιμώντων. The ἄγκοινα or anquina is mentioned by Cinna, apud Isidorum, xix. 4. 7, atque

eighteen loops of brailing-ropes—six ropes with three loops each, two halyards, a double fore-stay, two sheets, two braces, and a back-stay[180]. The inventories also shew that the three-banked ships were rigged differently some years before. There were then the *histos megas* and the *keraiai megalai* or large-mast and large-yard, and the *histos akateios* and the *keraiai akateioi* or boat-mast and boat-yard : there were also two timber *parastatai*, which probably were a pair of posts arranged as bitt-heads to support the foot of a mast that could easily be raised and lowered : and although four of the six sorts of ropes were the same, there were then *kaloi* instead of loops of *kalodia* and the *agkoina* was not double[181]. But whilst

anquina regat stabilem fortissima cursum, and by Lucilius, apud Nonium, p. 536, *funis enim præcisu' cito adque anquina soluta*. But here *anquina* should be read *ancyra*, the line meaning that the shore-cable was cut, and the anchor weighed : see note 166 on p. 73 for similar passages. Cinna's expression *anquina fortissima* might well denote the fore-stay, as that came to be the principal rope in the rigging : see note 202 on p. 94. The term χαλινός would thus remain for the back-stay, and seems suitable enough.

[181] Corp. Inscr. Attic. vol. ii, no. 795, col. d, ll. 31—42, κεφάλαιον παραστατῶν ἐπὶ ναῦς ⌐||||, κεφάλαιον ἱστῶν μεγάλων ΔΔ [...], κεφάλαιον κεραιῶν μεγάλων ἐπὶ ναῦς ΔΔ⌐|, κεφάλαιον ἱστῶν [ἀκα]τείων ⌐||, κεφάλαιον [κερ]αι[ῶ]ν ἀκατείων ἐπὶ ναῦς [...]. This forms part of a list of the gear for the three-banked ships in one division of the fleet in or about 352 B.C. Corp. Inscr. Attic. vol. ii, no. 794, col. b, ll. 1—10=no. 793, col. a, ll. 38—52, παραστατῶν ἀριθμὸς ΗΗΗΗ⌐||||· οὗτοι γίγνονται ἐπὶ ναῦς ΗΗΔΔ||||, [ἱστῶν μεγ]άλων ἀριθμ[ὸς ἐπὶ να]ῦς [..] ΔΔΔΓ, [κερ]αιῶ[ν] μεγά(λων) ἀριθμὸς ΗΗΗΗ⌐[Δ|]Ι· αὗται γίγνονται ἐπὶ ναῦς ΗΗΔΔΔΙ, [ἱστῶ]ν ἀκατείων ἀριθμὸς [ἐπὶ ναῦς...] ΔΔΔΔ||, [κεραιῶ]ν ἀκατεί(ων) ἀριθμὸ[ς Η⌐] ΔΓ||· αὗται γίγνον[ται] ἐπὶ ναῦς ⌐ΔΔΔ||| [καὶ μία] κεραία. no. 794, col. b, ll. 15—21=no. 793, col. a, ll. 61—65, [ἱ]στίων ἀριθμὸς [ἐπ]ὶ ναῦς ⌐ΔΔΔΔΓ||, [τοπεί]ων ἀριθμὸς ἐπὶ ναῦς [ἐντ]ελῆ ⌐ΔΔΔΓ|||| [καὶ] ἱμάντες ||, πόδες ||, ὑπέραι |||, ἄγκοινα |, [χ]αλινὸς |, κάλως ⌐|||. This forms part of a list of the gear for all the three-banked ships in the fleet in or about 356 B.C. Such lists, however, can only shew that masts of two kinds and yards of two kinds were in use concurrently —not that there was a mast and yard of each kind on every three-banked ship; for obviously these ships might not all be rigged alike, but some with a large mast and yard, and some with an akatian. But various entries in the inventories shew incidentally that the ships carried a mast and yard of each kind. Corp. Inscr. Attic. vol. ii, no. 791, l. 92, ἱστ μεγ and ἱστ ἀκ wanted for the Δελφινία, no. 794,

f 2

there were two kinds of masts and yards, there certainly was only one kind of rope of each sort and only one kind of sail : and the inscriptions give no hint that there was ever more than one set of ropes and one sail for a ship. Xenophon, however, mentions the two kinds of sails, *megala* and *akateia*, in speaking of Athenian three-banked ships in 373 B.C.: and both kinds might have continued in use for about sixteen years longer without appearing in the extant fragments of the inventories[182]. Still, the fact remains that the second mast and yard and the *parastatai* were retained in the Athenian navy for some years after the second sail and the second set of ropes had been discarded: and this is a curious

col. a, ll. 18—20, 27—29, κερ μεγ and ιστ ἀκ ready for the Εὐπρεπής, col. d, ll. 66—68, ιστ μεγ, κερ μεγ, ιστ ἀκ, κερ ἀκ, all lost by the Ταχεῖα, no. 798, col. b, ll. 16, 17, 26, ιστ μεγ, κερ μεγ and ιστ ἀκ now on board the Μεγίστη, ll. 31, 32, ιστ μεγ and ιστ ἀκ now on board the Σφενδόνη, no. 800, col. b, ll. 57, 58, ιστ μεγ and ιστ ἀκ now on board the Ἡγεμονία, no. 801, col. b, ll. 19, 20, κερ μεγ and κερ ἀκ now on board the Μακαρία, no. 803, col. b, ll. 53—55, ιστ μεγ, κερ μεγ and ιστ ἀκ lost by the Τρυφῶσα, col. c, ll. 62—64, ιστ μεγ, ιστ ἀκ and κερ ἀκ lost by the Δωρίς, ll. 87—90, ιστ μεγ, κερ μεγ, ιστ ἀκ, κερ ἀκ all lost by the Ὑγίεια: and so forth. There is clearly an error in the second of the lists above, where 454 παραστάται are allotted to 224 ships : the mason has put ‖‖‖‖ for ⌐‖‖ by repetition, the ships really numbering 227, each with two παραστάται. By some chance the Νίκη and the Ἐλευθερία once had three παραστάται on board, according to the entries in the inventories, no. 789, col. b, l. 3, no. 793, col. c, l. 22. But no other ships are credited with more than two; and the entries here may possibly be wrong. The παραστάται were certainly of timber, for in the inventories they are reckoned among the σκεύη ξύλινα : and as they were discarded simultaneously with the masts and yards described as μεγάλοι and ἀκάτειοι, they probably had some connexion with one or other of those masts or yards. Their name indicates that they were a pair of supports for something standing between them ; and such supports could not well be attached to a yard, or to any part of a mast except its foot. Most likely they were a pair of posts, to serve as bitt-heads, with the foot of a mast fixed on a pivot between them in such a way that this mast could easily be raised or lowered ; for the Athenian three-banked ships then had masts of that description. Xenophon, Hellenica, vi. 2. 29, φυλακάς γε μήν, τὰς μὲν ἐν τῇ γῇ (ὥσπερ προσήκει) καθίστη, ἐν δὲ ταῖς ναυσὶν αἰρόμενος αὖ τοὺς ἱστοὺς ἀπὸ τούτων ἐσκοπεῖτο. It is clear that there was only one ἱστίον and one set of τοπεῖα for each ship, since the phrase is ἐπὶ ναῦς in the second of the lists above, where the phrase would have been ταῦτα γίγνεται ἐπὶ ναῦς, had there been more than one. Unless there was more than one ἄγκοινα in a set of τοπεῖα, there must have been more than eight κάλως, for otherwise these τοπεῖα would have sufficed for ninety ships with one ὑπέρα to spare. But possibly there were two ἀγκοῖναι in place of the ἄγκοινα διπλῆ of later date.

fact. The extant fragments of the inventories do not mention thirty-oared war-ships until 330 B.C.: and then mention them so seldom that there are no parallel passages for correcting errors and omissions. But apparently these ships had a mast that could be raised and lowered; a pair of *parastatai* to support its foot; a yard formed of two spars; a sail; and the same six sorts of ropes, except that there were *kalodia* and not *kaloi*, and that the *agkoina* was not double[183]. The inventories shew clearly that all ships of the same rate in the Athenian navy were rigged in exactly the same way; and that their masts, yards, sails, etc., were interchangeable.

[182] Xenophon, Hellenica, vi. 2. 27, ὁ δὲ Ἰφικράτης. ἐπεὶ ἤρξατο τοῦ περίπλου, ἅμα μὲν ἔπλει, ἅμα δὲ πάντα ὅσα εἰς ναυμαχίαν παρεσκευάζετο· εὐθὺς μὲν γὰρ τὰ μεγάλα ἱστία αὐτοῦ κατέλιπεν, ὡς ἐπὶ ναυμαχίαν πλέων· καὶ τοῖς ἀκατείοις δέ, καὶ εἰ εὔφορον πνεῦμα εἴη, ὀλίγα ἐχρῆτο· τῇ δὲ κώπῃ τὸν πλοῦν ποιούμενος ἄμεινόν τε τὰ σώματα ἔχειν τοὺς ἄνδρας καὶ ἄμεινον τὰς ναῦς πλεῖν ἐποίει. This was in the spring of 373 B.C. The earliest fragments of the inventories in the Corp. Inscr. Attic. are no. 789, assigned to 373/2, and no. 789. b (appendix), assigned to 374/3: but there are no entries about sails until nos. 793 and 794, which are quoted in the last note. The large sails are mentioned again by Xenophon, Hellenica, i. 1. 13, Ἀλκιβιάδης δέ, εἰπὼν καὶ τούτοις διώκειν αὐτὸν ἐξελομένοις τὰ μεγάλα ἱστία, αὐτὸς ἔπλευσεν εἰς Πάριον, cf. 12, ἀνάγεσθαι ἤδη αὐτοῦ μέλλοντος ὡς ἐπὶ ναυμαχίαν. ii. 1. 29, Κόνων δέ, κατασχὼν ἐπὶ τὴν Ἀβαρνίδα τὴν Λαμψάκου ἄκραν, ἔλαβεν αὐτόθεν τὰ μεγάλα τῶν Λυσάνδρου νεῶν ἱστία. These events were in 410 and 405 B.C. See also Epicrates, apud Athenæum. xi. 23, κατάβαλλε τἀκάτεια, καὶ κυλίκια | αἴρου τὰ μείζω. This dates from about 375 B.C. There is an allusion here to hoisting and lowering the large sails and the akatians, and also an allusion to taking up and putting down the drinking-cups known as κυλίκια and ἀκάτεια. The κυλίκια were shaped like saucers, and could therefore be compared to a sail swelling out before the wind.

[183] Corp. Inscr. Attic. vol. ii, no. 812, col. a, ll. 6—11, τριακοντόρου Ξενοκλῆς Δεκελ(εεὺς) σκεύη ἔχει ξύλινα· ταρρόμ, πηδάλια, κλιμακίδας, κοντούς, ἱστούς, κεραίας, παραστάτας δύο· ἀπὸ τῆς Νίκης, Χαιρεστράτου ἔργον. This thirty-oared Νίκη is not to be confounded with the three-banked Νίκη mentioned in note 181 on p. 84. The mason has probably put ἱστούς for ἱστόν by mistake: he would easily be misled by the neighbouring plurals, and especially by κοντούς just before. A little thirty-oared ship was not very likely to be carrying two masts at a time when large ships of three and four banks were carrying only one; nor was any ship likely to carry two masts of the same kind—the masts would naturally differ in size and bear different names. The δύο after παραστάτας appears to be redundant. Corp. Inscr. Attic. vol. ii, no. 809, col. a, ll. 115, 116, καὶ ἱστίον τρι[ακοντ]όρου ἐποησάμε[θα], no. 807, col. c, ll. 42—45, καὶ τριακοντέρου, καλῴδια ἀδόκιμα △△△, πόδες ‖, ὑπέρα |, ἄγκοινα, ἱμάντες ‖.

At the time when akatian masts and sails were carried on the three-banked war-ships, the large sails used to be sent ashore whenever the ships were cleared for action[184]. Battles being fought without regard to wind, no ship could ever hoist a sail until she had abandoned all attempts at fighting and was trying to get away; and as the large sail had been sent ashore beforehand, she had then to hoist the akatian: so that 'hoisting the akatian' became a proverbial expression for running away. This expression occurs in a play by Aristophanes that was produced in 411 B.C.: and a century afterwards it was adopted by Epicuros in a saying that is quoted by Plutarch and parodied by Lucian[185]. The classic name *akateion* is also applied by Lucian to one of the sails on the merchant-ships of his own times: but apparently the name does not occur again in ancient literature[186]. Most probably, therefore, these masts and sails went out of use soon after they were discarded in the Athenian navy.

[184] Xenophon, Hellenica, i. 1. 13, ii. 1. 29, vi. 2. 27, already quoted in note 182. Thucydides also alludes to this practice of sending the large sails ashore before going into action, though he does not give these sails their name: vii. 24, καὶ χρήματα πολλὰ τὰ ξύμπαντα ἑάλω· ἅτε γὰρ ταμιείῳ χρωμένων τῶν Ἀθηναίων τοῖς τείχεσι πολλὰ μὲν ἐμπόρων χρήματα καὶ σῖτος ἐνῆν, πολλὰ δὲ καὶ τριηράρχων, ἐπεὶ καὶ ἱστία τεσσαράκοντα τριήρων καὶ τᾶλλα σκεύη ἐγκατελήφθη, viii. 43, οἱ δὲ Ἀθηναῖοι ταῖς ἐκ τῆς Σάμου ναυσὶ πάσαις, ὡς ᾔσθοντο τὰ τῆς ναυμαχίας, πλεύσαντες ἐς τὴν Σύμην...λαβόντες δὲ τὰ ἐν τῇ Σύμῃ σκεύη τῶν νεῶν, ἀπέπλευσαν ἐς τὴν Σάμον. These events were in 413 and 411 B.C.

[185] Aristophanes, Lysistrata, 61—64, Λ. οὐδ' ἃς προσεδόκων κἀλογιξόμην ἐγὼ | πρώτας παρέσεσθαι δεῦρο τὰς Ἀχαρνέων | γυναῖκας, οὐχ ἥκουσιν. Κ. ἡ γοῦν Θεογένους, | ὡς δεῦρ' ἰοῦσα, τἀκάτειον ἦρετο. Plutarch, de audiendis poetis, 1, πότερον οὖν τῶν νέων, ὥσπερ τῶν Ἰθακησίων, κηρῷ τινι τὰ ὦτα καὶ ἀτέγκτῳ κηρῷ καταπλάσσοντες ἀναγκάζωμεν αὐτούς, τὸ Ἐπικούρειον ἀκάτειον ἀραμένους, ποιητικὴν φεύγειν καὶ παρεξελαύνειν; non posse suaviter vivi secundum Epicurum, 12, ἐπαραμένους τὰ ἀκάτεια φεύγειν ἀπ' αὐτῶν κελεύουσι, sc. οἱ Ἐπικούρειοι. Lucian, quomodo historia conscribenda sit, 45, δεήσει γὰρ τότε ποιητικοῦ τινος ἀνέμου ἐπουριάσοντος τὰ ἀκάτεια καὶ συνδιοίσοντος ὑψηλὴν καὶ ἐπ' ἄκρων τῶν κυμάτων τὴν ναῦν.

[186] Lucian, Lexiphanes, 15, ἀλλὰ σὺ τὸ ὅμοιον εἰργάσω με ὥσπερ εἴ τις ὁλκάδα τριάρμενον ἐν οὐρίῳ πλέουσαν, ἐμπεπνευματωμένον τοῦ ἀκατείου, εὐφοροῦσάν τε καὶ ἀκροκυματοῦσαν, ἔκτοράς τινας ἀμφιστόμους καὶ ἰσχάδας σιδηρᾶς ἀφεὶς καὶ ναυσιπέδας, ἀναχαιτίζοι τοῦ δρόμου τὸ ῥόθιον φθόνῳ τῆς εὐηνεμίας. cf. Jupiter tragœdus, 46, οὔκουν ἔφερε μὲν ὑμᾶς τότε ἄνεμος ἐμπίπτων τῇ ὀθόνῃ καὶ ἐμπιπλὰς τὰ ἀκάτεια, ἢ οἱ ἐρέττοντες, ἐκυβέρνα δὲ εἷς τις ἐφεστὼς καὶ ἔσωζε τὴν ναῦν;

A mast termed *dolon*, with a sail of the same name, subsequently served for manœuvering before an action and for escaping after a defeat. According to Polybios, the Rhodian war-ships used dolons in an action in 201 B.C.: and he had read the admiral's despatch at Rhodes. And according to Livy, the Syrian and Roman war-ships also used them in actions in 191 and 190 B.C.: and he is here following the lost narrative by Polybios, who probably got his information about these actions from the Rhodian despatches[187]. Diodoros says that the Carthaginian war-ships used them in an action in 307 B.C.: but perhaps he is misquoting his authorities, for at that date the ships might have used akatians[188]. The dolons are mentioned again by Procopios in speaking of Byzantine war-ships in 533 A.D.; and he describes them as the little sails and distinguishes them from the large sails. The name must have been obsolete for centuries, and then resuscitated as a classic term for the smaller sort of mast or sail[189].

---

[187] Polybios, xvi. 15, ἐν τῇ περὶ Λάδην ναυμαχίᾳ δύο μὲν αὐτάνδρους πεντήρεις τῶν Ῥοδίων ὑποχειρίους γενέσθαι τοῖς πολεμίοις· ἐκ δὲ τοῦ κινδύνου μιᾶς νηὸς ἐπαραμένης τὸν δόλωνα διὰ τὸ τετρωμένην αὐτὴν θαλαττοῦσθαι· πολλοὺς καὶ τῶν ἐγγὺς τὸ παραπλήσιον ποιοῦντας ἀποχωρεῖν πρὸς τὸ πέλαγος· τέλος δὲ μετ᾽ ὀλίγων καταλειφθέντα τὸν ναύαρχον ἀναγκασθῆναι ταὐτὸ τοῖς προειρημένοις πράττειν......τῆς ἐπιστολῆς ἔτι μενούσης ἐν τῷ πρυτανείῳ, τῆς ὑπ᾽ αὐτοῦς τοὺς καιροὺς ὑπὸ τοῦ ναυάρχου πεμφθείσης περὶ τούτων τῇ τε βουλῇ καὶ τοῖς πρυτάνεσιν. Livy, xxxvi. 44, *quod ubi vidit Romanus, vela contrahit malosque inclinat, et, simul armamenta componens, opperitur insequentes naves. iam ferme triginta in fronte erant ; quibus ut æquaret lævum cornu, dolonibus erectis altum petere intendit.* 45, *neque ita multo post primum ab lævo cornu fuga cœpit. Polyxenidas enim ut virtute militum haud dubie se superari vidit, sublatis dolonibus effuse fugere intendit.* xxxvii. 30, *ceterum postquam alias circumventas, prætoriam navem Polyxenidæ relictis sociis vela dantem videre, sublatis raptim dolonibus, Ephesum petunt fuga.*

[188] Diodoros, xx. 61, ὁ δὲ τῶν Καρχηδονίων στρατηγός, ἁλισκομένης ἤδη τῆς ναυαρχίδος, ἀπέσφαξεν ἑαυτόν, προκρίνας τὸν θάνατον τῆς προσδοκηθείσης αἰχμαλωσίας. οὐ μὴν ἐφάνη γε εὖ βεβουλευμένος · ἡ γὰρ ναῦς φοροῦ πνεύματος ἐπιλαβομένη, τοῦ δόλωνος ἀρθέντος, ἐξέφυγε τὸν κίνδυνον.

[189] Procopios, de bello Vandalico, i. 17, τοῖς δὲ ναύταις ἐπήγγελλε παρακολουθεῖν τε ἀεὶ καὶ τοῦ στρατεύματος μὴ πολὺ διεστάναι, ἀλλ᾽ ἐπιφόρου μὲν γινομένου τοῦ πνεύματος χαλάσαντας τὰ μεγάλα ἱστία τοῖς μικροῖς, ἃ δὴ δόλωνας καλοῦσιν, ἕπεσθαι· λωφήσαντος δὲ παντελῶς τοῦ ἀνέμου βιάζεσθαι ὅσον οἷοί τε ὦσιν ἐρέσσοντας. This is clearly an adaptation of the passage in Xenophon, Hellenica, vi. 2. 27, already quoted in note 182 on p. 85.

A mast and sail termed *artemon* are mentioned by Lucilius a little before 100 B.C., and then by Labeo and the elder Seneca, who treat them as subordinate to the ordinary mast and sail[190]. In later times the artemon is mentioned by name in the Acts of the Apostles and also by Paulinus of Nola about 400 A.D.; while a subordinate sail is noticed by Juvenal and afterwards by Synesios, a contemporary of Paulinus[191]. These statements may all refer to merchant-ships: but a small sail is mentioned by Appian in narrating how some Roman war-ships got away after a defeat off Mylæ in 36 B.C., though unfortunately he does not give the sail a name[192].

Thus a second mast of some sort, artemon or dolon or akatian, was generally in use from 411 B.C. to 533 A.D. and perhaps before and after: but there is not anything to shew what difference there was between the akatian and the dolon, or the dolon and the artemon.

---

[190] Lucilius, apud Charisium, p. 99, *Arabus artemo.* Lucilius died about 100 B.C. The Pandects, l. 16. 242, *malum navis esse partem, artemonem autem non esse, Labeo ait: quia pleræque naves sine malo inutiles essent, ideoque pars navis habetur; artemo autem magis adiectamento quam pars navis est.* Seneca, contro-versiæ, vii. 1. 2, *ubi spes? in gubernaculo? nulla est. in remigio? ne in hoc quidem est. in comite? nemo repertus est naufragi comes. in velo? in artemone? omnia pæne instrumenta circumscisa sunt: adminiculum spei nullum est.* There is an emendation here, *artemone* for *arte;* and if that is right, Seneca distinguishes the ordinary sail (*velum*) from a sail termed *artemo,* just as Labeo distinguishes the ordinary mast (*malus*) from a mast termed *artemo.* Labeo and Seneca were both living at Rome in the reign of Augustus.

[191] Acts, xxvii. 40, ἐπάραντες τὸν ἀρτέμωνα τῇ πνεούσῃ, κατεῖχον εἰς τὸν αἰγιαλόν. Paulinus Nolanus, epistolæ, 49. 2, *malus ita prosilivit a vulnere, ut longe extra navem in undas expulsus tuto ceciderit. deinde, cum aut artemone armari oporte-bat, aut sentinam depleri, etc.* Juvenal, xii. 67—69, *inopi miserabilis arte cucurrit | vestibus extentis, et, quod superaverat unum, | velo prora suo.* cf. 53—55, *tunc, adversis urguentibus, illuc | recidit, ut malum ferro submitteret, ac se | explicat angustum.* Synesios, epistolæ, p. 163 D, ὑπαλλάττειν μὲν οὖν ἱστίον ἕτερον νόθον οὐκ εἴχομεν, ἠνεχυρίαστο γάρ· ἀνελαμβάνομεν δὲ αὐτὸ καθάπερ τῶν χιτώνων τοὺς κόλπους. This can only mean that they reduced the size of the ordinary sail until it would fit a smaller mast and yard. For χιτώνων κόλπους, cf. Herodotos, vi. 125. 2, 3; Polybios, iii. 33. 2; Æschylos, septem adversus Thebas, 1039. Pauli-nus died in 431 A.D., and Synesios a year or two before.

[192] Appian, de bellis civilibus, v. 111, ἁλισκομένων δὲ καὶ πιμπραμένων τῶν Καίσαρος νεῶν, αἱ μὲν ἀράμεναι τὰ βραχέα τῶν ἱστίων ἀπέπλεον εἰς τὴν Ἰταλίαν, τῶν παραγγελμάτων καταφρονοῦσαι κ.τ.λ.

The artemon must have been something between a fore-mast and a bowsprit with a spritsail on a spritsail-yard; for that is what is represented on the coins of 67 and 186 and 305 A.D. in fgs. 27 and 28 and 34, and in the reliefs and paintings of corresponding date in fgs. 26, 29, 31, 33, 35, 37 and 40. On the Roman war-ship of about 50 A.D. in fg. 35 there is not any mast beside the artemon; but the ship is here in action, and obviously the ordinary mast and sail have been taken down or sent ashore beforehand. The rule was still to send the ordinary sail ashore when a ship was cleared for action; and the ordinary mast must always have been lowered in a battle, for otherwise it would have snapped under the shock of ramming[193]. A third mast had come into use by about 50 A.D.; and this was presumably a mizen[194]. Perhaps a few of the largest merchant-ships were fitted with this mast; but normally there were only two.

[193] Plutarch, Antonius, 64, καὶ τοὺς κυβερνήτας τὰ ἱστία βουλομένους ἀπολιπεῖν ἠνάγκασεν ('Αντώνιος) ἐμβαλέσθαι καὶ κομίζειν. 66, ἀκρίτου δὲ καὶ κοινῆς ἔτι τῆς ναυμαχίας συνεστώσης, αἰφνίδιον αἱ Κλεοπάτρας ἑξήκοντα νῆες ὤφθησαν αἱρόμεναι πρὸς ἀπόπλουν τὰ ἱστία καὶ διὰ μέσου φεύγουσαι τῶν μαχομένων. Dion Cassius, l. 33, τοὺς γὰρ φεύγοντας, ἅτε καὶ ἄνευ ἱστίων ὄντες καὶ πρὸς τὴν ναυμαχίαν μόνην παρεσκευασμένοι, οὐκ ἐπεδίωξαν. These passages refer to the battle of Actium in 31 B.C.; and certainly imply that it then was customary to send the ordinary sail ashore on clearing for action. See also Livy, xxvi. 39, velis tum forte, improvidus futuri certaminis, Romanus veniebat, and Vegetius, iv. 43, navalis pugna tranquillo committitur mari, liburnarumque moles non ventorum flatibus sed remorum pulsu adversarios percutit rostris. For the lowering of the masts, see Polybios, i. 61, οἱ δὲ Καρχηδόνιοι, κατιδόντες τὸν διάπλουν αὐτῶν προκατέχοντας τοὺς Ῥωμαίους, καθελόμενοι τοὺς ἱστούς, κ.τ.λ., and Livy, xxxvi. 44, quod ubi vidit Romanus, vela contrahit malosque inclinat.

[194] Athenæos, v. 43, τριῶν τε ἱστῶν ὑπαρχόντων,...τῶν δὲ ἱστῶν ὁ μὲν δεύτερος καὶ τρίτος εὑρέθησαν· δυσχερῶς δὲ ὁ πρῶτος ἐν τοῖς ὄρεσι τῆς Βρεττίας εὑρέθη ὑπὸ συβώτου ἀνδρός. Pliny, xix. 1, iam vero nec vela satis esse maiora navigiis. sed cum vix amplitudini antennarum singulæ arbores sufficiant, super eas tamen addi velorum alia vela, præterque alia in proris et alia in puppibus pandi. Pliny speaks as though a three-masted ship were a thing of recent date; and Athenæos may really be describing a ship of Caligula's time or afterwards, though professing to describe a ship belonging to Hieron: see pp. 27—29. There is possibly an allusion to the three masts of a ship in the Corinthian jest recorded by Strabo, viii. 6. 20. As many as fifty masts and sails were carried on the biggest timber-rafts: see Theophrastos, historia plantarum, v. 8. 2, quoted in the note on rates on p. 122.

A topsail had also come into use by about 50 A.D. as part of the ordinary rig[195]. The ancients always knew that they improved the pace of a ship by carrying sail as high as possible, though apparently they did not understand the cause of this; but hitherto they had gained their object by hoisting up the yard[196]. Now they introduced a sail that was triangular in form, and spread it with its base along the yard and its apex at the top of the mast, as depicted on the Roman ship of about 200 A.D. in fg. 29, and less distinctly on those in fgs. 27, 32, and 39. The topsail being of this shape, no topsail-yard was needed; nor can such a yard be detected in the manuscript of about 500 A.D. in fg. 38, for obviously the scribe has combined the masts and yards belonging to both lines of ships in a convenient group above the upper line, simply to avoid confusion.

---

[195] Seneca, epistolæ, 77, *subito nobis hodie Alexandrinæ naves apparuerunt, quæ præmitti solent et nuntiare sècuturæ classis adventum: tabellarias vocant. gratus illarum Campaniæ aspectus est.　omnis in pilis Puteolorum turba consistit et ex ipso genere velorum Alexandrinas quamvis in magna turba navium intellegit. solis enim licet supparum intendere, quod in alto omnes habent naves.　(nulla enim res æque adiuvat cursum quam summa pars veli: illinc maxime navis urgetur. itaque quotiens ventus increbruit maiorque est quam expedit, antenna submittitur: minus habet virium flatus ex humili.)　cum intravere Capreas et promontorium ex quo " alta procelloso speculatur vertice Pallas," ceteræ velo iubentur esse contentæ: supparum Alexandrinarum insigne est.* cf. Seneca, Medea, 323—328, *nunc antennas medio tutas | ponere malo ; nunc in summo | religare loco, cum iam totos | avidus nimium navita flatus | optat, et alto rubicunda tremunt | suppara velo.* Lucan, v. 428, 429, *summaque pandens | suppara velorum perituras colligit auras.* Statius, silvæ, iii. 2. 27, *summis annectite suppara velis.* The top-sail is noticed by Pliny in the passage quoted in the last note, but he omits the name. Apparently *supparum* becomes σίφαρος in Greek. Epictetos, dissertationes, iii. 2. 18, βυθιζομένου δὲ τοῦ πλοίου, σύ μοι παρελθὼν ἐπαίρεις τοὺς σιφάρους. But possibly σιφάρους is here a corruption of σειραφόρους, the regular equivalent of *supparum* being παράσειρον. Lucian, navigium, 5, ὁ μὲν γὰρ ἄλλος κόσμος, αἱ γραφαὶ καὶ τοῦ ἱστίου τὸ παράσειρον πυραυγές, κ.τ.λ. Athenæos, v. 39, ὁ δὲ ἱστὸς ἦν αὐτῆς ἑβδομή-κοντα πηχῶν, βύσσινον ἔχων ἱστίον, ἀλουργεῖ παρασείρῳ κεκοσμημένον. This last passage refers to a vessel built by Ptolemy Philopator for his voyages on the Nile: but Athenæos is quoting from Callixenos, and he must be committing the ana-chronism of giving this vessel a type of sail that was not introduced until about two hundred years afterwards. The term παράσειρον can only denote a top-sail or a studding-sail; and there is not any trace of the use of studding-sails in ancient times. By their description of these παράσειρα as πυραυγές and ἀλουργές, Lucian and Athenæos confirm Seneca's description of the *suppara* as *rubicunda*.

Thus a full-rigged ship must now have had a main mast with a yard that carried a square sail below and a triangular sail above, a fore-mast or bowsprit with a yard and square sail only, and also a mizen with perhaps a similar yard and sail. The rigging had been developed to this point by about 50 A.D. at latest; but after that there was not any further progress, and the additional masts and sails were gradually discarded. Thus, while two masts and sails were carried on the Byzantine war-ships that made the attack on Carthage in 533 A.D., only one was carried on those that were equipped for the attack on Crete in 949 A.D. So the arrangement of the rigging as well as the arrangement of the oars had now reverted to the style in vogue among the Greeks some sixteen centuries before[197].

[196] Aristotle, mechanica, 7, διὰ τί, ὅσῳ ἂν ἡ κεραία ἀνωτέρα ᾖ, θᾶττον πλεῖ τὰ πλοῖα τῷ αὐτῷ ἱστίῳ καὶ τῷ αὐτῷ πνεύματι; ἢ διότι γίνεται ὁ μὲν ἱστὸς μοχλός, ὑπομόχλιον δὲ τὸ ἐδώλιον ἐν ᾧ ἐμπέπηγεν, ὃ δὲ δεῖ κινεῖν βάρος τὸ πλοῖον, τὸ δὲ κινοῦν τὸ ἐν τῷ ἱστίῳ πνεῦμα; εἰ δ' ὅσῳ ἂν πορρώτερον ᾖ τὸ ὑπομόχλιον, ῥᾷον κινεῖ καὶ θᾶττον ἡ αὐτὴ δύναμις τὸ αὐτὸ βάρος, ἡ οὖν κεραία ἀνώτερον ἀγομένη καὶ τὸ ἱστίον πορρώτερον ποιεῖ τοῦ ἐδωλίου ὑπομοχλίου ὄντος. This is copied by Vitruvius, x. 3. 5; eiusque vela cum sunt per altitudinem mediam mali pendentia, non potest habere navis celerem cursum: cum autem in summo cacumine antennæ subductæ sunt, tunc vehementiori progreditur impetu, quod non proxime calcem mali—quod est loco centri—sed in summo et longius ab eo progressa recipiunt in se vela ventum. Asclepiades says that the calx or πτέρνα was the bottom of the mast, and fitted into the ληνός—see note 199 on p. 92—so ληνός and ἐδώλιον seem to mean the same thing here. In its action as a lever, the mast could only drive the fore part of the ship deeper into the water as the leverage was increased. The fact is simply that the friction of the wind against the waves retards the lower currents of air more than it retards the currents above; so that, as Seneca says, minus habet virium flatus ex humili, epistolæ, 77, quoted in the last note.

[197] Porphyrogenitos, de cærimoniis, ii. 45, p. 389, ἐδόθη ὑπὲρ ἀγορᾶς τῶν πανίων τῶν ῥασιακῶν λόγῳ ποιήσεως ἀρμένων θ' ἀνὰ πηχῶν λ' τῶν θ' καραβίων τῶν Ῥῶς, καὶ ἑτέρων ἀρμένων β' ἀνὰ πηχῶν κη' τῶν β' μονερίων τῶν αἰχμαλώτων, σὺν τῶν δοθέντων πανίων ῥασιακῶν κατὰ περίσσειαν τοὺς αὐτοὺς Ῥῶς· ὑπὲρ πανίων διὰ τῶν ἀμφοτέρων ῥαρνδ'...ἐδόθη ὑπὲρ ἀγορᾶς σχοινίων λόγῳ κρυπτῶν ἐπικήρων καὶ ποδιοδρόμων τῶν αὐτῶν ια' ἀρμένων ,γ. p. 388, εἰς ἐξόπλισιν τῶν κ' δρομονίων,...ἄρμενα κ',...ἀναγοκατάγοντα σὺν τῶν ἱμανταρίων αὐτῶν κ'. These were the largest dromons then in use: see note 47 on p. 19. The ἄρμενα are here the sails; and apparently the ἱμαντάρια and ἀναγοκατάγοντα are the halyards and their blocks. The sheets and braces may be included in the phrase κρυπτῶν ἐπικήρων καὶ ποδιοδρόμων under names akin to πόδες and ἐπίκρια. See pp. 18, 19 as to the oars in use at this period; and p. 87 with note 189 as to the masts and sails in use in 533 A.D.

The mast was fitted with a military-top on the largest of these Byzantine war-ships, so that the men could shoot down missiles upon an enemy's deck[198]. And military-tops are represented on the masts of the Egyptian and Asiatic war-ships two thousand years before, as in fgs. 6 to 8. But on the Greek and Roman war-ships the masts were lowered during an engagement; and military-tops were consequently left to merchant-ships, the larger vessels of that class carrying them as part of their defence against the pirates. In these times the top was somewhat like a tub or cask, with space enough for two or three men to stand inside; and this was fastened round the mast a little way above

[198] Leo, tactica, xix. 7, ἀλλὰ καὶ τὰ λεγόμενα ξυλόκαστρα περὶ τὸ μέσον που τοῦ καταρτίου ἐν τοῖς μεγίστοις δρόμωσιν ἐπιστήσουσι περιτετειχισμένα σανίσιν, ἐξ ὧν ἄνδρες τινὲς τὸ μέσον τῆς πολεμίας νηὸς ἀκοντίσουσιν ἢ λίθους μυλικοὺς ἢ σίδηρα βαρέα, οἷον μάζας ξιφοειδεῖς, δι' ὧν ἢ τὴν ναῦν διαθρύψουσιν ἢ τοὺς ὑποκειμένους συνθλάσουσιν σφοδρῶς καταφερόμενα, ἢ τι ἕτερον ἐπιχύσουσιν ἢ ἐμπρῆσαι δυνάμενον τὴν ναῦν τῶν ἐναντίων ἢ τοὺς ἐν αὐτῇ πολεμίους θανατῶσαι.

[199] Athenæos, xi. 49, καρχήσιον. Καλλίξενος ὁ Ῥόδιος ἐν τοῖς Περὶ Ἀλεξανδρείας φησὶν ὅτι ποτήριόν ἐστιν ἐπίμηκες, συνηγμένον εἰς μέσον ἐπιεικῶς, ὦτα ἔχον μέχρι τοῦ πυθμένος κατήκοντα....Ἀσκληπιάδης δ' ὁ Μυρλεανὸς κεκλῆσθαί φησιν αὐτὸ ἀπό τινος τῶν ἐν τῇ νηὶ κατασκευασμάτων. τοῦ γὰρ ἱστοῦ τὸ μὲν κατωτάτω πτέρνα καλεῖται, ἢ ἐμπίπτει εἰς τὸν ληνόν· τὸ δ' οἷον εἰς μέσον, τράχηλος· τὸ δὲ πρὸς τῷ τέλει καρχήσιον. ἔχει δὲ τοῦτο κεραίας ἄνω συννευούσας ἐφ' ἑκάτερα τὰ μέρη, καὶ ἐπίκειται τὸ λεγόμενον αὐτῷ θωράκιον, τετράγωνον πάντη πλὴν τῆς βάσεως καὶ τῆς κορυφῆς· αὗται δὲ προὔχουσιν μικρὸν ἐπ' εὐθείας ἐξωτέρω. ἐπὶ δὲ τοῦ θωρακίου εἰς ὕψος ἀνήκουσα καὶ ὀξεῖα γιγνομένη ἐστὶν ἡ λεγομένη ἡλακάτη. There is clearly a misreading here, ἐπίκειται for ἔγκειται. Callixenos says that the wine-cup καρχήσιον contracted a little in the middle and had handles reaching down to the bottom, so Asclepiades must have said that the mast-head καρχήσιον consisted of a θωράκιον bulging a little at the top and bottom, with a pair of κεραῖαι curving up on either side. These κεραῖαι were presumably the hooks that carried the halyards: they could not be the yards, as those were straight. For the phrase τετράγωνον πάντη, cf. Corp. Inscr. Attic. vol. ii, no. 835, l. 70, κύλινδρος τετράγωνος πανταχεῖ. Thus its meaning is simply that there were not any projections or depressions in the sides of the θωράκιον between the two projections at the top and bottom. Athenæos, v. 43, τριῶν τε ἱστῶν ὑπαρχόντων,...ἦσαν δὲ κατὰ τοὺς ἱστοὺς ἐν τοῖς καρχησίοις, οὖσι χαλκοῖς, ἐπὶ μὲν τοῦ πρώτου τρεῖς ἄνδρες, εἶθ' ἑξῆς καθ' ἕνα λειπόμενοι· τούτοις δ' ἐν πλεκτοῖς γυργάθοις διὰ τροχιλίων εἰς τὰ θωράκια λίθοι παρεβάλλοντο καὶ βέλη διὰ τῶν παίδων. cf. 44, ἄστρων γὰρ ψαύει καρχήσια, καὶ τριελίκτους θώρακας μεγάλων ἐντὸς ἔχει νεφέων. In the inventories of the Athenian dock-yards an ἐπίθημα θωρακείου is mentioned as something belonging to a war-ship: see Corp. Inscr. Attic. vol. ii, no. 791, l. 31. But there is nothing to shew that this θωράκειον was part of a military-top.

the yard, the halyards working through a pair of hooks or rings which projected from its sides and served as blocks[199]. In the absence of a military-top these hooks or rings projected from the mast itself, as in fg. 13, where they crown the mast, or again in fg. 30, where the mast extends beyond, and forms a kind of topmast for carrying the triangular sail above the yard[200]. On merchant-ships the yards were strong enough for heavy weights to be hoisted to the ends and thence let fall on an assailant. And channels could therefore be defended by mooring merchant-ships at intervals across, and thus sending masses of lead and lumps of rock through the bottoms of any vessels that tried to run through[201].

[200] Pindar, Nemea, v. 51, ἀνὰ δ' ἱστία τεῖνον πρὸς ζυγὸν καρχασίου. The term ζυγόν must here denote the pair of hooks for the halyards; and so also *iuga* in Latin. Lucan, ii. 695, *dum iuga curvantur mali*, cf. v. 418, *hic utinam summi curvet carchesia mali*, sc. *Aquilo*. The hooks being known as horns, κεραῖαι—see last note—the καρχήσιον could be described as the thing with the horns, κερούχος or *ceruchus*. Ennodius, carmina, i. 7. 43, *lintea nam summis dum crispant nexa ceruchis*. Valerius Flaccus, i. 469, *temperet ut tremulos Zetes fraterque ceruchos*. Lucan, viii. 177, *instabit summis minor Ursa ceruchis*, x. 494, 495, *et tempore eodem | transtraque nautarum, summique arsere ceruchi*. But while *ceruchus* was thus in use in Latin, κερούχος gave place to κεροίαξ in classical Greek—see note 203 on p. 94—and afterwards to κάροιον, as in Leo, tactica, xix. 5. The terms *ceruchus* and κεροίαξ are always in the plural, but *carchesium* and καρχήσιον vary between the plural and the singular. Plutarch, Themistocles, 12, γλαῦκα δ' ὀφθῆναι τοῖς καρχησίοις ἐπικαθίζουσαν. Lucian, de mercede conductis, 1, ἤ τιν' ἄλλον ἐκ μηχανῆς θεὸν ἐπὶ τῷ καρχησίῳ καθεζόμενον, cf. navigium, 9, amores, 6. Apuleius, metamorphoses, xi. 16, *insigni carchesio conspicua*, sc. *malus*. Catullus, 64. 235, 236, *candidaque intorti sustollant vela rudentes, | lucida qua splendent summi carchesia mali*. See also Apollonios Rhodios, i. 565, κὰδ δ' αὐτοῦ λίνα χεῦαν ἐπ' ἠλακάτην ἐρύσαντες, where αὐτοῦ denotes ἱστοῦ. According to Asclepiades, the ἠλακάτη was the portion of the mast above the θωράκιον—see last note—so Apollonios can only mean that the yard was hoisted up to the καρχήσιον at the foot of the ἠλακάτη. Apparently, the ἠλακάτη was also termed the στυλίς, for three of the stars in the constellation of the Argo are placed ἐπὶ στυλίδος ἄκρας by Eratosthenes, catasterismi, 35, and *ad malum* by Hyginus, astronomia, ii. 36. Hyginus, however, may be confusing the stars that Ptolemy places πρὸς τῷ ἄκρῳ τοῦ ἱστοῦ and ἐν τῷ ἀκροστολίῳ, Almagest, viii. 1, Ἀργοῦς ἀστερισμός. The ἀκροστόλιον is suggested by the phrase in Plutarch, Pompeius, 24. 2, στυλίσι χρυσαῖς.

[201] Thucydides, vii. 38, διαλειπούσας δὲ τὰς ὁλκάδας ὅσον δύο πλέθρα ἀπ' ἀλλήλων κατέστησεν, ὅπως εἴ τις βιάζοιτο ναῦς, εἴη κατάφευξις ἀσφαλὴς καὶ πάλιν καθ' ἡσυχίαν ἔκπλους. 41, αἱ δὲ τῶν Συρακοσίων νῆες μέχρι μὲν τῶν ὁλκάδων ἐπεδίωκον· ἔπειτ' αὐτοὺς αἱ κεραῖαι ὑπὲρ τῶν ἔσπλων αἱ ἀπὸ τῶν ὁλκάδων δελφινοφόροι ἠρμέναι ἐκώλυον. Aristophanes, equites, 761, 762, ἀλλὰ φυλάττου, καὶ πρὶν ἐκεῖνον προσικέσθαι σου,

All the ropes in the rigging of a Roman merchant-ship seem to be represented in the reliefs of about 50 A.D. and 200 A.D. in fgs. 26 and 29 to 31. The mast is fitted with a set of shrouds, which slope a little aft and thus support it from behind as well as from the sides; while in front it is supported by a single fore-stay. This is a larger rope than any of the others[202]; and seems to be intended for lowering the mast towards the stern and hauling it up again, though on a merchant-ship the mast might well have been a fixture. The yard has two halyards in the middle and several pairs of lifts towards the end; and these lifts carry the topsail. There are braces to the yard; and there are sheets to the sail, and also a number of brailing-ropes. The bowsprit has two

πρότερον σὺ | τοὺς δελφῖνας μετεωρίζου καὶ τὴν ἄκατον παραβάλλου: scholia in locum, δηλοῦται δὲ καὶ ὑπὸ Φερεκράτους ἐν τοῖς 'Αγρίοις, ὅταν λέγῃ, ὁ δὲ δὴ δελφίς ἐστι μολιβδοῦς, δελφινοφόρος τε κέρδος, διακόψει τοὔδαφος αὐτῶν ἐμπίπτων καὶ καταδύων. These verses are corrupt; but some word like κέρας must be involved in κέρδος. Diodoros, xiii. 78, οἱ δ' ἐπὶ τῶν μεγάλων πλοίων ἐφεστῶτες ἐπέρριπτον ταῖς τῶν πολεμίων ναυσὶ τοὺς ἀπὸ τῶν κεραιῶν λίθους. 79, πλεῖστοι δ' ὑπὸ τῶν λιθοφόρων κεραιῶν ἔπιπτον, ὡς ἂν ἐξ ὑπερδεξίων τόπων βαλλόντων λίθους ὑπερμεγέθεις τῶν 'Αθηναίων. Athenæos, v. 43, τριῶν τε ἱστῶν ὑπαρχόντων, ἐξ ἑκάστου κεραῖαι λιθοφόροι ἐξήρτηντο δύο, ἐξ ὧν ἅρπαγές τε καὶ πλίνθοι μολίβου πρὸς τοὺς ἐπιτιθεμένους ἠφίεντο.

[202] Lucian, navigium, 5, ἡλίκος μὲν ὁ ἱστός, ὅσην δὲ ἀνέχει τὴν κεραίαν, οἵῳ καὶ προτόνῳ κέχρηται καὶ συνέχεται. cf. Æschylos, Agamemnon, 897, σωτῆρα ναὸς πρότονον. Synesios, epistolæ, p. 164 c, τὸ κέρας ἐπετρίγει, καὶ ἡμεῖς ᾠόμεθα προτονίζειν τὴν ναῦν. εἶτα κατεαγὸς μέσον ἐγγὺς μὲν ἦλθεν ἀπολέσαι πάντας ἡμᾶς, κ.τ.λ. Antipater in the Anthology, x. 2. 7, λαίφεα δ' εὐυφέα προτονίζετε. Synesios uses προτονίζειν for tightening the fore-stay to secure the mast, etc.; whereas Antipater uses it for letting the sail out far enough to touch the fore-stay. cf. Oppian, de piscatione, i. 227, λίνα πάντα περὶ προτόνοισι μέμυκε: Euripides, Hecuba, 113, 114, τὰς ποντοπόρους δ' ἔσχε σχεδίας, | λαίφη προτόνοις ἐπερειδομένας, Iphigeneia in Tauris, 1134—1136, ἀέρι δ' ἱστία προτόνοις κατὰ | πρῷραν ὑπὲρ στόλον ἐκπετάσουσι, πόδα | ναὸς ὠκυπόμπου, reading προτόνοις in place of πρότονοι or πρότονος. For πούς, see note 206 on p. 96.

[203] Aristotle, ethica Eudemia, iii. 1. 28, οὔτε γὰρ διὰ τὸ εἰδέναι τὰ φοβερὰ θαρροῦσιν οἱ ἐπὶ τοὺς ἱστοὺς ἀναβαίνειν ἐπιστάμενοι, ἀλλ' ὅτι ἴσασι τὰς βοηθείας τῶν δεινῶν. Cicero, de senectute, 6, alii malos scandant. Euripides, Hecuba, 1259— 1263, Π. ἀλλ' οὐ τάχ', ἤνίκ' ἄν σε ποντία νοτίς—Ε. μῶν ναυστολήσῃ γῆς ὅρους 'Ελληνίδος; Π. κρύψῃ μὲν οὖν πεσοῦσαν ἐκ καρχησίων. Ε. πρὸς τοῦ βιαίων τυγχάνουσαν ἁλμάτων; Π. αὐτὴ πρὸς ἱστὸν ναὸς ἀμβήσει ποδί. Lucian, navigium, 4, θαυμάζοντες ἀνιόντα τὸν ναύτην διὰ τῶν κάλων, εἶτα ἐπὶ τῆς κεραίας ἄνω ἀσφαλῶς διαθέοντα τῶν κεροιάκων ἐπειλημμένον, cf. Jupiter tragœdus, 48, καὶ ἐπὶ τὴν κεραίαν ἀναπηδῆσαι ῥάδιον. Ovid, metamorphoses, iii. 615, 616, quo non alius conscendere

halyards for the spritsail-yard ; and the spritsail and its yard would require sheets and brailing-ropes, braces and lifts. There are not any ratlines to the shrouds : and men had always to go aloft as best they could by climbing up the mast or any rope available[203].

The brailing-ropes were passed through rings upon the fore-side of the sail, and then through separate pulleys on the yard[204], as may be seen in fgs. 29 and 30; and from the yard they seem to have been carried to the stern and made fast to pins there, so that the steerer could manage them himself, whereas the larger ropes were attached to various windlasses about the ship and worked by his subordinates[205]. Curiously, the practice was always to brail up half the sail when the

summas | ocior antennas, prensoque rudente relabi. Galen, de usu partium, viii. 5, ἀλλὰ καὶ ὅσοι ταῖς κεραίαις τῶν πλοίων ἐπανίασι, πρότεροι τὴν γῆν καθορῶσι τῶν ἐν τῇ νηὶ πλωτήρων. In the passages just quoted from Euripides and Lucian the terms καρχησίων and κεροιάκων appear to be synonymous : see note 200 on p. 93. The terms κάλοι and *rudentes* could be applied to ropes of any kind, but generally were reserved for brailing-ropes. Virgil, Æneid, x. 229, *velis immitte rudentes,* cf. iii. 267, 682. Lucan, v. 426, 427, *totosque rudentes | laxavere sinus.* Lucian, amores, 6, εἶτ' ἀθρόας κατὰ τῶν κάλων τὰς ὀθόνας ἐκχέαντες. Satyrios Thyillos, in the Anthology, x. 5. 6, πᾶν λαῖφος ὕφεσθε κάλοις. See also the passages quoted in note 178 on p. 81.

[204] Synesios, epistolæ, p. 163 C, ὃ δὲ ἐποίει παρὰ πόδας τὸν κίνδυνον, οὐχ ἕτερον ἦν ἀλλ' ὅτι πᾶσιν ἱστίοις ἡ ναῦς ἐφέρετο, ὑποτεμέσθαι δὲ οὐκ ἦν, ἀλλὰ πολλάκις ἐπιχειρήσαντες τοῖς καλῳδίοις ἀπηγορεύκειμεν, τῶν τροχῶν ἐνδακόντων, κ.τ.λ.   p. 163 D, καὶ ἡ δρόσος ἐξισταμένη παρεῖχεν ἡμῖν κεχρῆσθαι τοῖς καλῳδίοις καὶ τὸ ἱστίον μεταχειρίζεσθαι.   p. 164 D, πάλιν δὲ δυσπειθὲς ἦν τὸ ἱστίον καὶ οὐκ εὔτροχον εἰς καθαίρεσιν. Synesios employs the phrase ὅλοις ἱστίοις, p. 160 C, as well as πᾶσιν ἱστίοις, p. 163 C. For the converse, see Aristophanes, ranæ, 999, 1000, ἄκροισι | χρώμενος τοῖς ἱστίοις, and Euripides, Medea, 524, ἄκροισι λαίφους κρασπέδοις.

[205] Plutarch, præcepta gerendæ rei publicæ, 15. 16, ὡς οἱ κυβερνῆται τὰ μὲν ταῖς χερσὶ δι' αὐτῶν πράττουσι, τὰ δ' ὀργάνοις ἑτέροις δι' ἑτέρων ἄπωθεν καθήμενοι περιάγουσι καὶ στρέφουσι. Lucian, navigium, 5, αἱ ἄγκυραι καὶ στροφεῖα καὶ περιαγωγεῖς καὶ αἱ κατὰ τὴν πρύμναν οἰκήσεις, θαυμάσια πάντα μοι ἔδοξε. Lucretius, iv. 905, 906, *multaque per trochleas et tympana pondere magno | commovet atque levi sustollit machina nisu.* These *trochleæ* and *tympana* are probably the στροφεῖα and περιαγωγεῖς, for the context is about a ship. Apollonios Rhodios, i. 566, 567, ἐπ' ἰκριόφιν δὲ κάλωας | ξεστῆσιν περόνῃσι διακριδὸν ἀμφιβαλόντες. The phrase ἐπ' ἰκριόφιν must here denote the stern, as in Odyssey, xiii. 74, already quoted in note 130 on p. 57. See also Oppian, de piscatione, i. 229, 230, πρύμνῃ δ' ἔπι πάντα χαλινὰ | ἰθυντὴρ ἀνίησι, and Valerius Flaccus, iv. 679, 680, *sed neque permissis iam fundere rector habenis | vela, nec eniti remis pote.* These *habenæ* or χαλινά are probably the brailing-robes ; and so also the κάλωες.

ship was put on either tack, the other half being thereby transformed into a triangle with base extending from the middle of the yard to the leeward end of it and apex terminating in the sheet below[206].

The sail used generally to be made of linen[207]; but the fibre of the papyrus and various other rushes was employed as well as flax in the manufacture of sail-cloth[208]. This cloth was probably of many different qualities; and two were

[206] Aristotle, mechanica, 8, διὰ τί, ὅταν ἐξ οὐρίας βούλωνται διαδραμεῖν μὴ οὐρίου τοῦ πνεύματος ὄντος, τὸ μὲν πρὸς τὸν κυβερνήτην τοῦ ἱστίου μέρος στέλλονται, τὸ δὲ πρὸς τὴν πρῴραν ποδιαῖον ποιησάμενοι ἐφιᾶσιν; ἢ διότι ἀντισπᾶν τὸ πηδάλιον πολλῷ μὲν ὄντι τῷ πνεύματι οὐ δύναται, ὀλίγῳ δέ, διὸ ὑποστέλλονται; προάγει μὲν οὖν τὸ πνεῦμα, εἰς οὔριον δὲ καθίστησι τὸ πηδάλιον, ἀντισπῶν καὶ μοχλεῦον τὴν θάλατταν. For ποδιαῖον read ποδωτόν, cf. Lycophron, 1015, ποδωτοῖς ἐμφορούμεναι λίνοις, sc. πνοαί. The passage shews that, when the yard was braced round, the sail was furled upon the arm that came aft, and left unfurled upon the arm that went forward. And clearly it was the arm to windward that was braced aft; for if this arm had been braced forward and carried the outstanding portion of the sail, the wind would have twisted the ship round until this portion of the sail had got to leeward of her. The manœuvre is described by Virgil, Æneid, v. 830—832, una omnes fecere pedem; pariterque sinistros, | nunc dextros, solvere sinus; una ardua torquent | cornua, detorquentque. The πούς or pes is mentioned frequently. Odyssey, x. 32; Pindar, Nemea, vi. 55—57; Sophocles, Antigone, 715—717; Euripides, Orestes, 706, 707; Lucian, Charon, 3; etc. Lucan, v. 427, 428; Catullus, 4. 19—21; Seneca, Medea, 320—322; Pliny, ii. 48; etc. This πούς, the corner of the sail, is not to be confounded with the πούς, the rope that held the corner: for which see notes 177 and 179 on pp. 81, 82.

[207] Æschylos, Prometheus, 468, λινόπτερ' εὗρε ναυτίλων ὀχήματα, sc. Προμηθεύς. Euripides, Iphigeneia in Tauris, 410, νάιον ὄχημα, λινοπόροισιν αὔραις, Hecuba, 1080, 1081, λινόκροκον | φᾶρος στέλλων. Oppian, de venatione, i. 121, λινοπτερύγων ὅπλα νηῶν. Apollonios Rhodios, i. 565, κὰδ δ' αὐτοῦ λίνα χεῦαν, sc. ἱστοῦ. Lucian, amores, 6, εἶτ' ἀθρόας κατὰ τῶν κάλων τὰς ὀθόνας ἐκχέαντες, ἠρέμα πιμπλαμένου τοῦ λίνου, κ.τ.λ. Meleager, in the Anthology, xii. 53. 8, οὔριος ὑμετέρας πνεύσεται εἰς ὀθόνας. Leonidas, ibid., x. 1. 6, πᾶσαν ἐφεὶς ὀθόνην. Lucilius, ibid., xi. 404. 4, διαπλεῖ σινδόν' ἐπαράμενος. Euripides, Phaethon, Fr. 2. 42, σινδὼν δὲ πρότονον ἐπὶ μέσον πελασσει. Athenæos, v. 39, βύσσινον ἔχων ἱστίον. cf. Herodotos, ii. 86, vii. 181, σινδόνος βυσσίνης. Livy, xxviii. 45, Tarquinienses lintea (dederunt) in vela. Virgil, Æneid, iii. 357, tumidoque inflatur carbasus austro, iv. 417, vocat iam carbasus auras. Ovid, heroides, 3. 58, te dare nubiferis linea vela notis, 7. 171, præbebis carbasa ventis, amores, ii. 11. 41, zephyri veniant in lintea pleni, metamorphoses, xi. 476, 477, totaque malo | carbasa deducit. Catullus, 64. 225, suspendam lintea malo, cf. 227, carbasus. Lucan, v. 428, obliquat lævo pede carbasa, cf. 430, lintea. All these terms, λίνον, linum, ὀθόνη, carbasus, σινδὼν and βύσσος, appear to be used promiscuously in reference to linen.

certainly in use in the Athenian navy about 330 B.C., the common sail being superseded by one of finer texture and higher price [209]. The edges of the sail used to be bound with hide; and the skins of the hyæna and the seal were especially in request for this, as there was a superstition among sailors that these would keep off lightning [210]. The ropes were sometimes made from strips of hide, but oftener from the fibre of the papyrus or from flax or hemp [211].

[208] Theophrastos, historia plantarum, iv. 8. 4, αὐτὸς δὲ ὁ πάπυρος πρὸς πλεῖστα χρήσιμος. καὶ γὰρ πλοῖα ποιοῦσιν ἐξ αὐτοῦ, καὶ ἐκ τῆς βύβλου ἱστία τε πλέκουσιν καὶ ψιάθους, κ.τ.λ. = Pliny, xiii. 22, ex ipso quidem papyro navigia texunt, et e libro vela tegetesque, etc. Herodotos, ii. 96, ἱστῷ δὲ ἀκανθίνῳ χρέονται, ἱστίοισι δὲ βυβλίνοισι. Pliny, xvi. 70, namque iis (scirpis) velificant, non in Pado tantum nautici, verum et in mari piscator Africus, præpostero more vela intra malos suspendens. In this passage Pliny uses intra as Herodotos uses ἔσωθεν in the passage quoted in note 178 on p. 81, and thus gives præpostero its literal meaning, the sail being set abaft of the mast.

[209] Corp Inscr. Attic. vol. ii, no. 807, col. a, ll. 55—58, [ἐ]ν νεωρίοις παρέδομεν [ἱ]στία, σὺν τῷ παλαιῷ, [ἐ]πὶ ναῦς ΗΗΡΔΔΔΓΙΙΙ. [τ]ούτων λεπτὰ ΡΔΔΙΙΙΙ.

no. 811, col. c, ll. 169—172, ἱστία λεπτὰ ΙΙ. ἀντὶ τούτων παρέδοσαν παχέα δύο.

ὑπὲρ τούτωμ προσοφείλουσιμ πρὸ[s] τὸ διάγραμμα ΗΗΗ.

[210] Plutarch, quæstiones convivales, iv. 2. 1, καὶ γὰρ ὁ γελώμενος οὑτοσὶ καὶ παροιμιώδης, ἔφη, βολβὸς οὐ μικρότητι διαφεύγει τὸν κεραυνόν, ἀλλ' ἔχων δύναμιν ἀντιπαθῆ, καθάπερ ἡ συκῆ καὶ τὸ δέρμα τῆς φώκης, ὥς φασι, καὶ τὸ τῆς ὑαίνης, οἷς τὰ ἄκρα τῶν ἱστίων οἱ ναύκληροι καταδιφθεροῦσι. Lucian, navigium, 4, παρὰ τὸν ἱστὸν ἐπὶ πολὺ ἔστημεν ἀναβλέποντες, ἀριθμοῦντες τῶν βυρσῶν τὰς ἐπιβολάς, κ.τ.λ. The sail itself was made of hide on the vessels in the Bay of Biscay. Cæsar, de bello Gallico, iii. 13, pelles pro velis alutæque tenuiter confectæ, sive propter lini inopiam atque eius usus inscientiam, sive eo (quod est magis verisimile) quod tantas tempestates oceani tantosque impetus ventorum sustineri ac tanta onera navium regi velis non satis commode posse arbitrabantur. cf. Dion Cassius, xxxix. 41, καὶ γὰρ ἱστία δερμάτινα εἶχον, ὥστε πᾶσαν τὴν τοῦ πνεύματος ἰσχὺν ἀπλήστως ἐσδέχεσθαι, Strabo, iv. 4. 1, ἦν γὰρ σκύτινα (τὰ ἱστία) διὰ τὴν βίαν τῶν ἀνέμων.

[211] Odyssey, ii. 426, ἕλκον δ' ἱστία λευκὰ ἐυστρέπτοισι βοεῦσιν. xii. 422, 423, αὐτὰρ ἐπ' αὐτῷ | ἐπίτονος βέβλητο, βοὸς ῥινοῖο τετευχώς. xxi. 390, 391, κεῖτο δ' ὑπ' αἰθούσῃ ὅπλον νεὸς ἀμφιελίσσης | βύβλινον, ᾧ ῥ' ἐπέδησε θύρας. Hermippos, apud Athenæum, i. 49, ταῦτα μὲν ἐντεῦθεν· κἄξ Αἰγύπτου τὰ κρεμαστά, | ἱστία καὶ βύβλους. Herodotos, vii. 25, παρεσκευάζετο δὲ καὶ ὅπλα ἔς τὰς γεφύρας βύβλινά τε καὶ λευκολίνου, ἐπιτάξας Φοίνιξί τε καὶ Αἰγυπτίοισι. cf. 34, τὴν μὲν λευκολίνου Φοίνικες, τὴν δ' ἑτέρην τὴν βυβλίνην Αἰγύπτιοι. Æschylos, Persæ, 69, λινοδέσμῳ σχεδίᾳ πορθμὸν ἀμείψας. Euripides, Iphigeneia in Tauris, 1043, οὗ ναῦς χαλινοῖς λινοδέτοις ὁρμεῖ σέθεν. Ovid, fasti, iii. 587, dumque parant torto subducere carbasa lino. Persius, v. 146, 147, tibi torta cannabe fulto | cœna sit in transtro?

T.   g

The sails used often to be coloured[212], a black sail being everywhere a sign of mourning, while a purple or vermilion sail was generally the badge of an admiral or a monarch; and on vessels employed as scouts in time of war the sails and ropes were dyed the colour of sea-water, so as to keep them out of sight.

In some cases the topsail seems to have been coloured, while the sail below was plain; and frequently a patchwork of colours was produced by using different stuffs in different sections of the ordinary sail, as shewn in the Egyptian ship of about 600 B.C. in fg. 12. Various inscriptions and devices used also to be woven on the sails, the titles and emblems of a Roman emperor being thus displayed upon his sail in characters of gold[213]. This practice is illustrated by the Roman relief of about 200 A.D. in fg. 29.

[212] Plutarch, Theseus, 17, πρότερον μὲν οὖν οὐδεμία σωτηρίας ἐλπὶς ὑπέκειτο· διὸ καὶ μέλαν ἱστίον ἔχουσαν, ὡς ἐπὶ συμφορᾷ προδήλῳ, τὴν ναῦν ἔπεμπον· τότε δὲ (Αἰγεὺς) ἔδωκεν ἕτερον ἱστίον λευκόν, κ.τ.λ. ὁ δὲ Σιμωνίδης οὐ λευκόν φησιν εἶναι τὸ δοθὲν ὑπὸ τοῦ Αἰγέως, ἀλλὰ "φοινίκεον ἱστίον ὑγρῷ πεφυρμένον πρίνου ἄνθει ἐριθάλλου." cf. Æschylos, septem adversus Thebas, 857, 858, μελάγκροκον | ναύστολον θεωρίδα, Philostratos, heroica, 9. 3, ἱστίοις μέλασι, 20. 25, μέλανα ἱστία. Athenæos, xii. 49, ἡ δὲ τριήρης ἐφ' ἧς (Ἀλκιβιάδης) κατέπλει, μέχρι μὲν τῶν κλείθρων τοῦ Πειραιέως προσέτρεχεν ἀλουργοῖς ἱστίοις, κ.τ.λ. cf. Plutarch, Alcibiades, 32, ἱστίῳ δ' ἀλουργῷ τὴν ναυαρχίδα προσφέρεσθαι τοῖς λιμέσιν, Antonius, 26, ἱστίων ἀλουργῶν ἐκπεπετασμένων. See also the passages quoted from Vegetius in note 89 on p. 35, from Suetonius in note 133 on p. 59, from Lucian, Athenæos and Seneca in note 195 on p. 90, and from Procopios and Pliny in note 214 on p. 99. Philostratos, imagines, i. 18, θύρως δ' οὑτοσὶ ἐκ μέσης νεὼς ἐκπέφυκε τὰ τοῦ ἱστοῦ πράσσων, καὶ ἱστία μεθῆπται ἀλουργῆ, μεταυγάζοντα ἐν τῷ κόλπῳ, χρυσαῖ δ' ἐνύφανται βάκχαι ἐν Τμώλῳ καὶ Διονύσου τὰν Λυδίᾳ. But here Philostratos is describing a picture of a ship, and may be thinking of the Peplos that was carried like a sail in the procession at the Panathenæa. Apparently the colours ἀλουργές and φοινίκεον differed only in their origin, one being obtained from the purple-fish, while the other (as Simonides remarks) was obtained from the ilex-berry. Lucian's πυραυγές is probably the same as Seneca's rubicundum; and this would be the colour of the rubrica or μίλτος mentioned by Procopios. The versicoloria of Pliny and Suetonius must be parti-coloured sails.

[213] Arrian, Fr. 19, apud Suidam, s. v. ναῦς:—καὶ ἐπ' ἄκρῳ τῷ ἱστίῳ τὸ βασιλικὸν ὄνομα, καὶ ὅσοις ἄλλοις βασιλεὺς γεραίρεται, χρυσῷ ἐγκεχαραγμένα. This refers to Trajan's ship on the Tigris. Apuleius, metamorphoses, xi. 16, huius felicis alvei nitens carbasus litteras voti intextas progerebat. ecce litteræ votum instaurabant de novi commeatus prospera navigatione. For the inscription v·l in fg. 29, see Corp. Inscr. Latin. vol. xiv, no. 2033; and also no. 456 for an inscription QQ·C·F·NAV upon a similar relief.

An admiral's ship was distinguished by some sort of flag in addition to any purple or vermilion sail that she might carry; and after dark a light was exhibited in lieu of the flag[214]. This light was simply for the guidance of the fleet, the admiral's ship leading the way, and the others requiring some indication of her course throughout the night. But in many fleets every ship was provided with a light; and here the admiral's ship must have carried her light in some distinctive place, or carried more than one, as was certainly the case in a Roman fleet in 204 B.C., where three lights were allotted to the admiral's ship and two to every transport, the ordinary war-ships carrying the single light[215]. An astute admiral would manage to mislead the enemy by screening or extinguishing the lights or setting them adrift on buoys[216].

---

[214] Herodotos, viii. 92, ὡς δὲ ἐσεῖδε τὴν νέα (Θεμιστοκλέος) ὁ Πολύκριτος, ἔγνω τὸ σημήιον ἰδὼν τῆς στρατηγίδος.   Appian, de bellis civilibus, v. 55, πλησίον τε ἦσαν ἀλλήλων ἤδη, καὶ αἱ ναυαρχίδες ἐκ τῶν σημείων ἐφαίνοντο, καὶ ἀλλήλαις προσέπλεον. ii. 89, οὐδενί τε ἐκφήνας ὅπη τὸν πλοῦν ποιήσεται, περὶ ἑσπέραν ἀνήγετο ἐπαγγείλας τοῖς λοιποῖς κυβερνήταις πρὸς τὸν λαμπτῆρα τῆς ἑαυτοῦ νεὼς καὶ μεθ' ἡμέραν πρὸς τὸ σημεῖον εὐθύνειν. cf. Diodoros, xx. 75, ἀκολουθεῖν τῇ στρατηγίδι νηὶ προσέχοντας τῷ λαμπτῆρι.   Xenophon, Hellenica, v. 1. 8, νυκτὸς δ' ἐπιγενομένης, φῶς ἔχων, ὥσπερ νομίζεται, ἀφηγεῖτο, ὅπως μὴ πλανῶνται αἱ ἑπόμεναι.   Procopios, de bello Vandalico, i. 13, τριῶν νεῶν, ἐν αἷς αὐτός τε καὶ ἡ θεραπεία ἔπλει, τὰ ἱστία ἐκ γωνίας τῆς ἄνω ἐς τριτημόριον μάλιστα ἔχρισε μίλτῳ, κοντούς τε ὀρθοὺς ἀναστήσας ἐν πρύμνῃ ἑκάστῃ ἀπεκρέμασεν ἀπ' αὐτῶν λύχνα, ὅπως ἔν τε ἡμέρᾳ καὶ νυκτὶ αἱ τοῦ στρατηγοῦ νῆες ἔκδηλοι εἶεν· αἷς δὴ ἔπεσθαι τοὺς κυβερνήτας ἐκέλευε πάντας.   Apparently the γωνία is here the mast-head, as in Herodotos, viii. 122. 2.   Pliny, xix. 5, tentatum est tigni linum quoque, et vestium insaniam accipere, in Alexandri Magni primum classibus, Indo amne navigantis, cum duces eius ac præfecti in certamine quodam variassent insignia navium: stupueruntque litora, flatu versicoloria implente. velo purpureo ad Actium cum M. Antonio Cleopatra venit, eodemque effugit. hoc fuit imperatoriæ navis insigne.   An admiral might display a coloured sail; but that could hardly be his σημεῖον or insigne, for no sail was carried in action.   Most likely he used a flag. Tacitus, historiæ, v. 22, prætoriam navem, vexillo insignem, abripiunt.   A lantern is represented on the three-banked ship on Trajan's column, hanging from the ornament above the stern.

[215] Livy, xxix. 25, lumina in navibus singula rostratæ, bina onerariæ haberent: in prætoria nave insigne nocturnum trium luminum fore.   These were the orders to Scipio's fleet on its voyage to Africa.

[216] Polyænos, v. 10. 2, λαμπτῆρας δ' ᾖρε τὸ πρόσθεν μέρος πεφραγμένους, ὅπως μὴ γνωρίζοιεν ἀπὸ τοῦ φωτὸς οἱ πολέμιοι τὸν ἐπίπλουν. cf. Philistos, Fr. 15, apud Pollucem, x. 116, ἐπαίρεσθαι λαμπτῆρας ἀντιπεφραγμένους.   Polyænos, vi. 11, καὶ νυκτὸς γενομένης ἐκέλευσεν ἆραι τοὺς λαμπτῆρας, οἷς αἱ τοῦ Διονυσίου νῆες εἴποντο.

g 2

A national flag, or something of the sort, used to be carried in battle by all the ships of a fleet, to distinguish them from ships belonging to the enemy[217]; and besides the flag that was distinctive of the admiral, a set of flags was carried on his ship for signalling. A purple flag was generally the signal for going into action, and there probably were flags of other colours; but attempts were made at semaphoring with a single flag[218], and occasionally the signal was given by flashing the sunlight from a shield[219]. In addition to the signal for going into action, there certainly were signals for getting under way, for altering the formation of the fleet by various manœuvres, for bringing to, for disembarking troops, and possibly for many other purposes[220]. Some flags are represented at the sterns of the Athenian ships of about 500 B.C. in fg. 19, and on the masts of the Roman ships of about 50 A.D. in fgs. 26 and 27.

μετὰ μικρὸν δὲ τούτους καθελόντες ἑτέρους καθῆκαν ἐς τὴν θάλατταν φελλοῖς μεγάλοις ἐφηρμοσμένους, κἀκ τοῦ φωτὸς ἐς τὸ πλάγιον ἐπιστρέψαντες ἔφθασαν, κ.τ.λ. Dion Cassius, xlix. 17, προεῖπε μέν σφισιν ὡς διὰ πελάγους τὸν πλοῦν ποιησόμενος, ἀποσβέσας δὲ τὸ φῶς ὃ ἐν τοῖς νυκτερινοῖς πλοῖς αἱ στρατηγίδες νῆες (ὅπως καὶ αἱ λοιπαὶ κατὰ πόδας αὐτῶν ἐφέπωνται) προδεικνύουσι, παρά τε τὴν Ἰταλίαν παρέπλευσε, κ.τ.λ. cf. Florus, iv. 8. 9, *fugiebat extincto prætoriæ navis lumine.*

[217] Appian, de bellis civilibus, v. 106, καὶ τὰ σημεῖα κατὰ ναῦς ἦρτο. Polyænos, viii. 53. 3, εἰ μὲν ἐδίωκεν αὐτὴ ναῦν Ἑλληνίδα, τὸ βαρβαρικὸν ἀνέτεινε σημεῖον, εἰ δὲ ὑπὸ Ἑλληνίδος νεὼς ἐδιώκετο, ἀνέτεινε τὸ Ἑλληνικόν, cf. 1, τὰ σημεῖα τὰ Περσικά. These can hardly be the same as the σημεῖα mentioned in note 150 on p. 67.

[218] Leo, tactica, xix. 41, τὸ δὲ σημεῖον ὑποσημαινέτω, ἢ ὀρθὸν ἱστάμενον, ἢ ἐπὶ δεξιὰ ἢ ἐπὶ ἀριστερὰ κλινόμενον καὶ ἐπὶ δεξιὰ πάλιν ἢ ἐπὶ ἀριστερὰ μεταφερόμενον, ἢ τινασσόμενον, ἢ ὑψούμενον, ἢ ταπεινούμενον, ἢ ὅλως ἀφαιρούμενον, ἢ μετατιθέμενον, ἢ διὰ τῆς ἐν αὐτῷ κεφαλῆς ἄλλοτε ἄλλως φαινομένης ἀλλασσόμενον, ἢ διὰ σχημάτων, ἢ διὰ χρωμάτων, οἷόν ποτε τοῖς παλαιοῖς ἐπράττετο. ἐν γὰρ πολέμου καιρῷ σημεῖον εἶχον τῆς συμβολῆς αἴροντες τὴν λεγομένην φοινικίδα. Diodoros, xiii. 46, καὶ τοῖς μὲν Λακεδαιμονίοις οὐδὲν ἐφαίνετο σύσσημον, τοῖς δ᾽ Ἀθηναίοις Ἀλκιβιάδης μετέωρον ἐποίησεν ἐπίσημον φοινικοῦν ἀπὸ τῆς ἰδίας νεώς, ὅπερ ἦν σύσσημον αὐτοῖς διατεταγμένον. xiii. 77, ἃ δὴ συνιδὼν ὁ Κόνων ἦρεν ἀπὸ τῆς ἰδίας νεὼς φοινικίδα· τοῦτο γὰρ ἦν τὸ σύσσημον τοῖς τριηράρχοις. cf. Polyænos, i. 48. 2, ἐπῆρε τὴν φοινικίδα· ἦν δὲ ἄρα μάχης σύνθημα τοῖς κυβερνήταις.

[219] Diodoros, xx. 51, Δημήτριος μὲν οὖν, τῶν ἐναντίων ἀποσχὼν ὡς ἂν τρεῖς σταδίους, ἦρε τὸ συγκείμενον πρὸς μάχην σύσσημον, ἀσπίδα κεχρυσωμένην, φανερὰν πᾶσιν ἐκ διαδοχῆς. Herodotos, vi. 115, τοῖσι Πέρσῃσι ἀναδέξαι ἀσπίδα ἐοῦσι ἤδη ἐν τῆσι νηυσί. Plutarch, Lysander, 11, κατὰ μέσον τὸν πόρον ἀσπίδα χαλκῆν ἐπάρασθαι πρῴραθεν ἐπίπλου σύμβολον=Xenophon, Hellenica, ii. 1. 27, ἆραι ἀσπίδα κατὰ μέσον τὸν πλοῦν.

On board a ship there was generally a lead for sounding ; and this seems to have been armed with grease to bring up samples of the bottom[221]. And it is said that ships were fitted with a pair of paddle-wheels for reckoning the distances they traversed ; the notion being that these wheels would be kept steadily in motion by the impact of the water on the paddles as the ship went on her course, and that her progress could therefore be computed from the number of revolutions they recorded[222]. But obviously this would be impracticable, unless the water were preternaturally smooth.

Ships generally were provided with a ladder or a gangway for people to come on board when the vessel was made fast to the shore. The ladder may be noticed at the stern of the Athenian ships of about 500 B.C. in fgs. 17 to 19 ; and this was probably its usual place, for it would be wanted hereabouts, as vessels usually were made fast by the stern. The

---

[220] Herodotos, vii. 128, ἐσβὰς ἐς Σιδωνίην νέα ἀνέδεξε σημήιον καὶ τοῖσι ἄλλοισι ἀνάγεσθαι. Thucydides, i. 49, συμμίξαντες δέ, ἐπειδὴ τὰ σημεῖα ἑκατέροις ἤρθη, ἐναυμάχουν. ii. 90, ἀπὸ σημείου ἑνὸς ἄφνω ἐπιστρέψαντες τὰς ναῦς μετωπηδὸν ἔπλεον. Xenophon, Hellenica, vi. 2. 30, ἐν δὲ τοῖς μεθ' ἡμέραν πλοῖς ἀπὸ σημείων τοτὲ μὲν ἐπὶ κέρως ἦγε, τοτὲ δ' ἐπὶ φάλαγγος, cf. 28. Dion Cassius, l. 31, καὶ μετὰ τοῦτο τὰ κέρατα ἐξαίφνης ἀμφότερα ἀπὸ σημείου ἐπεξαγαγὼν ἐπέκαμψεν. Polyænos, iii. 9. 63, ὡς δὲ ἤδη σύμμετρον ὑπέλαβεν εἶναι τὸ τῆς θαλάσσης βάθος, ἀνέτεινε τὸ σημεῖον τῆς ἐκβάσεως. Plutarch, Antonius, 67, ἐκείνη δέ, γνωρίσασα σημεῖον ἀπὸ τῆς νεώς, ἀνέσχε. Livy, xxxvii. 24, signo sublato ex prætoria nave, quo dispersam classem in unum colligi mos erat. Aulus Hirtius, de bello Alexandrino, 45, vexillo sublato, quo pugnandi dabat signum.

[221] Herodotos, ii. 5, ἔτι καὶ ἡμέρης δρόμον ἀπέχων ἀπὸ γῆς, κατεὶς καταπειρητηρίην πηλόν τε ἀνοίσεις καὶ ἐν ἕνδεκα ὀργυιῆσι ἔσεαι, cf. 28. Acts, xxvii. 28, καὶ βολίσαντες εὗρον ὀργυιὰς εἴκοσι, βραχὺ δὲ διαστήσαντες καὶ πάλιν βολίσαντες εὗρον ὀργυιὰς δεκαπέντε. Lucilius, apud Isidorum, origines, xix. 4. 10, hunc catapiratem puer eodem deferat unctum, | plumbi pauxillum rodus, linique metaxam. Statius, silvæ, iii. 2. 30, exploret rupes gravis arte molybdis.

[222] Vitruvius, x. 9. 5, traiicitur per latera parietum axis habens extra navem prominentia capita, in quæ includuntur rotæ diametro pedum quaternum, habentes circa frontes affixas pinnas aquam tangentes. 7, ita navis cum habuerit impetum aut remorum aut ventorum flatu, pinnæ quæ erunt in rotis tangentes aquam adversam, vehementi retrorsus impulsu coactæ versabunt rotas : eæ autem involvendo se agent axem, etc. Then, by means of cogged wheels, etc., a stone was dropped into a bronze pan at every four-hundredth revolution of the wheels outside. ita et sonitu et numero indicabit milliaria spatia navigationis. In thus reckoning that the ship would make 5000 ft. of headway during 400 revolutions of a wheel that was 4 ft. in diameter, Vitruvius is forgetting that water is not so firm as land

gangway was presumably a heavier structure than the ladder, if there was really any difference between the two; but the names seem to be used indiscriminately[223]. In the Athenian navy the war-ships carried two ladders apiece; and they also carried three poles of different sizes[224]. Such poles were needed whenever a ship had to be pushed off from the shore or kept at a distance from another ship: so they generally formed part of the outfit[225].

[223] Thucydides, iv. 12, καὶ ὁ μὲν (Βρασίδας) τούς τε ἄλλους τοιαῦτα ἐπέσπερχεν, καὶ τὸν ἑαυτοῦ κυβερνήτην ἀναγκάσας ὀκεῖλαι τὴν ναῦν ἐχώρει ἐπὶ τὴν ἀποβάθραν· καὶ πειρώμενος ἀποβαίνειν ἀνεκόπη ὑπὸ τῶν Ἀθηναίων, καὶ τραυματισθεὶς πολλὰ ἐλειποψύχησέ τε, καὶ πεσόντος αὐτοῦ ἐς τὴν παρεξειρεσίαν ἡ ἀσπὶς περιερρύη ἐς τὴν θάλασσαν. Diodoros, xii.'62, ἡ μὲν τριήρης ἐπώκειλεν, ὁ δὲ Βρασίδας ἐπιβὰς ἐπὶ τὴν τῆς νεὼς ἐπιβάθραν, κ.τ.λ. Plutarch, de gloria Atheniensium, 3, καὶ ὁ τὸν κυβερνήτην ἐπισπέρχων Βρασίδας ἐξοκέλλειν, καὶ χωρῶν ἐπὶ τὴν βάθραν, καὶ τραυματιζόμενος καὶ λιποψυχῶν καὶ ἀποκλίνων εἰς τὴν παρεξειρεσίαν. As a war-ship must have been beached stern forward on account of her ram, the term παρεξειρεσία must here denote the space abaft the oars, as in the passages quoted from Polyænos in note 170 on p. 75, not the space forward, as in those quoted from Thucydides in note 141 on p. 62. Herodotos, ix. 98, παρασκευασάμενοι ὧν ἐς ναυμαχίην καὶ ἀποβάθρας καὶ τὰ ἄλλα ὅσων ἔδεε, ἔπλωον ἐπὶ τῆς Μυκάλης. 99, προσσχόντες τὰς νέας ἀπέβησαν ἐς τὸν αἰγιαλόν. Lucian, dialogi mortuorum, 10. 10, εὖ ἔχει· ὥστε λῦε τὰ ἀπόγεια, τὴν ἀποβάθραν ἀνελώμεθα, τὸ ἀγκύριον ἀνεσπάσθω, κ.τ.λ. Polyænos, iv. 6. 8, ἄλλοι μὲν ἀνέσπων τὰ πρυμνήσια, ἄλλοι δὲ ἀνεῖλκον τὰς ἀποβάθρας, ἄλλοι δὲ ἀγκύρας ἀνιμῶντο. Euripides, Iphigeneia in Tauris, 1350—1352, οἱ δ᾽ ἐπωτίδων | ἀγκύρας ἐξανῆπτον, οἱ δὲ κλίμακας | ... | σπεύδοντες ἦγον διὰ χερῶν πρυμνήσια. In this passage there is obviously a lacuna. Theocritos, xxii. 30, 31, ἔνθα μιᾶς πολλοὶ κατὰ κλίμακος ἀμφοτέρων ἐξ | τοίχων ἄνδρες ἔβαινον Ἰησονίης ἀπὸ νηός. Arrian, anabasis, i. 19, κλίμακας φέρειν ἐπὶ τὰς πρῴρας τῶν τριηρῶν κελεύσας, ὡς κατὰ τὰ ἀπότομα τῆς νήσου, καθάπερ πρὸς τεῖχος, ἐκ τῶν νεῶν τὴν ἀπόβασιν ποιησόμενος. The κλίμακες and ἀποβάθρα seem to be distinguished in Latin as scalæ and pons respectively. Virgil, Æneid, x. 653, 654, forte ratis celsi coniuncta crepidine saxi | expositis stabat scalis et ponte parato, cf. 288. Statius, silvæ, iii. 2. 54, 55, iamque ratem terris divisit fune soluto | navita, et angustum deiecit in æquora pontem.

[224] Corp. Inscr. Attic. vol. ii, no. 793, col. a, ll. 28—37, [κλι]μακίδων ἀριθμὸς [Η]ΗΗΗΡΔΓ· [αὖτ]αι γίγνονται ἐπὶ [να]ῦς ΗΗΔΔΙΙ [καὶ] μία κλιμακίς. [κοντ]ῶν ἀρι[θμὸς Ρ̣Η]ΡΔΔΓΙΙ· [οὗτ]οι γίγνονται ἐπὶ [ν]αῦς ΗΗΔΔΓ καὶ κοντοὶ δύο, cf. no. 789, col. a, l. 21, κοντὸν μέγαν, no. 791, l. 29, κοντοῦ μικροῦ.

[225] Odyssey, ix. 487, 488, αὐτὰρ ἐγὼ χείρεσσι λαβὼν περιμήκεα κοντὸν | ὦσα παρέξ. Thucydides, ii. 84, καὶ ναῦς τε νηὶ προσέπιπτε καὶ τοῖς κοντοῖς διωθοῦντο. cf. Procopius, de bello Vandalico, i. 13, τοῖς κοντοῖς διωθούμενοι. Euripides, Iphigeneia in Tauris, 1350, κοντοῖς δὲ πρῷραν εἶχον. Virgil, Æneid, v. 208, 209, ferratasque trudes et acuta cuspide contos | expediunt. See also Tacitus, annales, xiv. 5, and Suetonius, Tiberius, 62, Caligula, 32.

A small boat used to be towed astern by every merchant-ship of any size, and also by the war-ships in the Roman navy ; and occasionally a merchant-ship took two or three. The boat was intended for the safety of the crew in case the ship were wrecked or had to be abandoned ; and ordinarily was used for communicating with the shore when the ship was lying some way out[226]. Apparently, the Roman and Byzantine merchant-ships had some means of hoisting up the boat[227]

[226] Demosthenes, in Phormionem, 10, ὁ δὲ Λάμπις ἀναχθεὶς ἐναυάγησεν οὐ μακρὰν ἀπὸ τοῦ ἐμπορίου. καὶ αὐτὸς μὲν ἀπεσώθη ἐν τῷ λέμβῳ, κ.τ.λ., in Zenothemin, 6, ῥίπτει ἑαυτὸν ('Ηγέστρατος) εἰς τὴν θάλατταν, διαμαρτὼν δὲ τοῦ λέμβου διὰ τὸ νύκτ' εἶναι, ἀπεπνίγη, 7, ἔπειθε (Ζηνόθεμις) τὸν πρῳρέα καὶ τοὺς ναύτας εἰς τὸν λέμβον ἐμβαίνειν καὶ ἐκλείπειν τὴν ναῦν τὴν ταχίστην, ὡς ἀνελπίστου τῆς σωτηρίας οὔσης καὶ καταδυσομένης τῆς νεὼς αὐτίκα μάλα. Anaxandrides, apud Athenæum, vi. 41, ὑμεῖς γὰρ ἀλλήλους ἀεὶ χλευάζετ', οἶδ' ἀκριβῶς · | ὄπισθεν ἀκολουθεῖ κόλαξ τῳ, λέμβος ἐπικέκληται. cf. Pliny, epistolæ, viii. 20. 7, sæpe minores maioribus velut cymbulæ onerariis adhærescunt. Plutarch, Demetrius, 17, προσέχειν μὲν οὐκ εἴασε τῇ γῇ τὸ πλοῖον, ἀγκύρας δ' ἀφεῖναι κελεύσας καὶ κατὰ ναῦν ἔχειν ἀτρέμα πάντας, αὐτὸς ἐμβὰς εἰς τὸ ἐφόλκιον ἐξῆλθε μόνος. Heliodoros, Æthiopica, v. 24, ἐπιτρέπομεν εἰς τὸ ἐφόλκιον εἰσβῆναι καὶ σώζειν αὐτούς, εἰ βούλεσθε...τῶν δ' εἰς τὸ σκάφος τὸ ὑπηρετικὸν ἄλλεσθαι καὶ διαδρᾶναι βουλευομένων. In the Acts of the Apostles, xxvii. 16, 30, 32—see next note—the term σκάφη is applied to the ship's boat in imitation of the Latin usage of scapha. Plautus, rudens, prologus, 75, de navi timidæ desuluerunt in scapham. The Pandects, xxxiii. 7. 29, Labeo :—si navem cum instrumento emisti, præstari tibi debet scapha navis. Paulus :—imo contra ; etenim scapha navis non est instrumentum navis ; etenim mediocritate, non genere ab ea differt ; instrumentum autem cuiusque rei necesse est alterius generis esse atque ea quæque sit ; quod Pomponio placuit, cf. xxi. 2. 44 and vi. 1. 3. Thus, as a rule, every ship had one boat and no more : but there were exceptions to this rule. Strabo, ii. 3. 4, κατασκευάσασθαι πλοῖον μέγα καὶ ἐφόλκια δύο λέμβοις λῃστρικοῖς ὅμοια. Athenæos, v. 43, ἐφόλκια δ' ἦσαν αὐτῇ τὸ μὲν πρῶτον κέρκουρος, κ.τ.λ. The Roman war-ships had boats as well as the merchant-ships : see Cæsar, de bello Gallico, iv. 26, de bello civili, ii. 43, iii. 24, 62, 101, and Aulus Hirtius, de bello Alexandrino, 46.

[227] Acts, xxvii. 16, νησίον δέ τι ὑποδραμόντες, καλούμενον Καῦδα, ἰσχύσαμεν μόλις περικρατεῖς γενέσθαι τῆς σκάφης · ἣν ἄραντες κ.τ.λ. 30, τῶν δὲ ναυτῶν ζητούντων φυγεῖν ἐκ τοῦ πλοίου καὶ χαλασάντων τὴν σκάφην εἰς τὴν θάλασσαν προφάσει ὡς ἐκ πρῴρης ἀγκύρας μελλόντων ἐκτείνειν,...32, τότε ἀπέκοψαν οἱ στρατιῶται τὰ σχοινία τῆς σκάφης, καὶ εἴασαν αὐτὴν ἐκπεσεῖν. cf. Paulinus Nolanus, epistolæ, 49· 1, rumpentibus (anchorarum) vinculis nautæ exterriti scaphulam demiserunt ; vel ut navi fortius continendæ renovatis et altius stabilitis anchoris subvenirent, vel ut seipsos, si possent, a discrimine navis eriperent. Agathias, iii. 21, νῆες δὲ φορτίδες μεγάλαι μετεώρους εἶχον τὰς ἀκάτους, καὶ ἀμφ' αὐτὰ δήπου τὰ καρχήσια τῶν ἱστῶν ἀνιμηθείσας καὶ βεβαιότατα αἰωρουμένας · ἄνω δὲ στρατιῶται εἰστήκεσαν, cf. 25, τῶν δὲ ταῖς ἀκάτοις ἐφεστηκότων.

instead of always towing it astern: and on the Roman
merchant-ships of about 200 A.D. in fgs. 29 and 31 the
halyards of the artemon, or bowsprit, seem to be attached to
something like a boat. It was now the custom to have one of
the crew constantly on duty in the boat, when towing astern,
in order to keep her under control and free from water[228].

[228] Petronius, satiræ, 102, *quin potius, inquam ego, ad temeritatem confugimus
et per funem lapsi descendimus in scapham præcisoque vinculo reliqua fortunæ
committimus?...nunc per puppim, per ipsa gubernacula delabendum est, a quorum
regione funis descendit qui scaphæ custodiam tenet. præterea illud miror, Encolpi,
tibi non succurrisse, unum nautam stationis perpetuæ interdiu noctuque iacere in
scapha, nec posse inde custodem nisi aut cæde expelli aut præcipitari viribus. quod
an fieri possit, interrogate audaciam vestram.* Gregory the Great, dialogi, iv.' 57,
ὁ ναύτης δὲ αὐτοῦ, Βάρακος ὀνόματι, ἐκυβέρνα τὸν κάραβον ὄπισθεν τοῦ πλοίου· τοῦ δὲ
σχοινίου κοπέντος, ἅμα τῷ καράβῳ ὃν ἐκυβέρνα ὑψωθείς, ἐν τοῖς κύμασιν ἀφανὴς ἐγένετο.
The Rhodian Law, in the Basilics, liii. 8. 46, ἐὰν κάραβος, ἀπὸ ἰδίου πλοίου τὰ
σχοινία διαρρήξας, ἀπόληται ἅμα τοῖς ἐμπλέουσιν ἐν αὐτῷ, ἐὰν οἱ ἐμπλέοντες ἀπό-
λωνται ἢ ἀποθάνωσι, τὸν μισθὸν τὸν ἐνιαυσιαῖον ἀποδιδότω ὁ ναύκληρος εἰς πλῆρες τοῦ
ἐνιαυτοῦ τοῖς τῶν ναυτῶν κληρονόμοις.

APPENDIX.

Actuariæ, Ἄκατοι.

These were small craft of all sorts. They were classed together in this fashion in compliance with a notion that ships might roughly be divided into three classes, men-of-war or long ships, merchant-men or round ships, and these boats or little ships. Thucydides, vii. 59, ἔκλῃον οὖν τόν τε λιμένα εὐθὺς τὸν μέγαν τριήρεσι πλαγίαις καὶ πλοίοις καὶ ἀκάτοις, ἐπ᾽ ἀγκυρῶν ὁρμίζοντες, κ.τ.λ. = Diodoros, xiii. 14, ἀκάτους τε γὰρ καὶ τριήρεις, ἔτι δὲ στρογγύλας ναῦς ἐπ᾽ ἀγκυρῶν ὁρμίσαντες. Plutarch, de tranquillitate animi, 3, ἀλλ᾽ ὥσπερ οἱ δειλοὶ καὶ ναυτιῶντες ἐν τῷ πλεῖν, εἶτα ῥᾷον οἰόμενοι διάξειν, ἐὰν εἰς γαῦλον ἐξ ἀκάτου, καὶ πάλιν ἐὰν εἰς τριήρη μεταβῶσιν, οὐδὲν περαίνουσι. Pindar, Nemea, v. 5, ἀλλ᾽ ἐπὶ πάσας ὁλκάδος ἔν τ᾽ ἀκάτῳ, γλυκεῖ᾽ ἀοιδά. Thus the ἄκατοι were distinguished from merchant-ships of every sort, and also from the three-banked ships, which were the typical warships. And this distinction was based upon their size; for at the time when the Athenian three-banked ships carried two masts—see note 181 on p. 83—these masts were styled ἱστὸς μέγας and ἱστὸς ἀκάτειος respectively, as though ἀκάτειος merely denoted inferiority in size. cf. Theophrastos, historia plantarum, v. 7. 2, τὴν δὲ τρόπιν (ποιοῦσι) τριήρει μὲν δρυΐνην, ταῖς δὲ ὁλκάσι πευκίνην, ταῖς δὲ ἐλάττοσιν ὀξυΐνην, where ἀκάτοις is replaced by ἐλάττοσιν.

Aulus Hirtius, de bello Alexandrino, 44, *nam cum ipse* (*Vatinius*) *paucas in portu naves longas haberet, navibus actuariis, quarum numerus erat satis magnus, magnitudine quamquam non satis iusta ad prœliandum, rostra imposuit.* Sisenna, apud Nonium, p. 535, *quibus occisis, actuarias ad viginti navis, item conplures onerarias incendunt.* Marcellus, in the Pandects, xlix. 15. 2, *navibus longis atque onerariis propter belli usum postliminium est: non piscatoriis, aut si quas actuarias voluptatis causa paraverunt.* Thus the *actuariæ*, like the ἄκατοι, were distinguished from the merchant-ships and from the war-ships; and Aulus Hirtius implies that the distinction was based upon their size.

There is plainly an error in the current reading of Livy, xxxviii. 38, *tradito et naves longas armamentaque earum : neve plures quam decem naves actuarias, quarum nulla plus quam triginta remis agatur, habeto: neve monerem ex belli causa, quod ipse illaturus erit* = Polybios, xxii. 26, ἀποδότω δὲ καὶ τὰς ναῦς τὰς μακρὰς καὶ τὰ ἐκ τούτων ἄρμενα καὶ τὰ σκεύη· καὶ μηκέτι ἐχέτω πλὴν δέκα καταφράκτων· μηδὲ τριακοντάκωπον ἐχέτω, μηδὲ ἐλαυνόμενον πολέμου ἕνεκεν, οὗ ἂν αὐτὸς κατάρχῃ, where both authors are quoting from the treaty of 189 B.C. In quoting from the treaty of 197 B.C. Livy says *naves tectas*, xxxiii. 30, while Polybios says καταφράκτους ναῦς, xviii. 27; so that in quoting from this treaty of 189 B.C. he must have said *decem naves tectas habeto : neve actuarias*. Consequently, the passage will not identify the *actuariæ* with the κατάφρακτοι but will only shew that these vessels often carried more than thirty oars. The term *actuarius* had a diminutive *actuariolus;* and this is applied to some ten-oared vessels by Cicero, ad Atticum, xvi. 3. 6, *conscendens e Pompeiano tribus actuariolis decemscalmis.*

The term ἄκατος could be applied to vessels that were small enough for the oars to be sculled in pairs, or to vessels that were large enough to require fifty rowers. Leonidas of Tarentum, in the Anthology, vi. 4. 6, καὶ τοὺς ἐξ ἀκάτων διχθαδίους ἐρέτας. cf. vii. 464. 1, ix. 242. 8, 279. 1, where Charon's boat is styled an ἄκατος. Lucian, veræ historiæ, i. 5, πεντήκοντα δὲ τῶν ἡλικιωτῶν προσεποιησάμην τὴν αὐτὴν ἐμοὶ γνώμην ἔχοντας, καὶ κυβερνήτην τὸν ἄριστον μισθῷ μεγάλῳ πείσας παρέλαβον, καὶ τὴν ναῦν—ἄκατος δὲ ἦν—ὡς πρὸς μέγαν καὶ βίαιον πλοῦν ἐκρατυνάμην. Apparently, the diminutive term ἀκάτιον could not be applied to such large vessels as those of fifty oars. Polybios, i. 73, παρεσκεύαζον δὲ καὶ τὰ περιλιπῆ τῶν πλοίων, τριήρεις, καὶ πεντηκοντόρους, καὶ τὰ μέγιστα τῶν ἀκατίων. This term was used in speaking of vessels that were carried about in carts or on men's shoulders. Thucydides, iv. 67, ἀκάτιον ἀμφηρικὸν ὡς λῃσταὶ εἰώθεσαν ἐπὶ ἁμάξῃ διὰ τῆς τάφρου κατακομίζειν τῆς νυκτὸς ἐπὶ τὴν θάλασσαν καὶ ἐκπλεῖν. Plutarch, Lucullus, 9, τῆς δὲ Δασκυλίτιδος λίμνης πλεομένης ἀκατίοις ἐπιεικῶς εὐμεγέθεσι, τὸ μέγιστον αὐτῶν ὁ Λούκουλλος ἀνελκύσας καὶ διαγωγὼν ἁμάξῃ πρὸς τὴν θάλατταν ὅσους ἐχώρει στρατιώτας ἐνεβίβασεν. See also Strabo, xi. 2. 12, quoted in the note on *camaræ* on p. 107. But the diminutive was not indispensable. Agathias, iii. 20, τὰς ἀκάτους, ὁπόσας ἐφ᾽ ἁμαξῶν ἐπήγετο, ἐς τὸν ποταμὸν ἐμβαλών.

In common parlance the term ἄκατος was used as vaguely as *boat* is used in English. Theognis, 457—459, οὔτοι σύμφορόν ἐστι γυνὴ νέα ἀνδρὶ γέροντι | οὐ γὰρ πηδαλίῳ πείθεται ὡς ἄκατος, | οὐδ᾽ ἄγκυραι ἔχουσιν. Critias, apud Athenæum, i. 50, Θήβη δ᾽ ἁρματόεντα δίφρον συνεπήξατο πρώτη· | φορτηγοὺς δ᾽ ἀκάτους Κᾶρες, ἁλὸς ταμίαι. Herodotos, vii. 186, τοὺς ἐν ταῖσι σιταγωγοῖσι ἀκάτοισι ἐόντας = vii. 184, τῶν σιταγωγῶν πλοίων καὶ ὅσοι ἐνέπλωον τούτοισι. Diodoros, xvii. 116, καὶ πλέοντος μετὰ τῶν φίλων ἔν τισιν ἀκάτοις, ἐφ᾽ ἡμέρας μέν τινας ἀποσχισθείσης τῆς νεὼς ἀπὸ τῶν ἄλλων σκαφῶν, ἐπλανήθη μόνος, κ.τ.λ. The diminutive term ἀκάτιον was used in the same vague way. Dion Chrysostom, oratio 72, p. 628, ὥστε καὶ ἐφ᾽ ἡμῶν ἴσως ῥηθῆναι εἰκότως, ὅτι πλεῖ πάντα ὁμοίως ἀκάτια καὶ πᾶσα βοῦς ἀροτριᾷ. And so also *acatium* in Latin. Pliny, ix. 49, *navigeram similitudinem et aliam in Propontide visam sibi prodidit Mutianus: concham esse acatii modo carinatam, inflexa puppe, prora rostrata : in hac condi nauplium*, where the phrase *acatii modo carinatam* merely expresses the fact that there was a ridge along the shell like the keel of a boat. It was clearly for a joke that the name *Acatus* was given to the great ship that brought the Flaminian obelisk to Italy : see note 71 on p. 27.

Barides, Βάριδες.

This term could be applied to ships or boats of any sort, provided that they hailed from Egypt or some other foreign country.

Æschylos, Persæ, 552, 553, Ξέρξης δὲ πάντ᾽ ἐπέσπε δυσφρόνως | βαρίδεσσι ποντίαις, 1074, 1075, τρισκάλμοισι | βάρισιν ὀλόμενοι, i.e. τριήρεσιν. Euripides, Iphigeneia in Aulide, 297, βαρβάρους βάριδας. Æschylos, supplices, 874, Αἰγυπτίαν γὰρ βᾶριν οὐχ ὑπερθορεῖ, cf. 836, 882. Propertius, iii. 11. 44, baridos et contis rostra Liburna sequi. The allusion is to Cleopatra's ships at the battle of Actium. Herodotos, ii. 96, τοῦτο γὰρ δὴ οὔνομά ἐστι τοῖσι πλοίοισι τούτοισι, sc. βᾶρις. He is speaking here of trading-vessels on the Nile: see also ii. 41, 179. Diodoros, i. 96, συμφωνεῖν δὲ καὶ τἄλλα τὰ παρὰ τοῖς Ἕλλησι καθ᾽ Ἅιδου μυθολογούμενα τοῖς ἔτι νῦν γινομένοις κατ᾽ Αἴγυπτον· τὸ μὲν γὰρ διακομίζον τὰ σώματα πλοῖον βᾶριν καλεῖσθαι, κ.τ.λ. cf. Leonidas of Tarentum, in the Anthology, vii. 67, Ἀΐδεω λυπηρὲ διηκόνε, τοῦτ᾽ Ἀχέροντος | ὕδωρ ὃς πλώεις πορθμίδι κυανέῃ, | δέξαι μ᾽, εἰ καί σοι μέγα βρίθεται ὀκρυόεσσα | βᾶρις, ἀποφθίμενον, τὸν κύνα Διογένην. The word was barit, bari, or baair in Egyptian.

Camaræ, Καμάραι.

These were boats of very light build, holding twenty-five to thirty men apiece. The stern was like the stem, and the oars were arranged for rowing either way. The bottom was rather flat, and the sides were so low that temporary bulwarks were needed in rough weather. These vessels were in use on the Black Sea in the First Century A.D. Strabo, xi. 2. 12, ζῶσι δὲ ἀπὸ τῶν κατὰ θάλατταν λῃστηρίων, ἀκάτια ἔχοντες λεπτά, στενὰ καὶ κοῦφα, ὅσον ἀνθρώπους πέντε καὶ εἴκοσι δεχόμενα, σπάνιον δὲ τριάκοντα δέξασθαι τοὺς πάντας δυνάμενα· καλοῦσι δ᾽ αὐτὰ οἱ Ἕλληνες καμάρας...... ἐπανιόντες δὲ εἰς τὰ οἰκεῖα χωρία, ναυλοχεῖν οὐκ ἔχοντες, ἀναθέμενοι τοῖς ὤμοις τὰς καμάρας ἀναφέρουσιν ἐπὶ τοὺς δρυμούς, ἐν οἷσπερ καὶ οἰκοῦσι, λυπρὰν ἀρούντες γῆν· καταφέρουσι δὲ πάλιν, ὅταν ᾖ καιρὸς τοῦ πλεῖν. τὸ δ᾽ αὐτὸ ποιοῦσι καὶ ἐν τῇ ἀλλοτρίᾳ. Tacitus, historiæ, iii. 47, camaras vocant artis lateribus latam alvum sine vinculo æris aut ferri conexam: et tumido mari, prout fluctus attollunt, summa navium tabulis augent, donec in modum tecti claudantur. sic inter undas volvuntur, pari utrimque prora et mutabili remigio, quando hinc vel illinc appellere indiscretum et innoxium est. By thus contrasting the latam alvum with the artis lateribus Tacitus implies that the bottom was broad considering the height of the sides, not that it was broad considering the size of the boat: so he hardly contradicts Strabo's statement that these boats were narrow.

Κάνθαροι, Κυκνοκάνθαροι, Κύκνοι.

These were merchant-ships of types that were in vogue among the Greeks in the Fourth and Fifth Centuries B.C. The κυκνοκάνθαροι were presumably of a type between the κάνθαροι and the κύκνοι. Nicostratos, apud Athenæum, xi. 48, A. ἡ ναῦς δὲ πότερ᾽ εἰκόσορός ἐστιν, ἢ κύκνος, | ἢ κάνθαρος; τουτὶ γὰρ ἐὰν πύθωμ᾽ ὅ τι, | αὐτὸς περανῶ τὰ πάντ᾽. Β. ἀμέλει κυκνοκάνθαρος. This indicates that these vessels all resembled an εἰκόσορος, and an εἰκόσορος was usually a large merchant-ship with twenty oars for auxiliary work: see note 51 on p. 20. Ships termed κάνθαροι are also mentioned by Sosicrates, ibid., λεπτὴ δὲ κυρτοῖς ἐγγελῶσα κύμασιν | αὔρα, κόρη Σκείρωνος, ἡσύχῳ ποδὶ | προσῆγε πρᾴως καὶ καλῶς τὸν κάνθαρον. Again by Menander, ibid., A. ὡς ἐς καλὸν | τὸν υἱὸν εὐτυχοῦντα καὶ σεσωσμένον | πρῶτος λέγω σοι, τόν τε χρυσοῦν κάνθαρον. | Β. ποῖον; Α. τὸ πλοῖον· οὐδὲν οἶσθας, ἄθλιε. | Β. τὴν ναῦν σεσῶσθαί μοι λέγεις; Α. ἔγωγε μὴν | τὴν ναῦν ἐκείνην, ἣν ἐποίησε Καλλικλῆς | ὁ Καλύμνιος, Εὐφράνωρ δ᾽ ἐκυβέρνα Θούριος. And by Aristophanes, pax, 143, τὸ δὲ πλοῖον ἔσται Ναξιουργὴς κάνθαρος. But there is not any further mention of ships termed κύκνοι or κυκνοκάνθαροι.

Caudicariæ or Codicariæ.

This name was given to vessels plying on the Tiber, and hence to those on other rivers. It was reputed to be an early Latin name for boats or ships.

Seneca, de brevitate vitæ, 13, *hoc quoque quærentibus remittamus, quis Romanis primus persuaserit navem conscendere?* Claudius *is fuit, Caudex ob hoc ipsum appellatus, quia plurium tabularum contextus caudex apud antiquos vocatur, unde publicæ tabulæ codices dicuntur et naves nunc quoque, quæ ex antiqua consuetudine commeatus per Tiberim subvehunt, codicariæ vocantur.* Varro, apud Nonium, p. 535, *quod antiqui pluris tabulas coniunctas codices dicebant; a quo in Tiberi navis codicarias appellamus.* The boatmen on the Tiber are mentioned frequently: *e.g.* Corp. Inscr. Latin. vol. xiv, no. 131, l. 7, *codicari nabiculari*, no. 170, l. 10, *codicarii navicularii*, no. 4234, l. 5, *codicarius*, vol. vi, no. 1759, l. 15, *caudicariis.* Sallust, apud Nonium, p. 535, *quam maximis itineribus per regnum Ariobarzanis contendit ad flumen Euphraten qua in parte Cappadocia ab Armenia diiungitur; naves codicariæ, occulte per hiemem fabricatæ, aderant.* Ausonius, idyllia, 10. 197, *navita caudiceo fluitans super æquora lembo.* This refers to the Moselle.

At Ostia, near the mouth of the Tiber, there was a guild of these boatmen with the title of *corpus splendedissimum codicariorum* : see Corp. Inscr. Latin. vol. xiv, no. 4144, l. 12.

Celoces, Κέλητες, Κελήτια.

These were small vessels built especially for speed, and hence styled race-horses. They served for carrying reports and orders and despatches, and taking officers of rank from place to place; and generally discharged the duties that are now allotted to a despatch-boat or admiral's-yacht. They were in use in most navies in the first five centuries B.C.

Thucydides, iv. 120, ἀποστᾶσι δ᾽ αὐτοῖς ὁ Βρασίδας διέπλευσε νυκτὸς ἐς τὴν Σκιώνην, τριήρει μὲν φιλίᾳ προπλεούσῃ, αὐτὸς δὲ ἐν κελητίῳ ἄποθεν ἐφεπόμενος, ὅπως εἰ μέν τινι τοῦ κέλητος μείζονι πλοίῳ περιτυγχάνοι, ἡ τριήρης ἀμύνοι αὐτῷ, ἀντιπάλου δὲ ἄλλης τριήρους ἐπιγενομένης οὐ πρὸς τὸ ἔλασσον νομίζων τρέψεσθαι ἀλλ᾽ ἐπὶ τὴν ναῦν, καὶ ἐν τούτῳ αὐτὸν διασώσειν. There is clearly an error here, κέλητος for κελητίου, or else κελητίῳ for κέλητι. The scholiast's paraphrase makes the vessel a κελήτιον in both instances; so his reading was κελητίου. Polybios, v. 94, αὖθις δ᾽ ὑποστρέψας, ἔπλευσε πρὸς Χάλκειαν· τῶν δ᾽ ἐκβοηθησάντων, ἐκυρίευσε δύο μακρῶν πλοίων αὐτάνδρων· ἔλαβε δὲ καὶ κέλητα περὶ τὸ Ῥίον Αἰτωλικὸν ὁμοῦ τῷ πληρώματι. Livy, xxi. 17, *naves longæ centum sexaginta, celoces duodecim.* So the κέλητες were reckoned among the small craft in a fleet. Polybios elsewhere speaks of them as vessels of a single bank, v. 62, καὶ πλοῖα τετταράκοντα· τούτων κατάφρακτα μὲν εἴκοσι διαφέροντα ταῖς κατασκευαῖς, ἐν οἷς οὐδὲν ἔλαττον ἦν τετρήρους· τὰ δὲ λοιπά, τριήρεις καὶ δίκροτα καὶ κέλητες, cf. Fr. 132, apud Suidam, s.v. ὑπερισθμίσας:—ταχὺ δέ, τοὺς κέλητας καὶ τὰς ἡμιολίας ὑπερισθμίσας, ἀνήχθη. Nor is he really contradicted herein by Ephippos, apud Athenæum, viii. 38, πέντε κέλητας πεντεσκάλμους. At this time the compounds formed from σκαλμός were used in reckoning the tholes vertically, and thus marked the number of banks of oars in a ship; so that πεντέσκαλμος denoted a ship of five banks, just as τρίσκαλμος denoted a ship of three banks: Æschylos, Persæ, 679, 680, ἐξέφθινθ' αἱ τρίσκαλμοι | ναῦς ἄναες, 1074, 1075, τρισκάλμοισι | βάρισιν ὀλόμενοι, cf. Polybios, xvi. 3, ταύτῃ δοῦσα πληγὴν βιαίαν κατὰ μέσον τὸ κῦτος ὑπὸ τὸν θρανίτην σκαλμόν, where θρανίτης σκαλμός must refer to the upper bank. But the verse occurs in a passage where Ephippos is mercilessly ridiculing the ostentation of Alexander the Great; and his statement that the king's κέλητες had five banks of oars—the largest number then in use— must not be taken a whit more seriously than the rest of his exaggerations.

Thucydides, iv. 9, οὐ γὰρ ἦν ὅπλα ἐν χωρίῳ ἐρήμῳ πορίσασθαι, ἀλλὰ καὶ ταῦτα ἐκ λῃστρικῆς Μεσσηνίων τριακοντόρου καὶ κέλητος ἔλαβον, οἳ ἔτυχον παραγενόμενοι· ὁπλῖταί τε τῶν Μεσσηνίων τούτων ὡς τεσσαράκοντα ἐγένοντο. Fully thirty of these men would be needed for the τριακόντορος, leaving barely ten for the κέλης. A four-oared κελήτιον is mentioned by Appian, de bellis civilibus, ii. 56, κελήτιον ὀξὺ καὶ κυβερνήτην τὸν ἄριστον ἔμελλον ἑτοιμάσειν, for the number of oars is fixed by Velleius, ii. 43, quattuor scalmorum navem una cum duobus amicis decemque servis ingressus = Plutarch, Cæsar, 38, εἰς πλοῖον ἐμβὰς τὸ μέγεθος δωδεκάσκαλμον, where the assertion that the boat was large enough for twelve oars seems to be based upon the story that Cæsar had twelve companions on this voyage. A two-oared κελήτιον is mentioned by Synesios, epistolæ, p. 165, ἧκεν ἐπὶ κελητίου δισκάλμου. At this time the compounds formed from σκαλμός were used in reckoning the tholes horizontally, and thus marked the number of oars in a ship of a single bank. They are used in this sense by Cicero, ad Atticum, xvi. 3. 6, tribus actuariolis decemscalmis, de oratore, i. 38, duorum scalmorum naviculam. And apparently also by Diodoros, xl. 1, δόγμα ἔγραψαν ὅπως οἱ Κρῆτες πάντα τὰ πλοῖα ἕως τετρασκάλμου ἀναπέμψωσιν εἰς Ῥώμην, and by Plutarch, Æmilius Paulus, 6, τὰς δὲ ναῦς ἀπάσας ἀφείλετο καὶ πλοῖον οὐδὲν αὐτοῖς τρισκάλμου μεῖζον ἀπέλιπε, cf. Theseus, 19, δόγμα κοινὸν ἦν Ἑλλήνων μηδεμίαν ἐκπλεῖν τριήρη μηδαμόθεν ἀνδρῶν πέντε πλείονας δεχομένην, where τριήρης refers to fighting-ships of any sort.

Xenophon, Hellenica, i. 6. 36, τῷ δ' Ἐτεονίκῳ ὁ ὑπηρετικὸς κέλης πάντα ἐξήγγειλε τὰ περὶ τὴν ναυμαχίαν. cf. Herodotos, viii. 94, for the story of a κέλης bringing a message θείῃ πομπῇ. Thucydides, i. 53, ἔδοξεν οὖν αὐτοῖς ἄνδρας ἐς κελήτιον ἐμβιβάσαντες ἄνευ κηρυκείου προσπέμψαι τοῖς Ἀθηναίοις. viii. 38, Θηριμένης μέν, παραδοὺς Ἀστυόχῳ τὰς ναῦς, ἀποπλέων ἐν κέλητι ἀφανίζεται. Appian, de bello Mithridatico, 33, ἐς κελήτιον ἐνέβη, καὶ ναῦν ἐκ νεώς, ἵνα λάθοι, διαμείβων, ἐπ' Ἀλεξανδρείας ἐφέρετο, sc. Λούκουλλος. The κέλητες and κελήτια, or other vessels doing the same work, were often described simply as ὑπηρετικά. Polyænos, i. 38. 4, Βρασίδας νυκτὸς ἐπιπλέων Σκιώνῃ, τριήρη φιλίαν προπλεῖν ἔταξεν, αὐτὸς δὲ ἐν ὑπηρετικῷ κατόπιν εἵπετο = Thucydides, iv. 120, αὐτὸς δὲ ἐν κελητίῳ ἄποθεν ἐφεπόμενος. Plutarch, Demosthenes, 29, διαπλεύσας ὑπηρετικοῖς καὶ ἀποβὰς μετὰ Θρακῶν δορυφόρων, Lysander, 10, πέμπων δὲ ὑπηρετικὰ παρὰ τὰς πρώτας τῶν νεῶν ἀτρεμεῖν ἐκέλευε καὶ μένειν ἐν τάξει. Demosthenes, in Polyclem, 46, ἀφικνεῖται ὑπηρετικόν, ἄγων ἄνδρα καὶ ἐπιστολάς. Polyænos, iii. 9. 36, ὑπηρετικὸν ἐκπέμψας (Ἰφικράτης) κομίζον ἐπιστολὴν πεπλασμένην. Æschines, de falsa legatione, 73, οὕτω δ' ἦν σφαλερὰ καὶ ἐπικίνδυνα τὰ πράγματα, ὥστε ἠναγκάσθη γράψαι ψήφισμα Κηφισοφῶν ὁ Παιανιεὺς ἐκπλεῖν τὴν ταχίστην Ἀντίοχον τὸν ἐπὶ τῶν ὑπηρετικῶν καὶ ζητεῖν τὸν στρατηγὸν τὸν ἐπὶ τῇ δυνάμει τεταγμένον. This last passage shews that in the Athenian navy these ὑπηρετικά formed a distinct class under one command. They are presumably the same as the ἄκατοι δημόσιαι of the inventories : Corp. Inscr. Attic. vol. ii, no. 808, col. d, ll. 74, 75, ἐπὶ τὰς ἀκάτους τὰς δημοσίας, πηδάλια. And these are termed *celoces publicæ* by Plautus, captivi, iv. 2. 92—94, *nam filium | tuom modo in portu Philopolemum vivom salvom et sospitem | vidi in publica celoce*, cf. miles gloriosus, iv. 1. 39, *hæc celox illiust quæ hinc egreditur internuntia.*

The *celoces* are mentioned also by Ennius, apud Isidorum, origines, xix. 1. 22, *labitur uncta carina per æquora cana celocis*, by Turpilius, apud Nonium, p. 533, *remulis sensim celox ab oppido processerat*, by Varro, ibid., *nautæ remivagam movent celocem*, and *procella frigida ne obruat celocem*, by Livy, xxxvii. 27, *piraticas celoces et lembos*, and perhaps by Velleius, ii. 73, *piraticis celetibus* or *sceleribus*. And there are puns on the name : Plautus, Pseudolus, v. 2. 12, *unde onustam celocem agere te prædicem*, asinaria, ii. 1. 10, *quo hanc celocem conferam*, Poenulus, iii. 1. 40, *obsecro, hercle, operam celocem hanc mihi, ne corbitam, date.*

Pliny, vii. 57, *celetem (invenerunt) Rhodii.* Possibly these Rhodian 'race-horses' were evolved from the Phœnician 'horses' mentioned on p. 113. As to the live race-horses of this name, see Pausanias, v. 8. 8, vi. 12. 1, and Pliny, xxxiv. 10.

Cercuri, Κέρκουροι

These were vessels of a type that was equally suitable for warfare and for commerce. They were in use throughout the Mediterranean from the beginning of the Fifth Century to the middle of the First Century B.C. The war-ships of this type were small, but the merchant-ships were occasionally of considerable size.

Herodotos, vii. 89, τῶν δὲ τριηρέων ἀριθμὸς μὲν ἐγένετο ἑπτὰ καὶ διηκόσιαι καὶ χίλιαι, 97. τριηκόντεροι δὲ καὶ πεντηκόντεροι καὶ κέρκουροι καὶ ἱππαγωγά, πλοῖα σμικρὰ συνελθόντα ἐς τὸν ἀριθμὸν ἐφάνη τρισχίλια. That refers to the Persian fleet in 480 B.C. Arrian, anabasis, vi. 2, ἦν δὲ τὸ ξύμπαν πλῆθος τῶν νεῶν, τριακόντεροι μὲν ἐς ὀγδοήκοντα, τὰ δὲ πάντα πλοῖα σὺν τοῖς ἱππαγωγοῖς καὶ κερκούροις καὶ ὅσα ἄλλα ποτάμια οὐ πολὺ ἀποδέοντα τῶν δισχιλίων. That refers to Alexander's fleet on the Hydaspes in 327 B.C. Diodoros, xxiv. 1, 'Ρωμαῖοι δὲ ναυσὶ μακραῖς διακοσίαις τεσσαράκοντα καὶ κερκούροις ἑξήκοντα καὶ πλοίων πλήθει παντοδαπῶν κατέπλευσαν εἰς τὴν Πάνορμον. This was in 250 B.C. Appian, de rebus Punicis, 75, ναυσὶ δὲ ἐφέροντο (οἱ 'Ρωμαῖοι) πεντήκοντα μὲν πεντήρεσιν, ἑκατὸν δ' ἡμιολίαις, ἀφράκτοις δὲ καὶ κερκούροις καὶ στρογγύλοις πολλοῖς. 121, καὶ ναυσὶ πεντήκοντα μὲν τριηρετικαῖς, κερκούροις δὲ καὶ μυοπάρωσι καὶ ἄλλοις βραχυτέροις πολλοῖς ἐξέπλεον, sc. οἱ Καρχηδόνιοι. This was in 149 B.C. and 146 B.C. Memnon, Fr. 37, apud Photium, p. 232, Μιθριδάτης δὲ ἄλλον τε στρατὸν συχνὸν παρεσκευάζετο, καὶ τριήρεις μὲν τετρακόσιοι, τῶν δὲ μικροτέρων νηῶν πεντηκοντέρων τε καὶ κερκούρων ἀριθμὸς ἦν οὐκ ὀλίγος. This was in 74 B.C. Livy, xxxiii. 19, *ipse (Antiochus) cum classe centum tectarum navium, ad hoc levioribus navigiis cercurisque ac lembis ducentis, proficiscitur.* This was in 197 B.C. In all these instances the *cercuri* are reckoned among the small craft in a fleet. Apparently, they were faster than ships of the line. Livy, xxiii. 34, *cercuros ad persequendam retrahendamque navem quum (Flaccus) misisset, primo fugere regii conati ; deinde, ubi celeritate victi cesserunt, tradunt se Romanis, etc.* That was in 215 B.C.

Plautus, mercator, i. 1. 87, 88, *ædificat navem cercurum et merces emit:* | *parata navi inponit, etc.*, Stichus, ii. 2. 42—45, *dum percontor portitores, ecquæ navis venerit* | *ex Asia, ac negant venisse, conspicatus sum interim* | *cercurum, quo ego me maiorem non vidisse censeo.* | *in portum vento secundo, velo passo pervenit,* and then follows an account of the cargo. Athenæos, v. 43, ἐφόλκια δ᾽ ἦσαν αὐτῇ, τὸ μὲν πρῶτον κέρκουρος, τρισχίλια τάλαντα δέχεσθαι δυνάμενος· πᾶς δ᾽ ἦν οὗτος ἐπίκωπος. A merchant-ship that carried 3000 talents, or 75 tons, was larger than most war-ships: see note 78 on p. 30. The πᾶς seems to mean that the oars were not merely auxiliary. The oars of a *cercurus* are noticed again by Lucilius, apud Nonium, p. 533, *iligneis pedibus cercurum conferet æquis.* There is probably a misreading, *cercurum* for *cerycem*, in another passage of Lucilius, ibid., *ad regem legatu' Rhodum, Ecbatanam ac Babylonem* | *ibo ; cercurum sumam.*

The name κέρκουρος is perhaps an adaptation of the Phœnician word which appears in Hebrew as *kirkârâh :* and the name of these ships would certainly be Semitic in origin, if they really were invented in Cyprus, as Pliny asserts, vii. 57, *cercurum* (*invenerunt*) *Cyprii.* The word *kirkârâh* is found in Isaiah, lxvi. 20, and is translated into English as *swift beast :* but the Septuagint gives σκιάδιον, which must denote a hood over a chariot, or else an umbrella.

Corbitæ.

These were merchant-ships of great size. They were in use among the Romans in the First and Second Centuries B.C.

Lucilius, apud Nonium, p. 533, *multa homines portenta in Homeri versibu' ficta* | *monstra putant ; quorum in primis Polyphemu' ducentos* | *Cyclops longu' pedes, et porro huic maiu' bacillum* | *quam malus navis in corbita maximus ulla,* where the allusion is to the Odyssey, ix. 319, 322—324, Κύκλωπος γὰρ ἔκειτο μέγα ῥόπαλον παρὰ σηκῷ......ὅσσον θ᾽ ἱστὸν νηὸς ἐεικοσόροιο μελαίνης, | φορτίδος, εὐρείης, ἥ τ᾽ ἐκπεράᾳ μέγα λαῖτμα· | τόσσον ἔην μῆκος, τόσσον πάχος εἰσοράασθαι, so that Lucilius means the largest merchant-ship imaginable. Cicero also speaks of a *corbita* as a merchant-ship : ad Atticum, xvi. 6. 1, *sed putabam, quum Rhegium venissem, fore ut illic* δολιχὸν πλόον ὁρμαίνοντες *cogitaremus, corbitane Patras an actuariolis ad Leucopetram Tarentinorum, ast inde Corcyram ; et, si oneraria, statimne freto an Syracusis.* Being merchant-ships, these vessels had only auxiliary oars, and could therefore make little progress in a calm. Plautus, Pœnulus, iii. 1. 3, 4, *sicut ego hos duco advocatos, homines spissigradissumos,* | *tardiores quam corbitæ sunt in tranquillo mari,* cf. 40, *obsecro, hercle, operam celocem hanc mihi, ne corbitam, date.* For the *celoces* see p. 108. There is a pun on *corbis* and *corbita* in Plautus, Casina, iv. 1. 20, 21, *gnovi ego illas ambas estrices ; corbitam cibi* | *comesse possunt,* unless *corbitam cibi* should be read *corbitant ubi.*

Cybææ.

These also were merchant-ships of great size. They were in use in Sicily in the First Century B.C.

Cicero, in Verrem, ii. iv. 8, *tametsi, rogatus de cybæa, tenetis memoria quid responderit : ædificatam publicis operis, publice coactis, eique ædificandæ publice Mamertinum senatorem præfuisse.* 9, *negent isti onerariam navem maximam ædificatam esse Messanæ? negent, si possint. negent ei navi faciundæ senatorem Mamertinum publice præfuisse? utinam negent.* 67, *hæc sum rogaturus. navem populo Romano debeantne? fatebuntur. præbuerintne prætore C. Verre? negabunt. ædificaverintne navem onerariam maximam publice, quam Verri dederunt? negare non poterunt.* cf. ii. v. 23, *non populo Romano reddita biremis, sed prætori donata cybæa.* These passages prove that a *cybæa* was a merchant-ship : nor is the contrary implied in ii. v. 17, *navem vero cybæam maximam, triremis instar, pulcherrimam atque ornatissimam, palam ædificatam sumptu publico, sciente Sicilia, per magistratumque Mamertinum tibi datam donatamque esse dico.* Cicero is arguing here that Verres had not only procured a merchant-ship from the Mamertines in place of a war-ship, but had made them build him a merchant-ship that was as big as a war-ship of three banks, when they were not bound to provide a war-ship of more than two banks.

The term *cybæa* may be equivalent to κυβαία or to κυπαία, the β and π interchanging easily. cf. Hesychios, s. v. κύπαι :—εἶδός τι νεώς, where κύπαι is probably a corruption of κυπαία.

Cymbæ, Κύμβαι.

These were vessels of a type invented in Phœnicia : but Latin authors applied the name to any boat.

Pliny, vii. 57, *cymbam* (*invenerunt*) *Phœnices*. Sophocles, Andromeda, Fr. 2, apud Athenæum, xi. 64, ἵπποισιν ἢ κύμβαισι ναυστολεῖs χθόνα ; The scene of the play was laid in Phœnicia, so Sophocles was likely to select Phœnician types of ships, and the ἵπποι certainly were Phœnician : see pp. 113, 114.

The name is common in Latin. Cicero, de officiis, iii. 14 ; Pliny, ix. 10, 12 ; Seneca, epistolæ, 51. 12 ; Lucan, iv. 136 ; Ovid, tristia, ii. 330, amores, iii. 6. 4, metamorphoses, i. 293, fasti, vi. 777 ; Virgil, georgics, iv. 195, 506, Æneid, vi. 303 ; Horace, odes, ii. 3. 28 ; Propertius, iii. 18. 24 ; Juvenal, ii. 151 ; etc.

Ἔπακτρα, Ἐπακτρίδες.

These were small vessels of a type that probably was meant for fishing, but suitable also for some purposes in warfare.

Xenophon, Hellenica, i. 1. 11, ἐνταῦθα δὲ καὶ Ἀλκιβιάδης ἧκεν ἐκ τῶν Κλαζομενῶν σὺν πέντε τριήρεσι καὶ ἐπακτρίδι. Agathias, iii. 21, ἐπακτρίδας τινὰς ἀμφιπρύμνους δέκα πληρώσαντες. Nicander, theriaca, 823, 824, ἐπεὶ μογερούς ἁλιῆας | πολλάκις ἐμβρύξασα κατεπρήνιξεν ἐπάκτρων, sc. μύραινα. The name seems to be connected with ἐπακτήρ, a fisherman.

Aulus Gellius, x. 25, *actuariæ, quas Græci* ἱστιοκώπους *vocant vel* ἐπακτρίδας. See p. 114 for the ἱστιόκωποι and p. 105 for the *actuariæ*. No doubt, all ἐπακτρίδες were *actuariæ* : but Aulus Gellius cannot be right in asserting that all *actuariæ* were ἐπακτρίδες. The *actuariæ* formed a large class which included the κέλητες, and if the ἐπακτρίδες had been the same as the *actuariæ*, there could hardly have been such vessels as ἐπακτροκέλητες.

Ἐπακτροκέλητες.

These were vessels of a type between the ἐπακτρίδες and the κέλητες. They were in use among the Greeks in the Fourth Century B.C., especially for piracy.

Aristotle, de interpretatione, 2, gives ἐπακτροκέλης as an example of a compound name. The ships themselves are mentioned by Æschines, in Timarchum, 191, ταῦτα πληροῖ τὰ ληστήρια, ταῦτα εἰς τὸν ἐπακτροκέλητα ἐμβιβάζει, and also by Deinarchos : see Harpocration, s. v. ἐπακτροκέλης :—Αἰσχίνης ἐν τῷ κατὰ Τιμάρχου. εἶδος δ᾽ ἐστὶ πλοίου σύνθετον ἔχον τὴν κατασκευὴν ἔκ τε ἐπακτρίδος καὶ κέλητος. ἦν δὲ ὡς ἐπίπαν ληστρικόν, ὡς καὶ Δείναρχος ἐν τῇ κατὰ Πολυεύκτου δοκιμασίᾳ.

Γαῦλοι.

These were the great merchant-ships in which the Phœnicians made their trading-voyages in the Mediterranean and Atlantic between the Third and the Sixth Centuries B.C., and perhaps before and afterwards. The shape of the ships is indicated by their name, for that was given to any tub.

Antiphanes, apud Athenæum, xi. 102, A. γαύλους ὁλοχρύσους. B. πλοῖα ; A. τοὺς κάδους μὲν οὖν | καλοῦσι γαύλους πάντας οἱ προγάστορες. Aristophanes, aves, 598, γαῦλον κτῶμαι καὶ ναυκλήρω, scholion, Καλλίμαχος :—Κυπρόθε Σιδόνιός με κατήγαγεν ἐνθάδε γαῦλος. Epicharmos, apud Athenæum, vii. 114, αὐτὸς ὁ Ποτιδὰν ἄγων γαύλοισιν ἐν Φοινικικοῖς | ἧκε καλλίστας σαγήνας. Herodotos, iii. 136, καταβάντες δ᾽ οὗτοι ἐς Φοινίκην καὶ Φοινίκης ἐς Σιδῶνα πόλιν αὐτίκα μὲν τριήρεας δύο ἐπλήρωσαν, ἅμα δὲ αὐτῆσι καὶ γαῦλον μέγαν παντοίων ἀγαθῶν. vi. 17, ὁ δὲ ἰθέως ὡς εἶχε ἔπλωε ἐς Φοινίκην, γαύλους δὲ ἐνταῦθα καταδύσας καὶ χρήματα λαβὼν πολλὰ ἔπλωε ἐς Σικελίην. viii. 97, ἐς τὴν Σαλαμῖνα (Ξέρξης) χῶμα ἐπειρᾶτο διαχοῦν, γαύλους τε Φοινικηίους συνέδεε, ἵνα ἀντί τε σχεδίης ἔωσι καὶ τείχεος, κ.τ.λ. Scylax, periplus, 112, οἱ δὲ ἔμποροί εἰσι μὲν Φοίνικες· ἐπὰν δὲ ἀφίκωνται εἰς τὴν νῆσον τὴν Κέρνην, τοὺς μὲν γαύλους καθορμίζουσιν, ἐν τῇ Κέρνῃ σκηνὰς ποιησάμενοι αὐτοῖς· τὸν δὲ φόρτον ἐξελόμενοι αὐτοὶ διακομίζουσιν ἐν μικροῖς πλοίοις εἰς τὴν ἤπειρον. These passages all date from before 250 B.C., and the ships mentioned therein are all Phœnician. The name γαῦλος occurs again in Plutarch, de tranquillitate animi, 3, ἀλλ᾽ ὥσπερ οἱ δειλοὶ καὶ ναυτιῶντες ἐν τῷ πλεῖν, εἶτα ῥᾷον οἰόμενοι διάξειν, ἐὰν εἰς γαῦλον ἐξ ἀκάτου, καὶ πάλιν ἐὰν εἰς τριήρη μεταβῶσιν, οὐδὲν περαίνουσι. But this does not prove conclusively that these vessels were still in use ; for Plutarch may here be quoting some old saying. The expression γαυλικὰ χρήματα or γαυλιτικὰ χρήματα stands for cargo in Xenophon, anabasis, v. 8. 1, cf. v. 1. 11, 12, 15, 16 ; and this indicates that the name γαῦλος might roughly be applied to any merchant-ship.

The name was probably of Phœnician origin, and was perhaps derived from gawal ; the island of Gozo, near Malta, being termed Γαῦλος in Greek and Gawal in Phœnician : see Corp. Inscr. Semit. part i, no. 132, ll. 1, 8, 'am G(a)w(a)l, plebs Gaulitana.

Hippi, Ἵπποι.

These were Phœnician merchant-ships with figure-heads of horses. They came into use in Phœnicia in very early times ; but afterwards were only to be found at Cadiz, where they were employed upon the fisheries along the African coast outside the straits. Some of them were of considerable size ; and apparently these could manage to double the Cape, for about 112 B.C. one of the typical figure-heads was brought to Egypt from a wreck on the east coast of Africa, and was attributed by experts to a ship from Cadiz.

T.   h

Strabo, ii. 3. 4, πάλιν οὖν (φησὶ Ποσειδώνιος) καὶ ὑπὸ ταύτης (Κλεοπάτρας) πεμφθῆναι τὸν Εὔδοξον μετὰ μείζονος παρασκευῆς. ἐπανιόντα δ᾽ ἀνέμοις παρενεχθῆναι ὑπὲρ τὴν Αἰθιοπίαν· προσφερόμενον δέ τισι τόποις ἐξοικειοῦσθαι τοὺς ἀνθρώπους μεταδόσει σιτίων τε καὶ οἴνου καὶ παλαθίδων, ὧν ἐκείνοις οὐ μετῆν, ἀντὶ δὲ τούτων ὑδρείας τε τυγχάνειν καὶ καθοδηγίας, ἀπογράφεσθαί τε τῶν ῥημάτων ἔνια. εὑρόντα δ᾽ ἀκρόπρωρον ξύλινον ἐκ ναυαγίου ἵππον ἔχον ἐγγεγλυμμένον, πυθόμενον ὡς ἀπὸ τῆς ἑσπέρας πλεόντων τινῶν εἴη τὸ ναυάγιον τοῦτο, κομίζειν αὐτὸ ἀναστρέψαντα πρὸς τὸν οἰκεῖον πλοῦν. σωθέντα δ᾽ εἰς Αἴγυπτον, οὐκέτι τῆς Κλεοπάτρας ἡγουμένης, ἀλλὰ τοῦ παιδός, ἀφαιρεθῆναι πάλιν πάντα· φωραθῆναι γὰρ νενοσφισμένον πολλά. τὸ δ᾽ ἀκρόπρωρον προφέροντα ἐς τὸ ἐμπόριον, δεικνύναι τοῖς ναυκλήροις, γνῶναι δὲ Γαδειριτῶν ὄν· τούτων γὰρ τοὺς μὲν ἐμπόρους μεγάλα στέλλειν πλοῖα, τοὺς δὲ πένητας μικρά, ἃ καλεῖν ἵππους, ἀπὸ τῶν ἐν ταῖς πρῴραις ἐπισήμων· τούτους δὲ πλεῖν μέχρι τοῦ Λίξου ποταμοῦ περὶ τὴν Μαρουσίαν ἀλιευομένους· ἀλλὰ τῶν δὴ ναυκλήρων τινὰς γνωρίσαι τὸ ἀκρόπρωρον ἑνὸς τῶν ἀπὸ τοῦ Λίξου ποταμοῦ πορρώτερον πλευσάντων καὶ μὴ σωθέντων ὑπάρξαν. ἐκ δὲ τούτου συμβαλόντα τὸν Εὔδοξον, ὡς δυνατὸς εἴη ὁ περίπλους ὁ Λιβυκός, κ.τ.λ. cf. Pliny, ii. 67, *in quo (sinu Arabico) signa navium ex Hispaniensibus naufragiis feruntur agnita*, where he seems to be referring to the story of Eudoxos, though he mentions a later date.

Pliny, vii. 57, *onerariam Hippus Tyrius invenit, lembum Cyrenenses, cymbam Phœnices, celetem Rhodii, cercurum Cyprii*. This can only mean that the Tyrians introduced the merchant-ships called Horses. Sophocles, Andromeda, Fr. 2, apud Athenæum, xi. 64, ἵπποισιν ἢ κύμβαισι ναυστολεῖς χθόνα; Sophocles was likely to select Phœnician types of ships, as the scene of the play was laid in Phœnicia ; and these ἵπποι and κύμβαι are the very ships that Pliny associates with the Phœnicians. Moreover, some vessels with figure-heads of horses are represented in Assyrian sculpture of about 700 B.C., as in fig. 9, and this indicates that the type was indigenous in that part of the world.

But ships of any sort could be described in metaphor as horses. Odyssey, iv. 708, 709, νηῶν ὠκυπόρων ἐπιβαινέμεν, αἴθ᾽ ἀλὸς ἵπποι | ἀνδράσι γίγνονται. Plautus, rudens, i. 5. 10, 11, *nempe equo ligneo per vias cærulas | estis vectæ?* Thus, in the legend of the taking of Troy through the stratagem of the Wooden Horse, there is perhaps a reminiscence of the capture of some seaport town by men concealed on board a ship, which had unwarily been admitted within the harbour : cf. Lydos, de mensibus, iv. 88, περὶ τοῦ δουρείου ἵππου ὁ Εὐφορίων φησὶ πλοῖον γενέσθαι τοῖς Ἕλλησιν ἵππον λεγόμενον. And the winged horse Pegasos may represent a ship with oars. Juvenal, iii. 117, 118, *ripa nutritus in illa, | ad quam Gorgonei delapsa est pinna caballi*, speaking of the river which flows through Tarsus. cf. Stephanos, s. v. Ταρσός :—Ἀλέξανδρος δὲ ὁ Πολυίστωρ (Ταρσὸν καλεῖσθαί φησι) διὰ τὸ τὸν Πήγασον ἵππον ἐκεῖ τὸν ταρσὸν κλάσαντα καὶ Βελλεροφόντην ἐν τῷ Ἀληίῳ πεδίῳ πλανηθῆναι. For the term ταρσός and the metaphor of the oars and wings see pp. 2, 3, 20 and note 52. The legend that Bellerophon tamed Pegasos at Corinth may refer to the initiative of the Corinthians in building ships with oars : as to which see p. 4.

Ἱστιόκωποι.

These were small vessels with a full complement of oars as well as sails. They were known by this name in the Second Century A.D.

Aulus Gellius, x. 25, *actuariæ, quas Græci ἱστιοκώπους vocant vel ἐπακτρίδας.* cf. Pollux, i. 103, ὁ ἐξ οὐρίας πλοῦς ἐστιν, εἰρεσίᾳ πλεῖν, ἀνέμῳ πλεῖν· εἴρηται δὲ καὶ ἱστιοκώπῃ, ἀλλὰ βέλτιον εἰρεσίᾳ καὶ πνεύματι. Merchant-ships trusted mainly to their sails and war-ships to their oars, and were thus distinguished from these vessels which trusted equally to both. See p. 105 for the *actuariæ* and p. 112 for the ἐπακτρίδες.

Ὑπηρετικά.

This name was given to the small craft in a fleet, or to any vessels in attendance on others of larger size.

Diodoros, xx. 82, εἶχε δὲ (Δημήτριος) ναῦς μακρὰς μὲν παντοίας μεγέθει διακοσίας, ὑπηρετικὰ δὲ πλείω τῶν ἑκατὸν ἑβδομήκοντα, xiii. 14, τριήρεις δὲ συνεπλήρωσαν (οἱ Συρακόσιοι) ἑβδομήκοντα τέτταρας· συμπαρείποντό τε τὰς ὑπηρετικὰς ἔχοντες ναῦς παῖδες ἐλεύθεροι = Plutarch, Nicias, 24, οὐκ αὐτοὶ μόνον ταῖς τριήρεσιν, ἀλλὰ καὶ τὰ παιδάρια πανταχόθεν ἐπιβαίνοντα τῶν ἁλιάδων καὶ ταῖς σκάφαις προσπλέοντα. See also Æschines, de falsa legatione, 73, and other passages quoted in the note on *celoces* on p. 109, especially Xenophon, Hellenica, i. 6. 36, ὑπηρετικὸς κέλης. Where Diodoros says ναῦς ὑπηρετικάς, xviii. 72, Polyænos says ὑπηρεσίαν ναυτικήν, iv. 6. 8. The term ὑπηρετικὸν σκάφος is applied to a ship's-boat by Heliodoros in the passage quoted in note 226 on p. 103, and is applied to a lighter by Strabo, v. 3. 5, καὶ γὰρ ἡ τῶν ὑπηρετικῶν σκαφῶν εὐπορία τῶν ἐκδεχομένων τὰ φορτία καὶ ἀντιφορτιζόντων ταχὺν ποιεῖ τὸν ἀπόπλουν.

Lembi, Λέμβοι.

These were small vessels of a type that was invented or perfected by the Illyrians in the Third Century B.C. They served for desultory warfare and for piracy; and differed from the regular war-ships in being relatively of larger beam, and carrying no ram.

Polybios, v. 109, Φίλιππος δὲ κατὰ τὴν παραχειμασίαν ἀναλογιζόμενος ὅτι πρὸς τὰς ἐπιβολὰς αὐτοῦ χρεία πλοίων ἐστὶ καὶ τῆς κατὰ θάλατταν ὑπηρεσίας, καὶ ταύτης οὐχ ὡς πρὸς ναυμαχίαν—τοῦτο μὲν γὰρ οὐδ' ἂν ἤλπισε δυνατὸς εἶναι, 'Ρωμαίοις διαναυμαχεῖν—ἀλλὰ μᾶλλον ἕως τοῦ παρακομίζειν στρατιώτας, καὶ θᾶττον διαίρειν οὗ πρόθοιτο, καὶ παραδόξως ἐπιφαίνεσθαι τοῖς πολεμίοις· διόπερ, ὑπολαβὼν ἀρίστην εἶναι πρὸς ταῦτα τὴν τῶν Ἰλλυριῶν ναυπηγίαν, ἑκατὸν ἐπεβάλετο λέμβους κατασκευάζειν, cf. 110. This was in 216 B.C. See also Polybios, ii. 3, 6, 8—12, iv. 16, 19, 29, v. 4, 95, 101, Livy, xxxi. 45, xxxii. 21, xxxviii. 7, xlii. 48, xliv. 30, xlv. 43, and Appian, de rebus Illyricis, 7, for λέμβοι in Illyrian fleets; and Polybios, xvi. 2, 4—7, xvii. 1, and Livy, xxxii. 32, xliv. 28, xlv. 10, 31, for λέμβοι in Macedonian fleets. These instances all fall between 231 and 168 B.C. Also see Livy, xxxiii. 19, xxxiv. 35, xxxv. 26, for λέμβοι in Syrian and Spartan fleets at that period; Polybios, i. 20, 53, for λέμβοι in Roman fleets a little before; and Diodoros xx. 85, for λέμβοι at the siege of Rhodes in 304 B.C. Polybios also speaks of some vessels on the Rhone as λέμβοι, iii. 42, 43, 46; but Livy abstains from rendering this by *lembi*, xxi. 26—28, and calls them simply *naves* or *naves actuariæ.*

The λέμβοι were always reckoned among the small craft in a fleet. Polybios, i. 20, οὐχ οἷον κατάφρακτος αὐτοῖς ὑπῆρχε ναῦς, ἀλλ' οὐδὲ καθόλου μακρὸν πλοῖον, οὐδὲ λέμβος οὐδὲ εἷς, xvi. 2, κατάφρακτοι τρεῖς καὶ πεντήκοντα, σὺν δὲ τούτοις ἄφρακτα, λέμβοι δὲ σὺν ταῖς πρίστεσιν ἑκατὸν καὶ πεντήκοντα, cf. 7. Livy, xxxii. 21,

h 2

centum tectæ naves, et quinquaginta leviores apertæ, et triginta Issaici lembi,
xxxiii. 19, *cum classe centum tectarum navium, ad hoc levioribus navigiis cercuris-que ac lembis ducentis,* xxxv. 26, *tres tectas naves, et lembos pristesque,* xxxvii. 27, *piraticas celoces et lembos.* They had not any rams. Livy, xxxii. 32, *cum quinque lembis et una nave rostrata.* The number of oars was variable. Livy, xxxiv. 35, quoting from the treaty between Rome and Sparta in 195 B.C., *neve ipse (Nabis) navem ullam præter duos lembos, qui non plus quam sexdecim remis agerentur, haberet.* Vessels of this class sometimes carried fifty men. Polybios, ii. 3, προσπλέουσι τῆς νυκτὸς ἑκατὸν λέμβοι πρὸς τὴν Μεδιωνίαν, ἐφ᾽ ὧν ἦσαν Ἰλλυριοὶ πεντακισχίλιοι, cf. Strabo, ii. 3. 4, λέμβον συμπηξάμενος πεντηκοντόρῳ πάρισον. But there was space on board for many men besides the rowers. Livy, xliv. 28, *octingenti ferme Gallorum occisi, ducenti vivi capti; equi, etc.... viginti eximiæ equos formæ cum captivis eosdem decem lembos; quos ante miserat, Antenor devehere Thessalonicam iussit.* Thus, upon the average, these vessels each took twenty men and two horses in addition to the crew; so they clearly were more roomy than the regular war-ships. Yet some were narrow enough for the oars to be sculled in pairs. Livy, xxiv. 40, *legati venerunt nuntiantes Philippum primum Apolloniam tentasse, lembis biremibus centum viginti flumine adverso subvectum, deinde, etc.* cf. Virgil, georgics, i. 201, 202, *qui adverso vix flumine lembum | remigiis subigit.*

At an earlier date the term had been applied to ship's-boats: see the passages quoted from Demosthenes and Anaxandrides in note 226 on p. 103. These authors were contemporary with Aristotle, so his πλοῖον λεμβῶδες, with its sharp prow, was presumably a boat of that sort: de animalium incessu, 10, στῆθος δὲ (τῶν γαμψωνύχων) ἰσχυρὸν καὶ ὀξύ, ὀξὺ μὲν πρὸς τὸ εὔπορον εἶναι, καθάπερ ἂν εἰ πλοίου πρῷρα λεμβώδους, ἰσχυρὸν δὲ κ.τ.λ. The small boats used for embarking on a ship are styled *lembi* by Plautus, mercator, i. 2. 81, 82, *dum hæc aguntur, lembo advehitur tuus pater pauxillulo; | neque quisquam hominem conspicatust, donec in navim subit,* ii. 1. 35, *inscendo in lembum atque ad illam navim devehor.* And as Plautus adapted his *Mercator* from Philemon's Ἔμπορος, this usage may date from the time of Aristotle. The term is applied to a fisherman's boat by Theocritos, xxi. 12, μήρινθοι κῶπα τε γέρων τ᾽ ἐπ᾽ ἐρείσμασι λέμβος, and also by Accius, apud Nonium, p. 534, *eo ante noctem extremam, retia ut perveherem et statuerem, | forte aliquando solito lembo sum progressus longius.* Vessels of this name are mentioned again by Sisenna, ibid., *Otacilium legatum cum scaphis ac lembis,* and by Turpilius, ibid., *hortari nostros ilico cœpi, ut celerarent lembum,* and *lembi redeuntes domum duo ad nostram adcelerarunt ratem.*

Pliny, vii. 57, *lembum (invenerunt) Cyrenenses.* That probably refers to the earlier vessels of this name, that were used as ship's-boats, etc.

Lenunculi.

This term was apparently a corruption of *lembunculi,* a diminutive of *lembi,* and hence applied to any small boats.

Sallust, apud Nonium, p. 534, *incidit forte per noctem in lenunculo piscantis.* Ammianus, xiv. 2. 10, *piscatorios quærunt lenunculos, vel innare temere contextis ratibus parant,* xvi. 10. 3, *anhelante rabido flatu ventorum lenunculo se commisisse piscantis,* where the allusion is to Cæsar's attempt to cross the Adriatic in an open boat. Tacitus, annales, xiv. 5, *nando* (*Agrippina*) *deinde occursu lenunculorum Lucrinum in lacum vecta villæ suæ infertur.* The term is applied to ship's-boats by Cæsar, de bello civili, ii. 43, *magistrisque imperat navium, ut primo vespere omnes scaphas ad litus adpulsas habeant......qui in classe erant, proficisci properabant: horum fuga navium onerariarum magistros incitabat. pauci lenunculi ad officium imperiumque conveniebant.* There were guilds of *lenuncularii* at Ostia near the mouth of the Tiber. Corp. Inscr. Latin. vol. xiv, nos. 250, 251, *ordo corporatorum lenunculariorum tabulariorum auxiliariorum Ostiensium*, no. 252, *o. c. l. pleromariorum a. O.*

Lintres.

These were small boats, chiefly for use on rivers.

Cæsar, de bello Gallico, i. 12, *ratibus ac lintribus iunctis transibant.* This refers to the Saône. cf. Ausonius, idyllia, 12, grammaticomastix, 10, *lintribus in geminis constratus, Ponto sit, an Pons?* Cæsar, de bello Gallico, vii. 60, *conquirit etiam lintres: has magno sonitu remorum incitatas mittit, etc.* That refers to the Seine. Livy, xxi. 26, *itaque ingens coacta vis navium est, lintriumque temere ad vicinalem usum paratarum; novasque alias cavabant ex singulis arboribus.* That refers to the Rhone. The *naves* and *lintres* of Livy are the λέμβοι and μονόξυλα of Polybios, iii. 42. Pliny, vi. 26, *regio autem, ex qua piper monoxylis lintribus Baracen convehunt, vocatur Cottonara.* These places were in India. Ovid, fasti, vi. 779, *ferte coronatæ iuvenum convivia lintres.* That refers to the Tiber. Cicero, pro Milone, 27, *lintribus in eam insulam* (*in lacu Prelio*) *materiem, calcem, cæmenta atque arma convexit.* See also Cicero, Brutus, 60, *motus erat is, quem et C. Iulius in perpetuum notavit, quum ex eo in utramque partem toto corpore vacillante quæsivit, 'quis loqueretur e lintre,'* ad Atticum, x. 10. 5, *ego vero vel lintriculo, si navis non erit, eripiam me ex istorum parricidio.* And also Ulpian, in the Pandects, iv. 9. 1. 4, *de exercitoribus ratium, item lintrariis nihil cavetur: sed idem constitui oportere, Labeo scribit,* sc. *quod de exercitoribus navium.*

Lusoriæ.

These were the war-ships constructed for the frontier rivers of the Roman Empire, as distinguished from those constructed for the high seas.

Vegetius, ii. 1, *classis item duo genera sunt, unum liburnarum, aliud lusoriarum. classibus* (*servantur*) *maria vel flumina.* iv. 46, *in Danubio agrarias cotidianis tutantur excubiis,* sc. *lusoriæ.* In the Theodosian Code, vii. 17, there is a law *de lusoriis Danubii* dated in 412 A.D. It fixes the strength of that fleet at 225 ships; and provides for the construction of thirty-one every year, so as to renew the whole fleet in about seven years. By Novel 24, dated in 443 A.D., the Emperor directs the *Magister Officiorum* to furnish an annual report from certain frontiers *quemadmodum se militum numerus habeat, castrorumque ac lusoriarum cura procedat;* and this order is repeated by Justinian in his Code, i. 31. 4. But while Justinian says vaguely *super omni limite sub tua iurisdictione constituto,* Theodosios says explicitly *tam Thraci, quam Illyrici, nec non etiam Orientalis ac Pontici limitis, Ægyptiaci insuper, Thebaici, Lybici:* and this suggests that *lusoriæ* were then in use upon the Euphrates and the Nile as well as the Danube. Ammianus, xvii. 2. 3, xviii. 2. 12, speaks of *lusoriæ* on the Meuse in 357 A.D., and on the Rhine in 359 A.D. Vopiscus, Bonosus, 15, speaks of them on the Rhine in 280 A.D. For an earlier use of the term, see note on *thalamegi* on p. 123.

Monoxyla, Μονόξυλα.

These were vessels of a single piece of timber, formed by simply hollowing out the trunk of a tree. They were in common use in many regions at many periods. Xenophon, anabasis, v. 4. 11, τριακόσια πλοῖα μονόξυλα, καὶ ἐν ἑκάστῳ τρεῖς ἄνδρας. These were on the Black Sea. Polyænos, v. 23, σκάφας τρεῖς μονοξύλους, ἑκάστην ἄνδρα ἕνα δέξασθαι δυναμένην. These were also on the Black Sea. Heliodoros, Æthiopica, i. 31, ἐπιβαίνει δὲ τοῦ σκάφους αὐτὸς καὶ ὁ Θέρμουθις καὶ τρίτος ὁ ἐρέτης· οὐ γὰρ πλείονας οἶά τε φέρειν τὰ λιμναῖα σκάφη ἀπὸ μόνου ξύλου καὶ πρέμνου παχέος ἑνὸς ἀγροικότερον κοιλαινόμενα. These were in the Delta of the Nile. Pliny, vii. 2, *arundines vero tantæ proceritatis ut singula internodia alveo navigabili ternos interdum homines ferant,* cf. xvi. 65. These bamboos were said to grow in India. Pliny, xvi. 76, *Germaniæ prædones singulis arboribus cavatis navigant, quarum quædam et triginta homines ferunt.* The inevitable parody is supplied by Lucian, veræ historiæ, ii. 26, οὕτω δὴ ἐμβιβάσας ὁ Ῥαδάμανθυς πεντήκοντα τῶν ἡρώων εἰς ναῦν μονόξυλον ἀσφοδελίνην παρήγγειλε διώκειν. For further allusions to the μονόξυλα, see Aristotle, historia animalium, iv. 8. 6, for the Mediterranean. Arrian, anabasis, i. 3, and Theophylactos, historia, vi. 9, for the Danube. Porphyrogenitos; de administrando imperio, 9, for the Dnieper and the Black Sea. Pliny, vi. 26, for the west coast of India, *monoxylis lintribus.* Polybios, iii. 42, for the Rhone : also Livy, xxi. 26, *cavabant (lintres) ex singulis arboribus.* Velleius, ii. 107, for the Elbe, *cavatum ex materia alveum.* Strabo, iii. 2. 3, for the Guadalquivir ; and iii. 3. 7, for the north coast of Spain.

Vessels of this sort were carried by the armies of the Roman Empire for the construction of floating-bridges. Vegetius, iii. 7, *sed commodius repertum est ut monoxylos, hoc est, paulo latiores scaphulas ex singulis trabibus excavatas, pro genere ligni et subtilitate levissimas, carpentis secum portet exercitus, tabulatis pariter et clavis ferreis præparatis. ita absque mora constructus pons, etc.* cf. ii. 25. Leo, tactica, xvii. 13, συμπηγνύουσι (οἱ καβαλλάριοι) γέφυραν ἢ διὰ ξύλων μεγάλων ἢ διὰ μικρῶν πλοιαρίων, τῶν λεγομένων μονοξύλων.

Myoparones, Μυοπάρωνες.

These were fighting-ships of no great size. They were in use throughout the Mediterranean in the First Century B.C. for warfare and for piracy. Apparently they were broader than the regular war-ships in proportion to their length, and therefore better able to keep the sea.

Appian, de bellis civilibus, v. 95, ἐδωρήσατο δὲ καὶ Ὀκταουΐα τὸν ἀδελφόν, αἰτήσασα παρ' Ἀντωνίου, δέκα φασήλοις τριηρετικοῖς, ἐπιμίκτοις ἔκ τε φορτίδων νεῶν καὶ μακρῶν· καὶ τὴν Ὀκταουΐαν ὁ Καῖσαρ χιλίοις λογάσι σωματοφύλαξιν, οὓς ἐπιλέξαιτο Ἀντώνιος = Plutarch, Antonius, 35, Ὀκταουΐα τῶν ὡμολογημένων χωρὶς ᾐτήσατο τῷ μὲν ἀδελφῷ παρὰ τοῦ ἀνδρὸς εἴκοσι μυοπάρωνας, τῷ δ' ἀνδρὶ παρὰ τοῦ ἀδελφοῦ στρατιώτας χιλίους. This was in 37 B.C. Appian and Plutarch are certainly referring to the same squadron, though they differ about its strength : so these statements of theirs would naturally define the μυοπάρωνες as vessels of a hybrid species between the long ships and the round ships. But the difficulty is that Appian has no obvious motive for employing a periphrasis here to describe the μυοπάρωνες, seeing that he elsewhere mentions them by name : de bello Mithridatico, 92, μυοπάρωσι πρῶτον καὶ ἡμιολίαις, εἶτα δικρότοις καὶ τριήρεσι, de rebus Punicis, 121, ναυσὶ πεντήκοντα μὲν τριηρετικαῖς, κερκούροις δὲ καὶ μυοπάρωσι καὶ ἄλλοις βραχυτέροις πολλοῖς. Moreover, in these passages he treats the μυοπάρωνες as ships of a single bank, and distinguishes them from ναυσὶ τριηρετικαῖς, whereas he describes the vessels in question as φασήλοις τριηρετικοῖς. But among those ναυσὶ τριηρετικαῖς he must include some five-banked ships that he has mentioned just before, πεντήρεις τε καὶ τριήρεις, and in another passage he uses the phrase σκεύη τριηρετικὰ for the gear belonging to ships of any number of banks from two to five, præfatio, 10, τριήρεις δὲ ἀπὸ ἡμιολίας μέχρι πεντήρους, πεντακόσιαι καὶ χίλιαι· καὶ σκεύη τριηρετικὰ διπλότερα τούτων : so that he could not mean by τριηρετικός that a ship had three banks of oars, or necessarily more banks than one. Apparently, he employs the term φασήλοις, like its equivalent in Latin, to denote a certain type of vessel that was not meant for warfare—see p. 120— and then adds τριηρετικοῖς to show that the type was so far modified that the vessels here were capable of fighting, though not entitled to rank with the regular war-ships, ναυσὶ τριηρετικαῖς—that they were, in fact, ἐπιμίκτοις ἔκ τε φορτίδων νεῶν καὶ μακρῶν. See note 60 on p. 23 for other examples of an intermediate type.

Vessels termed πάρωνες are mentioned by Polybios, Fr. 65, apud Suidam, s. v. πάρωνες :—ὁ δὲ ἔπλει, παράπλους ποιησάμενος τοὺς Σιδητῶν πάρωνας· ἧκον γὰρ 'Ροδίοις εἰς συμμαχίαν. And vessels termed parones and parunculi are mentioned in verses that are ascribed to Cicero by Isidore, origines, xix. 1. 20, tunc se fluctigero tradit mandatque paroni, and parunculis ad littus ludet celeribus. The μυοπάρωνες therefore bore a compound name : and a compound name would naturally be given to ships of an intermediate type.

The μυοπάρωνες are mentioned also by Sallust, apud Nonium, p. 534, duobus prædonum myoparonibus, and by Sisenna, ibid., navisque triginta biremis, totidem myoparonas. Again by Plutarch, Lucullus, 2, τρισὶν Ἑλληνικοῖς μυοπάρωσι, καὶ δικρότοις ἴσαις 'Ροδιακαῖς, 13, λῃστρικὸν μυοπάρωνα. Also by Cicero, in Verrem, ii. v. 34, si in prædonum pugna (quadriremis) versaretur, urbis instar habere inter illos piraticos myoparones videretur. 37, hic, te prætore, Heracleo archipirata cum quattuor myoparonibus parvis ad arbitrium suum navigavit. hic, te prætore, prædonum naviculæ pervagatæ sunt. cf. ii. i. 34, iii. 80, v. 28. And by Aulus Hirtius, de bello Alexandrino, 46, depressa scapha vulneratus tamen adnatat (Octavius) ad suum myoparonem. eo receptus, cum prælium nox dirimeret, tempestate magna velis profugit.

Orariæ, Oriæ, Oriolæ, Prosumiæ.

These were small craft employed on rivers and along the coast for traffic or fishing.

Pliny, epistolæ, x. 26, nunc destino partim orariis navibus partim vehiculis provinciam petere : nam sicut itineri graves æstus ita continuæ navigationi etesiæ reluctantur, cf. 28, orarias naviculas. Isidore, origines, xix. 1. 27, makes the word littorariæ, but probably without authority. Plautus, rudens, iv. 2. 5, 6, *salute oriæ, quæ in mari fluctuoso | piscatu novo me uberi conpotivit,* iv. 3. 81, *mea opera et labore et rete et oria,* trinummus, iv. 2. 100, 101, *immo oriola advecti sumus | usque aqua advorsa per amnem.* The *oriolæ* are identified with the *prosumiæ* by Aulus Gellius, x. 25, *prosumiæ vel geseoretæ vel oriolæ.* Nothing is known of the *geseoretæ:* but the *prosumiæ* are mentioned by Cæcilius, apud Nonium, p. 536, *cum ultro gubernator propere vertit prosumiam,* and again, *de nocte ad portum sum provectus prosumia.*

Phaseli, Φάσηλοι.

These were vessels of a type that was especially suitable for carrying people from place to place. They were in use throughout the Mediterranean in the First Centuries B.C. and A.D.

Catullus, 4. 1—5, *phaselus ille, quem videtis, hospites, | ait fuisse navium celerrimus, | neque ullius natantis impetum trabis | nequisse præterire, sive palmulis opus foret volare, sive linteo.* This vessel had brought Catullus from Bithynia to Italy. Cicero, ad Atticum, i. 13. 1, *accepi tuas tres iam epistolas: unam a M. Cornelio, quam Tribus Tabernis, ut opinor, ei dedisti; alteram, quam mihi Canusinus tuus hospes reddidit; tertiam, quam, ut scribis, anchoris sublatis, de phaselo dedisti.* xiv. 16. 1, *quinto Non. conscendens ab hortis Cluvianis in phaselum epicopum has dedi litteras.* Atticus was crossing the Adriatic from Brindisi, and Cicero was cruising in the Bay of Naples. Sallust, apud Nonium, p. 534, *et forte in navigando cohors una, grandi phaselo vecta, a ceteris deerravit; marique placido a duobus prædonum myoparonibus circumventa.* This great ship clearly was dependent on her sails, since she was helpless when becalmed; and Cicero's phrase *phaselus epicopus* implies that some *phaseli* were not *epicopi,* and had not any oars to help them along. Juvenal, xv. 127, 128, *parvula fictilibus solitum dare vela phaselis, | et brevibus pictæ remis incumbere testæ,* cf. Virgil, georgics, iv. 289, *et circum pictis vehitur sua rura phaselis.* These were the earthenware tubs that served as boats in Egypt, the ὀστράκινα πορθμεῖα of Strabo, xvii. 1. 4. So a *phaselus* might be of any size.

These vessels are mentioned frequently in Latin. Ovid, epistolæ ex Ponto, i. 10. 39, *fragili tellus non dura phaselo.* Horace, odes, iii. 2. 28, 29, *fragilemve mecum | solvat phaselon.* Seneca, Hercules Œtæus, 695, 696, *nec magna meas aura phaselos | iubeat medium scindere pontum.* Martial, x. 30. 12, 13, *nec languet æquor; viva sed quies ponti | pictam phaselon adiuvante fert aura.* Lucan, v. 518, *et latus inversa nudum munita phaselo,* sc. *domus.*

And they are mentioned occasionally in Greek. Appian, de bellis civilibus, v. 95, ἐδωρήσατο δὲ καὶ Ὀκταουία τὸν ἀδελφόν, αἰτήσασα παρ' Ἀντωνίου, δέκα φασήλοις τριηρετικοῖς, ἐπιμίκτοις ἔκ τε φορτίδων νεῶν καὶ μακρῶν. This passage has already been discussed in the note on the μυοπάρωνες on p. 118. Appian follows the Latin usage in treating the φάσηλοι as φορτίδες νῆες, and adds τριηρετικοί here to show that the vessels in question had something of the character of the μακραί. Strabo, however, reckons the φάσηλοι among the μακρὰ πλοῖα, and distinguishes them from the σκευαγωγά, in his account of the expedition of Ælius Gallus down the Red Sea in 25 B.C. Strabo, xvi. 4. 23, πρῶτον μὲν δὴ τοῦθ' ἁμάρτημα συνέβη τὸ μακρὰ κατασκευάσασθαι πλοῖα, μηδενὸς ὄντος μηδ' ἐσομένου κατὰ θάλατταν πολέμου. ὁ δ' οὐκ ἔλαττον ὀγδοήκοντα ἐναυπηγήσατο δίκροτα καὶ τριήρεις καὶ φασήλους. γνοὺς δὲ διεψευσμένος ἐναυπηγήσατο σκευαγωγὰ ἑκατὸν καὶ τριάκοντα, οἷς ἔπλευσεν ἔχων περὶ μυρίους πεζούς. By thus including these φάσηλοι among the μακρὰ πλοῖα, Strabo may perhaps imply that they were φάσηλοι τριηρετικοί, as Appian says, and in fact were μυοπάρωνες.

Pontones.

These were merchant-ships of a type that was in use on the south coast of France in the First Century B.C. Cæsar, de bello civili, iii. 29, *pontones, quod est genus navium Gallicarum, Lissi relinquit*, sc. *Antonius.* 40, *Lissum profectus* (*Cn. Pompeius*) *naves onerarias triginta a M. Antonio relictas intra portum aggressus omnes incendit.* The circumstances of the campaign suggest that these ships came from Marseilles.

At a later date the term denoted a pontoon. Paulus, in the Pandects, viii. 3. 38, *flumine interveniente, via constitui potest, si aut vado transiri potest, aut pontem habeat: diversum, și pontonibus traiiciatur.* cf. Ausonius, idyllia, 12, grammaticomastix, 10, *lintribus in geminis constratus, Ponto sit, an Pons?*

Pristes, Πρίστεις.

These were war-ships of no great size; yet large enough to carry rams. They were employed in Greek fleets in the Second Century B.C. The name denotes a shark.

Polybios, xvii. 1, παρῆν ὁ μὲν Φίλιππος ἐκ Δημητριάδος ἀναχθεὶς εἰς τὸν Μηλιέα κόλπον, πέντε λέμβους ἔχων καὶ μίαν πρίστιν, ἐφ᾽ ἧς αὐτὸς ἐπέπλει = Livy, xxxii. 32, *eo rex ab Demetriade cum quinque lembis et una nave rostrata venit.* Livy elsewhere mentions them by name, xxxv. 26, *tres tectas naves, et lembos pristesque*, xliv. 28, *cum quadraginta lembis, adiectæ ad hunc numerum quinque pristes erant.* They are again classed with the *lembi* by Polybios, xvi. 2, κατάφρακτοι τρεῖς καὶ πεντήκοντα, σὺν δὲ τούτοις ἄφρακτα, λέμβοι δὲ σὺν ταῖς πρίστεσιν ἑκατὸν καὶ πεντήκοντα. These instances fall between 201 and 168 B.C. Virgil, Æneid, v. 116, *velocem Mnestheus agit acri remige Pristin:* but *Pristis* is here the name of the ship.

The fish known as *pristis* was certainly a shark. Leonidas of Tarentum, in the Anthology, vii. 506, 3—10, ἢ γὰρ ἐπ᾽ ἀγκύρας ἔνοχον βάρος εἰς ἅλα δύνων, | Ἰόνιόν θ᾽ ὑγρὸν κῦμα κατερχόμενος, | τὴν μὲν ἔσωσ᾽· αὐτὸς δὲ μετάτροπος ἐκ βυθοῦ ἔρρων | ἤδη καὶ ναύταις χεῖρας ὀρεγνύμενος, | ἐβρώθην· τοῖόν μοι ἐπ᾽ ἄγριον εὖ μέγα κῆτος | ἦλθεν, ἀπέβρωξεν δ᾽ ἄχρις ἐπ᾽ ὀμφαλίου. | χἤμισυ μὲν ναῦται, ψυχρὸν βάρος, ἐξ ἁλὸς ἡμῶν | ἤρανθ᾽, ἥμισυ δὲ πρίστις ἀπεκλάσατο. Thus, the sailor had been diving to recover an anchor, and was just being hauled into the ship again, when the lower half of his body was bitten off and swallowed by a *pristis.* That was the act of a shark, and of no other fish. Aristotle, historia animalium, vi. 11. 10, οἱ μὲν οὖν γαλεοὶ καὶ οἱ γαλεοειδεῖς, οἷον ἀλώπηξ καὶ κύων, καὶ οἱ πλατεῖς ἰχθύες, νάρκη καὶ βάτος καὶ λειόβατος καὶ τρυγών, τὸν εἰρημένον τρόπον ζῳοτοκοῦσιν ᾠοκήσαντες. 12. 1, δελφὶς δὲ καὶ φάλαινα καὶ τὰ ἄλλα κήτη, ὅσα μὴ ἔχει βράγχια, ἀλλὰ φυσητῆρα, ζῳοτοκοῦσιν, ἔτι δὲ πρίστις καὶ βοῦς· οὐδὲν γὰρ τούτων φαίνεται ἔχον ᾠά, ἀλλ᾽ εὐθέως κύημα, ἐξ οὗ διαρθρουμένου γίνεται τὸ ζῷον, καθάπερ ἄνθρωπος καὶ τῶν τετραπόδων τὰ ζῳοτόκα. Here the πρίστις and βοῦς are distinguished from those κήτη which had φυσητῆρα in place of βράγχια, *i.e.* the marine mammals, or Cetacea. And they are also distinguished from some species of sharks, in that they were viviparous in the strictest sense, while these were ovo-viviparous: but this distinction seems dubious. The passage, however, refutes the opinion that the *pristis* was a whale. Linnæus was clearly in error in describing the saw-fish as *pristis antiquorum.* He probably took πρίειν in the sense of sawing, whereas it also refers to biting; and the shark is pre-eminently the biter.

Rates, Σχεδίαι.

These terms were applied to rafts of various kinds; also to floating-bridges; and occasionally to ships.

Rafts were used for moving timber from place to place: and sometimes were of immense size, requiring many masts and sails. Theophrastos, historia plantarum, v. 8. 2, μέγιστα δὲ (ξύλα) καὶ παρὰ πολὺ τὰ ἐν τῇ Κύρνῳ φασὶν εἶναι...διαβάντας δέ τινας ἀποτεμέσθαι πάμπολυ πλῆθος ἐκ τόπου βραχέος ὥστε τηλικαύτην ποιῆσαι σχεδίαν ἢ ἐχρήσατο πεντήκοντα ἱστίοις· οὐ μὴν ἀλλὰ διαπεσεῖν αὐτὴν ἐν τῷ πελάγει. Vitruvius, ii. 9. 14, *propterque pondus* (*larix*) *ab aqua non sustinetur ; sed cum portatur, aut in navibus aut supra abiegnas rates collocatur.* Such rafts would consist entirely of timber ; but others were floated on skins or jars or casks. Xenophon, anabasis, ii. 4. 28, οἱ βάρβαροι διῆγον ἐπὶ σχεδίαις διφθερίναις ἄρτους, τυρούς, οἶνον. This was on the Tigris. Pliny, viii. 6, *centum quadraginta duo* (*elephanti*) *fuere transvecti ratibus, quas doliorum consertis ordinibus imposuerat,* sc. *Metellus.* The passage was from Sicily to Italy, and the date was 251 B.C. See also Diodoros, xix. 54. 3, for transport of elephants from Megara to Epidauros on σχεδίαι in 315 B.C.; and Polybios, iii. 46, and Livy, xxi. 28, for transport of elephants across the Rhone on σχεδίαι or *rates* in 218 B.C. Lucan, iv. 420—422, *namque ratem vacuæ sustentant undique cuppæ,* | *quarum porrectis series constricta catenis* | *ordinibus geminis obliquas excipit alnos.* This raft was built for fighting ; so a large space was left open in the middle, for the rowers to work their oars there out of reach of missiles: 423—426, *nec gerit expositum telis in fronte patenti* | *remigium : sed, quod trabibus circumdedit æquor,* | *hoc ferit; et taciti præbet miracula cursus,* | *quod nec vela ferat, nec apertas verberat undas.*

The floating-bridges which the Persians threw across the Dardanelles and Bosporos are termed σχεδίαι by Æschylos, Persæ, 69, and by Mandrocles in the epigram quoted by Herodotos, iv. 88, and also by Herodotos himself, iv. 88, 89, vii. 36 ; and he applies the term to other floating-bridges, iv. 97, viii. 97. Livy, xxi. 47, *biduo vix locum rate iungendo* (*Pado*) *flumini inventum tradunt.* Strabo, xvii. 1. 16, καὶ σχεδία ἔζευκται ἐπὶ τῷ ποταμῷ, ἀφ' ἧς καὶ τοὔνομα τῷ τόπῳ, sc. Σχεδία. This refers to the toll-bar across the Canopic arm of the Nile.

Sea-going ships are described as ποντοπόρους σχεδίας by Euripides, Hecuba, 113. In the Odyssey, v. 251, Ulysses' boat is described as εὐρεῖαν σχεδίην, and Theocritos uses the phrase εὐρεῖαν σχεδίαν for Charon's boat, xvi. 41. Among the Roman poets *ratis* bore this meaning: Catullus, 63. 1, 64. 121 ; Virgil, georgics, ii. 445, Æneid, i. 43, iii. 192, iv. 53, v. 8, vi. 302 ; etc.

Speculatoriæ, Κατάσκοποι, *Tabellariæ.*

These were small vessels for reconnoitring and for carrying despatches. Apparently, they became a distinct class in the First Century B.C. In the Fifth

Century A.D. the hulls of these vessels and their sails and ropes used all to be painted the colour of sea-water, to keep them out of sight.

Livy, xxxvi. 42, *una et octoginta constratis navibus, multis præterea minoribus, quæ aut apertæ rostratæ aut sine rostris speculatoriæ erant, Delum traiecit.* Plutarch, Cato Minor, 54, ἦσαν δὲ πεντακοσίων μὲν οὐκ ἐλάττους αἱ μάχιμοι, λιβυρνικὰ δὲ καὶ κατασκοπικὰ καὶ ἄφρακτα παμπληθῆ, Pompeius, 64, ἦσαν γὰρ αἱ μάχιμοι πεντακόσιαι, λιβυρνίδων δὲ καὶ κατασκόπων ὑπερβάλλων ἀριθμός. For this use of μάχιμοι in place of κατάφρακτοι, cf. Pseudo-Callisthenes, i. 28, ναυπηγήσας λιβέρνους καὶ τριήρεις καὶ ναῦς μαχίμους ποιήσας. Livy and Plutarch both treat the scouts as a distinct class of vessels; but Polybios speaks as though the scouting was done by any vessels that were available. Livy, xxii. 19, *inde duæ Massiliensium speculatoriæ missæ retulerunt classem Punicam stare in ostio, etc.* = Polybios, iii. 95, προαπέστειλε κατασκεψομένας δύο ναῦς ταχυπλοούσας Μασσαλιωτικάς... διασαφούντων δὲ τῶν ἐπὶ τὴν κατασκοπὴν ἐκπεμφθέντων ὅτι περὶ τὸ στόμα, κ.τ.λ. Livy, xxx. 10, *intervalla fecit, qua procurrere speculatoriæ naves in hostem ac tuto recipi possent.* = Polybios, (xiv. 10), apud Suidam, s. v. ὑπηρετικοῖς:—βραχὺ διάστημα ποιῶν, ὥστε ὑπηρετικοῖς ἐκπλεῖν δύνασθαι καὶ διαπλεῖν. And Livy doubtless used *speculatoriæ* in transcribing from Polybios, i. 53, ὁμοίως δὲ καὶ τοῖς ἐκ τῶν Συρακουσῶν προαπεσταλμένοις ταμίαις ἀνήγγειλαν οἱ προπλεῖν εἰθισμένοι λέμβοι τὸν ἐπίπλουν τῶν ὑπεναντίων. The inference is that the scouts did not become a distinct class until after the time of Polybios; and that Livy is guilty of some anachronisms. They usually were small vessels. Livy, xxxv. 26, *ipse Philopœmen in levi speculatoria nave fugit,* xxx. 10, *speculatoriæ naves ac levia navigia.* Cæsar, de Bello Gallico, iv. 26, *speculatoria navigia.* The inscription mentioning *speculatores classis Misenensis* is a forgery: see Corp. Inscr. Latin. vol. x, no. 247*.

Seneca, epistolæ, 77, *subito nobis hodie Alexandrinæ naves apparuerunt, quæ præmitti solent et nuntiare secuturæ classis adventum: tabellarias vocant.* These vessels *quæ præmitti solent* answer to the προπλεῖν εἰθισμένοι of Polybios, i. 53. And the regular scouts also served as *tabellariæ.* Aulus Hirtius, de bello Africano, 26, *per catascopum (litteras) mittit.*

The term *exploratoriæ* is employed by Vegetius, iv. 37, *scaphæ tamen maioribus liburnis exploratoriæ sociantur, quæ vicenos prope remiges in singulis partibus habeant...ne tamen exploratoriæ naves candore prodantur, colore veneto, qui marinis est fluctibus similis, vela tinguntur et funes; cera etiam, qua ungere solent naves, inficitur: nautæque vel milites venetam vestem induunt.*

Thalamegi, Θαλαμηγοί.

These were house-boats of extraordinary size and splendour, constructed by the Ptolemies for their voyages upon the Nile.

Strabo, xvii. 1. 16, διέχει δὲ τετράσχοινον τῆς Ἀλεξανδρείας ἡ Σχεδία, κατοικία πόλεως, ἐν ᾗ τὸ ναύσταθμον τῶν θαλαμηγῶν πλοίων, ἐφ᾽ οἷς οἱ ἡγεμόνες εἰς τὴν ἄνω χώραν ἀναπλέουσιν, cf. 15, εὐωχοῦνται δ᾽ ἐν σκάφαις θαλαμηγοῖς. Suetonius, Julius Cæsar, 52, *nave thalamego pæne Æthiopia tenus Ægyptum penetravit.* Appian, præfatio, 10, θαλαμηγά τε χρυσόπρυμνα καὶ χρυσέμβολα, ἐς πολέμου πομπήν, οἷς αὐτοὶ διαπλέοντες ἐπέβαινον οἱ βασιλεῖς, ὀκτακόσια. This refers to the Ptolemies. Athenæos, v. 38, κατεσκεύασε δ᾽ ὁ Φιλοπάτωρ καὶ ποτάμιον πλοῖον, τὴν θαλαμηγὸν καλουμένην, τὸ μῆκος ἔχουσαν ἡμισταδίου, κ.τ.λ. Athenæos is quoting from Callixenos, and his account of the vessel seems untrustworthy throughout. Diodoros, i. 85, ἔπειτα (τὸν μόσχον) εἰς θαλαμηγὸν ναῦν οἴκημα κεχρυσωμένον ἔχουσαν ἐμβιβάσαντες, ὡς θεὸν ἀνάγουσιν εἰς Μέμφιν. This bull was the Apis.

The term *thalamegus* used sometimes to be replaced by *cubiculata* or *lusoria*. Seneca, de beneficiis, vii. 20, *cui triremes et æratas non mitterem, lusorias et cubiculatas et alia ludibria regum in mari lascivientium mittam.* Epiphanios, ancoratus, 106, ὡς ὁ Ἀντίνοος, ὁ ἐν Ἀντινόου κεκηδευμένος, καὶ σὺν λουσορίῳ πλοίῳ κείμενος ὑπὸ Ἀδριανοῦ οὕτως κατετάγη.

Tragi, Τράγοι.

These were vessels of a type invented by the Lycians. Sisenna, apud Nonium, p. 534, *prores actuariæ tragi grandes ac phaseli primo.* cf. Pollux, i. 83, ἔστι δέ τινα πλοῖα Λύκια λεγόμενα κριοὶ καὶ τράγοι. Plutarch, de mulierum virtutibus, 9, ἔπλει δὲ (Χίμαρρος) πλοίῳ λέοντα μὲν ἔχοντι πρῴραθεν ἐπίσημον, ἐκ δὲ πρύμνης δράκοντα, καὶ πολλὰ κακὰ τοὺς Λυκίους ἐποίει. As the Chimæra was a goat with a lion's head and a snake's tail, this vessel must have been a τράγος.

Vectoriæ, Ἐπιβατηγοί.

These were vessels for carrying passengers. They were not used for cargo. These names were applied to them in the Second Century A.D.

Ulpian, in the Pandects, xiv. 1. 1. 12, *quædam enim naves onerariæ, quædam (ut ipsi dicunt) ἐπιβατηγοί, id est vectorum ductrices, sunt......ut, ecce, sunt naves quæ Brundusium a Cassiopa vel a Dyrrhachio vectores traiiciunt, àd onera inhabiles.* Suetonius, Julius Cæsar, 63, *cum per angustias Hellesponti vectoria navicula traiiceret.* This was presumably a passenger-boat ; but Cæsar, de bello Gallico, v. 8, uses the phrase *vectoriis gravibusque navigiis* for vessels carrying troops and stores. See note on *phaseli* on p. 120 for other vessels of this class.

The boats from Brindisi to Durazzo connected the Appian Way from Rome with the Egnatian Way to Salonica and the East. Cassiopa lay at the northern end of Corfu, and was on the route from Italy to Greece.

INDEX TO SUBJECTS.

INDEX TO TECHNICAL TERMS.

GREEK.

INDEX TO TECHNICAL TERMS.

LATIN.

INDEX TO AUTHORITIES.

ANCIENT WRITERS.

COMPILATIONS.

INSCRIPTIONS.

INDEX TO ILLUSTRATIONS.

PLATE 1.

Fgs. **1** and **2**, boats on the Nile: about 2500 B.C. Mentioned on pp. 2, 78. From reliefs in the tomb of Meràb, a son of king Chufu of the Fourth Dynasty: now in the Berlin Museum. Copied from Lepsius, Denkmäler aus Aegypten, part ii, plate 22.

Fg. **3**, boat on the Nile, and fgs. **4** and **5**, Egyptian ships on the Red Sea: about 1250 B.C. Mentioned on pp. 2, 9, 10, 41, 56, 68, 75, 77, 78. From reliefs in the temple at Dêr el-Baḥari built by queen Mātkarā of the Eighteenth Dynasty: still in position. Copied from Mariette, Deir-el-Bahari, plates 6 and 12.

Fg. **6**, Egyptian war-ship in action in the Mediterranean, and fgs. **7** and **8**, Asiatic war-ships disabled and sinking: about 1000 B.C. Mentioned on pp. 2, 51, 56, 65, 79, 92. From a large relief on the temple at Medînet Habû built by king Rameses III of the Twentieth Dynasty: still in position. Copied from Champollion, Monuments de l'Égypte, vol. iii, plate 222.

PLATE 2.

Fg. **9**, vessel on the Tigris: about 700 B.C. Mentioned on p. 114. From a relief in the palace at Khorsabad built by king Sargon: now in the Louvre. Copied from Botta, Monument de Ninive, vol. i, plate 33.

Fgs. **10** and **11**, Phœnician war-ship and merchant-ship: about 700 B.C. Mentioned on pp. 4, 44, 49, 52, 64, 79. From a relief in the palace at Kouyunjik built by king Sennacherib: perhaps destroyed. Copied from Layard, Monuments of Nineveh, first series, plate 71.—In reply to an enquiry, Sir A. H. Layard has kindly sent me a note to say that he found the relief in too rickety a state to be removed, and covered it up again to keep it out of harm's way.

PLATE 3.

Fg. **12**, symbol for a ship: about 600 B.C. Mentioned on pp. 69, 79, 98. From a painted vase found in the Polledrara tomb near Vulci in Etruria: now in the British Museum. Drawn from the original.

Fg. **13**, war-ship: about 600 B.C. Mentioned on pp. 64, 68, 69, 79, 80, 93. From fragments of a painted vase found near the Dipylon at Athens: one fragment now in the Louvre, the other missing. Copied from the Monumenti dell' Instituto, vol. ix, plate 40.

Fg. **14**, part of a war-ship : about 600 B.C. Mentioned on p. 51. From a fragment of a painted vase found near the Dipylon at Athens : now in the Louvre. Copied from the Monuments Grecs, nos. 11—13, plate 4.

Fgs. **15** and **16**, two war-ships in action : about 550 B.C. Mentioned on pp. 49, 57, 64, 69. From a painted vase by Aristonophos found at Cære in Etruria : now in the New Capitoline Museum at Rome. Copied from the Monumenti dell' Instituto, vol. ix, plate 4.

PLATE 4.

Fgs. **17** and **18**, war-ship and merchant-ship : about 500 B.C. Mentioned on pp. 44, 56, 57, 65, 68, 75, 81, 101. From a painted vase found at Vulci in Etruria : now in the British Museum. Drawn from the original.

Fg. **19**, two war-ships : about 500 B.C. Mentioned on pp. 56, 65, 68, 69, 78, 81, 100, 101. From a painted vase by Nicosthenes found at Vulci in Etruria : now in the Louvre. Copied from the Journal of Hellenic Studies, first series, plate 49.

PLATE 5.

Fg. **20**, stern of a war-ship : about 500 B.C. Mentioned on p. 40. From a coin of Phaselis in Lycia. Drawn from a cast.

Fg. **21**, waist of a war-ship : about 400 B.C. Mentioned on pp. 40, 44, 45, 49, 50, 52. From a fragment of a relief found on the Acropolis at Athens : now in the Acropolis Museum. Drawn from a cast.

Fg. **22**, prow of a war-ship : about 300 B.C. Mentioned on pp. 40, 62, 69. From the remains of the pedestal of the great statue of Victory found at Samothrace : now in the Louvre. Copied from a photograph.

Fg. **23**, prow of a war-ship : about 300 B.C. Mentioned on pp. 40, 57, 62, 64, 68, 69. From a coin of Cios in Bithynia. Drawn from a cast.

Fg. **24**, sterns of three war-ships : about 200 B.C. Mentioned on pp. 36, 68. From a relief probably found in Rome : now in the Doges' Palace at Venice. Copied from a photograph.

Fg. **25**, prow of a war-ship : about 50 A.D. Mentioned on pp. 16, 44, 53, 60, 66, 68, 69. From a relief found in the temple of Fortune at Præneste : now in the Vatican. Copied from a photograph.

PLATE 6.

Fg. **26**, merchant-ship : about 50 A.D. Mentioned on pp. 40, 66, 67, 69, 78, 89, 94, 100. From a relief on the tomb of Nævoleia Tyche at Pompei : still in position. Copied from Niccolini, Case di Pompei, Sepolcro di Nevoleia Tyche.

Fg. **27**, merchant-ship : in 67 A.D. Mentioned on pp. 89, 90, 100. From a dated coin of Alexandria. Drawn from a cast.

Fg. **28**, merchant-ship : in 186 A.D. Mentioned on pp. 78, 89. From a dated coin of the emperor Commodus. Drawn from a cast.

Fg. **29**, merchant-ship, and fgs. **30** and **31**, parts of another : about 200 A.D. Mentioned on pp. 36, 40, 58, 66, 67, 78, 81, 89, 90, 93, 94, 95, 98, 104. From a relief found at Porto near the mouth of the Tiber : now in the private collection of Prince Torlonia at Rome. Copied from Guglielmotti, Delle due navi Romane, frontispiece.

Fg. **32**, merchant-ship: about 200 A.D. Mentioned on p. 90. From a relief on a sarcophagus found in the precincts of the Vatican : now in the Lateran Museum. Copied from a photograph.

Fg. **33**, merchant-ship : about 200 A.D. Mentioned on p. 89. From a relief found at Utica : now in the British Museum. Drawn from the original.

Fg. **34**, merchant-ship : in 305 A.D. Mentioned on p. 89. From a dated coin of the emperor Maximian. Drawn from a cast.

PLATE 7.

Fgs. **35** and **36**, two war-ships in a sham-fight : about 50 A.D. Mentioned on pp. 58, 68, 78, 89. From a fresco in the temple of Isis at Pompei : now in the Naples Museum. Copied from Niccolini, Case di Pompei, Tempio d'Iside, plate 4.

Fg. **37**, merchant-ship : about 250 A.D. Mentioned on pp. 69, 89. From a fresco in the Callistine Catacombs at Rome : still in position. Copied from G-B. de Rossi, Roma Sotterranea, vol. ii, plate 14.

Fg. **38**, war-ships : about 500 A.D. Mentioned on pp. 78, 90. From a manuscript of the Iliad in the Ambrosian Library at Milan. Copied from Mai, Homeri Iliados picturæ antiquæ, plate 32, with some corrections from a photograph.

Fg. **39**, ships in harbour at Classis : about 600 A.D. Mentioned on pp. 17, 90. From a mosaic in the church of S. Apollinare Nuovo at Ravenna : still in position. Copied from a photograph.

Fg. **40**, merchant-ship : date uncertain. Mentioned on pp. 69, 75, 89. From a fresco in one of the caves at Ajunta in India : still in position. Copied from a reproduction in the South Kensington Museum.

PLATE 8.

Fg. **41**, figure-head in bronze : about 50 B.C. Mentioned on p. 66. Found off Actium : now in the British Museum. Drawn from the original. One sixth of actual size.

Fg. **42**, prow of a war-ship : about 150 B.C. Mentioned on p. 65. From a coin of Leucas in Acarnania. Drawn from a cast.

Fig. **43**, auxiliary ram in bronze : about 50 B.C. Mentioned on p. 65. Found in Genoa harbour : now in the Armoury at Turin. Copied from the Archäologisches Jahrbuch, vol. iv, p. 12. One twelfth of actual size.

Fg. **44**, anchor : about 350 B.C. Mentioned on p. 71. From a coin, probably of Apollonia in Mysia. Drawn from a cast.

Fgs. **45** to **47**, portions of an anchor in lead : about 50 B.C. Mentioned on pp. 71, 72. Found off the coast of Cyrene : now in the British Museum. Drawn from the original. One sixteenth of actual size.

PLATE **1**

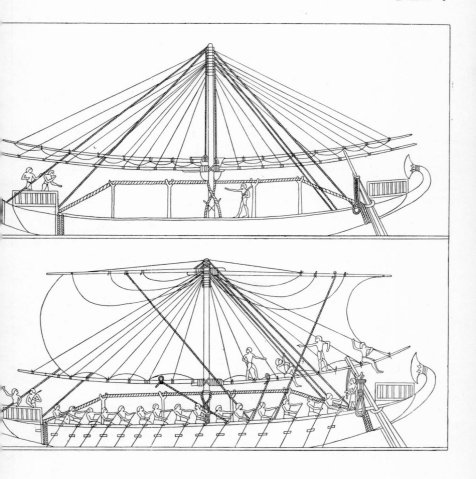

PLATE 1

PLATE **2**

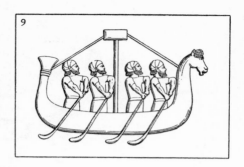

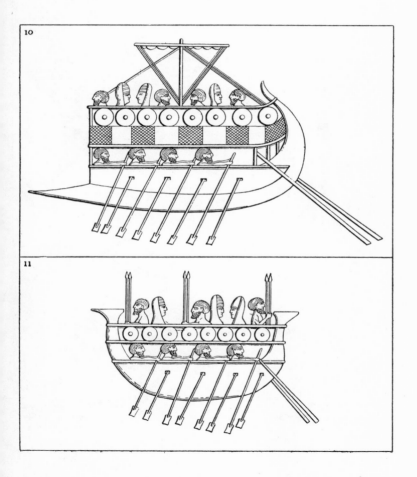

PLATE **3**

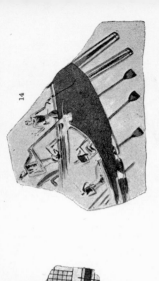

14

13

12

16

15

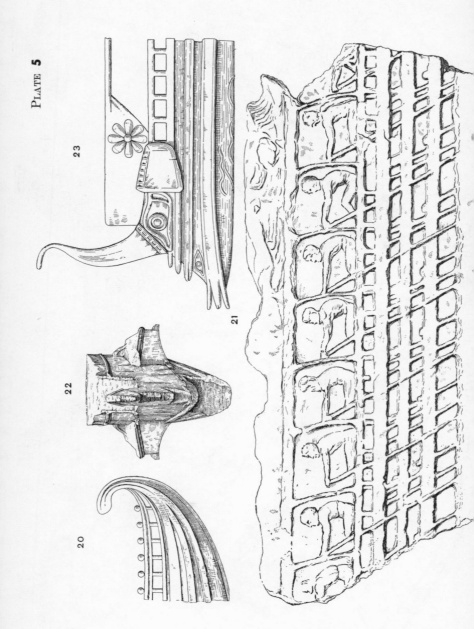

PLATE 5

PLATE **5.**

24

25

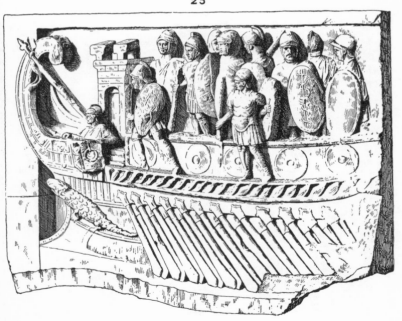

PLATE 6

26

29

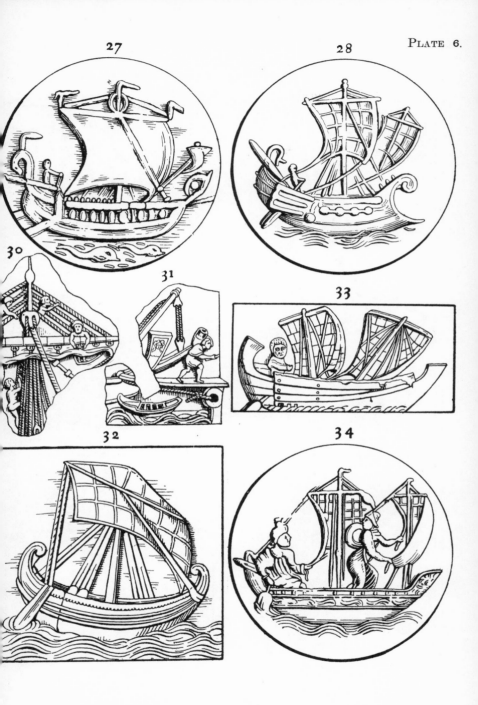

PLATE 6.

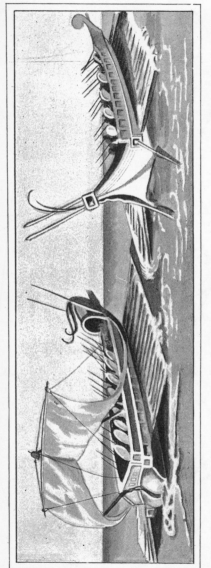

35

36

37

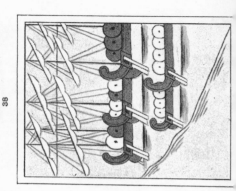

38

40

PLATE **8**

41

42

44

43

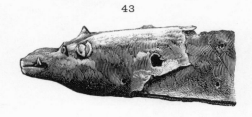

PLATE 8.

45

46

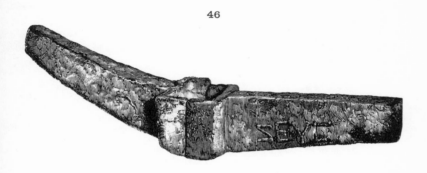

47

THE GREEK WARSHIP.

(*Journal of Hellenic Studies* 1905 xxv.)

I.

THE controversy as to the arrangement of the oars in ancient warships has been, in one aspect and with the due exceptions, a controversy between the scholars and the sailors, in which, while the sailors cannot well be wrong on their own ground, the same impossibility hardly applies to their opponents. When the practical seaman points out that superposed banks of oars, in the accepted [1] sense, are a frank impossibility, it is hardly a conclusive reply to tell him that his acquaintance with the authorities leaves something to be desired. It follows, that for anyone who, like the present writer, is convinced that the sailors are right, the real interest of the question is this: does the evidence compel me, or even invite me, to believe in a practical impossibility?

---

[1] By 'the accepted theory' in this paper I mean the group of solutions (they are legion) which, though differing in details of arrangement, agree in this, that a trireme had three banks of oars at a *substantial* interval one over the other, a quinquereme five, a dekeres ten, and so forth, each oar rowed by one man and the lowest bank fairly near the water. (I do not include Bauer, or so much of Assmann as relates to breit-polyereis.) All these solutions rest on a common basis and fall together if that be destroyed. The most important current expression of this theory, beside Mr. Torr's, is Assmann's hoch-polyeres theory (art. *Seewesen* in Baumeister and several papers, notably *Jahrb.* 1889, p. 91, *Zur Kenntniss der Antiken Schiffe*), followed by Droysen, *Griechische Kriegsaltertümer* in Hermann's Lehrbuch; Luebeck, *Das Seewesen der Griechen und Römer*, 2 vols. 1890; and Schmidt, *Ueber griechische Dreireiher*, 1899; to judge by Luebeck's article *biremis*, it will be adopted in the new Pauly-Wissowa. Bauer's theory (*Griechische Kriegsaltertümer* in Müller's *Handb. d. klass. Alt.-Wiss.*, 1893, and several papers), that a trireme had a *very slight* interval between the banks and that ships larger than triremes never had more than three banks but employed more than one man to an oar, is quite a separate matter. Important is Admiral Fincati's *Le Triremi*, 1881; a trireme had three oars to one bench, like a Venetian galley a zenzile. I unfortunately only know this book in Serre's translation, at the end of Vol. 1 of his *Marines de la guerre*, 1885 and 1891, from which I cite it. I cannot classify Admiral Serre; though accepted, I believe, in France, his views seem to bear little relation to the evidence. Weber's book *Die Lösung des Trierenrätsels*, published 1896, but written much earlier, with many blunders and mistranslations, contains ideas. A trireme had three men to an oar, a quinquereme five, etc. Accepted by Speck, *Handelsgeschichte*, 1900. Weber has no monopoly in mistranslations. The best exposition of the accepted theory prior to Assmann is probably that of Cartault, *La Trière Athénienne*, 1881. I understand he afterwards agreed with Bauer. While this paper was in the press two important articles appeared: one by Mr. Torr in Dar.-Sagl. s.v. *navis*, which seems to state his version of the accepted theory more definitely than was done in *Ancient Ships*; the other by Mr. A. B. Cook in Whibley's *Companion to Greek Studies*, who favours the Venetian theory, but not very decidedly. References to Torr in this paper are to *Ancient Ships* unless otherwise stated.

If it does, the fact obviously has a very real bearing on the question of the
degree of credibility to be attached to ancient history generally; and this

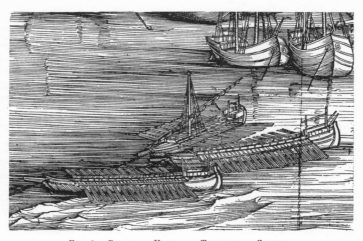

FIG. 1.—GROUP OF VENETIAN TRIREMES A ZENZILE.

From a wood-cut in the British Museum, dated 1500, by Jacopo de' Barbari. (Large view of
Venice, Mitchell Collection, 1895. 1. 22. 1195.)

seems to me to be the true importance of what has become known as the
'trireme-problem.' The object of this paper is simply to examine evidence,

FIG. 2.—SMALL PORTION OF A VENETIAN BIREME A ZENZILE, SHOWING THE ARRANGEMENT
OF THE ROWERS.

From a wood-cut in the British Museum, late fifteenth century (1866. 7. 14. 48*). This appears
to be a state galley, and is at rest, with the crew sitting in her.

and to try to ascertain primarily what quinqueremes and triremes were *not*,
with a view to clearing the ground: the period to be considered ends in

effect with Actium,[2] which closes an epoch in naval warfare. The positive conclusion appears to be that the Greek system was analogous to the Venetian, *i.e.* that a trireme was in the nature of a trireme a zenzile, and that the large ships of the last three centuries B.C. were galleys a scaloccio.[3]

Apart from the Athenian lists, which are conclusive for what they state, the evidence falls mainly into three classes; (1) historians and inscriptions, (2) scholiasts and lexicographers, (3) monuments. Class (1) varies in weight but includes all the best evidence. Class (2) has no independent value at all; at best it can only be used to illustrate Class (1). Where they disagree Class (1) must prevail. Probably Mr. Torr is right in saying that Class (2) can be neglected altogether. In Class (3) every item must be taken on its own merits; one may be of great value, another worthless. This class requires a more thorough going criticism than it has ever received or than I am competent to give.[4] Many supporters of the accepted theory are inconsistent; they may begin, like Assmann, by saying that Class (2) is not trustworthy; they always end by relying upon it. This paper is intended to be based primarily on Class (1). For obvious reasons I have had to consider Class (2) to a certain extent; I have never relied on it myself and I do not consider it evidence.

The following propositions seem to represent the facts of the case.[5]

A.—The terms thranite, zugite, thalamite, have nothing to do with the horizontal rows (or banks) of oars. The rowers were in three divisions, or squads, thranites astern, zugites amidships, thalamites in the bows. This applies to triremes and the larger polyereis.[6]

B.—The terms τρίκροτος δίκροτος and μονόκροτος refer primarily to these squads.

C.—There is no evidence of any kind, good or bad, for the dogma that, among Greeks and Romans, at all times and in all places, one man rowed one oar; but there is good evidence (1) that in the triremes of the Peloponnesian war one man rowed one oar and (2) that the same applies to the Athenian quadriremes and quinqueremes of the fourth century.

D.—There is some evidence (1) that in the first century B.C. more than one man sometimes rowed one oar and (2) that the larger polyereis were too

---

[2] I have had to notice the boats on Trajan's column, and one or two other matters, and, of course, writers of later date.

[3] A trireme a zenzile was one in which three men sat on one bench on the same level, one a little astern of the other, each rowing one oar, the three oars issuing through one opening side by side, and giving the appearance of a bundle of three oars (see Figs. 1 and 2). In the galley a scaloccio several men rowed each oar.

[4] The monumental evidence is often overrated. Even in the case of the best monuments,

one can never say how far the artist may have sacrificed truth of detail to artistic considerations. It will be considered under *E.*

[5] However little one wishes to dogmatise, one cannot always be writing in the potential mood and expressing every shade of proper reservation.

[6] By 'the larger polyereis' in this paper I generally mean quadriremes to dekereis both inclusive, nothing over a dekeres being heard of in action.

low in the water, too light, and of too simple an arrangement, to admit of the accepted theory being applicable to them.

E.—There is no good evidence, and very little bad, that can be made to refer to the accepted theory. There is none that necessitates, or even invites, this theory.

It remains to consider the evidence for these propositions,[7] and the conclusions to be drawn from them; and, finally, to consider the Athenian trireme.

A.

Polyaen. 5, 43. 'Calliades, overtaken by a swifter ship, kept using his steerage frequently, according as (the pursuer) tried to ram now from one side and now from the other, so that the pursuer, striking his steerage with her catheads, might not be able to ram by reason of her ram being over against his first (*i.e.*, sternmost) thranite oars.'[8] That is to say, as the boat behind made her shot, Calliades put on his steerage; the ram missed his stern and slid past it toward, pointing at, his sternmost oars, while the cathead struck his stern, and of course too high to do much harm; this checked the pursuer's way for the moment, and while she was straightening herself for another shot Calliades would gain a little on his new tack. The oars the ram pointed at were the first or endmost *thranite* oars. On the accepted theory they would have been the first or endmost oars of all three classes. The thranite oars therefore were in a group at the stern.

Polyaen. 3, 11, 14. Chabrias prepared a second set of steering oars for rough weather which he put out through the παρεξειρεσία beside the thranite oars (κατὰ τὰς θρανίτιδας κώπας). His avowed object was to prevent the steering oars leaving the water as the ship's stern lifted, and of course the oars that they were put out beside can only have been the sternmost oars. The thranite oars then are the sternmost oars. On Assmann's theory no sense can be given to the words 'the thranite oars' at all;[9] for as he supposes that the thranite oars were rowed through the

---

[7] *A* is very old as an *opinion*. *B* and a good deal of *D* (2) are new, I think. *C* (1) is given correctly by Bauer. *D* (1) is primarily Weber. In referring in this paper to Bauer's arrangement I mean his arrangement considered physically, *i.e.*, as a slight interval only between the rows, apart from questions like the meaning of thranite or παρεξειρεσία.

[8] τῷ τὴν ἐμβολὴν εἶναι κατὰ τὰς πρώτας θρανίτιδας κώπας. The only writer known to me who cites this passage is Breusing, *Die Lösung des Trierenrätsels*, 1889; and as he could not understand it at all, he said that the words from τῷ τὴν ἐμβολὴν to the end must be a gloss. If one may discard everything as a gloss that does not suit one's own theory, one

can prove anything. No one who has seen a bumping race, and watched the cox of the boat in front washing off the nose of the boat behind with his steerage, will have any difficulty in construing the passage. I quote Polyaenus throughout from Woelfflin-Melber. He made considerable use of Ephorus; but according to Melber, *Ueber den Quellen und der Wert der Strategemensammlung Polyäns*, (1885), the passages most material to this paper (5, 43; 3, 11, 7 and 12 and 13; 5, 22, 2) are derived from some earlier work on naval tactics.

[9] Assmann has to translate it (Baumeister, 1616) 'neben den *hintersten* Thranitenriemen,' which is not in the Greek.

παρεξειρεσία and the others through portholes below, if the steering oars were put through the παρεξειρεσία they could not be beside any oars *but* thranite oars, and the words are redundant and meaningless. The necessary sense is 'beside the sternmost oars.'[10]

Polyb. 16, 3 (battle of Chios). Philip's dekeres rams a trihemiolia[11] in the middle of the hull under the thranite 'thole.'[12] On the accepted theory this can only mean 'between the thranite and zugite banks.' The difficulty is twofold : (1) historians never (I think) mention the *height* at which a ship is struck : their references are always longitudinal, so to speak. They distinguish between blows ὕφαλα and ἔξαλα ; otherwise they appear to assume, as all monuments (and all reason) shows, that the ram, if not submerged, was near the waterline ; (2) even if the trihemiolia were lower than a trireme, the dekeres, if I am right as to its height, (see under *D*), cannot have had its ram placed as high as the 'zugite' bank ; while if the accepted theory be true, then, even if the trihemiolia were as high as a trireme, the far taller dekeres must have cut her right down with the stem and could not be said to ram her 'under' anything.—The passage is of course not conclusive.[13]

---

[10] This passage, unlike the former, is not evidence against anyone but those who accept Assmann's view (based on the monuments) of the παρεξειρεσία as an outrigger or 'oar-box' (Riemen-kasten) ; however, as it is conclusive that Assmann is right on this point, this is not very material. Chabrias' new steering oars were not where the old ones were. The new ones were through the παρεξειρεσία ; therefore, the old ones were not. But the old ones were in the usual place on the stern of the ship, as shewn by their lifting clear of the water ; therefore the old view, that by παρεξειρεσία is meant the stern (and bow) of the ship *beyond* the oarage, is untenable. The same conclusion is supported by *Peripl. Pont. Eux.* 3, the waves coming in not only through the oar-holes but over the παρεξειρεσίαι (where the reference *must* be to a *higher* point, not a *different* point) ; and by the frequent references to ships losing part of their παρεξειρεσία in action (Thuc. 7, 34 is a good instance). But the absolutely decisive passage is Polyaen. 3, 11, 13 ; Chabrias stretches skins over the παρεξειρεσία *of each side* of the ship (ὑπὲρ τὴν παρεξειρεσίαν ἑκατέρου τοίχου) and nails them to the deck above, thus making a φράγμα which prevented the waves washing in and the oarsmen looking out. Chabrias here improvised a cataphract. Assmann never really proved his own theory of the παρεξειρεσία ; at the same time there is nothing in Buresch's attack on it, *Die Ergebnisse der neueren Forschung über die alten Trieren* (*Woch. für klass. Phil.* 1891, No. 1).

[11] In a Rhodian inscription of the first half of the first century B.C. (*I.G.* xii. fasc. i. No. 43) trihemioliai are contrasted with cataphracts, and again triremes with aphracts ; suggesting that the trihemiolia was then a smaller or less important ship than a trireme. The form τριηρημιολία (Ath. 203 d) suggests that Photius is right in calling it a trireme ; if so, it was a light trireme evolved from a hemiolia (as to which see n. 22), as the trireme from the pentekontor. The suggestion that it means a ship of 2½ banks is the merest guesswork.

[12] κατὰ μέσον τὸ κύτος ὑπὸ τὸν θρανίτην σκαλμόν. Cited by Weber.

[13] As I shall often have to refer to the battle of Chios, I should note that some writers (*e.g.* Beloch, *Bevölkerung*, and Ihne) doubt the accuracy of Polybius' version, obviously drawn from Rhodian sources, that it was a defeat for Philip. But even if so, this cannot affect the details of single events, which are precisely given ; for even if the Rhodians wrote up an account of the battle for the honour of Rhodes and Theophiliscus, they would take all the more care to put in details that either did happen or might, consistently with nautical probability, have happened. The account of this battle is hardly affected by Polybius' supposed inaccuracies as to the first Punic war, for which his sources were far different. One cannot go into the case for Polybius in a note ; but I would point out (1) that, as to the numbers, no one, I think, has yet examined the numbers in the sea-fights generally up to Actium, and the only examina-

Is there any counter-evidence, i.e., evidence for the view that thranite refers to the men in the highest row or bank of a trireme, zugite to those in the middle row or bank, thalamite to those in the lowest, however the rows were arranged ? All that I have ever seen cited belongs (except Pollux) to Class (2) and is given below [14]; I know of no other.[15] I have collected these passages so that it may be seen at a glance that all of them (except the first half of Schol. *Frogs* 1074 and one from Eustathius and that from Pollux) represent *one* statement only, namely, that given in the latter half of Schol. *Frogs* 1074.

If the latter half of this Scholion on *Frogs* 1074 is all one sentence, what it says is ʻThe τάξις which is κάτω is the thalamites, that which is μέση is the zugites, that which is ἄνω is the thranites. *Therefore*, the thranite is astern, the zugite in the middle, the thalamite toward the prow.ʼ Everyone (except Weber) has omitted the οὖν. Now if οὖν means ʻ therefore,ʼ it follows of course that by ἄνω the Scholiast means ʻ astern ʼ and not ʻ above ʼ—the *consequence* of sitting ἄνω is that you sit astern—and by κάτω he means ʻ in the bows ʼ and not ʻ below.ʼ [16] Any supporter of the accepted

---

tion for part of the period that I know of—Kromayer, *Die Entwickelung der röm. Flotte vom Seeräuberkriege des Pompeius bis zum Schlacht von Actium* (Philol. 1897), p. 426—accepts the great numbers recorded for the war with Sextus Pompey ; (2) that to bring in the population question (Beloch, Serre) is surely to explain *obscurum per obscurius ;* (3) that the real exaggeration is not in the separate accounts of battles, which generally mention ʻ ships ʼ or ʻ cataphracts,ʼ but in the summing-up chapter (1, 63), where Polybius has used πεντήρεις when he ought to have said warships, as appears both from the separate accounts and from the *columna rostrata* (*C.I.L.* 1, 195) ; and (4) that Ihne's objection (*Röm. Gesch.*[2] 2, 47) that the Romans had ships before the first Punic war, neglects the obvious explanation that Polybius or his authority means no more in speaking of the creation of the Roman fleet than we might in speaking of the creation of the German fleet—a first serious bid for sea-power. See also n. 91.

[14] Schol. *Frogs* 1074 τῷ θαλάμακι· τῷ κωπηλατοῦντι ἐν τῷ κάτω μέρει τῆς τριηροῦς· τῷ θαλάμακι· οἱ θαλάμακες ὀλίγον ἐλάμβανον μισθὸν διὰ τὸ κολοβαῖς χρῆσθαι κώπαις παρὰ τὰς ἄλλας [Γ] τάξεις τῶν ἐρετῶν ὅτι μᾶλλον ἦσαν ἐγγὺς τοῦ ὕδατος. ‖ ἦσαν δὲ τρεῖς τάξεις τῶν ἐρετῶν· καὶ ἡ μὲν κάτω θαλαμῖται, ἡ δὲ μέση ζυγῖται, ἡ δὲ ἄνω θρανῖται. θρανίτης οὖν ὁ πρὸς τὴν πρύμναν, ζυγίτης ὁ μέσος, θαλάμιος ὁ πρὸς τὴν πρῷραν. (I cite down to ‖ from Rutherford's ed. of the scholia (1896); he does not give the latter half, which is therefore not in the *codex Ravennas*.

I cite it from the *codex Venetus.* In the former half, according to the facsimile published by the Hellenic Society, cod. *Ven.* omits Γ̄.) Schol. *Ach.* 162 τῶν ἐρεττόντων οἱ μὲν ἄνω ἐρέττοντες θρανῖται λέγονται, οἱ δὲ μέσοι ζυγῖται, οἱ δὲ κάτω θαλάμιοι. Hesych. θρανίτης ὁ πρὸς τὴν πρύμναν, ζυγίτης ὁ μέσος, θαλάμιος ὁ πρὸς τῇ πρῴρᾳ (so Suidas and Zonaras). Hesych. θαλάμιος ἐρέτης· ὁ κατωτάτω ἐρέσσων ἐν τῇ νηΐ θαλάμιος λέγεται, ὁ δὲ μέσος ζύγιος, ὁ δὲ ἀνώτατος θρανίτης. θαλάμιαι κῶπαι· οἱ κατωτάτω· καὶ οἱ ταύτην ἔχοντες τὴν χώραν θαλάμιοι λέγονται. Suidas. θρανίτης λεώς· τῶν γὰρ ἐρεττόντων οἱ μὲν ἄνω θρανῖται λέγονται, οἱ δὲ μέσοι ζυγῖται, οἱ δὲ κάτω θαλάμιοι· Etym. Mag. θαλαμίδιοι κῶπαι· ὁ κατώτατος ἐρέτης θαλάμιος λέγεται, ὁ δὲ μέσος ζύγιος, ὁ δὲ ἀνώτατος θρανίτης. Eustath. 1818, 52 ἔχει δέ, φησίν (Pausanias), οὗτος (thranite) τὴν ἄνω ἕδραν, τὴν δευτέραν ζύγιος, τὴν τρίτην θαλάμιος. 640, 11 θαλαμῖται καὶ θαλάμακες ἐρέται οἱ ὑπὸ τοὺς θρανίτας. Lastly Pollux 1, 87 καλοῖτο δ' ἂν καὶ θάλαμος οὗ οἱ θαλάμιοι ἐρέττουσι· τὰ δὲ μέσα τῆς νεὼς ζύγα, οὗ οἱ ζύγιοι καθῆνται· τὸ δὲ περὶ τὸ κατάστρωμα θρᾶνος, οὗ οἱ θρανῖται.—There is another scholion on *Frogs* 1074, given by Zuretti, *Scolii al Pluto ed alle Rane d'Aristofane dal codice Veneto 472 e dal codice Cremonense* 12229, I, 6, 28 : τρεῖς τάξεις ἦσαν ἐν τῇ τριήρει· οἱ μὲν πρῶτοι θρανῖται καλούμενοι, οἱ δὲ δεύτεροι ζυγῖται, οἱ δὲ τρίτοι θαλάμακες. Read with Eustath. 1818, 52, this illustrates the use of πρῶτος as sternmost in Polyaen. 5, 43 above.

[15] Unless it be Ar. *Mech.* 4, discussed under *F.*

[16] That ἄνω and κάτω mean ʻastern' and

theory must say then either that οὖν here means, not 'therefore,' but something indeterminate, such as 'well, then;' or else that the sentence is two separate scholia, combined in an unintelligent manner. Either is possible, though neither can be shewn to be correct; but in any case it is certain that this scholion and the similar passages depend on the meaning of ἄνω and κάτω.

Pollux 1, 87 is different, and suits my view at least as well as the accepted theory, even if Pollux be referring only to triremes, which we have no right to assume.

Remains Eustath. 640, 11. If this is not (as I think it is) Eustathius' own misunderstanding of κάτω, then the question arising is, are we to follow on the one hand Eustathius, or on the other Polyaenus (twice) and (in effect) Arrian (see *B*)? The answer admits of no possible doubt.

What it then comes to is this. In order to say that the terms thranite, zugite, and thalamite refer to longitudinal rows or banks one over the other, we must take the latter portion of the Scholion on *Frogs* 1074, say it is evidence, translate it in a way that, at best, cannot be shewn to be correct, and use the result, with the (possible) help of Eustathius, to overrule two passages in Polyaenus, possibly one in Polybius and (in effect) Arrian (see *B*); and having done this, we land after all in the difficulty in which everyone is landed by the fact that all the higher values, as shewn by that inconvenient tesserakonteres, only possessed the same three classes of oarsmen.[17] I may add that my view explains that thorn in the side of the accepted theory, the greater number of the thranite oars as compared with the zugite and thalamite oars, which the Athenian lists render certain.

B.

The terms that correspond to the division of the rowers on a warship into squads are τρίκροτος, δίκροτος, and μονόκροτος, which are usually referred to the (triple) beat of the three banks of a trireme, the (double) beat of the

---

'in the bows' has often been asserted but never proved. I believe it is correct, but my reason for thinking so is given in *B*; it has nothing to do with the Schol. on *Frogs* 1074. If it be correct, all the ἄνω and κάτω passages given in the note are disposed of conclusively.

[17] This forced Assmann to explain *e.g.* a dekeres as constituted by three superposed triads, each triad consisting (in superposition) of a thranite, zugite, and thalamite; with a lonely thalamite on the top. The τεσσερακοντήρης is legimate evidence so far as it goes. Since the inscription about the τριακοντήρης was found, no one can suppose it to be a bad joke of Callixenus': and the idea that it was a kind of flat-bottomed river barge (Assmann, Droysen, Torr) seems to me to be disposed of by the fact

that Philopator *had* such a barge (the θαλαμηγός of Ath. 204 d. *seq.*). If any one will read Athenaeus consecutively he will see that he puts side by side three monsters of three different types; the τεσσερακοντήρης (long ship), the θαλαμηγός (ποτάμιον πλοῖον), and Hiero's ship (round ship). The height of the tesserakonteres, on which rests the 'Mississippi steamer' theory, is given to the top of the ἀκροστόλιον, which (*race* Liddell and Scott) is *not* the gunwale, see Torr, 68. Those who treat δίπρωρος as ἀμφίπρωρος have forgotten the old Calais-Douvres; and the twin hull was only the logical outcome of the common practice of lashing two ships together to get a steady platform.

two banks of a bireme, and the (single) beat of the one bank of a μονήρης. There is no evidence for this whatever, and if it were true one ought to find τετρακίκροτος and so forth, forms that never occur. The conventional explanation of their non-occurrence, given by Graser and repeated by Cartault and Luebeck, *viz.*, that the larger polyereis did not appear to an *observer from the side* to have more than a *triple* beat, is futile; why did any ship, *from the side*, appear to have more than a single beat?[18] The words must apply to some arrangement which was threefold and no more; and it can hardly be a coincidence that precisely the same point arises over the words thranite, zugite, and thalamite.

The important passage is Arr. *Anab.* 6, 5, 2,[19] generally cited, together with a note that δίκροτος = διήρης, to shew how near to the water was the lower bank of a bireme. The explanation is unfortunate, as Alexander had no biremes with him. Indeed they were not in use in his time. No one seems to have considered this preliminary point.

To take things in order. Arr. *Anab.* 5. 8, Alexander carries his ships over from the Indus to the Hydaspes, triakonts in three sections, the smaller boats in two. 6, 1. He builds on the Hydaspes many triakonts and hemioliai, also horse-transports and other transports. 6, 2. The fleet that started down the Hydaspes, according to Ptolemy, consisted of eighty triakontors, together with horse-transports, cercuri, and river boats, some being native boats, and some newly built. 6, 5, 2. (At the junction of the Hydaspes and the Acesines) the cargo boats (στρογγύλα) came through the rapids safely; but the warships (μακραί) suffered, as they were lower in the water, and those of them that were δίκροτοι had their κάτω oars not much above the water; and two were lost. 6, 14. He builds more ships in the land of the Malli. 6, 15, 1. He receives some more triakontors and some cargo boats (στρογγύλα). 6, 15, 4. He refits. 6, 18, 3. On his expedition from Patala to the sea he takes the swiftest of the hemioliai, all the triakontors, and some cercuri. 6, 18, 4. The waves get up and he loses some triakontors. Arr. *Ind.* 19. On the Hydaspes, Alexander had about 800 vessels, both warships (μακραί) and cargo boats (στρογγύλα) and horse-transports and food-transports. 23. Nearchus loses two warships (μακραί) and a cercurus, in a storm. 31. Nearchus (requiring a good ship for special service) sends a triakontor—the island story. No other writer adds anything.[20]

Two things come out strongly from this: (1) the important warships were the triakontors; (2) the *only* warships were the triakontors and hemioliai, for Arrian does not count a cercurus[21] as μακρά (*Ind.* 23). The warships

---

[18] If there was a visible triple beat on *any* view, what becomes of the stock comparison with the wings of a bird?

[19] ὅσαι τε δίκροτοι αὐτῶν (*i.e.* τῶν μακρῶν νεῶν) τὰς κάτω κώπας οὐκ ἐπὶ πολὺ ἔξω ἔχουσαι τοῦ ὕδατος.

[20] Curtius, Diodorus, and Justin are silent. Plutarch (*Alex.* 63) says he built πορθμεῖα κωπήρη καὶ σχεδίας.

[21] For cercurus see Torr *s.v.*; a type equally suited for warfare or commerce, but always reckoned among the small craft of a fleet; he has a lot of evidence. Weber's idea that a cercurus was a trireme is a mere mistranslation of App. *Pun.* 121.

then that were δίκροτοι were either triakontors or hemioliai. But whatever δίκροτος means, it is certain that a hemiolia was not δίκροτος.[22] The ships that were δίκροτοι then were triakontors, i.e., μονήρεις of fifteen oars aside. Consequently, δίκροτος does not primarily mean a bireme, whatever the lexicographers say, and does not therefore refer to the double beat of a bireme's two banks of oars, supposing it to have had such.

If then δίκροτος does not mean ' double-beating,' [23] it can only mean ' double-beaten.' Now συγκεκροτημένοι is the common term for a trained crew, 'beaten together,' or 'welded together'—(we sometimes say ground together); δίκροτος therefore means 'double-welded,' a ship whose crew is trained in, or falls into, two squads.[24]

Now we can get at the meaning of ἄνω and κάτω. A triakontor had two squads of rowers, and, though single-banked, the oars were distinguished as those κάτω from those something else, presumably ἄνω. In relation to the oarage, therefore, κάτω and ἄνω mean fore and aft; [25] and this is confirmed by the usage of κατά and ἀνά.[26] This explains the Schol. on Frogs 1074, in

---

[22] App. Mith. 92 the pirates originally (πρῶτον) used myoparones and hemioliai, later (εἶτα) δικρότοις and triremes, i.e., when they organised themselves. This is conclusive ; and overrules Hesych. ἡμιολία· ἡ δίκροτος ναῦς, where the definite article makes nonsense anyhow. I want to make this clear, because the accepted explanation of ἡμιολία is a ship with 1½ banks. There is not a shred of evidence for this ; it rests on the fact that ἡμιόλιος means 1½. I might say that hemiolia means a ship of 1½ squads, which has at least the support of Photius s.v. οὗ τὸ ἡμιόλιον μέρος ψιλὸν ἐρετῶν ἐστὶ πρὸς τὸ ἀπ' αὐτοῦ μάχεσθαι. The certain thing is that it was a pirate ship (Arr. Anab. 3, 2, 4, App. Mith. 92, Phot. s.v.), and a typical one (Theophr. Char. 25, 1), and could be classed with the little myoparones, which were certainly single banked (evidence Torr 119) ; it was a favourite for surprises (Diod. 19, 65, Polyaen. 4, 7, 4) ; and the latter passage also shews it was small, the object of Demetrius being to display the minimum of force. Pirates, whose heads depended on their speed, would not go in for fancy arrangements of oars.

[23] The word occurs in the active sense once, in a chorus (Eur. I. T. 407), δικρότοισι κώπαις, of the Argo, (a traditional single-banked ship, Ap. Rhod. 1, 394 seq.), where it refers to the beat of the oars on either side of the ship. This shews that in Euripides' time it cannot have been a technical term for the beat of two banks on the same side of the ship.

[24] The same causes which compelled the Venetians to divide the crew of a trireme into

3 squads and work as a rule in relays (Fincati p. 167) would have compelled the Greeks also to do this. Part of a crew did row alone, (Thuc. 3, 49 ; Polyaen. 5, 22, 4 ; Xen. Hell. 6, 2, 29) ; but these passages do not shew which part. If, however, when not in action, one squad only rowed at a time, as at Venice, it is explained how the Athenian horse-transports, with 60 oars only, kept up with triremes.

[25] i.e., when used as technical terms ; for Thuc. 7, 65 (the Syracusans covered with hides τὰς πρῴρας καὶ τῆς νεὼς ἄνω) might refer to the upper works of the ship. As to οὐκ ἐπὶ πολὺ ἔξω ἔχουσαι τοῦ ὕδατος, the forward oars would of course suffer most in the bad water. But it may be that these triakontors, built for a river, were even lower in the water than usual, and anyhow they would be heavily laden. Some were lost going down from Patala

[26] ' In the Odyssey κατά is the regular word for motion inwards, ἀνά for motion outwards ;' Mr. J. L. Myres, J.H.S. xx. p. 140 sq. For later Greek, Mr. A. P. Oppé, J.H.S. xxiv. p. 225 sq. Mr. G. F. Hill kindly furnished me with these references. If the ship was generally entered from the stern, this would explain why κάτω should be fore and ἄνω aft ; and at Athens anyhow she would be entered from the stern, if launched bow first ; see Prof. E. A. Gardner, Ancient Athens, p. 553. This is also borne out by the ordinary term for 'to come forward,' ἀναφέρειν τὴν κώπην, which shows that ἀνά is motion toward the stern.

the sense required by the natural reading of the Greek,[27] and all the other evidence of Class (2) cited n. 14, except perhaps the one passage in Eustathius, which, as we have seen, must be treated as overruled. The conclusion reached under section A is thus strongly supported.

It is of course also possible that in some ships the forward squad sat, or once sat, rather lower on the whole than the after squad.[28] If this were so, the thranite oars would on the whole be rather the longest; and if the Athenian trireme resembled the Venetian triremes in Fig. 1, this may perhaps explain the statement in the Athenian lists that of some condemned thranite oars ten were serviceable for the zugites.[30] Once κάτω had come to mean 'forward,' the term would remain, even if in historical times the difference was slight, or even non-existent; how many centuries have passed since 'forecastle' or 'starboard' had any real meaning?

But to return to δίκροτος. When Hesychius says that a διήρης ναῦς was also called δίκροτος, is he wrong? Or is the more accurate Pollux (1, 82) wrong in treating διήρης and δίκροτος as separate ships? I think both are right. I will assume here for a moment the result arrived at in section E, that (subject to the meaning of δίκροτος) there is no evidence for the use of biremes until well on in the first century B.C.; the question then is, is there any passage in which δίκροτος must mean a bireme? I think there can be no doubt that it means something different from and larger than a μονήρης, but smaller than a trireme, in App. Mith. 92 (see n. 22); and it will be fairest therefore to assume that to Appian generally δίκροτος

---

[27] Incidentally, this may suggest that Schol. Frogs 1074 represents a genuine tradition, i.e., one descended from a time when men knew the technical meaning of κάτω; for of course I do not suppose that the Scholiast knew this, any more than Eustathius, and all that I can attempt to shew is what the word meant to Arrian, or rather to Ptolemy.

[28] Bauer, Neue Philol. Rundschau 1895, p. 265, 'in Schräg vom Hinterschiff zum Vorschiff abfallender Linie augeordneten Ruderpforten,' which may well be right. It is clearly shewn in the Venetian triremes in Fig. 1. See Aesch. Agam. 1617, and n. 80.

[29] The inclination of the παρεξειρεσία to the long axis of the ship (n. 118) would furnish another explanation. The longest oars of the tesserakonteres were thranite oars, as the reference to the lead shows (Ath. 203 f); but as we have no idea how she was arranged, it is useless either suggesting explanations of this or drawing deductions from it as to triremes. All her thranite oars were not of the same length.

[30] C.I.A. vol. 2 part 2, 791 l. 56—θρανιτίδων τούτων ἀποφαίνει δ δοκιμαστὴς ζυγίας Δ. If the number of the θρανίτιδες that were

ἀδόκιμοι were extant, we might have something to go on as to the relative lengths; for as most oars go at the leather, or point of contact, then if only a few could be used as ζυγίαι we should know that any theory (like Assmann's explanation of the Lenormant relief) which made the zugite oars less than two-thirds of the length of the thranite, was, on this ground alone, untenable. The higher pay of the thranites probably had nothing to do with the length of the oar, (that is a Scholiast's guess), but was merely one sign of the greater consideration they enjoyed; and the primary reason no doubt (apart from any question of their more probably being burgesses) was that it depended largely on them, as the stern oars, whether the boat was 'together' and kept her pace. Great importance was attached to the manning of the stern benches in a mediaeval galley, as Jurien de la Gravière shews. The Athenian lists do not really prove anything at all as to the relative length of the oars, as we do not know why those ten were condemned; and we have no right to make them mean that all thranite oars were longer than all zugite oars, still less that they were much longer.

means bireme, which (incidentally) takes us back to the first Mithridatic war (*Mith.* 17). How then came a word, which at the end of the fourth century was applied to a triakontor, to mean a bireme ?

The first standard warship was the pentekontor, invented in 704 B.C.,[31] from which was afterwards evolved the trireme. By the time of Demosthenes the pentekontor was no longer in regular use,[32] shewing that the trireme did its work and did it better: But the lighter triakontor was in full use throughout the fourth century[33]; and by the end of this century we find frequent mention of another light ship of a different type, the first[34] of many borrowings from pirates, the hemiolia,[35] from which perhaps was again evolved a sort of light or abnormal trireme, the trihemiolia.[36] The hemiolia and triakontor, however, run side by side as light warships, shewing that neither could do the other's work ; presumably the speedier hemiolia could not ram. Philip V. introduced another light pirate ship, the Illyrian lembos,[37] which combined with great speed the power of ramming, and obviously effected something like a revolution in naval warfare (battle of Chios, 201 B.C.). The last mention, I think, of the triakontor in history is in the treaty between Rome and Antiochus III., 188 B.C.[38] The lembos then, doing the triakontor's work and doing it better, presumably tended to drive out the triakontor ; and perhaps we shall not be far wrong if we guess that some one thereupon took a leaf out of Philip's book,[39] 'double-banked' his triakontors, and so evolved the bireme,[40] which would still be as much a ναῦς δίκροτος as the original triakontor had been, possessing two squads only. As the triakontor vanished, the term δίκροτος remained adhering (without ambiguity) to the bireme ; and probably by the time that Appian

---

[31] See Kroker, *Die Dipylon-vasen* (*Jahrb.* 1886), with whose account (p. 106 *seq.*) of the first evolution of the warship I agree, as against Pernice's criticism in *Ath. Mitth.* 17 (1892), p. 306.

[32] It does not occur in the Athenian lists, and plays no part in battles again. I do not mean it was not built at all ; Mithridates *e.g.* had a few, and see Polyb. 1, 20, 14 (the Italiot states), 25, 7, 1 (Egypt).

[33] Athenian lists ; Arrian *l.c.* and 7, 19 ; Polyaen. 3, 9, 63 ; etc.

[34] If indeed the triakontor was not originally a pirate, Thuc. 4, 9.

[35] See n. 22.

[36] See n. 11.

[37] Demetrius had lemboi at the siege of Rhodes (Diod. 20, 85), but we do not hear of them in action (if Diodorus be correct neither he nor Ptolemy put μονήρεις into line at Salamis, and so cannot say if they were the Illyrian lemboi or not. Polyb. 1, 53, 9, and 3, 46, 5 (Hannibal crossing the Rhone) add nothing, and earlier mentions of lemboi refer to ship's boats. Polybius is clear as to Philip's

fleet of lemboi being almost a new thing (5, 109, σχεδὸν πρῶτος τῶν ἐν Μακεδονίᾳ βασιλέων) and as to his tactics at the battle of Chios being new. We may conclude that if he was not actually the first to introduce the Illyrian lembos he was the first to perceive its possibilities and to use it in a fleet action.

[38] Polyb. 21, 45 μηκέτι ἐχέτω πλὴν ι' κατα-φράκτων· μηδὲ τριακοντάκωπον ἐχέτω ἐλαυνό-μενον κ.τ.λ. Livy 38, 38 has run the two together (neve plures quam decem naves actuarias nulla quarum plus quam triginta remis agatur habeto), while App. *Syr.* 39 mentions cataphracts only.

[39] See post, n. 94 as to Philip's 'lembi biremes,' and 'double-banking.'

[40] Precisely the 'galeotta' of Furtenbach. No doubt someone experimented with biremes before triremes were invented. But these experiments remained without effect (witness the silence of Herodotus, Thucydides, and the Athenian lists, and indeed of all writers prior to Caesar) and have nothing to do with the biremes known to history, which appear first in the 1st century B.C. See under *E.*

and Arrian wrote the fact that the word had once applied to a triakontor had really been forgotten, and would have been lost, had not Arrian fortunately simply copied down Ptolemy. The above explanation is of course guesswork, but (I think) reasonable and consistent guesswork.[41]

As to μονόκροτος and τρίκροτος. These words, unlike δίκροτος, really were ambiguous, and therefore little used. Many ships were μονόκροτοι—not divided into squads; and apart from Xen. *Hell.* 2, 1, 18,[42] the word is found only once.[43] Similarly, τρίκροτος would apply, not only to triremes, but to all the larger polyereis; the word occurs thrice only, in Aristeides, Niketas, and Clement of Alexandria; they throw no light on its meaning.

C.

I have failed to trace either the genesis of, or any scrap of evidence that will support, the dogma that among Greeks and Romans, at all times and in all places, one man rowed one oar—a dogma that is responsible for three quarters of the nonsense written about the larger polyereis. Many writers are content to refer to the evidence as 'well-known,' generally a sign that there is not any; as given by Assmann and Luebeck, the proofs are Thuc. 2, 93; Polyaen. 3, 9, 63; Leo *Tactica* 19, 8; all the monuments.

Thuc. 2, 93 [44] is conclusive evidence for this, and for this only, that in

---

[41] It may be objected that the bireme of Octavian's time was a 'Liburnian.' Biremes are mentioned in history earlier than Liburnians, which is all I require; but it is as well to be clear about the Liburnian. In origin, it was another of the light swift pirate-craft of the Adriatic (App. *Ill.* 3), if indeed it was not the lembos under another name; and the fact that under the Empire the Liburnian was built, first as a bireme (App. *Ill.* 3, Lucan 3, 534—note Lucan's 'crevisse,' it had grown) and later as a trireme, etc. (Veget. 4, 37), which nobody doubts, only shews that there were biremes of two different builds running parallel, the Liburnian bireme evolved from a Liburnian and the dicrotos bireme evolved from a triakontor (just as earlier there were the trireme and the trihemiolia); see *C.I.L.* 5, 1956 which mentions a 'bicrota' called Mars and a 'Liburna' called Clupeus. When Appian (*Ill.* 3) says that *in his time* light δίκροτα were called Liburnians he shews, either that the two builds had become confounded, or (more probably) that he was ignorant of the process by which the δίκροτος bireme had been evolved, and that for him δίκροτον was simply 'bireme.'

[42] This passage is a good instance of one which explains equally well on *any* theory and is useless to cite. Other good instances are Polyaen. 5, 22, 4 and the drowning thalamites

of App. *b.c.* 5, 107.

[43] Strabo 7, 325. ἀνέθηκε Καῖσαρ τὴν δεκαναΐαν ἀκροθίνιον, ἀπὸ μονοκρότου μέχρι δεκήρους. He uses the word to mark the fact that the trophy began, not only with a μονήρης, but with the smallest kind of μονήρης.

[44] λαβόντα τῶν ναυτῶν ἕκαστον τὴν κώπην κ.τ.λ. Bauer alone has put this correctly. As regards triremes, the passage is conclusive as against Weber (three men to an oar) who has to mistranslate it, and Serre (three banks, but in action only the top bank rowed by three men to an oar), for then Brasidas would not have troubled to take the other oars with him on a mere raid. The large number of oars for a trireme given in the Athenian lists also certainly presupposes one man to an oar. Weber has to say a trireme carried two spare sets, which (apart from the question of weight) is improbable, seeing that the account of battle after battle assumes that a ship with a crippled ταρσός is out of action. The spare oar question is not, however, easy; see *e.g.* the Hippia (*C.I.A.* vol. 2 part 2, 802 c. 6) which is said to have a ταρρὸς δόκιμος (not, however, ἐντελὴς δόκιμος) though five oars are broken. Probably Assman's solution is the best (reviewing Schmidt in *Berl. Phil. Woch.* 1900, No. 43); the περίνεῳ oars were deck sweeps, carried for use in a ship left crippled. I may add that,

the triremes of the Greek states at the time of the Peloponnesian war one man rowed one oar. One is ashamed to have to state anything so elementary.

Polyaen. 3, 9, 63 refers explicitly to triakontors and to no other ships; and Leo *Tact.* 19, 8 refers explicitly to the Byzantine dromones of Leo's own time and to no other ships. Neither passage has the least bearing on the question : as Luebeck at least saw.

As to the monuments. It sounds well to say that no monument shews more than one man to an oar, provided that the hearer be not acquainted with the scantiness, the inadequacy, and the obscurity of the monumental evidence. As every monument that shews rowers is called a bireme or a trireme, this obviously has no bearing on the question of the larger polyereis, of which we are not supposed to possess any representation at all.[45]

But although there is not one bit of evidence for this dogma, which should long ago have been relegated to the limbo of things forgotten, there is evidence from the Athenian lists which proves that, *at Athens in the time of Demosthenes,* the oars of a trireme could form part of the ταρρός of a quadrireme and the oars of a quadrireme part of the ταρρός of a quinquereme :[46] Böckh called attention to this. Now quadriremes are common enough in the later lists, and remained in use at any rate for some time, for there were 30 Athenian quadriremes in Demetrius' fleet at Salamis (306 B.C.), and as they were posted on the left wing, on which Demetrius had massed his strength, they were presumably good efficient ships. We therefore get to this, that toward the end of the fourth century an Athenian quadrireme had one man to one oar, and similar quinqueremes were being experimented with.[47] But though not in use at Athens, quinqueremes had been known and used at Syracuse since Dionysius I. ;[48] and therefore perhaps we may, or ought to, say generally of the quadriremes and quinqueremes of the fourth century B.C. that they had one man to one oar and were, in fact, enlarged from, and similar to, triremes,[49] as shewn by the transference of equipment generally (σκευή) from one to the other at Athens. However, beyond the fact that the Athenian quadriremes were efficient, all the evidence we possess that throws any light on the nature of any of the larger polyereis is later than the fourth century,[50] or rather is not earlier than the building by

with a παρεξειρεσία half carried away, no spare oars but deck sweeps would (on the view I take of a trireme) have been of much use. Possibly however a trireme rowed 25 groups of 3 oars each side, and carried some half dozen spare oars of each class.

[45] And if we had, it would be a cataphract, and so could not shew any rowers.

[46] *C.I.A.* vol. 2 part 2, 812 a 35 : οὖ[το]s τὴμ μὲν τετρήρη ἀποδέδ[ακ]εν τὰ δὲ σκεύη ὀφείλει διὰ τὸ [ἐπὶ] πεντήρη κατασταθῆναι. The σκεύη here include the ταρρός which had been previously mentioned. 812 c 143 *seq.* 'Ηδεῖα. . . . . [οὖ]τος τὴν τριήρη ἀποδέδω[κεν διὰ τὸ

ἐπ]ὶ τετρήρη καθεστηκέναι [τὰ δὲ σκέυ]η ὀφείλει (here follow the συντριήραρχοι) σκεύη ἔχουσι ξύλ[ινα ἐντελῆ]. . . There is another passage to the same effect, and the filling up of the lacunae is quite certain. Incidentally, this disposes of every reconstruction of a trireme which cannot be expanded into a quinquereme.

[47] Rarely mentioned, and only in the last extant list.

[48] Diod. 14, 41.

[49] Here we undoubtedly meet Assmann's breitpolyereis.

[50] I shall find it convenient to talk of ships of the fourth century, prior to Antigonus' fleet,

Antigonus and Demetrius of the fleet which afterwards fought victoriously at Salamis. Meanwhile there is no evidence for any ship larger than a hexeres [51] prior to this fleet of Antigonus'; and I fancy that even the mention of hexereis is probably an anticipation of events.

D.

Taking the battle of Salamis (306 B.C.) for the moment as a convenient mark of time, what evidence can we get as to the larger polyereis later than this battle? So far as we have gone, we are at liberty to suppose more than one man to one oar in the larger polyereis in the last three centuries B.C., subject to this, that, as in a fourth century πεντήρης one man rowed one oar, we must not suppose that the same word at a later time had a different meaning unless evidence appears to that effect. I give in this section such evidence as I know of as to the larger polyereis in the last three centuries B.C., the effect of it being to make it probable that they were galleys a scaloccio of some kind with more than one man to an oar, and to make it, I think, reasonably certain that the accepted theory is quite at variance with the facts. [52]

(a) Some men in some ships stood at the oar, and were therefore rowing oars a scaloccio. It was the chief merit of Weber's book to call attention to the passage in Appian that proves this. When the sea got up (he says), Salvidienus' inexperienced crews could neither *keep their feet* nor 'come forward.' [53] Note that Appian is not caring about informing the reader whether they stood or sat; he merely uses ἐστῶτες as an illustration, by the way, of how bad the tide was; he refers to it as to a well-known thing. Such a reference can hardly ever be anything but correct. Unfortunately, the

---

simply as ships of the fourth century. It will not create any confusion. For our purpose the third century begins with Salamis.

[51] Aelian *V.H.* 6, 12 : Dionysius II. had a fleet of 400 ships, hexereis and quinqueremes ; this is of course impossible, and it must mean 'including hexereis and quinqueremes'; see Diod. 16, 19. Even so, the statement as to hexereis is extremely improbable, seeing that Alexander never had anything larger than a quinquereme. Very possibly Dionysius II. had built one hexeres on the fourth century system (whatever it was), as a 'royal ship.' The statement of Pliny *N.H.* 7, 56, that Alexander invented the dekeres, is valueless ; see Luebeck 1, 17 n. 6 and Droysen 272 n. 3, who give the evidence as to Alexander's fleets. It is precisely what *would* get stated about Alexander, and is on a level with Curt. 10, 1, 19, the 700 heptereis carried over in sections to the Euphrates ; this last is refuted, were refutation necessary, by Arr. *Anab.* 7, 19, who gives the correct version (from Aristobulus).

[52] Many writers have *assumed*, on the ground of practical necessity, that in the larger polyereis more than one man rowed one oar ; but that is another matter. Serre and Weber try to shew that Ap. Rhod. 1, 396 means two men to an oar ; but there is no foundation whatever for this. The passage, a straight-forward one, had already been correctly explained by Cartault.—Possibly the Delos ship of Paus. 1, 29, 1 would be in point, if one knew what the passage meant ; but I cannot translate it, and Frazer's translation 'decked for nine banks of oars' conveys no meaning to me. Pausanias had of course heard of higher values, and therefore the ship was abnormal in some way ; νικήσαντα does not mean 'larger than' but 'more curious than.'

[53] *b.c.* 4, 85 (battle between Sextus Pompey and Salvidienus) ; οὔτε ἑστῶτες βεβαίως ὑπὸ ἀηθείας, οὔτε τὰς κώπας ἔτι ἀναφέρειν δυνά-μενοι.

size of Salvidienus' ships is not stated, though they are said to be larger and heavier than those of Sextus : we must therefore consider the alternatives, taking two things as fixed points, *viz.*, that for serious work no man ever stood at an oar if he could possibly sit, and that five men to one oar cannot all sit through the stroke.

First, can the ships in question be merely triremes ?

Fincati gives an account of the Venetian zenzile triremes, three men on a bench rowing three oars ; extremely long oars, with leaded handles ; he gives the lengths as 32, 30½, and 29 feet, and proves these extraordinary figures from Venetian arsenal-lists. Obviously, with such oars the stroke must have been a slow one ; and Fincati states (p. 167) that they rowed a stroke called monta e casca, rise and fall.[54] Were then the ships of Salvidienus in question triremes, rowing the stroke called rise and fall ?

This can I think be disproved. The oars of a trireme, whatever their exact length, were certainly very short compared to the Venetian, perhaps not more than half the length ;[55] and there would be no point in rowing so cumbersome a stroke, for with the shorter oars the crew of a trireme could certainly have rowed sitting. That they *did* row sitting is clear from this, that on occasion they could row a really fast stroke,[56] which would not be possible except sitting. And if they ever could and did row sitting they would certainly do so when it was rough. What applies to triremes applies a fortiori to smaller ships.

Suppose then that Salvidienus' ships were quinqueremes on the model of the fourth century Athenian quinquereme. Then, taking two other fixed points, *viz.*, that three of the ordines were identical with those of a trireme, and the oars in the other two only slightly longer,[57] we again get the fact that the men could have, and therefore would have, rowed sitting, or at most in the case of the longer oars with some such slight lift from the seat as some men are apt to give in the first stroke of a race. This might conceiv-

---

[54] 'Vogue dans laquelle la force sur l'aviron est produite presque tout entière par le poids du rameur, qui, monté debout sur la pédague ou sur le banc qui précède, se jette en arrière, et, tirant à lui son aviron, va tomber assis sur son propre banc.' The lead may have been used to meet the difficulty of the oars being of different proportionate lengths inboard. How this was met in a Greek trireme does not appear ; the only actual reference to lead is with regard to the thranite oars of the τεσσερα-κοντήρης.

[55] The length of the περίνεῳ oars, 4.4 m., is the only one actually known, but this supplies a kind of limit. Schmidt has an interesting attempt to work out the measurement from the data as to the Athos canal in Herodotus and Demetrius of Skepsis ; he makes the longest oars in a trireme 3.3 m. outboard.

[56] There are of course a great many references to spurting, and the common name for it, ῥοθιάζειν, implies a fast enough stroke to make a good deal of splashing. The celebrated feat of an Athenian trireme, which swung round a merchantman and rammed her pursuer (Thuc. 2, 91) implies a quick lively stroke and a power of backing water on one side only quickly and forcibly. And the fact that a crew could only last a short time in action (*e.g.*, Polyaen. 3, 10, 12, Diod. 13, 77, Frontinus 2, 5, 47) conclusively implies a fast stroke. Chabrias, training rowers for a trireme, trained them sitting ; Polyaen. 3, 11, 7 : and *cf.* Aristophanes' reference to 'that which fought at Salamis.'

[57] See n. 110.

ably satisfy the passage in Lucan *Phars.* 3, 543, ' in transtra cadunt et remis pectora pulsant,' but it will not satisfy Appian's ἐστῶτες.

If then the ships were quinqueremes or higher values *differing* from the quinqueremes of the fourth century—and no other alternative now remains—the only reasonably probable explanation of Appian is that enough men rowed one oar for some at least to be on their feet some part of the stroke—if not throughout it—*i.e.*, five men to an oar.[58] I regret the conclusion, as it involves saying that πεντήρης meant one thing in the fourth century and another in the first; but we have seen that this was certainly the case with δίκροτος, and we shall find other reasons for supposing it to be correct. Incidentally, Appian is conclusive, I think, against a theory such as that a quinquereme was a three-banked ship with oars rowed by 2, 2, and 1 men respectively; for 2 men can sit to any oar.

(*b*) The larger polyereis were not only of very shallow draught,[59] but low in the water also. The shallow draught is now generally admitted; the lowness in the water (a necessary consequence, by the way), requires consideration.

Polyb. 2, 10. The Illyrians, fighting with the Achaeans, lashed their lemboi together by fours and let the Achaeans ram. As soon as an Achaean ship was held fast by its ram the Illyrians leapt on her deck (ἐπιπηδῶντες ἐπὶ τὰ καταστρώματα) and in this manner captured four quadriremes and sunk a quinquereme. The quinquereme then was but little higher than the small light lemboi.[60]

Polyb. 16, 4 (battle of Chios again). It would have gone hard with the Macedonians had they not stationed lemboi among their cataphracts : as soon as the battle became a mêlée, and the Rhodians could no longer manœuvre, the lemboi attacked them, even meeting them bow to bow : this the Rhodians met in a workman-like way.[61]   I shall come to this

---

[58] There is a fine picture of a mediaeval quinquereme, with 5 men to an oar, on Pl. VII. of Furtenbach's *Architectura Navalis,* 1629 ; with a huge outrigger, and the oarsmen on their feet. A good description of such a quinquereme in Bigge, *Der Kampf um Candia in den Jahren* 1667–1669 (Kriegsgeschichtliche Einzelschriften, Heft 26, 1899), p. 130 : the men worked in three relays, as in a trireme. I owe the reference to these writers to the kindness of Mr. W. C. F. Anderson. For the scaloccio galleys generally, see Admiral Jurien de la Gravière, *Les derniers jours de la marine à rames,* 1885 ; the different strokes in use (none rowed sitting) are described p. 231 *seq.*, the best of commentaries on Appian and on Lucan, *Phars.* 3, 543.

[59] Quinqueremes run ashore and the crews depart, Polyb. 1, 51 ; 3, 96 ; etc. Attalus' royal flagship at the battle of Chios (size not given, but following the usual Hellenistic practice [see too Beloch, *Gr. Gesch.* iii. pt. 2,

p. 428 n. 2] it would be the largest he had, and he had quinqueremes) runs ashore and the king and his crew *departed* (ἀπεχώρησε) ; Philip tows her off uninjured (Polyb. 16, 6 and 7). Diodorus 20, 47, Demetrius sails to Cyprus and draws his ships ashore and surrounds them with a palisade and ditch ; he had heptereis and hexereis, and no preparation made for drawing them up. Frontinus 1, 5, 6, Duilius' ships (quinqueremes anyhow) cross a boom at Syracuse. Ath. 204 c, the dock of the tesserakonteres was only four cubits deep. Livy 30, 25 is not against this ; the quinquereme there was damaged because driven ashore *at full speed.*

[60] Lembos small and cannot have had more than one bank : Livy 34, 35, and evidence collected by Torr *s.v.*

[61] ἐμπιπτόντων αὐτοῖς τῶν λέμβων ποτὲ μὲν εἰς τοὺς ταρσούς . . . ποτὲ δὲ πάλιν εἰς τὰς πρῴρας . . ., κατὰ δὲ τὰς ἀντιπρῴρους συμπτώσεις ἐποίουν (the Rhodians) τι τεχνικόν.

presently. Polybius is speaking here of the Rhodian wing. The Rhodians and Attalus together had in action three triremes, nine trihemioliai, and sixty-five cataphracts, by which larger ships than triremes are here meant; and 16, 5, shews plainly that the Rhodian ships attacked by the lemboi were, or included, quinqueremes. A lembos then could meet a quinquereme bows on, and the two must therefore have been of approximately equal height. On the accepted theory it would be like a destroyer trying to ram a cruiser bow to bow.

Caesar *b.g.*, 3, 14. The sterns of the ships of the Veneti (which were real ships, not galleys, though shallow bottomed) were higher than the tops of the turres on Caesar's galleys. The size of Caesar's galleys is not given, but as they carried turres they cannot have been small ones.

Plut. *Ant.* 67. Eurykles in a Liburnian pursues Antony, then on Cleopatra's flagship, converses with him, and threatens him with a spear. Plutarch evidently conceived of the heights as not unequal, especially as Eurykles then attacks the second Egyptian flagship and spins it round like a top (περιερρόμβησε). Add perhaps Diod. 20, 50 (battle of Salamis in Cyprus): those on deck spear their enemies in the water; and Val. Max. 1, 8, b, 11: a rower, engaged in baling out a Tyrian hexeres, was swept overboard by a wave. As they had no pumps,[62] he must have been baling from the deck with a bucket; presumably she was very shallow.

Now as to the evidence generally quoted for the *height* of the larger polyereis, *viz.*: Livy 30, 25, Cic. *Verr.* 2, 5, 34, Orosius 6, 19, Dio Cass. 50, 33; (I know of no other; no one, I think, has thought it advisable to cite Vergil on Actium).

Livy 30, 25. Three Carthaginian quadriremes attack a Roman quinquereme; she was too speedy to ram, and the men in their armour could not board her as she was the taller ship.[63] The height here is of course only relative to a quadrireme; and as you could board a quinquereme from a lembos you could of course do so from a quadrireme. Unless the point is the word armati, the most probable explanation is, that she had her turres on board.[64] Anyhow, the passage affords no evidence for the supposed considerable *actual* height of a quinquereme.

Cic. *Verr.* 2, 5, 34. Cleomenes ran away from the pirates, and the

---

[62] One of the wonders of Hiero's ship was the water-screw invented for her by Archimedes, Ath. 208 f.

[63] Sed neque rostro ferire celeritate subterlabentem poterant neque transilire armati ex humilioribus in altiorem navem.

[64] First mention of turres, battle of Chios (201 B.C.) Polyb. 16, 3, πυργούχων (unless πυρσούχων be the correct reading). The best commentary on Livy here is the battles of Mylae and Naulochos in App. *b.c.* 5. At Mylae, though some of Sextus' ships carried towers, they were on the whole much lower

and lighter than Agrippa's; and the point of Sextus' epigram (108), that he had been storming forts, not fighting ships, was Agrippa's turres. He gave orders τι προσθήσειν ἐς τὸ τῶν νεῶν ὕψος, and by the *height* of the ships turres are clearly referred to, for at Naulochos all his ships carried turres, and could only be distinguished from Agrippa's by the war-paint (121). This seems to shew that altiorem is quite satisfied by turres. The accounts of Actium shew the difficulty of boarding ships carrying turres.

pleader's case is to magnify his force so as to emphasise his cowardice. His quadrireme, the only navis constrata in the squadron, would, if he had joined battle, have appeared as big as a town among the pirates' myoparones. There is of course nothing in this bit of rhetoric about urbis instar the moment the context is read.

Orosius 6, 19 [65] and Dio C. 50, 33. The Orosius passage was taken by Assmann to prove that the height of a dekeres (dekereis being the largest ships in Antony's fleet) was 10 feet. What Orosius says is that Antony's dekereis were *actually* 10 feet high; which is quite another thing. Antony's ships created the impression of being the largest ever seen, as appears in every account of the battle; according to Dio Cass. 50, 23, Antony, being aware that Octavian had crushed Sextus Pompey by sheer size and weight,[66] resolved so to crush Octavian, and outbuilt him; a good deal of the speech put into Antony's mouth before the battle by Dio (50, 18) is taken up with boasting of the size and height of his ships and their towers, on the disadvantages of which Octavian in his turn expatiates (50, 28). If these monster dekereis were 10 feet high, what was the height of an ordinary dekeres, and how low in the water was an ordinary quinquereme? Supposing Orosius to be correct, a sentence more decisive against the accepted theory was never written. Then Dio 50, 33; when the fleet was broken up, and each of Antony's ships was surrounded, it was like forts or islands being besieged—a consistent part of the picture, but implying nothing further as to height; the reference in τείχεσι is to the turres,[67] to which also Orosius' measurement might possibly refer.

(c) A warship, of shallow draught and low freeboard, very long, was light and crank.[68] Livy 36, 44; two of Polyxenidas' ships attack Livius' flagship; he wishes to throw grapnels, and bids his men steady their ship for the encounter by keeping their oars in the water.[69] Any rowing man will see at once what kind of a 'ship' this implies. Plut. *Ant.* 67, before cited: a Liburnian spins the Egyptian flagship [70] round like a top. Demetrius' heptereis are drawn ashore anywhere; and Archimedes' grapnel could lift a

---

[65] Classis Antonii centum septuaginta navium fuit quantum numero cedens tantum magnitudine praecellens. *Nam* decem pedum altitudine a mari aberant.

[66] Battles of Mylae and Naulochos in App. *b.c.* 5; and see n. 64; Dio Cass. 48, 47, 4 and 49, 1, 2: the evidence is overwhelming that for a few years there was a great race in building; not only as regards height, but more especially in weight and thickness, see Plut. *Ant.* 65, 66. I do not know why it is believed that Octavian had only light ships at Actium. He had the fleet with which he had crushed Sextus; up to hexereis, Florus 2, 21 (4, 11). Plut. *Ant.* 62 is responsible for the other view; probably adopted to rub in the moral.

[67] Whether Sextus in fact ever spoke of τειχομαχῆσαι or not, it became a commonplace; see τειχομαχία in Plut. *Ant.* 66.

[68] Polyaen. 3, 11, 13 (if the rowers sprang up in a hurry they might upset the ship), presumably refers to a trireme; nor do I lay stress on Lucan, *Phars.* 3, 665: if she took in drowning men she might turn over.

[69] quum inferrentur, demittere in aquam remos ab utroque latere remiges stabiliendae navis causa jussit. App. *Syr.* 22, gives 3 Syrian ships, not 2, and says that it was they who tried to grapple Livius.

[70] Size not given, but the flagship of any Hellenistic monarch was always the largest obtainable.

quinquereme half out of the water.　Arr. *Anab.* 7, 9, Alexander has quinqueremes carried in sections from the Mediterranean to the Euphrates.

(*d*) The arrangement of a quinquereme was simple; there was none of the complexity of structure that five superposed banks would involve.[71] At the battle of Chios the Rhodians met in a workmanlike manner the lemboi which rammed them bow to bow: they sunk their own rams under water, and so, while struck above the waterline themselves, they struck their enemy beneath it.[72] Polybius is explicit that they did this *during* the fight; besides, they cannot have gone into battle with their hulls weighted down, as it is stated that at the beginning of the action their pace enabled them to row round their opponents. The only way a ship can lower its *whole* freeboard during action is by taking in water, as was done *e.g.* by the Huascar when bombarding Callao; this is out of the question, as quinqueremes cannot have had double bottoms, and also had no pumps. They lowered their rams then by shifting ballast forward, either live[73] or dead;[74] whence it follows that the system of oars was such that, with the bow depressed and the stern raised, the ship could still be rowed enough to keep her stem on to a speedy enemy. How this could be done in a boat having five superposed banks is incomprehensible; and any one who thinks that it could ought to work it out and demonstrate it. It implies some system in which, on the spur of the moment, changes of level and angle can be met; and this certainly implies among other things that all the oars were a reasonable height above the normal waterline, a state of facts demanded also, not only by common sense, but by the evidence that exists of changes in the waterline.[75] On the accepted theory, the lowest portholes forward of

---

[71] This is presupposed by the pace at which a fleet could be built; for which there is plenty of evidence (no doubt sometimes exaggerated) beside the first Punic war. Elaborate arrangements for building were not required; Dio Cass. 48, 49, Octavian built ships ἐν πάσῃ τῇ παραθαλασσίῳ 'Ιταλίᾳ; and no doubt the building of the Argo in Ap. Rhod. 1, 363 *seq.* is copied from current Egyptian practice.

[72] n. 61 (continues) αὐτοὶ μὲν γὰρ ἔμπρῳρα τὰ σκάφη ποιοῦντες ἐξάλους ἐλάμβανον τὰς πληγάς, τοῖς δὲ πολεμίοις ὕφαλα τὰ τραύματα διδόντες ἀβοηθήτους ἐσκεύαζον τὰς πληγάς.

[73] Like a modern racing yacht. See Frontinus 1, 5, 6; Duilius, to get his ships (including presumably quinqueremes) over the boom at Syracuse, shifts the troops aft, thus raising his bows, and goes at the boom at full speed, shifting the troops forward again at the critical moment. If this be true, a ship with bow raised and stern depressed, *i.e.* with every angle altered, could still get on a good deal of pace. It has, I understand, been demonstrated that a torpedo boat rushing an

ordinary floating boom at full speed may be expected to 'jump' it without doing herself any serious injury.

[74] Cf. Arr. *Anab.* 2, 19. If this be so, it implies that the ballast was easily got at during action.

[75] Those who speak of a row of portholes of 10 inches (25 m.) (Assmann) or any such height above the (normal) waterline cannot really have thought what this would mean. Leaving practical considerations aside, the waterline was no more a constant quantity then than now. Polyb. 1, 60–62, the Carthaginian ships were much hampered by being loaded down with corn and stores which Hanno had trusted to put ashore before engaging. Diod. 20, 49 and 83, Demetrius mounts on the prows of his ships great catapults (τοὺς τρισπιθάμους τῶν ὀξυβελῶν), and of course ballasted the sterns accordingly. So Duilius' corvi. App. *b.c.* 5, 121, Sextus Pompey's men throw over the turres when escaping, shewing that they had been too low in the water. See too an appendix to Kromayer's article in *Philol.* for 1897, before

these Rhodian ships must have gone under water. This passage, in my opinion, certainly requires these quinqueremes to have been scaloccio galleys of 5 men to an oar, with the oars a reasonable height above the (normal) waterline.

(e) Finally there is Livy 28, 30.[76] Caught in some eddies, a Roman quinquereme nevertheless held her way better than the Carthaginian triremes, and was more manageable; and Livy's second reason no doubt is right; there was more *power* behind the oars, and the fact that she was normally slower than the triremes had become immaterial. A greater number of one man oars would not have helped in the eddies relatively to the triremes; the required meaning is more power to *each* oar. She must then have been a scaloccio galley.

W. W. TARN.

---

cited, on the great numbers of troops that could be carried at a pinch.—I do not give cases, like Marcellus' sambucae before Syracuse, where the ships were not in action: though Marcellus' quinqueremes could still be rowed : Polyb. 8, 4(6).

[76] Quinqueremis Romana, seu pondere tenacior, seu pluribus remorum ordinibus scindentibus vortices, quum facilius regeretur, duas triremes suppressit, etc. (For ordines remorum see under *E*). A little before, Livy had said she was slower than a trireme. Fincati p. 158 : according to Nicolo Surian (1583) a quadrireme a scaloccio could beat a trireme a scaloccio but not a trireme a zenzile. It is just possible that these triremes were a scaloccio (n. 120) and owed their pace to the greater skill of the Carthaginians ; but I think most improbable.

Ancient stone anchor from port of Piraeus. Naval Museum of Greece.

THE GREEK WARSHIP.

E.

THE evidence considered under *D* makes it, I think, impossible that the accepted theory can be true as regards the larger polyereis of the first three centuries B.C., which clearly were galleys a scaloccio of some sort. If what is put forward under *A* be true, the *reason* why the accepted theory was invented [77] and has been so largely believed disappears. Nevertheless, there is still room for evidence that will support the accepted theory as to triremes generally, the quadriremes and quinqueremes of the fourth century, and the biremes of the first; and the theory may be true, even if the words thranite, zugite, and thalamite do refer to another arrangement.

For a trireme, said Cartault, the evidence is overwhelming. Unfortunately he omitted to mention what it was, and with the best will in the world I have been unable to discover it. Assmann (1610) relied solely on the monuments. Luebeck however gives Schol. on Aelian's *Tactica*, Schol. on *Frogs* 1074 (see under *A*), Arr. *Anab.* 6, 5, 2 (see under *B*), Pollux 1, 87 (see under *A*), and *Frogs* 1074. Let me add Livy 33, 30, Aesch. *Agam.* 1617, Luc. *Phars.* 3, 529 *seq.*

The Scholion on Aelian [78] (which I do not consider evidence) would be quite well satisfied by a galley, whether one a zenzile or one a scaloccio, in which the rows of rowers, taken as parallel to the long axis of the ship, should rise somewhat from the side of the ship toward the long axis. The phrase 'exstructi remigis' of Luc. *Phars.* 3, 530 [79] may well refer to the same thing;

---

[77] According to Luebeck, its first modern supporter was Scaliger, relying on Schol. *Frogs*, 1074. But it existed when De Baif wrote in 1536.

[78] ἡ μονήρης καὶ διήρης καὶ ἐφεξῆς κατὰ τοὺς στίχους τοὺς κατὰ τὸ ὕψος ἐπ' ἀλλήλοις. Should anyone think I am unfair to the scholiasts, I would now refer to the chapters entitled 'The explaining of obsolete words' and 'The explaining of matters of fact' in Dr. Rutherford's recent volume *A Chapter in the History of*

Annotation.
[79]   Validaeque triremes
Quasque quater surgens exstructi remigis ordo
Commovet, ...
Celsior at cunctis Brúti praetoria puppis
Verberibus senis agitur molemque profundo
Invehit et summis longe petit aequora remis.

while the ' summis...remis' of line 537, translated of course as 'thranite' oars, really answers to celsior two lines earlier; Brutus' hexeres was higher than the other ships and its oars were (necessarily) the highest and longest in the fleet. *Agam.* 1617 [80] may only mean that the thalamite squad were, or had once been, somewhat nearer the water than the zugite squad, as is probable enough; unless νερτέρᾳ be a mere convention. *Frogs* 1074,[81] taken literally, is of course dead against every version of the accepted theory, except Graser's: it no more suits Assmann than it does Bauer, Fincati, or Weber; moreover that θαλάμαξ = θαλαμίτης is mere Scholiast's guesswork. It is undoubtedly a bit of slang; Fincati refers to a similar expression in the Venetian dialect, and probably a professor of argot could parallel it in every language.

There remains Livy, 33, 30.[82] Bauer (p. 462) and Weber have recognised the truth of the old view that the larger polyereis were named from rows of *rowers*; but the use of ordines remorum (or versus remorum) requires clearing up. It is obvious that, on *any* theory, it was a matter of indifference in a trireme, with one man to one oar, whether one said ordines remorum or ordines remigum. The Romans seem to have inclined to ordines remorum, the Greeks to στοῖχοι ἐρετῶν. When the galleys a scaloccio came in, ordines remorum ceased to be correct, but people went on using it; instances of such 'survivals' are common enough in English. This is strongly borne out by a passage in Florus, which has not been cited : 2, 21 (4, 11) Antony's ships at Actium had a senis in novenos *remorum* ordines, Octavian's a binis *remigum* in senos ordines. They were of course built on the same system; it was indifferent which phrase was used.[83] Ordines remorum then means only ' rows,' like ordines.

The only two phrases in all this that are of much use to an upholder of the accepted theory are Lucan's exstructi remigis and the Scholion on Aelian. One cannot build a theory on one epithet in a poet, and both phrases are, I think, easily explicable; but in case anyone should suggest that I find it convenient to say that the Scholion on Aelian (whatever it may mean) is not evidence, I would·point out that, if I may cite scholia, there is one on Thuc. 7, 40, 5 which almost settles the question.[84]

---

[80] σὺ ταῦτα φωνεῖς νερτέρᾳ προσήμενος
κώπῃ, κρατούντων τῶν ἐπὶ ζυγῷ δορός ;
We have here a reference to a ship in which the zugite was the most important person, and so not a trireme ; and as it is too early for a bireme, it bears out section *B* ; it was a μονήρης δίκροτος. The importance of the zugite here came from his being the stern oar ; see n. 30. Is it not possible however that the contrast is between oarsmen and fighting men, with a play upon δορός ?

[81] προσπαρδεῖν ἐς τὸ στόμα τῷ θαλάμακι. Anyone inclined to take this literally should read Jurien de la Gravière's remarks in *La Marine des Anciens.*

[82] Quam sexdecim versus remorum agebant. A translation of ἐκκαιδεκήρης in the corresponding passage in Polybius.

[83] This may help to explain Lucan's ' senis verberibus ' (n. 79) which refers to *one* hexeres only, and should on the accepted theory be sex verberibus, if it were to refer to the beat of the six banks. It means ' with sixfold strokes ' ' strokes worked (or made) by six (men) apiece.' Lucan's quadriremes have not four ordines, but a fourfold ordo.

[84] Thuc. 7, 40, 5 the Syracusans in boats ἐς τοὺς ταρσοὺς ὑποπίπτοντες τῶν πολεμίων νεῶν. Schol. ὑποδυόμενοι ὑπὸ τοὺς ταρσούς. If the schol. be right, as Bauer supposed, the accepted

Now as to the monuments. Breusing was the first to call for a thorough-going criticism. How badly it was (and is) wanted anyone can see who will refer to the astounding cases of misuse given by Mr. Torr in his preface (p. ix) : and these are by no means the only instances.[85]

Omitting coins and Trajan's column, we are supposed to have about 15 representations of biremes, 3 of triremes, and none of larger ships. Of the 'triremes,' only one really matters, the so-called Lenormant relief in the Acropolis Museum at Athens (possibly fourth century).[86] The 'biremes' fall into two groups, one belonging to the seventh and sixth centuries, the other to Hellenistic and Roman times. The most important of the latter group are the prow from Samothrace, in the Louvre (the only monument we can check by written evidence); the ship from the Temple of Fortune at Praeneste, in the Vatican Museum ; and the Palazzo Spada and Ludovisi ships.

I do not count the river boats on Trajan's column. If any one cites them in proof of superposed banks, I may also cite them as proof that the upper oars were rowed over, or through, a fretwork railing, the lower without port-holes ; that the rowers used their oars like Canadian canoe paddles,[87] had

---

theory is in a bad way, of course. But the schol. must be wrong. The same phrase in Dio Cass. 50, 32, 8 clearly means driving the ship across the ‚oars so as to break them ; he adds καὶ τὰς κώπας συναράσσοντες ; and warships could not go *under*. Cf. Polyb. 16, 4, 10 ἐμπιπτόντων ἐς τοὺς ταρσούς.

[85] See Bauer 367 n. 1 on the so-called Malay bireme. See also two startling sections of tri-remes in Kopecky, *Die Attischen Trieren* (1890) plates 21 and 22, which he calls ‘sehr be-achtenswerthe Abbildungen alter Schiffe,’ from Rondelet. ‘Die erste (fig. 21) ist der Abdruck einer Medaille’ etc. On turning up Rondelet (1820) I found, of course, they were Rondelet's own sections, the most worthless of guesswork ; of fig. 21 Rondelet does not even pretend to figure, or refer to, any original, but merely labels it ‘ after a medal.’

[86] The two triremes in the Naples Museum, figs. 1676 and 1691 in Baumeister, the first from Pompeii and the other from Puteoli, are, I think, of no great value, as the top oars could hardly reach the water ; but the way the oars are laid in threes, one actually upon the other, can be meant for nothing but three oars to a bench all issuing in a sheaf from one opening. The spirited Isis-temple ships, the only ones that give any idea of the general look of an ancient warship, are of no value for the ‘problem.’ I have not seen any representation of the Ulubad ‘ bi-reme ’ ; but according to *B.C.H.* 12, 190 the oars (14 in number) are in groups of two, side

by side. If not a moneres, it would seem to add little to what can be learnt from the Palazzo Spada ship. Two recent discoveries, the ship on a metope of the Treasury of the Sicyonians at Delphi (see Assmann in *Jahrb.* 1905, p. 32), and a graffito on the wall of a tomb near Anfushi bay in Egypt, to which Mr. G. F. Hill kindly referred me (Dr. G. Botti in *Bull. de la Soc. Archéol. d'Alexandrie* (1902) p. 13 seq. and Admiral Blomfield *ib.* p. 37), do not bear on the problem of the oars ; though the latter ship (called late Ptolemaic) is interesting as showing a further development of the navis ignifera used by the Rhodians in 190 B.C.

[87] Every oarsman will sympathise with Arenhold, *Die historische Entwicklung der Schiffstypen* (1891), when he says bluntly that every monument on which the oars ‘ganz steil in's Wasser tauchen’ is self-condemned. I would like to say the same of every similar reconstruction, and of every monument which shews an oarsman grasping the oar from under-neath and with no possibility of getting his feet against anything. Mr. G. C. V. Holmes, *Ancient and Modern Ships* (1900), suggests that the monuments shew that the art of row-ing was *not* understood till the Liburnian came in. But some mediaeval pictures also shew the oars at an absurd angle ; *e.g.*, C. A. Levi, *Navi Venete*, pls. 28 and 31 ; and it seems incredi-ble that any people should row for centuries without discovering the proper angle for the oar to make with the water.

one hand *under* the handle, and sat bolt upright at the end of the stroke, and that a bireme had only eight oars aside, and a long list of other absurdities. The oars of the 'trireme,' in particular, are just plastered on anyhow; and it is an open boat. 'The design' says Mr. Torr 'makes little pretensions to accuracy.' It is high time that it vanished from the text books.

And I need hardly say that I do not count dal Pozzo's sketch, interesting as it is; for it is not known from what it is taken.[88]

The prow from Samothrace. Assmann has been much praised for calling this a bireme. But, apart from the question whether the holes seen in the monument are really portholes,[89] if one assumes, as certainly Assmann does, and I think every one else, that the monument celebrates Demetrius' victory at Salamis, certain consequences seem to follow as matter of history, which must be considered.

In Alexander's lifetime quinqueremes were the highest value in use.[90] Somewhere between his death and the first Punic war the change of system that introduced the scaloccio galley (see section *D*) must have taken place :[91] and as the higher values undoubtedly took their origin as fighting machines from the time when Antigonus the One-eyed resolved to build a fleet and command the sea (Diod. 19, 58 and 62), we shall not be far wrong in assuming that the change of system originated at the same time (though this is not perhaps very material), both alike being due to the inventive mechanical genius that made Demetrius famous as the Besieger of Cities. Demetrius with the new fleet, including seven heptereis and ten hexereis,[92] beside smaller values, sailed for Cyprus, and met Ptolemy, who (naturally) had nothing larger than quinqueremes, at Salamis. Demetrius massed his strength, including all his heptereis and hexereis, on his left wing, which he led in person on a hepteres; and the picture given by Diodorus of Demetrius in

---

[88] Graser published it (*Arch. Zeit.* 1874 vol. 32, p. 71). It is now in the British Museum (Dept. of Gr. and Rom. Antiq.) It is certainly not a drawing of the Lenormant relief.

[89] Two slits in the παρεξειρεσία, on which Eins, *Das Rudern bei den Alten* (1896), has based what appears to be an attractive theory of the διέκπλους. I have not seen his book. Torr follows Graser in saying the holes are for ropes for an anchor : but if so they should be further forward. If they are not portholes, this hepteres had seven men to an oar, as the monument shews that no oars could be rowed anywhere except through, or resting on, the παρεξειρεσία.

[90] With a possible reservation in favour of one or more hexereis in Sicily, n. 51.

[91] Polybius has been so abused for saying that the Romans had no experience of building quinqueremes and required a Carthaginian model, that I feel the utmost diffidence in suggesting that the basis of the story is merely

that the Carthaginians had got the new system and the Romans had not. Polybius does *not* say that they copied a stranded quinquereme ; he says (1, 20, 15) that they built their whole fleet (*i.e.* quinqueremes and triremes) on the model of a stranded *cataphract*. Ihne's criticism (*Röm. Gesch.*[2] 2, 49), that they had Syracusan models to hand, is beside the point. We, for instance, had many English models to hand in the Napoleonic war ; yet I have read that we often copied the lines of French prizes.

[92] According to Diod. 19, 62, three ennereis and ten dekereis were built. This may be an anticipation ; anyhow, they did not go into action. Plutarch gives no details of size. Beloch, *Gr. Gesch.* iii. 1, 159 n. 1, defends Diodorus' account, as against Niese, and says it is the best picture of a sea-fight of the time that we possess. This seems to overlook the battle of Chios just a century later.

action on the stern of his big ship, rejoicing in the battle, with his three armour-bearers fallen round him, is not only entirely in character with all that we know of Demetrius, but is the sort of picture that becomes traditional and gets handed down correctly. He gained a crushing victory, due to his own big ships which he had led in person (his other wing was defeated); and we might know, even if Diodorus had not expressly said so, that Demetrius, being such as he was, could not help sending the biggest ship he had to carry the news to his father. The impression the big ships made in the Hellenistic world was great; Demetrius built bigger and bigger; Lysimachus tried to rival him;[93] in mere size the Ptolemies soon went far ahead of all competitors. And in the face of this, how *can* the prow of Samothrace represent anything but Demetrius' hepteres, any more than a monument of Trafalgar could represent any ship but the Victory? And if this prow be a hepteres, the accepted theory goes by the board at once as regards heptereis.

Assmann's selection of a bireme to explain this monument seems most unfortunate. He calls it the 'swift Aviso' sent to carry the news. But Diodorus (20, 53) says a hepteres (τὴν μεγίστην ναῦν) was sent: and one cannot advance by throwing over even Diodorus without good reason and taking to guesswork. If it is to be a bireme, one must begin by showing that it has nothing to do with the battle of Salamis. But the real point is that there is no evidence for the use of biremes at all till far later. I may well have missed some inscriptions; but subject to this, I believe that διήρης hardly occurs in Greek at all, and not before Pollux (second century A.D.); biremis is not found in Latin literature before Caesar and Cicero, or referring to an earlier period than theirs[94]; δίκροτος has already been dealt with,[95] and only takes us back to the Mithridatic wars.

There is then no reason for calling the prow of Samothrace a bireme. Its elucidation as such is a good instance of a method which seems to me a wrong one.

The Dipylon 'biremes' have been explained as a first attempt at perspective,[96] and this may be true; but they may also be due simply to the

---

[93] Lysimachus' great okteres, the λεοντο-φόρος, is said to have distinguished itself in the sea-fight between Ptolemy Keraunos and Antigonus Gonatas; Memnon 13 = *F. H. G.* 3, 534, τὸ ἐξαίρετον ἔφερεν. The change of system obviously came in before this ship was built, whatever Memnon's description exactly means.

[94] Livy 24, 40 (nuntiantes, Philippum primum Apolloniam tentasse, lembis biremibus centum viginti flumine adverso subvectum) is an apparent instance to the contrary. But we know all about these lembi, which Philip had built on the Illyrian model (Polyb. 5, 109) and which fought so well at the battle of Chios; and they were certainly not biremes (n. 60). The explanation is flumine adverso; they were

going up stream and to get more power the oars had been double-banked for the occasion. Double-bank, 'to provide . . . with two rowers for each oar'; see Murray's *Dict. s.v.* I wish to thank my friend Mr. Colin Campbell for calling my attention to this word, which he tells me is still in use, and which aptly explains this puzzling passage. As to Pliny 7, 56, see Appendix.

[95] See n. 40.

[96] Pernice, *Geometrische Vase mit Schiffdar-stellung* (*Jahrb.* 1900, p. 92), on the ship published by the late Dr. A. S. Murray, *J.H.S.* 1899 (vol. 19), 198. I gather that in 1900 Pernice no longer held the view he had taken in 1892 as to the fragments of dipylon-ships,

desire of a very crude artist to show two sets of oars because he *knew* that a ship had a set on each side.[97] It is difficult to see how any one ever took such a ship as that in *J.H.S.* 1899, Pl. VIII., for a bireme of two superposed banks; for even an artist of the Dipylon period may be supposed to have known that oars should be able to reach the water and not stop short in mid-air. And if, as Pernice, Helbig, and von Wilamowitz have supposed, these Dipylon ships are Athenian, how came Athens to return for a couple of centuries to the more humble ships of a single bank? A question often asked and never answered. Assmann avoids it by calling the Dipylon ships Phœnician.

There are three Assyrian reliefs from the palace of Sennacherib, one in the British Museum, and two figured but not brought home by Layard, of which one has no ram. These shew oars in two rows, at no great interval of height, arranged in a zigzag thus $\cdot \: \cdot \: \cdot \: \cdot \: \cdot \: \cdot \: ,$ the lower oars in the intervals of the upper ones. The same thing is shewn on two ships on an Athenian B.-F. vase of about 500 B.C. (*B.M. Vases*, B. 436), and possibly in the ship on an Etruscan B.-F. vase (*B.M. Vases*, B. 60), though this latter is of little value for the arrangement of the oars. None of these ships can be biremes, which are unknown to every writer before Cæsar. The silence of Thucydides, who gives a sort of history of shipbuilding, is most material.

The Praenestine 'bireme.' According to Assmann, this relief belongs to the time of Augustus; according to Torr, to about 50 A.D. It shews two superposed banks with a very small interval between them; perhaps it would be more correct to say it shews the arrangement $\cdot \: \cdot \: \cdot \: \cdot \: \cdot \: \cdot \: .$ The higher bank issues from the outside of, the lower from the under part of, the παρεξειρεσία. The distance between the banks is too small for the accepted theory, to which it gives no support; but if it is in fact a bireme, then it may support Bauer's theory for *biremes of the early empire.* Whether it really is a bireme seems to me, I confess, very doubtful. Biremes were undoubtedly light and swift; but, allowing that in this relief, if to scale, the oars would be longer and the men smaller, it remains anything but a light or speedy-looking ship; compare it with the Isis-temple ships, for instance. Then it carries a turris. We do not know that a bireme never carried a tower, certainly; but we do not know that it did; I think the smallest ship referred to with a turris is Eudamus' quadrireme at Side (Livy 37, 24), and after all one can only argue from the facts that are known.

Figs. 5 and 6 in his article in *Ath. Mitth.* 17. Assmann claims to have refuted Pernice, (*Arch. Anz.* 1901, p. 98); and his point, that the Dipylon chariots shew one horse *beyond* and not *over* the other, is a fair one. But he does not (apparently) deal with the three things that seem conclusive, viz. :—(1) the supposed upper deck has no supports ; (2) the supposed upper oars are cut off short on reaching the (supposed lower) deck, *i.e.*, fall on the other side of it ; and (3) the steersman is lower than the supposed upper rowers.

[97] It is well known that almost all beginners will try to draw, not what they see, but what they know to be there. A case exactly in point appears to me to be the idea of some savages, that a drawing in profile represents half a man only. This would meet Assmann's point about the chariots. It is easy to shew the further horse *beyond* the other, but very difficult thus to shew the further oarsmen.

The Palazzo Spada and Ludovisi reliefs.[98] These are Roman copies of
the same Hellenistic original, of unknown date. The arrangement resembles
that in Fig. 2, *ante*, and the original may have been a bireme ; but it may
just as well have had several men to an oar. And the two copies do not
agree. If it was a bireme, then Luebeck's definition in Pauly-Wissowa is
wrong, for its oars form one line in the water and not two.

Now as to the ' bireme ' question generally. If the holes in the prow
of Samothrace are portholes, and supposing that the Praenestine ship is
not a biremis at all, but a large admiral-ship, as is possible—note the laurel-
wreath —we get a breit-polyeres system in which two oars appear at unequal
levels, a hepteres, *e.g.*, being rowed by three and four men to the oars respectively ; again as at Venice.[99] This seems to me quite possible, and would
explain the fact that every monument that we possess which shews or appears
to shew any form of superposition (except the two ships at Naples, Trajan's
column, and the Dipylon vases) never shews anything but two rows arranged
thus ·.·.·.·. ; and we may perhaps imagine, founding ourselves on
the Assyrian reliefs and the black-figure vases mentioned before, that such
an arrangement of two rows has nothing whatever to do either with banks
or ordines or the terms ending in -ηρης, but is merely an arrangement of old
standing in the Eastern Mediterranean, applicable in many forms. As we
possess very many references to triremes, quadriremes, and quinqueremes,
and (omitting inscriptions of the Empire) very few indeed to biremes, to call
nearly every monument a bireme is a historical absurdity. I would suggest
that from early times there were two arrangements ; in one the oars issued
from the ship in a straight, in the other in a zigzag, line ; from the former
was developed the trireme ; the latter, perhaps in abeyance in the 5th and
4th centuries, was again utilised, perhaps with modifications, for some of the
larger polyereis of Hellenistic and Roman times. This seems at any rate
worth consideration.[100] We have to explain Demetrius' hekkaidekeres somehow
and two oars of eight men apiece would be more feasible than one of sixteen[101]. As to what the zigzag arrangement precisely means, I have no
theory ; what is and is not mechanically possible in the way of alternation
must be left to others to say. I merely note the lines on which it would

---

[98] Schreiber, *die Hellenistische Reliefbilder*,
Pls. 10 and 23[a] respectively. See the two
together in Dar.-Sagl. s. v. navis.

[99] For such a hepteres at Venice, Fincati,
p. 196. It does not however appear if the oars
in the Venetian ship were at unequal levels.

[100] Though I do not accept Bauer's hypo-
thesis of the larger polyereis, I thoroughly
agree with his conclusion ; '[Meiner Hypothese
zufolge] ist es unmöglich, den Typus eines
Schiffes nach der Zahl der auf einer Darstel-
lung sichtbaren Ruderreihen zu bestimmen '
(p. 463).

[101] Nothing larger than a dekeres is known
to have gone into action ; nor does it appear

that in mediaeval times more than ten men
to an oar were ever known. It is possible
that the performance of Demetrius' hekkaidekeres, which so pleased Plutarch's authority,
(*Dem.* 43 τὸ τάχος καὶ τὸ ἔργον ἀξιοθεατότερον
τοῦ μεγέθους), was only a ' contractor's trial '
with a picked crew and very favourable con-
ditions. Yet Philadelphos' extraordinary fleet
(Ath. 203d) cannot have been merely for
shew ; though the account may be exaggerated,
as Beloch supposes. Livy's translation of
ἐκκαιδεκήρης (n. 82) seems to dispose of the
otherwise attractive view that the higher terms
were arbitrary and merely denoted so much
extra tonnage.

21

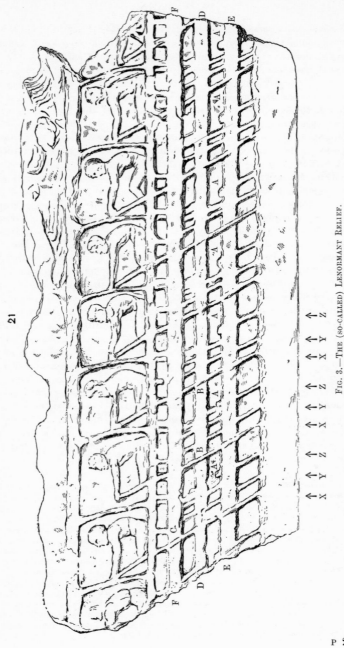

FIG. 3.—THE (SO-CALLED) LENORMANT RELIEF. The lettering is mine.

Reproduced by the kind permission of Mr. Torr from the plate in his 'Ancient Ships.'

appear that the 'bireme' problem must be solved, if due regard be paid to the evidence; and I rather think that the bireme is the key to the whole matter. For instance, I know of no evidence that the oars of any ship ever formed two distinct lines in the water, let alone more than two.[101a]

There remains the so-called Lenormant relief, (Fig. 3), which has (unfortunately) caught the popular imagination as the one remaining representation of a trireme, largely owing no doubt to the inaccurate representations originally published. As soon as accurate plates were available, the idea that Y and Z were the oars of the two lower banks was seen to be untenable in its original form, which took both Y and Z across the timber E E and made A A the portholes of the lowest bank Z Z.[102] Assmann accordingly, while still calling Y and Z the 'zugite' and 'thalamite' oars, has to place their ports below or under E E, (there is no sign of such ports in the relief itself), and to treat the design in effect as an abnormal trireme, with a very long 'thranite' bank and two stunted lower banks of almost equal length; and this explanation has been largely accepted.

If we take the relief as it now is, and if it is to be a trireme, no explanation but Assmann's is possible, as I think will appear from the subjoined letter[103] from Mr. R. Carr Bosanquet, who, in reply to some questions of mine, kindly examined the original for me, not knowing for what purpose I required it done. As to the matter of paint, or low relief, now lost, this is of course a double-edged weapon; and I submit that it is indisputable, either that we must take the relief as we find it, or that we must say that it is too worn to draw any deductions from, one way or the other. The *raised* lumps A A cannot of course be portholes, as Assmann saw.

Granted, however, that, if this relief is to be a trireme, Assmann's explanation is, on the facts before us, the only possible one, it is not easy to take it seriously. Why are we entitled to invent portholes, when the relief

---

[101a] One of Weber's points is the single line in the water.

[102] Even as late as 1896 Eins is said to have taken Y, and Haack (whose paper I have also not seen) Y and Z, across EE. Since this went to press, I see that the older view is still taken by Torr in Dar.-Sagl, and by Mr. E. Conybeare, *Triremes*, 1904.

[103] 'No sign of Y and Z crossing *over* the transverse pieces. The surface is much weathered and perished, and they may have done so in very low relief, now lost—or even in paint; no doubt the thing was made far more intelligible by the colouring (of which naturally no trace remains, but it must have been there). AAA are rounded knobs projecting vertically above the transverse strip E, but with their faces in the same plane as the face of E.' . . .

'I think Torr's drawing (which I have examined since looking at the stone) exaggerates the disturbed surface of the water; there is a raised lump where X meets the water in the case of oarsmen 1, 3, 4. No such lump in the case of Y and Z; but this must not be pressed.' All these points come out clearly on a cast in the Inner Temple Library, which also shews another point referred to by Mr. Carr Bosanquet, and not appearing in Fig. 3, *viz.*, that X seems to pass over F in the case of oarsmen 3, 6, and 8, as well as 1. The raised lump in the water round X, as compared with the smoothness where Y and Z meet it, is most distinct in this cast. The figure in Baumeister, reproduced by Luebeck, is from a cast in Berlin, but is (admittedly) much touched up and 'completed.'

does not shew them, and when there is no evidence, monumental or otherwise, for portholes [104] low down on the ship's side in a polyeres? How, if we are to invent them, can they be placed 10 inches, or even a foot,[105] above the normal waterline, where the least sea would prevent the oarsmen from clearing the water, and where a slight roll, or some change in the waterline,[106] would send them under water altogether? And how, if we do place them there, could the oars be got in and out quickly in the face of the enemy, as was done?[107] And why, if this be an Athenian trireme, has it no παρεξειρεσία, which is well attested by Thucydides for the fifth century and Polyaenus for the fourth? And why are Y and Z to be distinguished from the precisely similar streak (not lettered) running parallel to the upper part of Y, which cannot by any possibility be an oar?

Neither are we justified in supposing this to be an abnormal trireme. There probably *was* another type, the trihemiolia;[108] but short of elucidating this relief as a trihemiolia, should anyone care to, we are bound to suppose that triremes, at one and the same time, were all of one type as regards the arrangement of the oars.[109] Fifth century : Thuc. 2, 93 ; Brasidas led over the Isthmus crews from the fleet of the allies, furnished by a number of different states ; they all brought their oars, confident that these would fit the Megarian triremes at Nisaea ; and they did. Fourth century : for Athens alone the lists are conclusive. For Athens and Sparta, excerpta Polyaeni 40, 2, Iphicrates deceives the Laconisers of Chios by sailing in κόσμῳ Λακωνικῷ : had there been a difference in oarage he could not have hidden

---

[104] Even Mr. Torr's storehouse of quotations fails here. Herod. 5, 33 (which I shall come to presently) is certainly not such evidence. Pollux' τρήματα is quite satisfied by openings in the παρεξειρεσία ; and none other appear on the Praenestine and Palazzo Spada ships, and perhaps I may add on the prow of Samothrace. (The portholes *are* however low on the Delphi ship, which is a moneres ; but the gunwale is low also). θαλαμία is not connected with thalamite, technically, and does not mean the thalamite ports, but any port (Ar. *Ach.* 553) or any opening (Ar. *Peace*, 1232).

[105] Torr, p. 45, who takes AAA as the thalamite portholes, about one foot above the water, but points out the difficulty of squeezing in the rowers.

[106] See section *D* (*d*), and n. 75.

[107] Polyaen. 5, 22, 2. Note that the oars were not merely drawn inboard, but taken right out. The same manœuvre in Polyaen. 1, 47, 1 ; 3, 11, 3 ; excerpta Polyaeni 57, 9. This is obviously dead against the portholes being covered with leather bags, the only alleged support for which is the Praenestine ship. There is no proof that the Athenian ἀσκώματα

were such ; the only passage is Zonaras, who shews his ignorance by saying that the ἀσκώματα were fastened to the oars, the Athenian lists shewing that they were fastened to the trireme. Pollux 1, 88 τὸ πρὸς αὐτῷ τῷ σκαλμῷ δέρμα ἄσκωμα is more likely to be correct. But I suppose that the notion that the most intelligent people in the world first 'honeycombed' the sides of their triremes with holes larger than a man's head, and then covered the holes with leather bags to keep out the water, will die very hard. Why some of the text book writers believe that the oars were put out from the inside, blades first, instead of having the handles passed in from outside, is to me a puzzle. It also seems to me to be a grave question whether oars could be rowed at all through the *sides* of a boat as light as a trireme without pulling her to pieces in a short time.

[108] See n. 11.

[109] I do not mean more than 'at the same time.' We cannot for instance prove that the arrangement of the fourth century was that of the first. See however under *F*. Some writers assume a new arrangement of oars to explain each monument.

it, but must have betrayed himself at once. So exc. Pol. 58, 3. And as a general maxim of warfare, the same in exc. Pol. 57, 1. We *do* hear of considerable differences between the models of different states, both as to triremes and quinqueremes, but always in one respect only, weight or stoutness; a difference of oarage is never hinted at.

But the real objection to Assmann's view is, that it demands (judging by eye) an upper bank of oars that shall be more than twice the length of the two lower banks. Such a ship is impossible; for if one thing be more certain than another, it is that oars of different lengths, where the difference bears more than a certain proportion to the length, cannot be rowed together, by one man to an oar, so as to be of any real use or turn out an efficient ship. That they might be rowed together in a certain way for a short time I do not deny; but the huge increase in the ratio of dead weight to power would at once put an end to all idea of speed or efficiency.[110]

The Lenormant relief is, in fact, a moneres, and a simple one, as Bauer has always said;[111] and Y and Z are part of the hull.

F.

I trust I have now made probable the five propositions with which I started. The deductions from them—remembering that we have to do with reasonable probabilities only and not certainties—are, first, that a quinquereme of the last three centuries B.C. was a comparatively light galley of five men to an oar; secondly, that the ships from hexereis to dekereis may have been similar galleys of so many men to an oar, or may have been some other form of scaloccio galley, *e.g.*, one rowing two sets of oars in the arrangement ∴ ∴ ; and thirdly, that Roman biremes may well have been nothing but double-banked monereis, perhaps modified a little; this last however is mere opinion.

It is however pretty clear on the evidence that the accepted theory

---

[110] I am bound to refer to this controversy, on which so much has been written in Germany, and which has produced the greatest gem of the whole trireme-literature, the theory that the 'thalamites' may have taken 4 strokes and the 'zugites' 2 to the 'thranites' 1, *because* a pianist can play in three-time with one hand and four-time with the other. Given more than a certain proportionate difference in length, it is matter of mathematical demonstration, as well as practical knowledge, that the oars cannot be rowed together by one man to each oar so that each oar should do its best and each man pull his weight, *i.e.* his own and his share of the ship's; and therefore each added bank after the first means a relative loss in power, owing to the

disproportionate increase in dead weight. Schmidt here *almost* takes up the position that, if practical oarsmanship forbids his deductions, so much the worse for practical oarsmanship : the 'thranites' had '*erheblich längere* Riemen. . . . Um diesen Schluss kommen wir nun einmal nicht herum, wir mögen uns drehen und wenden, wie wir wollen. Die namhaft *verschieden langen* Riemen, also auch *alle ihre Konsequenzen*, sind feststehende Thatsache' (p. 17 ; italics mine). Once more, whatever thranite means, there is no evidence of any sort that the thranite oars were *much* longer than the others.

[111] Bauer remained of the same opinion after examining the original ; see his review of Schmidt in *Neue Phil. Rundschau*, 1900 p. 301.

cannot apply to any of the above ; but the question of the trireme, Greek and Roman, and of the quadriremes and quinqueremes of the fourth century, is still open.

Herod. 7, 36 : Xerxes' bridge over the Hellespont was laid on triremes and pentekontors. They were therefore of approximately equal height; and this seems to me very strong against the accepted theory, as regards Phoenician and Ionian triremes of 480 B.C.

Assuming the similar low elevation of an Athenian trireme, which is also a necessary consequence of its shallow draught, there remain only two theories, those of Bauer and Fincati respectively. To adopt Bauer's, one has to say, first, that the Praenestine ship is a bireme, and, secondly, that one can argue from a Roman bireme of the time of Octavian to a Greek trireme of the time of Pericles. Both these views are feasible enough, and I think therefore that Bauer's theory must remain a possible one. But for my part I do feel a great difficulty in arguing from a given monument to a ship of four centuries earlier. It is a question of individual opinion, no doubt ; a rowing galley has only limited possibilities of development, and the great pace at which ancient fleets were built, indubitable even if exaggerated in detail, may well point to stereotyped models ; but if I am right as to biremes not being in use till the first century B.C., I do not feel that they can have much bearing on the Athenian trireme. If this should be correct, the direct evidence for Bauer's view of the Athenian trireme has gone. Moreover I do not think Bauer claims that his view will explain the fourth century quadriremes and quinqueremes, which must be explained ; and it may be that Fincati's will.[112]

Was a trireme then in the nature of a zenzile galley, with three men on a bench ?

Galen, *de usu part.* 1, 24. Why are the fingers of different lengths and the middle one the longest ? In order that when they close round an object the ends may come equal. So in triremes [113] the ends of the oars all fall even (*i.e.*, make one line in the water) though the oars are not of equal length ; for there too (*i.e.*, in the trireme as well as the hand) the μέσαι are made the longest (note that he refers to the *oars* and not only to the inboard portions) *for the same reason.* These last words can only mean ' in order that the ends of the oars may form one straight line like the ends of the fingers.' Now if any oars were the longest, considered as a group, it was the thranite oars,

---

[112] Fincati seems clear that no zenzile galleys larger than triremes were in use at Venice ; but it is generally asserted, on Pantera's authority, that quinqueremes a zenzile were used. In Pantera's time the zenzile galley was only a memory. A thing might however be feasible with the shorter Athenian oars that was not so ·with the Venetian. How many difficulties would be avoided if one could only agree with Beloch (*Gr. Gesch.* 2, 470) that the

Athenian lists do not really prove that the oars of a trireme were used for a quadrireme.

[113] καθάπερ οἶμαι κἂν ταῖς τριήρεσι τὰ πέρατα τῶν κωπῶν εἰς ἴσον ἐξικνεῖται, καίτοι γ' οὐκ ἴσων ἁπάντων ὄντων. καὶ γὰρ οὖν κἀκεῖ τὰς μέσας μεγίστας ἀπεργάζονται διὰ τὴν αὐτὴν αἰτίαν.—πέρατα cannot of course refer to the *handles*, which did not, and could not, come εἰς ἴσον on any conceivable theory, except Graser's.

and not those amidships (zugite). μέσαι then is not zugite (probably if he had meant zugite he would have said zugite); and the μέσαι had [114] to be longest so as to get all the ends level. μέσαι then are the oars of the horizontal row or ordo nearest to the middle line of the ship drawn from stem to stern, and the trireme known to Galen was a breit-polyeres, probably in the nature of a zenzile galley; [115] for the oars, if the ordines were distinguished by their position relative to the long axis of the ship, must have been all on a level, or thereabouts.

Now arises the question, is Galen an independent authority or is he using or referring to Aristotle (*Mech.* 4)? [116] First, let us assume that he is using Aristotle.

As the text stands, Aristotle begins by saying (1) that the μεσόνεοι do most work ; (2) that the fulcrum of the oar-lever is the thole. (2) is of course wrong in fact ; if then (1) was right in fact, the μεσόνεοι must in fact have had the longest oars ; and, if the passage is to agree with Galen, as explained above, the μεσόνεοι must *also* have had more oar inboard than the others, and so Aristotle says : ἐν μέσῃ δὲ τῇ νηὶ πλεῖστον τῆς κώπης ἐντός ἐστιν. So far all is plain sailing. Then come the following words, explaining μέσῃ ; καὶ γὰρ ἡ ναῦς ταύτῃ εὐρυτάτη ἐστίν, ὥστε πλεῖον ἐπ' ἀμφότερα ἐνδέχεσθαι μέρος τῆς κώπης ἑκατέρου τοίχου ἐντὸς εἶναι τῆς νεώς, *i.e.*, μέσῃ means amidships, and the whole passage, as a source for Galen, becomes nonsense. The rest of the chapter (allowing for the mistake as to the fulcrum) is excellent sense and suits Galen very well. If then Galen was using this chapter, he was using a text in which the words καὶ γὰρ ἡ ναῦς, etc., did not occur, and I may therefore strike out these words as a gloss. But perhaps these words do suit Galen, and it is only my explanation of Galen that is wrong ? This, I think, is forbidden by Galen's words, διὰ τὴν αὐτὴν αἰτίαν.

Suppose now that Galen was not using or referring to Aristotle. He is then an independent authority ; but one must attempt to construe the more important Aristotle on the basis of the words καὶ γὰρ ἡ ναῦς, etc., forming part of the text. The passage refers to the inboard length of the oars ἐν μέσῃ τῇ νηΐ. νηΐ here is either confined to a moneres or not. If it is, as is often assumed, then the passage construes well enough, but has no bearing whatever on the accepted theory, or my theory, or any other theory. But if νηΐ refers to, or includes, a trireme (as it obviously must), then, (if the words καὶ γὰρ ἡ ναῦς, etc., be included) μέσῃ means amidships, μεσόνεοι mean what I call zugites, and my zugites do more work than my thranites : and as this

---

[114] This (the word αἰτία) is conclusive against μέσαι here meaning amidships, whatever theory we adopt as to the trireme ; for the oars amidships would not *have* to be the longest to make the ends come level ; indeed if they were the longest the ends would *not* come level. It seems equally conclusive against Conybeare's view that μέσαι means the middle of three superposed banks.

[115] The explanation is substantially Fincati's, though he does not apply it to Galen. He says they had two zenzile triremes at Venice, in one of which the oars formed one even line in the water. To the same effect is Aristot. de part. anim. 4, 10—the handle of the κώπη μεσόνεως traverses a greater space.

[116] The chapter is too long to cite in a note.

will not do, the passage must be taken to shew that the term 'zugites' means a row or ordo, and not a squad; this is of course against me.[117] Assuming then for a moment that it *does* shew that the zugites were an ordo (and it does not matter now whether we take the accepted theory, or Bauer's, or Fincati's, they all agreeing that the zugites were an ordo), we land in a very grave difficulty over the παρεξειρεσία. This must of course have formed a straight line parallel (more or less) to the long axis of the ship, and not a curved line following the ship's side, one object being to give the oars all along approximately equal leverage throughout each ordo;[118] and if so, the oars amidships of any ordo could not be longer inboard (*i.e.*, from the σκαλμός) than the others of the same ordo in any ship, such as a trireme, which carried a παρεξειρεσία, the σκαλμοί being of course in the παρεξειρεσία. If then this is well founded, μέση cannot mean amidships, and therefore μεσόνεοι must have the same meaning as in Galen,[118a] and I may omit the words καὶ γὰρ ἡ ναῦς, etc., as a gloss added by some one who was ignorant of the παρεξειρεσία and was thinking of a ship with a curved side. If this be done, Aristotle means what Galen means. I do not then myself think that Aristotle is against me: but I hope I have stated the difficulty fairly.

I need only refer to two other passages. Polyaen. 3, 11, 7; Chabrias, training some new men, took out the triremes' oars, and placing on the beach great logs (ξύλα μακρά), so that the men sat one by one (ὥστε ἐφ' ἕνα καθῆσθαι), thus taught them. I think the natural meaning is that in the trireme they did not sit ἐφ' ἕνα (else why be at pains to mention that they so sat on the beach?), but ἐπί some other number, *i.e.*, ἐπὶ τρεῖς, three on a bench; but I cannot press this. Herod. 5, 33. If a trireme was a zenzile galley, with the three oars issuing side by side from one opening, we can explain what Skylax' head was put through. The idea of a porthole for one oar larger than a man's head is not only unlikely in itself,[118b] but flatly contradicted by every published monument known to me that shews portholes: and Herodotus does *not* speak of the man's head as being near the water, as many seem to assume.

The evidence then, for what it is worth, though terribly scanty and unsatisfactory, does lend colour to the idea that, as regards triremes, Fincati is, in the main outlines, right:[119] and we come round once more to the

---

[117] The argument under *B, C, D*, and *E* is independent of the meaning of 'zugite.'

[118] This was the object of the telaro in the mediaeval galley, and of the first importance, as Jurien de la Gravière points out. It gave the boat, seen from above, the look of a parallelogram with two projecting ends; see the frontispiece and pl. 7 in Furtenbach, also the rearmost trireme in Fig. 1, *ante*. If I am right, then the παρεξειρεσία itself, though possibly inclining (as from stern to bow) somewhat

toward the long axis of the ship, must have been somewhat broader at the bow end than amidships; and this agrees well with Thuc. 4, 12, where Brasidas falls wounded and swooning on to the παρεξειρεσία and does not roll off.

[118a] I take μεσόνεοι to be a technical term; something like vogue-avante.

[118b] Even Assmann now doubts it; *Jahrb.* 1905, p. 89.

[119] Fincati could at least claim that his boat would go: according to a writer in the

conclusion to which we have been tending throughout this paper, that the course of development in the Aegean was very similar to that which took place later in the Adriatic.[120] Differences in detail, of course, there must have been;[121] but the conclusion as a whole does not seem to be in conflict with common sense.

One thing however seems to me to be abundantly clear: no evidence has yet been put forward that compels, or even seriously invites, us to believe in the accepted theory: and it is to be remembered that the burden of proof is on those who uphold that theory.

W. W. TARN.

APPENDIX.

I have received from Mr. Cecil Torr a number of critical notes on both parts of the above article, and by the courtesy of Mr. Torr and of the editors of this Journal it has been arranged that the substance of them shall be here published, with my replies. Mr. Torr's remarks are given verbatim as far as possible, in inverted commas.

p. 139. If the rowers were in three divisions, 'how did they get their names? I conceive that the thalamites sat in the thalamos, or hold ; the zugites sat on the zuga, or beams, which formed the upper limit of the hold ; and the thranites sat on thrani, or thranyes, which were seats above the beams.'——There is I think no evidence for these thrani ; and as to thranites, I should adopt Prof. Ridgeway's suggestion (*Class. Rev.* 1895, p. 166), and derive the term from θρῆνυς, the elevated step or platform at the *stern* on which stood the helmsman. As to thalamites, when an open boat first began to be partly decked, there would be a thalamos or cabin in the *bows* ; hence the name. In Timaeos ap. Ath. 2, 37d θάλαμοι are the cabins of a merchant ship ; and I know of no passage where the word simply means 'hold.' Pollux 1, 87 says that the ἔδαφος τῆς νεώς was called κύτος καὶ γάστρα καὶ ἀμφιμήτριον, and that in the part where the thalamites sat it was also called θάλαμος.

Academy, 1883 p. 219, it attained the great speed of 9 miles an hour, *i.e.*, nearly three-quarters of the pace of an average University crew from Putney to Mortlake. Unfortunately I have never seen any details of what the boat exactly was.

[120] So far as we have gone, there has been nothing to lead one to distinguish the Roman trireme from the Greek. It is however just possible that in Polyb. 1, 20, 15, we have a reference to a trireme a scaloccio ; the Romans, he says, built their whole fleet (quinqueremes and triremes) to a Carthaginian model ; and if, as suggested in this paper, the quinqueremes had 5 men to an oar, these Roman triremes *may* have had 3. This would only accord still further with what happened at Venice, where

triremes on both systems are said to have been built. But even were this so, the scaloccio trireme (if I am right as to Galen's meaning) was not the one that survived in the Aegean. At Venice, the galleys a scaloccio killed the trireme a zenzile.

[121] The length of the oars, for instance. It might be attractive guesswork that the bench rose a little from the ship's side inboard and that the oars had separate portholes very close together ; this would much resemble Bauer's theory, I think, and might be a useful subject for experiment. It has been suggested by Mr. Cook, whose citation of the τρίσκαλμοι νᾶες of Aesch. *Pers.*, 679, for the zenzile trireme is most happy, as a reference to Fig. 2 (*ante*) will shew.

pp. 140, 141. Polyaen. 5, 43 and 3, 11, 14 ; Polyb. 16, 3. 'The Athenian triremes had sixty-two oars in the thranite (or highest) bank, fifty-four oars in the zugite (or middle) bank, and fifty-four in the thalamite (or lowest) bank. Consequently, the thranite bank of oars was longer than either the zugite or the thalamite bank. And this would naturally be the case, for all three banks would start from abaft the catheads, and the thranite (or highest) bank could extend further back toward the stern than the other two banks, owing to the sharpness of the run in ancient ships.' The three passages in question refer 'to the part of the stern to which the thranite bank extended.'——The numbers 62, 54, and 54, are the highest of various numbers given for triremes by the Athenian lists ; but it does not follow that all these oars were in use at once. However, if Mr. Torr could shew that Calliades' ship was an Athenian trireme, and that a trireme had three superposed banks, his explanation might do for Polyaen. 5, 43. It cannot apply to the *trihemiolia* in Polyb. 16, 3, which was rammed κατὰ μέσον τὸ κύτος ; and Polyaen. 3, 11, 14 depends on the meaning of .παρεξειρεσία ; see post.

p. 140. 'In rendering Polyaen. 5, 43, the word πηδάλιον is taken three times to mean " steerage " and once to mean " stern." It really means " steering-oar." The phrase τὸ πηδάλιον ἔσχαζε is translated " kept using his steerage." It means "kept lifting his steering-oar out of the water," *i.e.* ceasing to use it for steering.'——' Stern ' does not occur in my rendering of Polyaenus, but in my own account of what happened, and is not meant for a translation of πηδάλιον. There is no instance, I think, of σχάζω meaning ' to lift.' It means ' to cut ' ; and when it is used in the phrase κώπην σχάζειν, ' to stop rowing,' the meaning is that the oar is (naturally) dropped flat on the water, so that the edge of the blade cuts through the surface ; this was known to the Scholiast on *Clouds* 107 σχάσαι γὰρ δεῖ καὶ ὥσπερ διαστεῖλαι καὶ διασχίσαι τὸ ὕδωρ τὴν κώπην, though he is mistaken in adding ἐρέσσουσαν. From this meaning again are derived two others (ἀπὸ μεταφορᾶς τῶν ἐρεσσόντων) ; simply ' to stop,' and simply ' to drop' (Xen. *Kyn.* 3, 5). ἔσχαζε τὸ πηδάλιον is then ' he kept dropping his steering-oar into the water,' *i.e.* making use of it ; and this is the only rendering of the passage that makes sense, for Calliades must have turned his own ship now to one side and now to the other in order to avoid the enemy καθ' ὁπότερον ἂν ἐμβάλλειν μέλλοι. No doubt it was a technical term.

p. 141. Note 10. ' "The new steering-oars were through the παρεξειρεσία : therefore, the old ones were not." This does not follow. Polyaenus says διὰ τῆς παρεξειρεσίας κατὰ τὰς θρανίτιδας κώπας. He is specifying a point in the παρεξειρεσία further forward than the position of the old steering-oars, namely, the point to which the thranite oars extended. Then as to παρεξειρεσίαι in *Peripl. Pont. Eux.* 3, "the reference *must* be to a *higher* point, not a *different* point," *i.e.* from κατὰ τὰς κώπας. Of course, it is a *higher* point, because the ships were higher out of water at the ends (παραξειρεσίαι) than in the middle (κατὰ τὰς κώπας). But, unless it is a different point, the passage is meaningless. Then, Thucydides vii. 34 is made to mean exactly the reverse of what it does mean. The ships met the others bow to bow (ἀντίπρῳροι) and were damaged in the parts next the bow (παρεξειρεσίαι). It is unfair to Thucydides to make him say that the ships met bow to bow and thereby damaged themselves amidships. "But the absolutely decisive passage is Polyaenus, iii. 11, 13. Chabrias stretches skins over the παρεξειρεσία of each side of the ship and nails them to the deck above, thus making a φράγμα which prevented the waves washing in and the oarsmen looking out." If the sea had been abeam, he would only have put the skins along the windward side of the ship. As he put them *on each side* of the ship, it must have been a head sea or a following sea ; and, as one of his objects was to prevent the rowers seeing the approaching waves, it must have been a following sea, for the rowers faced aft. In fact, there was a following sea in which his ship was likely to be pooped, and he protected her at the stern (παρεξειρεσία).'——I think there is no passage in which παρεξειρεσία must mean stern or bow, and cannot mean an outrigger or some analogous structure. I grant that *Peripl. Pont. Eux.* 3 can be taken either way ; and that Polyaen. 3, 11, 14 is not quite conclusive ; though if παρεξειρεσία be the stern, why is it mentioned at all ? And how is διά to be construed ? Did Chabrias cut a hole in the timbers of the poop ? (*Anc. Ships* fig. 36 illustrates *how* he put out his new steering-oars, I think.) Thuc. 7, 34 states that no Athenian ship sank, but seven became ἄπλοι, ἀναρραγεῖσαι τὰς παρεξειρεσίας. It is incredible that none sank if their bows were torn open. Two triremes ramming bow to bow would rarely meet stempost to stempost with accuracy ; the stems would slide each past the other, and carry away the forepart of the opponents' outrigger, which extended most of the ship's length. (I said nothing about 'amidships.') This was why the Syracusans strengthened their ἐπωτίδες, *i.e.* the forward ends of the outriggers. Cf. the distinction between ἀναρρῆξαι τὴν παρεξειρεσίαν and ἀναρρῆξαι τὴν πρῴραν in Pollux 1, 124. Polyaen. 3, 11, 13 is decisive that the παρεξειρεσία was something extending along each side of the ship so far as the rowers extended. Chabrias stretched skins ὑπὲρ τὴν παρεξειρεσίαν ἑκατέρου τοίχου (which in silver Greek can only, I submit, mean the παρεξειρεσία *of* each side of the ship), and nailing them to the deck above made a φράγμα πρὸς τὰς παρεξειρεσίας (plural), which (among other things) prevented the men getting wet and prevented them seeing the waves, οὐχ ὁρῶντες διὰ τὴν τοῦ φράγματος πρόσθεσιν. No arrangement on the *stern* could possibly have this effect, apart from the reference to cataphracts in φράγμα ; and Chabrias could not possibly have carried out his idea *at sea*, with a crew so nervous that he was afraid of their upsetting the boat. The old interpretation of παρεξειρεσία as stern or bow is in fact a guess of the scholiast on Thucydides from the look of the word, τὸ παρὲξ τῆς εἰρεσίας.

Mr. Torr then refers to Dr. Assmann's view of the παρεξειρεσία, which I have adopted, as being based on a misinterpretation of the prow of Samothrace, the projections on which (as in *Ancient Ships*) he calls cat-heads, comparing a coin of Cios (*Anc. Ships* fig. 23).——I have nothing to add to what I have said on this monument. But if one can prove the outrigger from the texts, it lends much support to Dr. Assmann's view that what the monument shews is an outrigger.

pp. 142, 143. 'I am not concerned with evidence of class (2). But Pollux 1, 87, shews by his mention of θάλαμος, ζυγά, and κατάστρωμα that he supposed the banks of rowers to be superposed.'——The most that can be claimed for Pollux is, that he can be read to suit either theory, like many other passages. But he does not refer to triremes only ; he is speaking generally ; and for three centuries the standard warship had been the quinquereme. As to there being three classes *only*, Mr. Torr says 'The men in the highest bank of the tesserakonteres were called thranites, as was to be expected ; but nothing whatever is known about the names for the men in the other banks in the tesserakonteres, or any other ships of higher rank than triremes.'——One cannot *disprove* this ; but we have no right to confine Pollux 1, 87 and 119 to triremes, and most recent writers have taken the simple view, that in all ships there were only three classes. It is a pity that the text of Polyb. 26, 7, 10 is corrupt.

pp. 143, 144. 'The forms "τετρακίκροτος and so forth" may not occur, but their equivalents do. Aelius Aristeides, *Rhodiaca* p. 341 δικρότους καὶ τρικρότους καὶ εἰς ἑπτὰ καὶ εἰς ἐννέα στοίχους.'——ἑπτὰ στοίχους is septem ordines, which we know (from Livy and Eutropius) would be the translation of ἑπτήρης ; it is not ἑπτακίκροτος. In the second century A.D. δίκροτοι *were* probably biremes ; and τρικρότους is used here for 'triremes' because the writer has just used τριήρεις for 'warships.' A professional rhetorician like Aristeides could not write τριήρεις ὑπῆρχεν ἰδεῖν, διήρεις καὶ τριήρεις καὶ εἰς ἐπτήρεις καὶ ἐννήρεις, which is what he *means* ; he has done all he can to vary the *sound*, that is all.

pp. 144, 145. App. *Mith.* 12. 'There is nothing there to shew that the term δίκροτος excludes hemiolia. I conceive that δίκροτος includes hemiolia as well as the true bireme and the bireme of the Liburnian type. Appian's statement is that the pirates gave up using myoparones, and took to using δίκροτοι of other sorts besides the hemioliai, and also triremes.' Then follows the explanation of hemiolia as a two banked ship given in *Ancient Ships*, for which there is no evidence.——As this is important, I quote Appian (Mendelssohn). πειρατὰς ... οἱ τὸ μὲν πρῶτον ὀλίγοις σκάφεσι καὶ μικροῖς οἷα λῃσταὶ περιπλέοντες ἐλύπουν, ὡς δὲ ὁ πόλεμος ἐμηκύνετο, πλέονες ἐγίγνοντο καὶ ναυσὶ μεγάλαις ἐπέπλεον. ... ἀντὶ τῆς γῆς ἐκαρποῦντο τὴν θάλασσαν, μυοπάρωσι πρῶτον καὶ ἡμιολίαις, εἶτα δικρότοις καὶ τριήρεσι κατὰ μέρη περιπλέοντες. To the man who wrote this, ἡμιολία and δίκροτος are mutually exclusive terms ; and Mr. Torr's explanation is forbidden by the Greek.

pp. 144, 145. Arr. *Anab.* 6, 5, 2. 'The context shews that these δίκροτοι were hemioliai. By making the statement refer to triakontors, instead of hemioliai, the author has to shew that κάτω does not mean lower ; and he does not seem to me to shew it.'—— Once it is established from Appian that the hemiolia is not δίκροτος, the meaning of κάτω follows with almost mathematical precision.

p. 146.   Mr. Torr claims διήρης and δίκροτος in Pollux 1, 82 as synonyms. It is not very important; but no doubt by the second century A.D. they were practically synonyms.

p. 150. App. *b.c.* 4, 85. 'Some ships got into the whirlpool at Scylla, and the crews were upset, not being used to it. It seems forcing the translation to say that the men were knocked off their legs rather than off their seats.'——I submit that οὔτε ἑστῶτες βεβάιως cannot possibly refer to sitting.

p. 154.   'Oros. 6, 19 is quoted as if he were contrasting Antony's dekereis with other dekereis, whereas he is contrasting them with the ships in Octavian's fleet which were all smaller than dekereis.'——Very possibly this is right ; but it does not affect the other evidence for the size of Antony's ships. They must have resembled galeasses.

Note 80.   'See *Anc. Ships* p. 57, n. 131' which states that ζυγόν in *Agam.* 1618 is some bench at the stern.

p. 205.   'Florus ii. 21 (iv. 11) uses remorum and remigum indifferently, because there was one man to one oar.'

p. 206.   'The Trajan column trireme cannot be ignored. It is not true that the oars " are just plastered on anyhow." They are clearly intended to be arranged *in quincuncem*

. . .
. . .   which is the natural developement of the zigzag · . · . · . . that

you mention in the biremes.'——But what the monument *shews* is not a quincunx at
all, but . · · . ; and is not that 'anyhow' ?

p. 207.   The prow of Samothrace. 'Your argument for the hepteres, which you develop at so much length, does not seem to have very much foundation. How can one assume that it has anything to do with Demetrius' victory at Salamis ? And why should Nike be travelling about on one of Demetrius' ships rather than her own ? Her ship was a familiar thing before that date ; see *Revue Arch.* 26 (1895) p. 161.' ——Mr. Torr's article in the *Revue Arch.* gives two figures of Nike, one on, and one hovering over, the prow of a ship ; but there is nothing to suggest that the ship is Nike's own ship. Is there any other evidence ? As to the Nike of Samothrace, Demetrius' well-known coins shew that she was set up to commemorate some victory of his by sea, and we know of no other but Salamis ; had there been any other of importance, Plutarch would hardly have passed it over.

Note 94.   'I conceive that these lembi were narrow enough to have the oars sculled in pairs.'——No doubt biremis *can* mean a sculling boat ; but had Philip two complete fleets of lembi ? Or did he put sculling boats into line against the Rhodian quinqueremes at Chios ?

p. 209. The Dipylon ship *J.H.S.* 1899, Pl. 8. 'I doubt if it is a bireme. I am in favour of its being a ship of a single bank with περίνεῳ oars rowed from the κατάστρωμα.'
——I by no means exclude the idea that (say) a state ship might have been thus rowed ; I believe there is a case at Venice, and possibly Antigonos' τριάρμενος was something of the kind. But in the case of this Dipylon ship the explanation does not seem to meet any of the three difficulties given in n. 96.

p. 209. As to biremes being unknown to every writer before Caesar. 'Damastes (apud Plin. vii. 56 (57), 207) attributes the invention of biremes to the Erythraeans ; and Damastes was a contemporary of Herodotus. Also in the catalogue of the ships *Il.* 2, 509, 510, there is a pretty clear allusion to biremes.'——The allusion in the Iliad is merely to ships with 120 men each. As to Pliny. It is not a case of Damastes *apud* Plinium, but of an assertion of Pliny's own, even supposing Damastes of Sigeum to be meant ; and Pliny's list is quite untrustworthy. 'Biremem Damastes Erythraeos fecisse : triremem Thucydides Aminoclem Corinthium (our Thucydides says nothing of the sort, see 1, 13, 2 ; it is Pliny's own interpretation of him) ; quinqueremem Mnesigiton Salaminios (directly contradicted by the circumstantial account in Diodorus) ; ab ea (hexeres) ad decemremem Mnesigiton Alexandrum Magnum (almost certainly untrue, see note 51). In the face of this kind of thing, Pliny's statement as to Damastes is of very slight value. No doubt a bireme was experimented with before a trireme ; my point is that it never came into use *at all* in early times, while Mr. Torr thinks it did, and was driven out by the trireme. Then why no reference to it ?

p. 209. 'If Sennacherib's ships are not biremes, what are they ?'——I do not know. But if the pentekontor was really not invented till 704 B.C., they cannot be *long* ships at all. I think they are *round* ships (see figs. 10 and 11 in *Anc. Ships*) beginning to be adapted for fighting ; two have rams, one has none.

Mr. Torr does not comment on the difficulty I have felt and expressed over the bireme question generally.

'Lenormant relief. I have no doubt at all about the accuracy of what you call the older view. "The *raised* lumps A A cannot of course be portholes." They presumably are portholes with ἀσκώματα. "And Y and Z are part of the hull." Similar reasoning would make X part of the hull ; which it certainly is not. Why should not Y and Z cross E E (the lower waling piece) just as much as X crosses D D and E E (the two waling pieces) and F F (the gunwale) ? If the relief disproves one, it disproves the other.

'I presume you admit that X are oars rowed against tholes on the gunwale F F, and that D D and E E are the waling pieces. Then one gets the ports (with ἀσκώματα) of the third bank just where one expects to find them, namely between the two waling pieces and vertically below the tholes of the first bank. One would expect to find the ports of the second bank between the upper waling piece and the gunwale. The difficulty of course is that the oars of the second bank (Y) seem to go right up to the lower side of the gunwale. Now there is a double set of supports under the gunwale, one running down to the upper waling piece and the other running down to the lower waling piece. One explanation is that the sculptor was rather careless, and continued the oars (Y) as far as the gunwale in the same way as these supports. Another explanation is that these supports imply that the gunwale projected a little way over the side of the ship, and thus hid the portholes.

'I think my diagram, D. and S., fig. 5275, helps one to understand this relief.'
——I submit that this is reconstruction, not explanation ; precisely as fig. 5275 in Dar.-Sagl. is. The monument shews that X crosses D D, E E, and F F, and does not shew that Y and Z cross E E : that is the point. One cannot reconstruct a relief on the footing that it has to shew three banks, and then use it as evidence that there *were* three banks.

Note 107. 'Polyaen. 5, 22, 2 is not conclusive that the oars could be got out quickly. Diotimos would begin getting his oars out as soon as the enemy saw his hulls, say five miles off. The stratagem would answer only so long as his ships were hull down. But the passage seems to me to shew that the oars could not have been passed in from the outside, as you suggest. Pollux, I think, is wrong ; the thing that he mentions was called τροπός or τροπωτήρ and κωπητήρ, not ἄσκωμα.'—— Diotimos must have let the enemy come close up, or he could have got back to harbour ; but I have omitted the words ' is conclusive ' from the note. But the *practical* difficulty of getting out the oars at all, whether from inside or otherwise, in a trireme arranged on the accepted theory is to my mind prohibitive. Whether Pollux here be right or wrong (I think he is right), there is no real evidence for the current view of the ἄσκωμα. Its use was to lessen friction.

n. 107. 'The latter part of this note seems to rest on a misconception. The portholes did not serve as rowlocks. The oars were rowed against tholes.'——By all means. My difficulty, *i.e.* the strain on the ship's timbers, remains (she was very lightly built) ; and I should like an expert opinion. I am thinking of the way a racing eight strains in spite of every precaution.

p. 215. Herod 7, 36. ' Probably the bridge had longer supports where the supports rested on pentekontors than where they rested on triremes.'——Perhaps. The bridge was laid on great cables. No doubt it may be possible to get round the question of *height* as regards a trireme ; it is with the quinquereme that it becomes so formidable.

p. 215. Galen. Mr. Torr is inclined to think that he is referring to one *tier* of the trireme's oars only and also to the aspect of the oars inside the ship. The word αἰτία I think forbids this, as I have shewn (n. 114). It also assumes that there *were* tiers, which is rather the point at issue.

p. 216. As to Aristotle. I do not reproduce Mr. Torr's criticism because (given his premisses) everyone will agree. If there was no such thing as an outrigger, and if Galen is not using Aristotle, (these are his premisses), then μεσόνεοι *are* the men amid-ships, and Aristotle is against my view under A. But if either of these premisses be false, my argument holds. Anyhow Mr. Torr does not claim that Aristotle supports the theory of superposed banks, for he says ' Aristotle is stating a general proposition, *i.e.* he refers to any tier of oars (it does not matter whether the ship had one or more).'

p. 217. Polyaen. 3. 11, 7 ἐφ' ἕνα. ' I take this to mean that each pair of rowers (port and starboard) sat on the same piece of timber, instead of sitting on separate seats. Cf. Leo, *Tactica* 8 and Ap. Rhod. 1, 395, 396 quoted in *Anc. Ships*, notes 46 and 110.'——Neither of these passages refers to triremes, and I doubt if the above explains ἐφ' ἕνα ; but I have said that I cannot press the passage.

Finally, Mr. Torr considers it hazardous to say that something which existed in the mediaeval type existed in the ancient type unless one can shew that it existed also in the intermediate or Byzantine type. But I claim neither continuity of tradition nor identity ; only analogy.

Mr. Torr sums up as follows :—

' As to your propositions.

A. I do not see that you have any evidence at all for the assertion, " thranites astern, zugites amidships, thalamites in the bows." Your evidence is only that the thranites were furthest astern. And there is quite another explanation of that, namely, that the thranite bank, which had sixty-two oars, reached further aft than the zugite and thalamite banks, which had only fifty-four.

B. To establish this translation of the terms τρίκροτος, etc., you would have to show that δίκροτος and ἡμιολία are mutually exclusive in App. *Mith.* 92, and that κάτω does not mean *lower* in Arr. *Anab.* vi. 5, 2.

C. Of course, there is a danger in generalizing from a limited number of instances ; but, I think, people were aware of that already.

D. I cannot find anything in your paper to support D (1), and hardly anything in support of D (2). Of course, D (2) is really a question for a naval architect ; and I fancy he would decline to express an opinion without more *data* than can be given him.

E. This is supposed to be dealt with in Part II., but I do not see that you have really tackled the question.'

W. W. TARN.

TRIREMES

(An article by Arthur Bernard Cook, published in *Classical Review* xix, 1905, pp. 371-376)

How did the ancient Greeks row their triremes? A score of scholars have in modern times answered the question in as many different ways, and the Germans have come to speak of it as 'the trireme-puzzle' (*das Trierenratsel*). This divergence of opinion is of course due to the inadequate nature of the evidence available. The monuments, including bas-reliefs, vase-paintings, and coins, are, in view of the comparative importance of the subject, not only scanty but also singularly inconclusive: their value is, indeed, largerly destroyed by the undoubted presence of those elements of uncertainty—artistic convention and artistic ignorance. Literary allusions escape the first, if not the second, of these draw-backs, but only to suffer from other and perhaps worse defects: for a literary allusion is, in the nature of the case, partial and incomplete— no merely verbal description of a vessel can ever make us realise what she looked like when afloat; besides, nautical language abounds with terms that are peculiarly apt to be misunderstood by the landsman, and the well-meaning historian (let alone the scholiast or lexicographer) is likely enough to use words that will prove at best ambiguous, at worst misleading, to his readers. All these sources of error have combined to vitiate ancient testimony with regard to the rowing of the trireme. Fortunately, however, there is in addition to the witness of the monuments and of literature a third order of facts, which may be termed evolutionary evidence. And I venture to hold that those who have had recourse to it, those who have argued back from what mediaeval triremes *were* to what classical triremes *must have been*, of course at the same time keeping their eyes open for the monuments and their ears for the literature, have, in point of fact, come nearest to a solution of the problem.

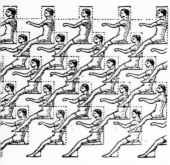

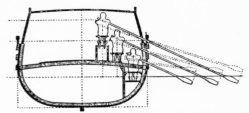

 NGEMENT OF MEN IN GRASER'S
QUINQUEREME.[9]

SECTION OF LEMAÎTRE'S TRIREME.

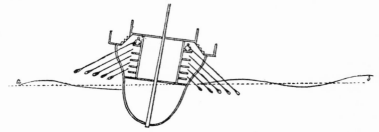

GRASER'S QUINQUEREME AT SEA.

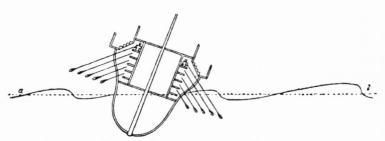

GRASER'S QUINQUEREME IN A GALE.

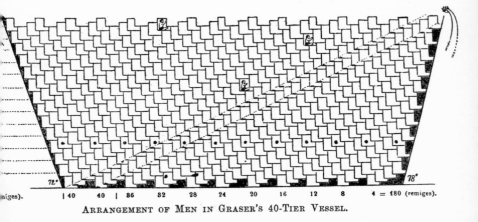

ARRANGEMENT OF MEN IN GRASER'S 40-TIER VESSEL.

In this brief paper I do not propose to investigate a score of different theories. For practical purposes they may be grouped under three heads according to the main principles involved:

(1) The trireme was rowed by three superimposed (or at least superposed) tiers of rowers, every rower pulling a separate oar through a separate port.

(2) The trireme was rowed by a single tier of rowers, every oar being pulled by three men.

(3) The trireme-rowers were so arranged that every three men sat on one bench (stepped or otherwise) pulling three oars, attached to three tholepins, through one common rowlockport.

The first of these views must be called the orthodox view; for it is still given in the handbooks and taught in the schools, so that most educated persons, indeed most scholars, if asked 'How were triremes rowed?' would reply 'By three tiers of rowers, one above the other.' Nevertheless this opinion is the least tenable of the three, simply because a vessel so constructed could not answer its purpose. Any practical boat-builder would scout the idea. And it needs but a few moments' reflection to convince the veriest land-lubber that the difficulties inherent in this solution are insurmountable. To begin with, if there are three superposed tiers of oars, by which I mean tiers separated by a height of two or more feet, either the lowest tier must consist of oars that are very short or the highest tier must consist of oars that are very long. But oars that are very short would be of little or no use for rowing a vessel as big as a trireme; and oars that are very long could only be rowed with a long slow stroke, whereas it is known that trireme-rowers could make a short quick stroke, in fact could make an effective spurt.[1] Hence it should be inferred, on the one hand that the three tiers of oars cannot have differed greatly from each other in point of length,[2] and on the other hand that even the longest of them cannot have been much longer than modern racing-oars.[3]

Again, if we assume three superposed tiers, either the lowest tier must be so near the water as to be constantly in

---

[1] This is shown by Mr. W. W. Tarn in an interesting and valuable paper on 'The Greek Warship' (*Journal of Hellenic Studies* 1905 xxv. 151 n. 56). [Ed. Note: See pp. 154-195 of the present edition].

[2] On this point see further Dr. A. Bauer in I. Muller's *Handbuch d. klass. Altertumswissenschaft* iv. 1. 3. p. 368 f.

[3] Triremes carried certain supplementary or spare oars called περίνεῳ. These were 9 or 9½ cubits long in 373-372 B.C. (IG. II. 789a 14, 22, 51, 55). Of other oars no exact measurements are recorded.

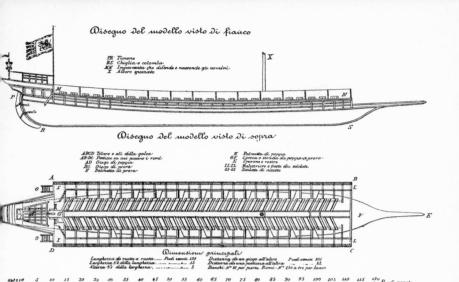

Disegno del modello visto di fianco

FR· Timone
BS· Chiglia o colomba
MN· Impavesata che difende e nasconde gli uomini
X· Albero spezzato

Disegno del modello visto di sopra

ABCD Telaro e ali della galea
AB·DC Ponticce su cui posano i remi
AD Giogo di poppa
BC Giogo di prora
F Palmetta di prora

H Palmetta di poppa
GF Cortia o strada da poppa a prora
E Sperone o rostro
LL·LL Balzatore o sette dei soldati
GI·GI Scaletta di accesso

Dimensioni principali

Lunghezza da ruota a ruota... Piedi veneti 139
Larghezza 5/9 della lunghezza... » 15
Altezza 52 della larghezza... » 5

Distanza da un giogo all'altra Piedi veneti 101
Distanza di un giogo all'altra... » 32
Banchi N° 25 per parte. Remi N° 150 a tre per banco

5 10 15 20 25 30 35 40 45 50 55 60 65 70 75 80 85 90 95 100 105 110 115 120 Piedi veneti

ELEVATION AND PLAN OF FINCATI'S VENETIAN TRIREME.

Fincati—TRIREMI

CROSS-SECTION OF TRIREME WITH PARTIAL UPPER DECK.

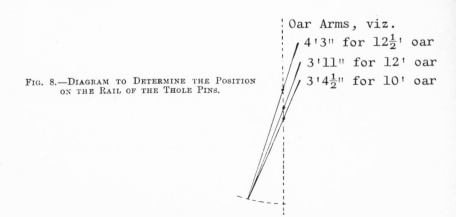

FIG. 8.—DIAGRAM TO DETERMINE THE POSITION
ON THE RAIL OF THE THOLE PINS.

Oar Arms, viz.
4'3" for 12½' oar
3'11" for 12' oar
3'4½" for 10' oar

danger of shipping a sea, or the highest tier must be so far above the water as to be worked at a most unmanageable angle. Dr. Assmann, for example, on the strength of a very debateable Greek relief and a quite imposible Roman one, would have us believe that the lowest tier of a sea-going trireme was only nine or ten inches (0.25 m.) above the water.[4] This, even if we grant a rather problematical leather-bag protection for the port-holes,[5] implies a decidedly narrow free-board. Others prefer Scylla to Charybdis. M. Lemaitre, for instance—and he is by no means an extremist in the matter—thinks that the oars were worked at an angle of 27 degrees as shown in the annexed cut.[6] In opposition to this and other such speculations Dr. Bauer rightly protests[7] that the oars should make with the surface of the water as acute an angle as possible, a requirement frankly incompatible with a theory that separates the three tiers of rowers by a considerable vertical interval.[8]

Dr. Assmann[9] states that triremes and the like 'were built mainly for smooth, calm water.' But, even if we may postulate halcyon weather, the rowing of a ship with superposed tiers must have been a precarious business. The slightest irregularity on the part of any individual oarsman might involve his neighbours of another tier, and so reduce the whole broadside to confusion. A fortiori, if the wind got up, the best-trained crew in the world would soon be floundering in inextricable chaos.

Moreover, with oars of markedly different length and therefore of markedly different sweep, the simplest operation would be much complicated. Imagine, for example, the difficulty of keeping time—a point first made by Barras de la Penne, who commanded the fleet of Louis XIV.[10] Dr. Breusing,[11] director of the Naval Academy at Bremen, shows that,

---

[4] See his article 'Seewesen' in Baumeister's *Denkmaler d. klass. Altertumswissenschaft*. iii. 1609.

[5] On which see *e.g.* J. Kopecky *Die attischen Trieren* Leipzig 1890 p. 67 f.

[6] From the *Revue archeologique* 1883 III. i. pl. 7, fig. 2,

[7] In I. Muller's *Handbuch* iv. 1. 3 p, 365 f,

[8] *E.g.* the theories of Graser *de veterum re navali* 1864, A. Cartault *La triere athenienne* 1881, E. Assmann 'Seewesen' in Baumeister's *Denkmaler* 1888 and 'Zur Kenntniss der antiken Schiffe' in *Arch. Jahrb.* 1889, E. Lubeck *Das Seewesen der Griechen und Romer* 1890, J. Kopecky *Die attischen Trieren* Leipzig 1890, C. Torr *Ancient Ships* Cambridge 1894 and 'navis' in Daremberg et Saglio *Dict. des ant.* 1904.

[9] In Baumeister's *Denkhaler* iii. 1609.

[10] See A. Bauer in I. Muller's *Handbuch* iv. 1. 3 p, 364,

[11] A. Breusing *Die Losung des Trierenratsels* Bremen 1889 p. 113 ff.

if we assume (as we have a right to do) an angle of 20 degrees between oar and water, an allowance for each oar of a quarter length inboard as against three-quarters length outboard, and a sweep of some 60 degrees, then a minimum vertical interval of 2 feet between the tiers of rowers will demand oars of 8, 16, and 24 feet in length; and consequently (*a*), while a rower in the lowest tier pulls his oar-handle 2 feet, a rower in the middle tier must pull 4 feet, and a rower in the upper tier 6 feet, which means that the lowest rower must sit, the second stand, the third pace to and fro; (*b*) further, while the lowest moves his oar-blade 6 feet, the second must move his 12, and the third 18! Nor can this logic be evaded by supposing either that the two upper tiers reduced their sweep from 18 and 12 feet respectively to 6 in order to suit the lowest tier, or that the lowest tier rowed 4 strokes and the middle tier 2 while the highest rowed 1. Both these assumptions, as Dr. Bauer[12] has proved, only lead to further mechanical difficulties and disabilities.

But nothing daunts the faith of the armchair navigator. Not only does he suppose that triremes were rowed on this preposterous system, but he proceeds to deal in similar fashion with vessels of 4, 5, 6, 7, 8, 9, 10, etc. tiers. The thing becomes humorous. Life on board Graser's quinquereme, even with a sea like a mill-pond, must have been full of incident. But fancy a capful of wind, perhaps with the added excitement of a sea-fight. Weber's sketches,[13] of the result are decidedly charitable! The climax of absurdity is, however, not reached till we try to picture Graser's 40-tier vessel, bearing in mind the fact that, as built by Ptolemy Philopator (222-204 B.C.), she drew less than 4 cubits of water![14]

Some critics, [15] disgusted at such puerilities, have gone to the opposite extreme and maintained that Greek war-ships never had more than a single tier of oars. The trireme, quadrireme, quinquereme, etc. were rowed, they say, by means of large sweeps each pulled by 3, 4, 5, etc. men, as the case might be. Now this theory is far from improbable when applied to vessels of the 6-fold, 8-fold, etc. type, which were all built by the Ptolemies, or by those who had come into

[12] *See* his argumentation in I. Muller's *Handbuch* iv. 1. 3 p. 366 f.

[13] L. Weber *Die Losung des Trierenratsels* Danzig 1896 p. 4 figs. 14, 15.

[14] This is implied by the contemporary author Callixenus of Rhodes, as quoted by Athenaeus 5. 37,—a point to which Mr. C. Torr *Ancient Ships* 1894 p. 9 justly called attention.

[15] *E.g.* L. Weber *Die Losung des Trierenratsels* Danzig 1896, Speck *Handelsgeschichte* 1900.

frequent connexion with them, and may therefore have been mere adaptations of the ordinary Nile-barge.[16] Even the 40-fold vessel becomes credible, if we can assume that its enormous sweeps, the largest of which measured 38 cubits, were each worked by a team of 40 men, of whom 20 pulled while 20 pushed.[17] But this conveniently simple theory cannot be made to cover the case of triremes, at any rate during the best days of Greek independence; for Thucydides[18]—an unimpeachable authority—definitely asserts that on one occasion (in 429 B.C.) the Peloponnesian crews marched overland from Corinth to Megara, 'taking every man's his oar, his cushion,[19] and his tholebight.' It would need a mental acrobat to dodge the implication that, at the time of the Peloponnesian War, Greek triremes had one man to each oar. Further, Mr. W. W. Tarn,[20] following Boeckh has pointed out that according to the Athenian dock-yard lists, the oars of a trireme could form part of the equipment of a quadrireme, those of a quadrireme part of the equipment of a quinquereme. Mr. Tarn reasonably concludes that quadriremes and quinqueremes, at least of the fourth century B.C., had likewise one man to one oar, being in fact wholly analogous to triremes.

But if the theory of three superposed tiers, in which each oar is pulled by one man, and the theory of a single tier, in which each oar is pulled by thee men, are alike discredited, we must commence *de novo* our attempts to answer the question—How after all were triremes rowed? It remains to attack the problem, so to speak, from the opposite end; and this is what several writers have done with no small measure of success.

Rear-admiral Fincati[21] of the Italian fleet has, by the aid

---

[16] This argument is developed by the present writer in Whibley's *Companion to Greek Studies* 1905 p. 490 ff. See also the weighty considerations adduced by Mr. W. W. Tarn in the *Journal of Hellenic Studies* 1905 xxv. 150-156.

[17] Vice-admiral Julien de la Graviere *La marine des Ptolemees et la marine des romains* i. 6 assigns to each oar of this leviathan a team of 20 men, 10 pulling and 10 pushing. But the title τεσσαρακοντήρης can only be justified by doubling these numbers.

[18] Thuc. 2. 93.

[19] I follow the scholiast *ad loc.*, who states that τὸ ὑπηρέσιον meant the fleece on which rowers sit to avoid abrading their persons'—a notion ridiculed by Breusing *Die Losung des Trierenratsels* p. 109 ff.

[20] *Journal of Hellenic Studies* 1905 xxv. 149.

[21] L. Fincati *Le triremi* ed. 2 Rome 1881. I have used both the original book (kindly lent to me by my friend Mr. Wigham Richardson) and the French translation of it given at the end of Rear-admiral Serre's *Les marines de guerre* Paris 1885 p. 154 ff. Fincati's work is that of a scholar and an enthusiast.

of documents in the archives of Genoa and Venice, proved that mediaeval galleys called *triremi* were from the thirteenth to the end of the sixteenth century very commonly equipped *a zenzile, i.e.* with a system of grouped oars, three oars and three oarsmen being assigned to each bench. The official descriptions leave no room for doubt (*galee armate ad tres remos ad banchum—galie armate a tre remi per bancho—galie da tre ordini di remi*—*galie da tre remi e tre homeni per bancho*) ; and contemporary paintings agree with them. Fincati was indeed able to produce detailed drawings and a model of a Venetian trireme of the year 1539. He did more than that; for he took a long-boat from his arsenal, fitted it out with 10 benches each accommodating 3 rowers, who pulled their 3 oars attached to 3 thole-pins through a common aperture, and so demonstrated to the satisfaction of all and sundry the principle on which the triremes of mediaeval Italy were rowed. Arguing (and the argument is sound) that nautical traditions are handed down with little alteration from century to century, he concluded that the triremes of the ancients did not differ essentially from those of Sicily, Genoa, and Venice —a conclusion in which Pantera, captain of the Papal galleys, had long since forestalled him.[22] Fincati further proved that in the course of the sixteenth cenury this system of grouped oars (*a zenzile*) was gradually replaced by a system of large sweeps (*di scaloccio*) rowed by several men each—in fact that mediaeval galleys underwent precisely the same evolution which we have already noticed in the case of ancient Greek vessels.

Fincati's views have commended themselves to more than one recent writer on the subject.[23] But, while a general adhesion to the principles that he enunciated may, perhaps must, be granted, there is still room for some differences of opinion. Indeed that astute mariner himself contemplated the possibility that an ancient trireme *a zenzile* might have its oars grouped in several distinct fashions. Mr. Tarn, for example, holds that the terms *thranite, zygite, thalamite* had nothing to do with the horizontal rows or banks' of oars, but denoted three divisions or squads of rowers, the *thranites* being astern, the *zygites* amidships, the *thalamites* in the bows. He refers the words τρίκροτος, δίκροτος, and μονόκροτος primarily to these squads, denying that they are equivalent to τριήρης,

---

[22] Pantera *Armata Navale* Rome 1614. See Fincati *op. cit.* p. 58 f,, Serre *op. cit.* p. 198.

[23] *E.g.* Mr. H. F, Brown in *The Academy* Sept, 29, 1883, p, 219 f,, Mr. W. W. Tarn in the *Journal of Hellenic Studies* 1905 xxv. 139, myself in Whibley's *Companion to Greek Studies* Cambridge 1905 p. 486 ff.

διήρης, and μονήρης respectivly. He further interpets κάτω and ἄνω in relation to the oarage as 'fore' and 'aft,' and apparently supposes that the three rowers of each group of trireme-oars on a single bench at the same level. I confess I am not convinced by the arguments that he adduces on any of these points, though to attempt a refutation of them would exceed my present limits. But this at least may here be said: Mr. Tarn's views admittedly presuppose that many of the most learned Greeks (grammarians, scholiasts, and lexicographers) were wrong in what they said about these matters. Personally I am not prepared to abandon Pollux, Eustathius, Hesychius and Co. without an effort at reconciliation. Mr. Tarn agrees that in the Venetian trireme *a zenzile* three men sat 'one a little astern of the other,' *en echelon* in fact. This, as I have elsewhere pointed out, expains the statement of the scholiast on Aristophanes *Frogs* 1074: 'The *thranite* then is the rower towards the stern; the *zygite* the rower in the middle; the *thalamius* the rower towards the prow.' If now we further suppose that the rowers' bench was in three steps or levels, we satisfactorily account for all passages cited in proof of superposed tiers, *e.g.* the scholiast on Aelian quoted by Graser[24]: 'A vessel is called μονήρης, διήρης, etc. according to the number of her banks rising one above the other' (κατὰ τοὺς στίχους τοὺς κατὰ τὸ ὕψος ἐπ' ἀλλήλοις). Besides, it is easy to explain the terms θαλαμίτης, ζυγίτης, θρανίτης: the *thalamite* was the man who rowed nearest the port-hole (θαλαμιά); the *zygite*, he who sat next him, originally on the beam (ζυγόν); the *thranite*, he who worked the longest oar by rising on a stool (θρᾶνος) to gain force for his stroke.

I believe, therefore, that the tririme-problem was in effect half-solved by Rear-admiral Fincati who first established the analogy of the Venetian trireme *a zenzile,* and half-solved too by Dr. Bauer who rightly insisted that the three banks of a trireme must be but a very slight distance apart (certainly less than two vertical feet).[25] It will only be completely solved, when an adequate and indisputable representation of and adequate and indisputable representation of an ancient trireme is discovered. In default of that much-to-be desired solution it seems worth while to attempt a reconstruction along the lines here laid down. But at this point I resign my pen in favour of Mr. Wigham Richardson, whose theoretical knowledge and practical experience qualify him for the task in a quite unusual degree. ARTHUR BERNARD COOK.

[24] Graser *de veterum re navali* § 4.

[25] A. Bauer in I. Muller's *Handbuch* iv. 1. 3 p. 368.

FIG. 9.—THE HALF-MODEL SEEN LONGITUDINALLY FROM THE INSIDE.

FIG. 10.—CROSS-SECTION OF THE HALF-MODEL.

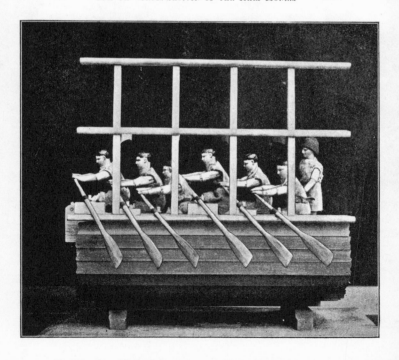

FIG. 11.—THE HALF-MODEL WITH THE UPPER PLANKING REMOVED.

SECTIONAL HALF MODEL OF A TRIREME

(Description and remarks by Wigham Richardson, published
in *Classical Review* xix, 1905, pp. 376-377)

The half model as photographed was made by Mr. Thorup
of the Neptune Works to a scale of one inch to the foot. It
represents a section, for a length of 6 rowers, of a trireme as
interpreted by Mr. A. B. Cook. It is a *sectional half model*
so as the better to show the internal structure and arrangements (Figs. 9, 10, 11).

I entirely agree with the learned author of the foregoing
article that the usual description of triremes cannot be re-
garded seriously. His explanation is the only one I have met
with which seems to solve the problem, and my firm (Swan,
Hunter, and Wigham Richardson) have had great pleasure in
making a model to represent his views.

From a shipbuilder's point of view there seem to be no
two ways about the problem.

Granted that the sheds at Munychia were about 150 ft.
long and 20 ft. wide, we may assume that the triremes built
in them were from 140 to 150 ft. long and about 16 ft. beam.

We also know that they used to be beached, so that probably their draught of water was from 4 to 5 ft.

Further, the sets of row boats cannot be spaced less than
about 3 ft. apart, but by placing them stepwise an extra man
can be got in between each, without fouling each other. I
confess that even this arrangement does not give the 85 rowers
a side in a length of 150 feet, but it nearly approximates to
that number. Moreover, the said number of 170 rowers is
named at a later date than the Battle of Salamis, and the
triremes may have been somewhat longer.

Again, oars must be nearly horizontal, so in the model the
gunwale is 12 inches above the water line.

The middle oars are 12 ft. long, which is about the length
for the racing boats at Oxford and Cambridge; the shorter
are 10 ft., and the longer oars are 13½ ft. In the modern
lifeboat the oars are up to 16 ft. in length, and this length
would be equally suitable for a trireme as interpreted by Mr.
Cook.

In order to give each rower the same stroke, whatever
the length of the oar, the centres of the thole-pins must be
shown *on the model*, and this arrangement leads to a wide

gunwale-rail, which doubtless was considered important for strength, see Fig. 8.

Mr. Cook has expressed a doubt whether or not there was a complete deck, but doubtless such an obvious feature would be adopted sooner or later, for, to say nothing of largely increasing the longitudinal strength, it provides a shelter for the rowers as well as a fighting platform for soldiers, or, as we should style them, marines, The Cross-Section, Fig. 12, shews a *partial* upper deck. This arrangement is a very probable one, and it has the further advantage of allowing the main deck to be raised to the level of the gunwale so that it would free itself at once from any sea coming aboard. Nautical readers will appreciate this point. Mr. Cook thinks that originally three oars (thranite, zygite, and thalamite) were arranged between every two ribs or uprights, as in the case of the Venetian galleys, but that when the trireme came to be completely decked more numerous supports for the deck may have become necessary.

The nomenclature of modern ships is notoriously erratic. For example, a *double banked launch* would hardly suggest to the uninitiated that the phrase indicates a large ship's boat with two men to each oar! If the Greek nautical terms were similar, the task of the commentators must be arduous indeed.

The first sketch of the model was submitted to my old friend Sir Gainsford Bruce, a scholar and an accomplished yachtsman, and he wrote with reference to the representations on ancient monuments as follows:—

'I think it quite possible that the ancient artists who depicted ships, like the old heralds who drew lions, had never seen what they professed to represent.'

In conclusion, may I note that in all ages it has been a question how to secure the greatest possible power in a ship. In the large Cunard steamer now building at Wallsend this problem has involved many months of laborious calculation, but if we consider 5 men as equal to 1 horse power the steamer of to-day is more than two thousand times more powerful than the Athenian trireme.   WIGHAM RICHARDSON.

TRIREMES

(A letter by Cecil Torr, published in *Classical Review* xix, 1905, p. 466)

Like many other recent writers on this subject, Messrs. Richardson and Cook have misconceived the nature of the problem. We do not want to know how they would build a trireme. We want to know how triremes actually were built. And, if we are to know this, we must take account of these five points at least:—

I. The remains of the Athenian docks show that the triremes were not more than 150 ft. long and 20 ft. wide.

II. Vase-paintings, coins, etc. show that oars were confined to about three-fifths of the length of the ship, not extending further forward than the cat-heads nor further aft than the steering-gear.

III. Inscriptions show that the Athenian triremes had 62 thranite oars, 54 zygite oars, and 54 thalamite oars.

IV. The Kouyunjik relief and several vase-paintings depict vessels with two tiers of oars arranged in this way • • • • • •

V. The Acropolis relief and the relief on Trajan's Column depict vessels with three tiers of oars arranged in this way • • • • • •that is, *in quincuncem*.[1]

There can be very little doubt about the arrangement of the oars. The difficulty is about the arrangment of the rowers. And the difficulty is aggravated by Messrs. Cook and Richardson, p. 199, when they make the midship-section of a trireme just like the midship-section of a modern steel-built steamer. If the midship-section of a trireme was something like the midship-section of a mediaeval galley, the difficulty nearly disappears.

Suppose that the vessel's sides curved sharply outward, and that the rowers' seats were fixed against the vessel's sides, so that the middle line of the vessel was nearer to the thalamites than to the zygites, and nearer to the zygites than to the thranites:[2] the rowers could then work three tiers of oars *in quincuncem* without any inordinate difference in the lengths of the oars or in the heights of the tholes above the water-line.

This, I think, may prove to be the true solution of the problem. At present the problem is insoluble, because we have not got sufficient information. And it is mere waste of time to give solutions that run counter to the information that we have got.

CECIL TORR

[1]See the diagram in my article *navis* in Daremberg & Saglio's *Dictionnaire des Antiquites,* Fig. 5275 on p. 29 of fascicule 36.

[2] *Ibid.* Fig. 5270 on p. 27.

THRANITE, ZUGITE, AND THALAMITE

(An article by W. W. Tarn, published in *Classical Review* xx, 1906, pp. 75-77)

Mr. A. B. Cook, in his recent article 'Triremes' in *Classical Review*,[1] xix, 1905, pp. 371-6, does not accept the old view which I have lately put forward[2] as to the meaning of the above terms, viz., thranites astern, zugites amidships, thalamites in the bows. I should like briefly to indicate how difficult it seems to me to be for anyone who accepts the reconstruction of Messrs. Cook and Richardson (which I for one greatly admire as a workable arrangement, whether it be an Athenian trireme or not) to adhere to the orthodox meaning attached to these terms. My view really does not 'presuppose that many of the most learned Greeks were wrong,' whatever some of their modern interpreters may be.[3]

First, Pollux. After mentioning numerous sizes of warships, up to the εἰκοσήρης and so forth, he proceeds to treat of them as a whole, as warships; and when he says that there were three classes of rowers he refers to warships generally and not merely to triremes. To refer this statement to triremes only, as has been done by so many writers, is a curious example of the false perspective induced by too much Thucydides. The trireme was (speaking roughly) the 'ship of the line' for about a century and a half (Salamis to Alexander); the quinquereme and the larger galleys for about three centuries (Alexander to Actium). That the latter period is half a blank to us is immaterial; it was not a blank to Pollux; looking back, Pollux would see the trireme somewhat as we

[1] [Ed. Note: see p. 196-204 of the present edition].

[2] 'The Greek Warship,' *J.H.S.* vol. xxv, 1905, pp. 137 and 204. These remarks are supplemental to the analysis of the evidence there given, to which I refer once for all. [Ed. Note: see p. 154-195 of the present edition].

[3] One must sift one's evidence reasonably; if two statements conflict, one must go. (A clear instance in *J.H.S.* vol. xxv, 1905, p. 145, note 22, where one has to choose between Appian and Hesychius.) Mr. Cook naturally does the same. For instance, Eustathius says the thalamites are *under* (ὑπὸ) the thranites: Mr. Cook discards this as directly as I do: see his model. (Is it possible that ὑπὸ should mean 'forward of,' comparing Polyb. 16, 3, ὑπὸ τὸν θρανίτην σκαλμόν, where 'forward of' would make far better sense than 'under'?) As a fact, I have discarded extremely little.

see Drake's ships, the quinquereme somewhat as we see
Nelson's. I do not abandon Pollux: I rely strongly on him.
Pollux 1, 87 θάλαμος οὗ οἱ θαλάμιοι ἐρέττουσι. The thalamites sat then in some particular part of the ship. Mr. Cook's
'thalamites' do not.

Polyaen. 5, 222, 4. Diotimus, having landed part of his
crews, made the remainder work now the thalamite, now the
zugite, now the thranite oars,[4] to deceive the enemy on shore.
If the thranites, etc., were *squads*, as I think, the enemy
could easily see which set of oars moved. If the thranite
oars, etc., were superposed banks of a substantial interval
(orthodox theory), then (leaving out of account the practical
difficulties of the manœuvre) the enemy might still see which
bank was moving. But if the thranite, zugite, and thalamite
oars were respectively merely every third oar of a level row
(to an observer *from outside* the oars of Mr. Cook's model
would appear to leave the ship in a level row, particularly if
she were a cataphract), the enemy could never distinguish
for a minute which set was being used (again omitting the
practical difficulties).

App. *b.c.* 5, 107. Agrippa rams Pappias' flagship[5] κατὰ
τὴν ἐπωτίδα, 'forward of the end of the outrigger,' and tears
her open; the men in the towers are thrown out, the sea
rushes in, and of the rowers the thalamites are all killed
(πάντες ἀπελήφθησαν), but the rest (οἱ ἕτεροι) burst the deck
and swim out (ἐξενήχοντο). If the thalamites sat forward,
and the ship plunged, they would be the first to drown (so
Weber). If they sat below the others, they might still
drown while the rest escaped supposing the ship not to plunge
but to settle (orthodox view). But there is no possible way
in which a ship resembling Mr. Cook's could sink without
the outside row (his 'thalamites') having at least as good a
chance of escape as the others.

IG. II, 791, l. 56.[6] There is a simpler explanation of this
than the one I suggested. I doubt now if it refers to shorten-
ing at all. Of a number of (discarded) thranite oars 'the
dokimastes passes 10 as zugite': that is, they were weak, too
weak for the stern oars. I do not think it has anything to

---

[4] ἀνὰ μέρος ὁτὲ μὲν τὰς θαλαμίας, ὁτὲ δὲ τὰς ζυγίας, ὁτὲ δὲ τὰς
θρανίτιδας κώπας ἀναφέρειν.

[5] Of course not a trireme, at that date. It is worth noting that, even
if this ship were only a quadrireme (as was, *e.g.*, the Roman flagship at
Side), the passage would be quite inconsistent with Dr. Assmann's arrangment, which would make the top bank of a quadrireme also 'thalamites.'

[6] θρανιτίδων τούτων ἀποφαίνει ὁ δοκιμαστὴς ζυγίας Δ.

do with the question of the supposed greater length of the thranite oars.

Arist. *Mech.* 4 (as I have shewn at length) can only be made to support the orthodox view on the assumption that the tholes were not arranged (as from stern to bow) in a straight line (or lines), but in a curved line (or lines) following the curve of the ship's side. Quite apart from proof of the existance of an 'outrigger,' I think that any practical man would decline to consider such an assumption; it is so obvious that equality of leverage throughout was a prime necessity in a Greek galley as much as in a mediaeval one.

Supposing then that I am absolutely wrong as to the meaning of ἄνω and κάτω (and any one who thinks this ought, I submit, to be prepared with some alternative explanation of Arr. *Anab.* 6, 5, 2, which one can treat seriously), there is still quite sufficient evidence to overrule the much quoted statement in the scholion to *Frogs* 1074 (on which Mr. Cook relies), on any canon of sound criticism.[7] Personally, of course, I believe this scholion to be quite correct: what I believe to be incorrect is the interpretation put on it by those who hold the orthodox theory.

I should like to add a word as to the five points recently stated by Mr. Torr in this *Review* (vol. xix. p. 207); for two of them (Nos. 3 and 5) are not well founded. The Athenian lists do not shew that the Athenian triremes had 62 thranite, 54 zugite, and 54 thalamite oars. They perhaps shew that, during the few years they cover, no trireme had *more* oars of each class; they do not shew that no trireme had less, or that all were in use at once. And the Acropolis relief and the Trajan's column relief do *not* shew an arrangement *in quincuncem*, as anyone can see by looking at them. The quincunx is Mr. Torr's own idea of what these reliefs ought to shew; and no evidence for it exists, so far as I knew; for the monuments shewing ships of two rows are no more evidence for the existence of a ship of three rows than are men with two hands evidence for the existence of men with three. I have gone fully into the details of these monuments elsewhere; but I should like to add one point as to the 'trireme' of Trajan's column. I take it to be an axiom that we cannot say arbitrarily of a given monument that it is right on one point of fact and wrong on another, merely because it suits us to do so. Consequently, supposing this monument to have any bearing

---

[7] There is an alternative, viz., to say that the writers of the second century A.D. did not know what they were talking about. But anyone saying this must never cite scholia.

at all on the oarage of a trireme, it also shews a trireme to have been an open boat with eight rowers a side; which is absurd. It cannot therefore be evidence for anything connected with a trireme.

The fact is that the orthodox theory of three superposed tiers depends essentially, now as ever, on the one scholion, and on an interpretation of that scholion which (at best) cannot be shewn to be correct, and which, if it were correct, would merely render the scolion inconsistent with Pollux and other evidence; quite apart from the general question of the evidential value of these scholia, a value which now, I suppose, is at a greater discount than ever.

What an Athenian trireme precisely was will probably never be known; but as I have been very glad to find myself in substantial agreement with Mr. Cook as to the limits within which the arrangement of the oars must lie—limits which exclude the orthodox theory—I cannot help regretting that he has hampered himself with the orthodox view of the meaning of thranite, zugite, and thalamite, a view that appears to be a legacy from the time when some people thought that the trireme-problem could be solved as a thing by itself, without reference to the trireme's place in the evolution of the larger warship. Had the facts as to the larger warships always been borne in mind, we might not also have seen a theory that involves a mathematical miracle gain such wide acceptance.

W. W. TARN

TRIREMES

(A letter by Cecil Torr, published in *Classical Review* xx, 1906, p. 137)

Mr. Tarn says (*Classical Review*[1] xx, 1906, p. 77) that two points of mine (*Classical Review*[2] xix, 1905, p. 466) are not well founded. He asserts :—

'The Athenian lists do not shew that the Athenian triremes had 62 thranite, 54 zugite, and 54 thalamite oars. They perhaps shew that, during the few years they cover, no trireme had *more* oars of each class; they do not shew that no trireme had less, or that all were in use at once.'

[1][Ed. note: See p. 210 of the present edition.]
[2][Ed. note: See p. 207 of the present edition.]

Pay was provided for 200 men on every trireme.[3] This seems to show that, in giving 200 oars to a trireme,[4] the lists are giving the regulation number. Moreover, the lists deal with sets of oars (ταρροὶ) for triremes on the basis of all the triremes being alike.[5]

He also asserts :—

'And the Acropolis relief and the Trajan's column relief do *not* shew an arrangement *in quincuncem*, as anyone can see by looking at them. The quincunx is Mr. Torr's own idea of what these reliefs ought to shew.'

As vessels are depicted with two tiers of oars arranged in this way . . . ., one would expect to find vessels with three tiers of oars arranged in this way. And that is precisely what one finds on Trajan's column, if one does not overlook the fracture that fixes the position of the second of the thalamite oars, now broken off.

As for the Acropolis relief, it is quite beyond dispute that the tholes of the thranite oars are vertically above the port-holes of the thalamite oars. The port-holes of the zygite oars are hidden by the projecting gunwale; but it is clear that they are approximately in the positions that would complete the quincunx.

Mr. Tarn says of Trajan's column :—

'Supposing this monument to have any bearing at all on the oarage of a trireme, it also shews a trireme to have been an open boat with eight rowers a side; which is absurd. It cannot therefore be evidence for anything connected with a trireme.'

The sculptor had to deal with a corkscrew relief at a very great height above the eye, the trireme being more than half-way up the column. And he did the right thing, namely, seized the essentials and made them very clear, and then indicated the remainder as best he could in the space at his disposal.

The sculptor depicted a number of vessels with two tiers of oars, and one vessel with three tiers; and on this vessel he depicted the admiral's lantern.[6] He thus brought out the

---

[3] Thus in Thucydides a talent a month a ship (vi. 8) makes a drachm a day a man (vi. 31), and in Xenophon (*Hell*. i. 5) thirty mnas a month a ship makes three obols a day a man.

[4] The 200 oars were 62 thranite, 54 zygite, 54 thalamite, and 30 perineoi.

[5] See, for instance, IG, II', 808, col. b. 11. 1 ff.

[6] For the admiral's lantern see Xenophon, *Hell*. v. 1. 8; Diodoros, xx. 75; Appian, *de bel. civ.* ii. 89; Livy, xxix, 25; Procopios, *de bel, Vand.* i. 13.

fact that there was a trireme as flagship to this fleet of
biremes; but the size and the position of the relief made it
impossible for him to give a detailed study of the ship and
all its crew.

CECIL TORR.

TRIREMES

(A letter by Philip H. Newman, published in
Classical Review xx, 1906, p. 280)

Mr. Cecil Torr (*Classical Review* xx, 1906, p. 137) has
disposed most satisfactorily of the question of the ships on
Trajan's column affording evidence of construction, I trust,
once and for all. It should be recognised now, that there is
no more reliability in the artistic compromises with actuality
in the monument alluded, to, than is to be found upon coins.

Mr. Torr will forgive me, however, if I cannot accept as
obvious, or 'quite beyond dispute,' that 'in the Acropolis
relief the tholes of the thranite oars are vertically above the
portholes of the thalamite oars.' This greatly depends whether
or not the old reading of the bas relief is maintained, *i.e.* as
to 'oars passing over the gunwale to the water.' Surely
the Acropolis—which I take to be our most important and
authentic reference on this subject of Triremes—is capable
of another, and—in my mind—much more practical interpretation. It will be observed that the projection of the
shadow of the upper wale is much greater than those of the
lower wales of the ship, and seems to indicate not merely a
gunwale, but a gallery of some amplitude,—*through which*
and *not over*, the oars descend to the sea. I will leave it to
Mr. Torr to arrange a quincunx, if he thinks it necessary, or
attaches more importance to it than the great mechanical
gain of a shortened oar which his reading presents.

At all events it does not conflict with those internal arrangements of the vessel scantily derivable from Classical writers,
and moreover supplies authority for the frequent occurrence
of galleries or important projections in vessels in the illustrations of ancient shipping in early printed books, such as
Lazare de Baif's *De Re Navali* (Basle, 1537).

That my view is an obvious one I will not say, because it

[1][Ed. Note: See p. 211-213 of the present edition.]

has been generally overlooked, but I submit it to Mr. Torr with the conviction that upon searching and unprejudiced examination he will probably confirm the result of my own.

PHILIP H. NEWMAN.

TRIREMES

(A letter by Cecil Torr, published in *Classical Review* xx, 1906, p. 324)

It surely is 'quite beyond dispute' that 'in the Acropolis relief the tholes of the thranite oars are vertically above the portholes of the thalamite oars.' If I rightly understand Mr. Newman's observations, (*Classical Review*[1] xx, 1906, p. 280), his point is that, if we had a section of the ship at right-angles to the plane of this relief, these tholes would not be vertically above these portholes. But I have not asserted that they would.

Mr. Newman says that 'the shadow of the upper wale is much greater than those of the lower wales of the ship, and seems to indicate not merely a gunwale, but a gallery of some amplitude.' It does not seem to me to indicate more than a gunwale. And there is this difficulty about the gallery :— The remains of the Athenian docks show that the triremes were not more than 20 ft. in width. If the triremes had a gallery 'of some amplitude' on each side of the hull, the hull itself would be so narrow that it would hardly have capacity enough to hold the crew or displacement enough to float its weight.

CECIL TORR.

[1][Ed. Note: See p. 213-214 of the present edition.]

SELECT BIBLIOGRAPHY

Adcock, F. E., *The Greek and Macedonian Art of War*. Berkeley, Calif. 1962.

Alexandris, K. A., *Sea Power in Ancient Greek History*. Athens 1950. (in Greek).

Anderson, R. C., *Oared Fighting Ships*. London 1962.

Anderson R. & R. C., *The Sailing Ship*. London & N.Y. 1947.

Assman, Ernst. "Kritisches im Sachen des antiken Seewesens," I. II. in *Berl. Phil. Woch.* 11, 1891, pp. 36-37.

——————, "Die neueste Erklärung der Trieren, Penteren, U.S.W.," in *Berl. Phil. Woch.* 10, 1890, pp. 639 ff.

——————, "Seewesen," in Baumeister, *Denkmäler des klassischen Altertums* III. Munich 1889, pp. 1593-1639. (cf. also *Jahrb. des Kais. deutsch. arch. Instituts* 1886, p. 315; 1889, p. 91; 1892, p. 42).

Barnett, R. D., "Early Shipping in the Near East," in *Antiquity* 32, 1958, pp. 220-30.

Bass, George F., "Underwater Archaeology: Key to History's Warehouse," in *National Geographic* 124, No. 1, July, 1963, pp. 138-155.

Bassett-Lowke, W. J. & Holland, G. *Ships and Men*. 1946.

Bauer, Adolf, *Die Kriegsschiffe der Griechen*. Munich 1890.

Blinkenberg, Chr., *Triemiolia*. Copenhagen 1938.

Boeckh, A., *Urkunden über das Seewesen des Attischen Staates*. Berlin 1840.

Borhegyi, S. de, *Ships, Shoals and Amphoras. The Story of Underwater Archaeology*. New York 1961.

Boreaux, Cf. *Études de nautique égyptienne*. Cairo 1925.

Bouvet de Cresse, *Histoire de la marine des tous les peuples depuis la plus haute antiquité jusqu'à nos jours*. 2 vols. Paris 1824.

Brehier, L., "La marine de Byzance du VIIIe au XIe siècle," in *Byzantion* 19, 1949, pp. 1-16.

Breusing, A., *Die Lösung des Trierenrätsels*. Bremen 1889.

——————, *Die Nautik der Alten*. Bremen 1886.

Brewster, Frank, "The Arrangement of Oars in the Trireme," in *Harvard Studies in Class. Phil.* 44, 1933, pp. 205-225.

Bridge, Admiral Sir Cyprian, *Sea Power and Other Studies.* London 1910.

British Museum Guide to the Exhibition on Greek and Roman Life. 3rd ed. London 1929. *Shipping,* pp. 17-23.

British Museum, *The Sutton Hoo Ship Burial* (8th rp.) London 1961.

Bury, J. B., "The Naval Policy of the Roman Empire in Relation to the Western Provinces from the seventh to the ninth century," in *Cent. Nasc. di Mich. Amari,* vol. 2. Palermo 1910, pp. 21-34.

Busley, R., *Die Entwicklung des Segelschiffes.* Berlin 1920.

——————, *Schiffe des Altertums.* Berlin 1918.

Cary, M. & Warmington, E. H., *The Ancient Explorers.* New York 1929.

Cartault, Augustin Georges Charles, *La Triére Athenienne (Étude d'archéologie navale).* Paris 1881.

Casson, L., *The Ancient Mariners.* London 1959.

——————, "Fore and Aft Sails in the Ancient World," in *The Mariner's Mirror* 42, 1956, pp. 3-5.

——————, "Hemiolia and Triemiolia," in *Journal of Hellenic Studies* 78, 1958, pp. 14-18.

——————, The Illustrated History of Ships & Boats. N.Y. 1964.

——————, "The Isis and her Voyage," in *Trans. & Proc. Amer. Phil. Assn.* 81, 1950, pp. 43-56.

——————, "The Sails of the Ancient Mariner," in *Archaeology* 7, 1954, pp. 214-219.

——————, "The Size of Ancient Merchant Ships," in *Studi in onore di Aristide Calderini e Roberto Paribeni* I, Milan, 1956, pp. 231-238.

——————, "Speed under Sail of Ancient Ships," in *Trans. & Proc. Amer. Phil. Assn.* 82, 1951, pp. 136-148.

Chatterton, E. Keble, *The Marvels of the Ship, etc.* Philadelphia 1921.

——————, *Sailing Ships: The Story of Their Development from the Earliest Times to the Present Day.* London 1909.

Clausetti, E., *Navi e Simboli marittimi sulle monete dell'antica Roma.* Rome 1932.

Clark, F. W., *The Influence of Sea Power on the History of the Roman Republic.* Menasha, Wisc. 1913.

Clowes, G. S. L., *Sailing Ships. Their History and Development, as illustrated by the collection of ship models in the Science Museum.* London 1930-1932. (rep. 1951)

Cohen, L., "Evidence of the Ram in the Minoan Period," in

American Journal of Archaeology 42, 1938, pp. 486-494.

Cook, A. B., "Ships," in *Companion to Greek Studies,* ed. L. Whibley. Cambridge 1931. pp. 567-588.

Cotterill, C. C. & Little, E. D., *Ships and Sailors, Ancient and Modern.* London 1868.

Cousteau, Captain J. Y., *The Living Sea.* New York 1963.

───────────, *The Silent World.* New York 1953.

Custance, Admiral Sir Reginald, *War at Sea — Modern Theory and Ancient Practice.* London 1919.

Davison, J. A., "The First Greek Triremes," in *Classical Quarterly* 41, 1947, pp. 18-24.

Dolley, R. H., "The Warships of the Later Roman Empire," in *Journal of Roman Studies* 38, 1948, pp. 47-53.

Droysen, Johann Gustav, *Die griechische Kriegsschiffe in Heerwesen und Kriegfuehrung der Griechen.* Freiburg 1889.

Dunbabin, T. J., "Minos and Daedalus in Sicily," in *Papers of the British School at Rome* 16, 1948, pp. 1-18.

DuSein, A., *Histoire de la marine de tous les peuples depuis les temps les plus reculés jusqu'à nos jours.* Paris 1863.

Duval, P. M., "La forme des navires Romains d'après la mosaïque d'Althiburus," in *Mel. d'Arch. et d'Histoire* 61, 1949, pp. 119-149.

Eichler, F., *Des Reliefs des Heroon von Griesch. Tryser.* Vienna 1950.

Faulkner, R. O., "Egyptian Seagoing Ships," in *Journal of Egyptian Archaeology* 26, 1940, pp. 3-9.

Fiennes, Gerard, *Sea Power and Freedom. A Historical Study.* New York 1918.

Fincati, L., *Le Triremi.* Rome 1883.

Fletcher, R. A., *Warships and Their Story.* London 1919.

Foucher, L., *Navires et Barques sur des Mosaïques de Sousse, etc.* Tunis 1957.

Gomme, A. W., "A Forgotten Factor of Greek Naval Strategy," in *Essays in Greek History and Literature.* Oxford 1937, pp. 190-203.

Grace, V. R., *Amphoras and the Ancient Wine Trade.* Princeton 1961.

Graeffe, F., "Studien zur Marinegeschichte des Altertums," in *Hermes* 57, 1922, pp. 430-449.

Graser, B., *Die Altesten Schiff darstellungen auf Münzen.* Berlin 1870.

───────────, *Die Gemmen d.k. Museum zu Berlin mit Darstellungen antiken Schiffe.* Berlin 1867.

───────────, *Das Model eines athenischen Funfreihenschiffes.* Berlin 1866 (1873).

Graser, B., "Das Trierenrelief der Akropolis," in *Berliner archaologische Zeitung.* Berlin 1864.

—————————, *Untersuchungen über das Seewesen des Altertums.* Göttingen 1870.

—————————, *De veterum re navali.* Berlin 1864.

Heidenreich, R., "Zum Biremenrelief aus Praneste," in *Rom. Mitt.* 51, 1936. pp. 337-346.

Hornell, J., "Naval Activity in the Days of Solomon and Rameses III," in *Antiquity* 21, 1947, pp. 66-73.

—————————, "Sea Trade in Early Times," in *Antiquity* 15, 1941, pp. 233-256.

Hyde, W. W., *Ancient Greek Mariners.* New York 1947.

Jal, Auguste, *Archéologie navale.* 2 vols. Paris 1840.

—————————, *La Flotte de Cesar.* Paris 1861.

—————————, *Glossaire Nautique: Repertoire polyglotte de termes de marine anciens et modernes.* Paris 1848.

Jane, Fred T., *Heresies of Sea Power.* London 1906.

Jurien de la Graviere, *Les derniers jours de la marine à rames.* Paris 1885.

—————————, *La marine des Anciens,* Paris 1890.

—————————, *La marine des Ptolemées et la marine des Romains.* 2 vols. Paris 1885.

—————————, "La marin des Byzantins," in *Revue des Deux Mondes* 65, 1884, pp. 130-158.

Kirk, G. S., "Ships on Geometric Vases," in *Annual of the British School at Athens* 44, 1949, pp. 93-153.

Knorringa, H., *Emporos: Data on Trade and Traders in Greek Literature from Homer to Aristotle.* Amsterdam 1926.

Kopecky, Josef, *Die attischen Trieren.* Leipzig 1890.

Koster, A., *Das antike Seewesen.* Berlin 1923.

—————————, *Schiffahrt und Handelsoerkelir des ostlichen Mittelmeers im 3 und 2 Jahr-tausend v. Christ.* Leipzig 1924.

—————————, *Studien zur Geschichte des antiken Seewesens.* Leipzig 1934. (repr. 1963).

La Berge, Camille de & Mowat, R., *Études sur l'organisation des flottes romaines.* Vienna 1887.

Lallemand, Ferdinand. *The Cruise of the Dolphin.* London 1957.

Landstrom, Bjorn. *The Ship.* 1961.

Lehmann-Hartleben, Karl, *Die Antiken Hafenaulagen des Mittelmeeres.* Leipzig 1923.

Lindsay, W. S., *History of Merchant Shipping and Ancient Commerce. 4 vols.* London 1874.

Lubeck, E., *Das Seewesen der Griechen und Römer.* Hamburg 1890-1891.

Mahan, Rear-Admiral Richard T., *The Influence of Sea Power upon History*. Boston 1903.

Marinatos, Sp., "La Marine Creto-Mycenienne, in " *Bull. Corresp. Hellenique* 67, 1933, pp. 170-235.

Miltner, F., "Das praenestinische Biremenrelief," in *Jahreshefte des Osterreichischen Archaeologischen Instituts* 24, 1929, pp. 88-111.

—————————, "Seewesen," in Pauly-Wissowa, *Real Encyclopediae* Supp. V. 1931, pp. 906 ff.

—————————, "Die Meerengenfrage in der griechischen Geschichte," in *Klio* 28, 1935, pp. 1 ff.

Moll, F., *Das Schiff in der bildenden Kunst*. Berlin 1929.

Morrison, J. S., "The Greek Trireme," in *The Mariner's Mirror* 27, 1941, pp. 14-44.

—————————, "Notes on Certain Greek Nautical Terms and on Three Passages in I. G. II² 1632," in *Classical Quarterly* 41, 1947, pp. 122-135.

Neumann, K., "Die byzantinische marine," in *Historische Zeitschrift* 45, 1898, pp. 1-23.

Newman, Philip H., "Ancient Sea Galleys, with remarks on the method of propusion of the Greek Trireme," in *Trans. Royal Soc. of Literature,* 2nd ser. 33, 1915, pp. 205-231.

Ormerod, H. A., *Piracy in the Ancient World*. Liverpool 1924.

Papagiannopoulos, Andrew, *"A Guide to the Naval Museum of Greece,"* (repr. from *Hos*) Athens 1961. (in Greek).

—————————, "The Nautical Life of the Ancient Greeks," in *Polemon* (Suppl. No. 2) Athens 1958. (in Greek).

Persson, A. W., "Die hellenistische Schiffbaukunst und die Nemischiffe," in *Opuscula Archaeologica* 1, 1935, pp. 129-163.

Rhados, K. N., *On the Finds of Antikythera . . . Underwater Searches for the Discovery of Antiquities*. Athens 1910. (in Greek).

Riley, W. E. & Gomme, L., *Ship of the Roman Period Discovered on the Site of the New County Hall*. London 1912.

Rodgers, William L., *Greek and Roman Naval Warfare*. London 1937.

—————————, *Naval Warfare Under Oars*. Annapolis 1939.

Roerie, G. la & Vivielle, Commander J., *Navires et Marins de la rame à l'helice*. 2 vols. Paris 1930.

Rubin de Cervin, G. M., "The Roman Galley of the Tibertine Island," in *The Mariner's Mirror* 40, 1954. pp. 309-311.

Rumpf, F., *Römische Fragmente*. Winckelmann's programme 95. Berlin 1935. (on the Lenormant relief).

Schmidt, K., *Die Namen der attischen Kriegsschiffe*. Leipzig 1931.

Schmidt, M., "Berichte über das Seewesen im Altertum," in Bursiau's, *Jahresberichte für Klassischen Altertumswissenschaft* 73, 1892, pp. 92-113.

Schwarz, Tjard, *Die Entwicklung des Kriegschiffbaues*. Berlin 1909.

Segre, M., "Dedica votiva dell'equipaggio di una nave Rodica," *Clara Rhodos* 8, 1930, pp. 225-244.

Serre, Le Contre-Admiral Paul, *Les marines de guerre de l'antiquitè et du moyen âge*. 2 vols. Paris 1885.

——————————, *Études sur l'histoire militaire et maritime des grecs et des romains*. Paris 1888.

Shepard, A. M., *Sea Power in Ancient History*. London 1925.

Silburn, P. A., *The Evolution of Sea Power*. London 1912.

Smith, J., "On the Ships of the Ancients," in his *Voyage and Shipwreck of St. Paul*. London 1848.

Solla Price, Derek J. de, "An Ancient Greek Computer," in *Scientific American* 200, 1959, (no. 6), pp. 60-67.

Starr, C. G., "The Ancient Warship," in *Classical Philology* 35, 1940, pp. 353-374.

——————————, *The Roman Imperial Navy 31 B.C. — A.D. 324*. Cornell Studies in Classical Philology. Ithaca 1941.

Steinitz, Francis, *The Ship, Its Origin and Progress*. London 1849.

Stevens, W. O. and Westcott, A., *A History of Sea Power*. New York 1920.

Tarn, W. W., "The Fleets of the First Punic War," in *Journal of Hellenic Studies* 27, 1907, pp. 48-60.

——————————, "The Dedicated Ship of Antigonus Gonatas," in *JHS* 30, 1910, pp. 209-222.

——————————, *Hellenistic Military and Naval Developments*. Cambridge 1930.

——————————, "The Oarage of Greek Warships," in *Mariner's Mirror* 19, 1938, pp. 52-74.

——————————, "The Roman Navy," in *Companion to Latin Studies*, ed. J. E. Sundys Cambridge 1910, pp. 489-500.

——————————, Review of Rodgers, *Greek and Roman Naval Warfare*, in *Classical Review* 52, 1938, p. 76.

Tenne, A., *Kriegsschiffe zu den Zeiten der alten Griechen und Römer*. Oldenburg 1915.

Thiel, J. H., *Studies on the Growth of Roman Sea Power in Republican Times*. Amsterdam 1946.

——————————, *A History of Roman Sea Power Before the Second Punic War*. Amsterdam 1954.

Throckmorton, Peter, "The Bronze Age Ship." in, *The Atlantic* 213, 1964, (No. 6), pp. 96-116.

——————————, *The Lost Ships*, New York 1964.

Throckmorton, P., "Oldest Known Shipwreck Yields Bronze Age Cargo," in *National Geographic* 119, (No. 5), May, 1962.

_____, "Thirty Three Centuries Under The Sea," in *National Geographic* 115, (No. 5), May, 1960.

Thursfield, J. R., *Naval Warfare*. Cambridge 1913.

Torr, C., "Navis," in Daremberg-Saglio, *Dict. d'Antiquités Grecques et Romaines*. IV, 1. Paris 1904, pp. 246-406.

Ucelli, G., *Le Navi di Nemi*. Rome 1950. 2nd ed.

Ure, P. N., "Early Athenian Sea Power," in *The Origin of Tyranny*, Cambridge 1922, pp. 321-331.

Vogel, W., *Die Namen der Schiffe*. Berlin 1912.

Voigt, C., "Der Schiffsbug von Samothrace," in *Schiffbau*, 1912.

_____, "Das System der Riemen-Ausleger in klassischen Altertum," in *Wassersport* 7, 1889, pp. 632 ff.

Wallinga, H. T., *The Boarding Bridge of the Romans*. Groningen 1946.

Warre, E., "Navis," in Smith's *Dictionary of Greek and Roman Antiquities*. 3rd ed. 1891, pp. 208-224.

Weber, L., *Die Lösung des Trierenrätsels*. Danzig 1896.

Williams, R. T., "Early Greek Ships of Two Levels," in *Journal of Hellenic Studies* 78, 1958, pp. 121-130.

TABULAE CURATORUM NAVALIUM

CIA or IG II	IG II²
789	1607
789b	1606
790	1608
791	1604
792	1605
792b	1610
——	1609
793	1611
794	1612
795	1613
796	1614
797	1615
798	1616
799	1617
800	1618
801	1619
802	1620
802b	1621
803	1622
804	1623
——	1624 (*SEG* III. 137)
805	1625
806	1626
807	1627
808 (+ *add.* p. 515)	1628
809	1629
810	1630
811	1631
812	1632

TABULAE CURATORUM NAVALIUM Supplement

SEG	III. 137	= IG II² 1964
	III. 138	
	X. 142	= Lex navalis, fin. saec. V
		(cf. Oliver, *Hesperia* 4, 1935, 14 - 19)
	X. 353-356	= Catalogi navales, c.a. 430
		(353. I.G. II² 1604* attigit D. M. Robinson, *A.J.A.* 41, 1937, 294 356. Catalogus navalis, a. 406 cf. Broneer, *Hesperia* 2, 1933, 393; *ibid.* 4, 1935, 164)
	XIII. 48	= IG II² 1624
	XVI. 132	= IG II² 1609
		(370/69 Sealey, *Phoenix* 11, 1957, 95 ff.)

Vase in the form of a prow of a trireme. British Museum. 4th century B.C.

Transfer of cargo from one ship to another. Mosaic in Ostia, 2nd century A.D.

Mosaic floor advertising the shipping firm of Karalis in Ostia. 3rd century A.D.

Merchant ships in harbor with Ostia lighthouse in background. Floor mosaic in Ostia. 3rd century A.D.

Fisherman's hut and canoes on the river Nile. Mosaic from Palestrina in Rome National Museum. 3rd century A.D.

PLATE C

Terra cotta model of merchant ship found in Amathus, Cyprus. British Museum.

Terra cotta votive vessels from Amathus, Cyprus. British Museum.

PLATE E

Roman ship entering a harbor. Relief on a Roman lamp. British Museum.

Plate F

Portion of relief from Trajan's column in Rome. The emperor disembarks, having crossed the Adriatic in a bireme.

PLATE G

Remains of a Roman ship, 3rd century A.D. Found in mud of the Thames. London Museum.

Bronze cheniskos from model of Roman ship found in Roman fort of London. *b. and c.* [in]scribed bronze model of Roman warship bearing the Greek name 'Ammilla' found in [Lon]don. British Museum. *d, e, f.* Gold medallion found near Arras, France. Obverse: bust of [Co]nstantius Caesar. Reverse: One of Caesar's galleys on Thames and Caesar riding into [Lon]don. *ca.* 296 A.D. Arras Museum.

PLATE I

Artist's conception of a pentekontoros (light Greek warship) based on the representations
of the kylix in the British Museum shown on page 145.

Model of a pentekontoros. Naval Museum of Greece.

PLATE K

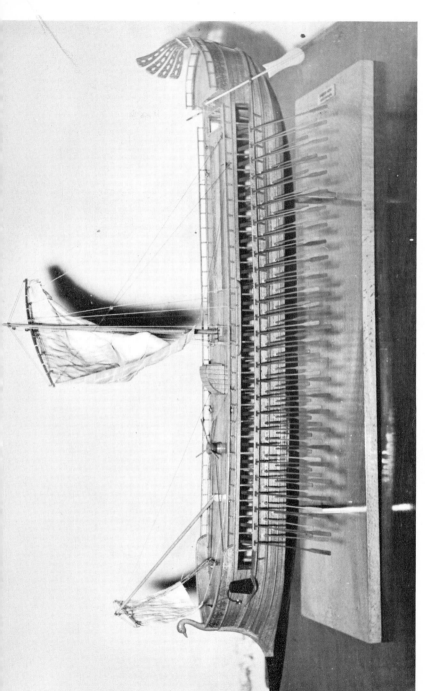

Model of a Greek trireme. Naval Museum of Greece.

PLATE M

MODELS OF ANCIENT ANCHORS. *a.* Bronze age, 800 B.C. from pottery decoration found in Malta. *b.* Sardinia, 650 B.C. *c.* Euxine (Black Sea), 450 B.C., from a coin, *d.* Euxine, 400-375 B.C. from a coin. *e.* Syria, 300-160 B.C. from a coin. *f.* Roman, 20 A.D. from the Arch of Tiberius. *g.* Norway, 700 A.D. *h.* Roman, 40 A.D., found in Lake Nemi. *i.* Medieval, 1066 A.D. from Bayeux Tapestry. *j.* Roman, 40 A.D. from ship found in Lake Nemi. Exhibit in Franklin Institute, Philadelphia.

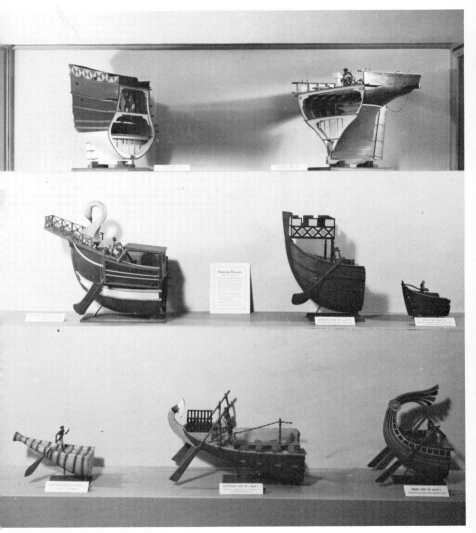

MODELS OF STEERING DEVICES. *Top row.* *l.* Ship of 1625. *r.* Ship of 1820. *Center row.* *l.* Roman ship of 50 A.D. *ctr.* Ship of 1100 A.D. *r.* Boat of 1325 A.D. *Bottow row.* *l.* Egyptian boat, 2500 B.C. *r.* Greek ship, 500 B.C. Exhibit in Franklin Institute, Philadelphia.

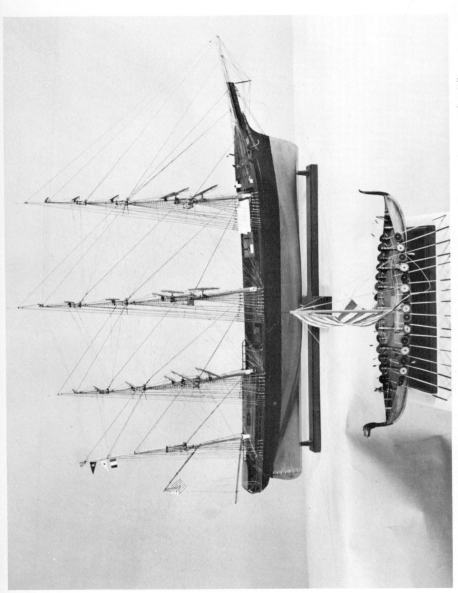

Model of a Viking ship, *ca.* 800 A.D. found at Gokstad, Norway. The vessel measured 79'2". Behind is a 282' Barque of the late 1880's. Franklin Institute, Philadelphia.

Model of Egyptian ship of the 4th Dynasty, *ca.* 2900 B.C. From the collections of the Commercial Museum, Philadelphia, Pennsylvania.

PLATE Q

Model of Egyptian Nile boat, *ca.* 2500 B.C. From the collections of the Commercial Museum, Philadelphia, Pennsylvania.

Model of Egyptian merchant ship, *ca.* 1500 B.C. Mariners' Museum, Newport News, Virginia. Cf. Pl. I.4. page 141.

PLATE S

Model of Egyptian merchant ship, *ca.* 1500 B.C. From the collections of the Commercial Museum, Philadelphia, Pennsylvania. Cf. Pl. I.4, page 141.

Model of a 'Philistine' ship, *ca.* 12th century B.C. From the collections of the Commercial Museum, Philadelphia, Pennsylvania. Cf. Pl. I.7, page 142.

PLATE U

Model of a Phoenician ship, *ca.* 13th c. B.C.? From the collections of the Commercial Museum, Philadelphia, Pennsylvania. Cf. Pl. E.

Model of a Homeric ship, 11th century B.C. From the collections of the Commercial Museum, Philadelphia, Pennsylvania.

PLATE W

Model of a Babylonian Sea Horse, 800 B.C. From the collections of the Commercial Museum, Philadelphia, Pennsylvania. Cf. Pl. 2.9, page 143.

Model of Phoenician galley, 7th century B.C. From the collections of the Commercial Museum, Philadelphia, Pennsylvania.

PLATE Y

Model of a Greek Trireme. Inset. Cross-section of same. From the collections of the Commercial Museum, Philadelphia, Pennsylvania. Cf. Pl. 5.20-23, page 146.

Model of a Greek merchant ship, 500 B.C. From the collections of the Commercial Museum, Philadelphia, Pennsylvania. Cf. Pl. 4.18, page 145.

PLATE AA

Model of a Carthaginian galley, 5th century B.C. From the collections of the Commercial Museum, Philadelphia, Pennsylvania.

Model of a Roman merchant ship, 2nd century A.D. From the collections of the Commercial Museum, Philadelphia, Pennsylvania. Cf. Pl. 6.29, page 148.

PLATE CC

Model of a Roman merchant ship, 1st century A.D. Mariners' Museum, Newport News, Virginia. Cf. Pl. B.; Pl. 6.27-34, page 149.

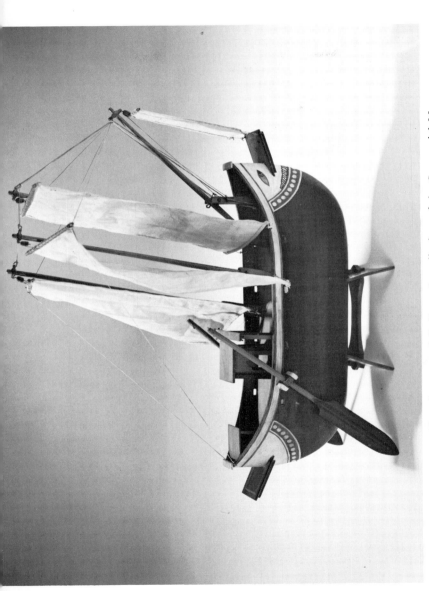

Model of Persian ship, 7th century A.D. From the collections of the Commercial Museum, Philadelphia, Pennsylvania. Cf. Pl. 7,40, page 151.

PLATE EE

Model of a Byzantine dromon. 10th century A.D. Naval Museum of Greece.

2284-14-14
22-91
5/78

11